Public Finance and Economic Growth

Finances Publiques et Croissance Economique

PUBLIC FINANCE AND ECONOMIC GROWTH

FINANCES PUBLIQUES ET CROISSANCE ECONOMIQUE

Proceedings of the 37th Congress of the International Institute of Public Finance
Tokyo, 1981

Dieter Biehl
Karl W. Roskamp
Wolfgang F. Stolper
Editors

Wayne State University Press, Detroit 1983

Library of Congress Cataloging in Publication Data

International Institute of Public Finance. Congress
37th : 1981 : Tokyo, Japan)
Public finance and economic growth—Finances publiques et croissance économique.

English and French.
Includes bibliographical references.
1. Finance, Public—Congresses. 2. Economic development—Congresses. I. Biehl, Dieter. II. Roskamp, Karl W. III. Stolper, Wolfgang F. IV. Title. V. Title: Finances publiques et croissance économique.
HJ236.I59 1981 339.5′2 83-12447
ISBN 0-8143-1750-2
ISBN 0-8143-1751-0

Manufactured in the United States of America.

Officers of the Board of Management 1982
Membres du Comité de Direction 1982

International Institute of Public Finance

A Brief Survey of Historical and Current Matters

The International Institute of Public Finance was founded in Paris in 1937. It held two conferences before the Second World War, and members have since met at least once a year from 1947 until the present. The Institute now has over 800 members from some 50 countries, and annual conferences are normally attended also by some non-members with a special interest in the particular topic.

The aims of the Institute are scientific. Its objectives include in particular: the study of Public Finance and Public Economics, the research and publications in both of these areas, the establishment of scientific contacts and exchange of knowledge and experience between persons of all nationalities. The Institute is exclusively and directly concerned with the furthering of public interest. The activities of the Institute have been recognized on an international level by the Economic and Social Council of the United Nations, which conferred upon it the Statut Consultatif B.

The Institute provides a forum for those concerned with problems of public economics, broadly defined. It has over the years aspired to sustain high academic standards. In the selection of topics and their investigation, it has directed itself towards matters of practical importance and towards issues of implementation, as well as of principle. The membership embraces both academic economists whose prime interests are in teaching and research, and public officials who face the problems "on ground": the unifying characteristic is acceptance of a proper standard of intellectual rigor.

Membership is essentially individual though corporate subscriptions are welcome. The Institute is proud of the involvement in its activities of members from countries of all kinds of political persuasion and all levels of economic development.

The Institute is governed by a Board of Management whose decisions require approval by the general assembly of members, with a President and Vice-Presidents elected for a period of three years. The Institute is administered by an Executive Committee (present membership, Professor Jean-Claude Dischamps, President, Paris; Professor André van Buggenhout, Brussels; Professor Victor Halberstadt, Leyden; Professor Karl W. Roskamp, Detroit).

All questions concerning the Institute should be directed to:

Mrs. B. Schneider, Executive Secretary
International Institute of Public Finance
University of Saarland
D-6600 Saarbrücken 11
West Germany

Institut International de Finances Publiques

Un aperçu de son passé et de ses activités actuelles.

L'Institut International de Finances Publiques fut fondé à Paris, en 1937. Il tint deux congrès avant la dernière guerre mondiale. En 1947, il put réunir à nouveau ses membres et, depuis, ceux-ci se sont rencontrés au moins une fois par an aux quatre coins du globe. L'Institut compte, aujourd'hui, plus que 800 membres appartenant à 50 pays et ses congrès annuels sont régulièrement suivis non seulement par ceux-ci mais également par des non-membres intéressés par tel ou tel sujet.

Les buts poursuivis par l'Institut sont purement scientifiques. Ses objectifs incluent en particulier: l'étude des finances publiques et de l'économie publique, la mise en oeuvre de recherches et la publication de travaux dans ces domaines ainsi que l'établissement de contacts scientifiques et l'échange de connaissances et d'expériences entre des personnes de toute nationalité. L'Institut est guidé exclusivement et directement par le souci de l'intérêt général. L'Institut a vu sa mission reconnue, sur le plan international, par le Conseil économique et social des Nations-Unies, qui lui a conféré le statut consultatif B.

L'Institut offre un terrain de rencontre pour les spécialistes intéressés par les problèmes d'économie publique, au sens large du terme. Le maintien d'un niveau scientifique très élevé est pour ses responsables une préoccupation permanente. Dans le choix des sujets et la manière de les traiter, il s'attache aussi bien aux problèmes théoriques qu'aux problèmes pratiques et à leurs solutions. Ses membres sont des spécialistes universitaires et de la recherche scientifique, et des hauts fonctionnaires qui assument d'importantes responsabilités. Tous sont d'un niveau intellectuel notoirement reconnu.

L'Institut est composé essentiellement de membres individuels et il réunit dans ses activités des personnalités de pays relevant de tous les systèmes d'organisation politique et de tous les niveaux de développement économique.

La direction de l'Institut est assurée par un Comité de Direction conformément aux orientations définies par l'Assemblée Générale des membres. Son administration incombe à un Comité Exécutif actuellement composé de:

Président, le Professeur Jean-Claude Dischamps, Paris.

Vice-Présidents, les Professeurs André van Buggenhout, Bruxelles, Victor Halberstadt, Leyden, et Karl W. Roskamp, Détroit.

Toute question relative à l'Institut est à adresser à:

Madame B. Schneider, Secrétaire, Administrative,
Institut International de Finances Publiques
Université de la Sarre
D-6600 Saarbrücken 11
(R.F.A.)

Tokyo Congress 1981
Welcoming Address by the President of the IIPF

Professor Horst-Claus Recktenwald

For the first time in the history of the International Institute of Public Finance our worldwide Congress is being held in Asia. It is indeed a great event for all of us who have the opportunity to visit our host country Japan, a land of warm hospitality and much vitality. We are deeply impressed and thankful for the admirable efforts our Japanese colleagues and friends have made in the preparation and organization of this year's World Congress of Public Finance.

I am pleased that we have chosen the right topic for the right place at the right time, namely Public Finance and Growth. Yet the good timing is more or less accidental. We have had good luck; as is well known, economists as forecasters are often only as trustworthy as planners or prophets. However this may be, here in Tokyo we shall deal with some basic issues. We shall deal with them independently of their topicality or current interest.

As professionals we are often so deeply immersed in our subject that we are likely to forget to adapt the name of our discipline and of our international society in response to fundamental changes. As insiders know too well and outsiders know too little, Public Finance is surely only one aspect of the subject to be treated here. Public Finance is indeed a somewhat anachronistic term. Even Public Economics or Fiscal Economics would be too narrow concepts for our discipline, that fascinating branch of the social sciences with a great future promise. As I see it, it has a bright future as an integral part of classical Political Economy as Adam Smith or Joseph Schumpeter used this term. The topic of this Conference and the titles of our Congress volumes published so far illustrate and underline my statement. Of course, what counts in our competitive world of scholars is in the end the quality of analytical results and not a formal label—yet the latter should not be misleading.

Public Finance, Growth and Inflation are interdependent phenomena which deeply influence the material well-being of mankind, today and tomorrow. All spheres of activities are touched. Even national and international institutions of sciences and research are nowadays affected by these factors—as many of us have just experienced struggling with budgetary constraints. The recent summit meeting of major industrial nations in Ottawa, Canada, has revealed some nagging problems in the area of Economic Growth some of which we shall intensively discuss in the week to come.

The range of our investigation will be wide. It will start with the main causes of the mentioned phenomena and end with optimal measures to come to grips with them, a controversial subject closely studied by many modern monetarists and fiscalists in different economic systems. In the more macroeconomic context of positive and normative theories there are embedded complex urban growth problems, a major concern of fiscal economists and administrators, particularly here in Japan. A special Working Session of this Congress is devoted to these important issues.

Comfortable ignorance, to be sure, is not a monopoly of economists. Yet there are important fields in General and Fiscal Economics in which our analytical insights and our empirical knowledge are rather limited. In spite of remarkable efforts and much progress during the last decades, there are still a few proverbial toolboxes which are quite empty or only partly filled. I draw the attention to the desolate state of our knowledge with respect to: (a) the proper integration of public sector activities in national income accounting systems, especially as Gross National Product is now often used as an indicator of growth and (or) welfare, (b) old-fashioned budget and accounting systems—sometimes pure cameralistics—leading to a primitive revenue-expenditure paradigm, which contributes little or nothing to the understanding of efficiency and equity effects in a personal, inter-temporal or regional context. Neither does it enlighten us on regional redistribution of costs and benefits. Finally the usefulness of what has been handed down to us. The wisdom of past days must be used with circumspection: neither Ricardo's chapter "On Machinery" nor Keynes's "General Theory" provide today a sufficient foundation for comprehending and coping with stagflation and rapid innovations of all kinds.

I submit four types of unanswered questions: (1) How much does the modern state through its inefficient use of resources contribute to the economic and political schizophrenia called "stagflation"? (2) How do neoclassical and neo-Keynesian models actually work and how can they help us to understand a world in which wage rates are permanently outrunning labor productivity? (3) How can neo-Keynesians recommend a still larger public debt in an important country in which the heavy financial burden of the budget is evident and in which the government's scope and structure of activities is fettered by sky-high interest rates? Which public project has a net productivity of 13% or more, the present rate of interest? (4) What do we really know about tax incentives for investment and consumption under 1981 conditions and not under those of 1931, 1950 or 1960?

Confronted with these encompassing problems, I feel confident that our discussions will be stimulating, challenging and fruitful. There should be many good results. I myself am positive and optimistic by nature. I feel that history and observation teach us that man's imagination, his ability to use the faculties of his mind and the power of his will overcome in the end all difficulties.

I'm convinced that our Congress will be both profitable and valuable to all participants. It will be characterized by mutual understanding and goodwill.

On behalf of the whole International Institute of Public Finance membership and others who attend this Congress, I cordially thank once more all persons and institutions in Japan who have contributed generously in the preparation of this friendly gathering of economic and fiscal experts from all over the world. We are thankful to our gracious hosts. We consider it a privilege to be invited to this beautiful country which has its roots in a venerable, ancient culture and which is, on the other hand, on the forefront of technical progress and industrial enterprise.

Once more, I say: Thank you all, Arigato gozaimasu.

Contributors

Professor Kul B. Bhatia, *Professor of Economics, Department of Economics, The University of Western Ontario, London, Ontario, Canada N6A 5C2*

Professor Albert Breton, *Institute for Policy Analysis, University of Toronto, 150 St. George Street, Toronto, Canada M5S 1A1*

Professor Geoffrey Brennan, *Center for Study of Public Choice, Virginia Polytechnic Institute and State University, Blacksburg, Virginia 24061 U.S.A.*

Professor James Buchanan, *Center for Study of Public Choice, Virginia Polytechnic Institute and State University, Blacksburg, Virginia 24061 U.S.A.*

Professor Christophe Chamley, *Professor of Economics, Department of Economics, Cowles Foundation for Research in Economics, Yale University, Box 2125, Yale Station, New Haven, Connecticut 06520 U.S.A.*

Professor Aldo Chiancone, *University of Venice, Via M. Macchi 33, I-20124 Milano, Italy*

Professor Béla Csikós-Nagy, *President of the National Office for Prices and Material, Titular Professor, Karl Marx University, Varosmajor u. 26-C, Budapest XII, Hungary*

Professor Robert Eisner, *Professor of Economics, Department of Economics, Northwestern University, Evanston, Illinois 60201 U.S.A.*

Professor David I. Fand, *Professor of Economics, Department of Economics, Wayne State University, Detroit, Michigan 48202 U.S.A.*

Dr. Otto Gadó, *Former President of the National Planning Office, Tárnok u. 13, H-1014 Budapest, Hungary*

Professor Yannis M. Ioannides, *Associate Professor of Economics, Boston University, School of Management, 704 Commonwealth Avenue, Boston, Massachusetts 02215 U.S.A.*

Professor Peter M. Jackson, *Director, Public Sector Economics Research Centre, Leicester University, Leicester LE1 7RH, England, U.K.*

Professor S. K. Kuipers, *Professor of Economics, University of Groningen, Rijksuniversiteit, Faculteit der Economische Wetenschappen, Hoogbouw W.S.N., Universiteitscomplex Paddepoel, Postbus 800, The Netherlands*

Professor Russell Mathews, *Director, Centre for Research on Federal Financial Relations, The Australian National University, Copland Building, P.O. Box 4, Canberra, A.C.T. 2600, Australia*

Professor Dr. Manfred Neumann, *Professor of Economics, Universität Erlangen-Nürnberg, Robert-Koch-Str. 16, D-8560 Lauf, Federal Republic of Germany*

Professor William A. Niskanen, *Advisor to the President, The President's Council of Economic Advisers, The White House, Washington, D.C. 20515 U.S.A.*

Professor Mancur Olson, *Professor of Economics, Department of Economics, University of Maryland, College Park, Maryland 20742 U.S.A.*

Professor Rémy Prud'homme, *Université de Paris (Val de Marne), Institut d'Urbanisme de Paris, Avenue du Général de Gaulle, F-94010 Créteil CEDEX France*

Professor Dr. Dr.h.c. Karl W. Roskamp, *Professor of Economics, Department of Economics, Wayne State University, Detroit, Michigan 48202 U.S.A.*

Professor Ryuzo Sato, *Professor of Economics, Brown University, Department of Economics, Providence, Rhode Island 02912 U.S.A.*

Professor Hirofumi Shibata, *Professor of Economics, Department of Economics, Osaka University, Toyonaka, 560, Japan*

Professor Carl S. Shoup, *Professor Emeritus, Columbia University, P.O. Box 4, Sandwich, New Hampshire 03270 U.S.A.*

Professor Wolfgang F. Stolper, *Professor Emeritus, Department of Economics, The University of Michigan, Ann Arbor, Michigan 48109 U.S.A.*

Professor Guy Terny, *Professor of Economics, Director, G.R.E.P., Université de Paris X, Résidence d'Ursines, 1, Allée Louis Roveyaz, F-78140 Vélizy-Villacoublay, France*

Professor Claude Vedel, *Université de Paris II, 23 Rue des Vallées, 91800 Brunoy, France*

Professor Jack Wiseman, *Director, Institute of Social and Economic Research, University of York, Heslington, York, Y01 5DD, England, U.K.*

Professor Dr. Horst Zimmermann, *Fachbereich Wirtschaftswissenschaften, Abteilung für Finanzwissenschaft, Universität Marburg, Am Plan 2, D-Marburg/Lahn, Federal Republic of Germany*

Professor A. H. van Zon, *Professor of Economics, University of Groningen, Rijksuniversiteit, Faculteit der Economische Wetenschappen, Hoogbouw W.S.N., Universiteitscomplex Paddepoel, Postbus 800, Groningen, The Netherlands*

Preface

The topic of the 37th Congress of the International Institute of Public Finance, held in Tokyo, Japan, in September, 1981, was "Public Finance and Economic Growth." It was an important and timely one.

During the 1970's the pace of economic growth had in most countries markedly slowed down. The somewhat euphoric feeling of many economists in the 1960's to have mastered timehonored, difficult problems impeding continued economic expansion and high level prosperity, gave way to sober reassessments. Events like the energy crises, rampant inflation accompanied by rising unemployment, capital shortages, an apparent slowing down of technical progress in important sectors, radically changed demographic developments, surging social expenditures and record budget deficits were ominous forebodings that economic growth could not be taken for granted. Growth is not something which is generated in a smooth, predictable, mechanical manner and staying with us for decades. It turned out that it is by its very nature much more like a fragile plant, difficult to get started, troublesome to nurture but easy to hamper. Many economists ruefully conceded that economic growth is far more intricate than expected. Clearly, it is not only a matter of the demand side but the supply side as well. It was recognized that growth, on which in our days the present and future welfare of nations and individuals, and perhaps even their survival in a troublesome world hinges, is still an elusive phenomenon, intensively studied but only partly understood. It is easy to see why this should be so. Economic growth is a complicated, multifaceted phenomenon requiring the successful interactions of a variety of factors in the right place at the right time. These factors are of an economic, political, sociological, technological and cultural nature and their interactions are in some cases direct and obvious, in others indirect and subtle, they are sometimes swift and sometimes slow and protracted.

Considerable efforts have been made to better understand and come to grips with the phenomenon of growth. It is too important an aspect of a nation's life for governments to remain aloof from, let alone, to ignore it. Governments as a rule not only desire economic growth but often actively try to promote it through public policy measures, which frequently fall within the domain of public finance. There are important relationships between economic growth and public finance.

A number of papers presented were devoted to normative growth theory, others dealt with actually observed growth processes and tried to derive new knowledge from these. Scholars from our gracious host country contributed greatly to these endeavors, drawing on the experience of Japan's remarkable economic growth in the post World War II period.

If economic growth was the Leitmotif of the Congress, it was natural for public finance experts to ask how precisely their specialty fits into all of this. The central question was how governments in market economies can enhance economic growth, to what extent, at what time? Is it possible to design for a market economy tax and expenditure measures to promote economic growth? Will these be compatible with the working of a market economy which relies on entrepreneurship and incentives to innovate and take risk in order to generate increases in output and labor productivity? Should governments leave the growth process essentially to private initiative and restrict its interventions to a few "market-conform" ones? Or should they try to cooperate, in a more or less paternalistic manner perhaps, with private enterprises, and influence the growth process through budgetary decisions? These are central and difficult questions; no consensus exists on the answer. In fact, at the time of the Congress two important industrial countries, the United States and France, had embarked upon rather different courses to stimulate economic growth. While the Reagan administration stressed private initiatives, the Mitterand government relied heavily on public policy measures. The extent to which a government in a socialist country can influence economic growth is another difficult matter.

Public policy measures including budgetary measures to stimulate economic growth, often entail monetary effects. At a time when many countries experienced double digit inflation, budget deficits incurred to further growth were not very palatable. Clearly the fiscal-monetary interactions had to be carefully evaluated. But this requires a knowledge of how modern economies work. Does the neoclassical model, the Keynesian model, or perhaps some other model, provide a proper description of the interactions of monetary and real variables? Several papers were devoted to this subject.

It was also recognized that public measures to stimulate economic growth have a number of other important aspects, to wit: equity considerations, environmental effects, problems of intergovernmental relationship and, possibly, social and cultural repercussions. There are difficult problems in this area and efforts were made to throw new light on these.

The discussions during the Tokyo Congress proved to be stimulating and productive. To be sure, they revealed the need for a better insight in the growth process. Yet even within the limits of our present knowledge the potential role of public finance in the growth process was delineated and brought into sharper focus. The present volume provides the reader with a rich menu of thought provoking contributions.

The Congress was sponsored by the Science Council of Japan, the Japanese Association of Fiscal Science, the Union of National Economic Associations in Japan, the Japan Economic Research Institute, and the West German Deutsche Forschungsgemeinschaft.

It is a pleasure to thank the many people, too numerous to mention individually, who have contributed to the success of the Congress and who have made the publication of this volume possible: the members of the Scientific Committee for the Tokyo Congress who prepared the program; the authors and discussants of the papers; our Japanese hosts; and the referees of the papers. We specifically mention only Madame Bernadette Dischamps, Maître Assistant á l'Université Paris II for careful translations; Mrs. Birgit Schneider of the University of Saarbrücken, the Secretary of the International Institute of Public Finance; and Mrs. Barbara Bendert, Mrs. Margot Demarais, and Mrs. Alice Nigoghosian, all of Wayne State University, who bore the thankless burden of final manuscript preparation.

Dieter Biehl
Karl W. Roskamp
Wolfgang F. Stolper
Editors

President of the International Institute of Public Finance—responsible for the 37th Congress: Professor Horst Claus Recktenwald, Federal Republic of Germany

Members of the Scientific Committee for the 37th Congress were:

Dieter Biehl, Chairman, Federal Republic of Germany
Karl W. Roskamp, Executive Vice President, United States of America
Otto Gadó, Hungary
Motokazu Kimura, Japan
André Middelhock, Netherlands

Contents

The Growth of Government and the Growth of the Economy

William A. Niskanen

I. Introduction

A specter is haunting public finance—the specter of irrelevance. As the primary professional community specializing in the analysis of government spending and taxation, we have only a vague understanding of the two most important fiscal issues of our time: What explains the relative growth of the government? What explains the decline in the real growth of the economy? We do not lack for theories to explain either condition. Indeed, there are almost more theories than facts. The relative size of government has been increasing almost continuously, almost everywhere. The rate of growth of the industrial economies has been declining almost continuously during the last fifteen years, almost everywhere. Without a solid understanding of either condition, we have little basis for understanding the mutual relations between these two conditions.

As an economic adviser to the President of the United States, I am specially sensitive to our poor understanding of these conditions. President Reagan has initiated a Program for Economic Recovery that is based, in large part, on a reduction of the relative role of the federal government in the U.S. economy. Although some of the major elements of this program have recently been approved, many of the details have yet to be developed. The choice of measures to control federal spending and to increase economic growth, however, depends more on the causes of spending growth and the decline in economic growth than on the fact of these conditions. For this reason, it is important to summarize our rudimentary understanding of these conditions.

Public Finance and Economic Growth. Proceedings of the 37th Congress of the International Institute of Public Finance. Tokyo, 1981, pp. 1–14

II. The Growth of Government

The Recent U.S. Experience

The government share of national output has increased most rapidly during recessions and wars. One must control for these and other intermittent conditions affecting government spending to isolate the longer-term conditions that have affected spending growth. Table 1 summarizes the rates of real growth of government spending in the United States between 1965 and 1979, both cyclical-peak nonwar years. Total government spending, in constant dollars, increased at a 4.4 percent annual rate; for comparison, real GNP increased at a 3.4 percent annual rate. The composition of government spending changed substantially. Real defense spending was roughly constant, including the additional budget cost from the termination of conscription. Real transfer payments increased at a 7.9 percent annual rate. Real spending for state and local services increased at a 4.9 percent annual rate, in part, financed by the rapid increase in real federal grants. Real federal spending increased slightly faster than real state spending from their own tax sources. Annual variations in the spending growth rates have been substantial. In 1980, for example, real government spending increased at a 5.9 percent rate, reflecting the effects of a brief recession and the political pressures of an election year.

The Causes of Government Spending Growth

Conditions Leading to Overspending. First, it is important to distinguish those conditions that lead the government budget to be too large from those conditions that appear to have caused spurts of growth at particular times. Several important conditions lead the government budget to be too large, distort the composition of programs, and reduce the efficiency of governmental activities. Since these conditions, however, have long been characteristic of the American political system, they do not explain the timing, composition, and magnitude of budget growth.

Concentrated Benefits, Diffused Costs. Americans are far better organized to press special interest demands for more spending than to enforce the general interest in spending control. Almost every trade association, profession, union, state, and major city is represented by a Washington lobby. Each of these groups has an incentive to press

Table 1

Annual Rates of Real Growth of Government Spending in the United States: 1965–1979*

Function	*Federal*	*State and Local*	*Total*
Total	4.6%	5.0%	4.4%
Defense	0.2%		0.2%
Civil Services	2.7%	4.9%	4.5%
Transfers	8.4%	5.8%	7.9%
Grants	8.9%		8.9%
Other	3.8%		3.1%

*Nominal spending in each category divided by the GNP deflator.

for more specific benefits even if the costs to the broader American community are higher. Legislators have an incentive to be most responsive to those groups that are concentrated in their constituency, because most of the costs accrue to voters in other districts.

Concentrated Costs, Diffused Benefits. The other side of the same coin is that few groups have an incentive to press for general spending control and government efficiency, because the costs are borne by these groups and the benefits are diffused among all the taxpayers. For the same reason, legislators do not have an adequate incentive to promote general interest legislation and to monitor government performance, because most of the benefits accrue to voters in other districts. Most people recognize the need for general interest legislation, effective monitoring, etc., but few people, in or out of government, have a private incentive to promote such measures.

The Organization of the Legislatures. Most law originates in program-specialized monopoly committees. These committees also have the primary oversight responsibility in each program area. Moreover, legislators choose to serve on those committees that most directly affect their constituents. This leads each committee to be dominated by those members that represent the highest relative demands for each program. Given the scale and complexity of contemporary government, most of the work of the legislature is performed by these committees and their staffs, and their monopoly of each program area increases their power relative to that of the rest of the legislature.

Bureaucratic Supply. Most government services are supplied by program-specialized monopoly bureaus. The private incentives of each bureaucrat are usually served by expanding the discretionary budget and size of his bureau. The combination of these conditions leads to inefficient performance and budgets that are larger than that preferred by the majority of the legislature.

Budgetary Practices. Several characteristics of government budgets contribute to inefficient resource use. Agencies have an incentive to spend every dollar in their current budget to avoid the risk of a budget reduction in the next year; this has often led to an unusually high rate of spending in the last few months of each fiscal year and conspicuous waste. In addition, agency budgets are not comprehensive—they do not include all of the cost of current programs. Most government budgets, for example, do not include any rent on land, structures and other capital assets acquired in previous years; this leads agencies to hoard capital which, in many cases, would have higher value in other uses. In addition, agency budgets do not reflect all of the future costs of present programs. The federal civil service pensions, for example, are substantially underfunded and military pensions are completely unfunded. This leads the budget to understate the current cost of programs and leads to a growing share of the total budget that is an uncontrollable obligation of prior decisions.

These conditions can and should be corrected. Such corrections would reduce the total budget and increase governmental efficiency. Since these conditions have been characteristic of the American political system from the earliest years, the rapid growth of government spending in recent years must be attributable to other conditions.

Economic Conditions Contributing to Budget Growth. A substantial part of the growth of government spending can be explained by the same set of conditions that determines the demand for private goods and services—relative prices, real per capita income, population, and other conditions that may affect the demand for specific services.

A closer examination of the government spending growth from 1965 through 1979 provides a basis for understanding this issue. The effects of the several economic conditions are drawn from studies of state and local spending and from earlier federal experience.

The real unit cost of government services increased at a 1.1 percent annual rate, reflecting a higher rate of pay increases and a lower rate of productivity growth than in the general economy. This increase in real unit costs probably caused an annual real increase in government spending of about 0.4 percent or about 9 percent of the total increase.

Real per capita GNP increased at a 2.5 percent annual rate. This increase in real income probably caused an annual increase in real government spending of about 1.8 percent or about 42 percent of the total increase.

The total U.S. population increased at an annual rate of about 0.9 percent. Government spending appears to increase in rough proportion to population, indicating that there are no realized economies of the population served by government services. The population increase, thus, probably caused an annual real increase in government spending of about 0.9 percent or about 20 percent of the total increase.

The combined effect of these three conditions, thus, appears to have caused real government spending to increase at a 3.1 percent rate, slightly lower than the increase in real GNP and about 70 percent of the total increase. The remaining government spending growth must be attributed to other conditions specific to this period.

The composition of spending growth during this period provides a clue to these other conditions. Real federal spending for defense and civil services is almost fully explained by the economic conditions and a decline in the number of armed forces overseas. Real federal transfers and grants, however, increased at an annual rate that was 2 to 3 times the rate attributable to economic conditions. Real state and local spending for goods and services are almost fully explained by the economic conditions and the rapid increase in federal grants. The special condition was the rapid increase in federal transfers and grants, and one must turn to other causes to explain this condition.

Political Conditions Contributing to Budget Growth. Any attribution of government spending growth to political conditions, of course, is even more speculative, because it is difficult to conduct the sort of quantitative analysis that is the basis for the estimates of the economic effects. Informed observers, nevertheless, have identified three political conditions that help explain the rate and composition of government spending growth since 1965.

Broadening the Franchise. The right to vote in federal elections has been formally extended four times—to black males in 1870, to women in 1919, to citizens of the District of Columbia in 1961, and to 18-year-olds in 1972. In general, the broadening of the franchise has had little effect on the demands for federal spending. One would not expect current voters to voluntarily extend the franchise to any group that is expected to threaten their interests. In addition, the three later extensions did not significantly change the expected family income of voters. The United States has had a relatively broad franchise for its whole history without triggering a rapid increase in federal spending until the last fifty years.

The delayed extension of the federal franchise to black males had a more significant effect, because this group has a lower expected income than other voters. Although black males were formally included in the federal franchise in 1870, the voting rights of blacks were often denied or restricted by the poll tax and other local measures which were removed only in the mid-1960s. An extension of the franchise to any group with a lower expected income increases the demand for transfers and social services. Whether the government is responsive to these demands, in turn, depends on whether the effective constitution authorizes such measures. A necessary condition for a broad consensus on federal spending control will be to convince the black community and other lower income groups that their interests are better served by increasing economic growth than by increasing government spending.

Changes in the Effective Constitution. Our formal Constitution enumerates a small set of powers (or functions) that the federal government may perform. Moreover, the Bill of Rights strengthens these limits: "The powers not delegated to the United States by the Constitution, nor prohibited by it to the States, are reserved to the States respectively, or the people." The nature and intent of these limits could hardly be clearer. And no subsequent amendment has added to the enumerated federal spending powers.

Today, however, many federal spending programs and regulatory activities have no formal constitutional basis. Our effective constitution has been changed to read: The federal government is authorized to exercise all powers not prohibited to it by the Constitution. Moreover, this change has been rapid and recent. Although there was some erosion of these limits from the earliest years, total domestic spending by the federal government seldom exceeded one percent of national output through the 1920s. The New Deal, of course, was the first massive breach of these limits. It was rationalized as a temporary necessity in an economic crisis and, in fact, many New Deal laws, programs, and agencies expired with the end of the depression. The few new federal programs introduced from World War II through the early 1960s were at least rationalized in terms of the enumerated powers. The Great Society began the first massive breach in these limits in a noncrisis period. The flood of domestic legislation since 1965 did not even pay lip service to the enumerated powers. Many of these new functions may be most worthy, but the federal government has assumed these powers by an extra-constitutional process of constitutional change.

The reasons why the effective constitution was changed are not clear, but the consequences are obvious. There are now few aspects of American life which are immune to the exercise of federal powers. There is probably no way to put the genie back in the bottle with respect to the specific exercise of these new powers. The breakdown of the formal constitutional limits on federal powers, however, strengthens the case for a new amendment limiting the relation of total spending and national output.

The Weakening of Political Parties. For most of American history, the major political parties were the primary institution to provide any discipline on elected officials who act in ways not consistent with the interests of the party. This discipline was exercised primarily through the party role in selecting candidates for office. This role restrained the proliferation of programs that served the interersts of individual politicians at a larger cost to the interests of others in their party. This role also reduced the problems of reaching agreement within the legislature and between the administration and the legislature.

Three developments in recent decades, however, have significantly weakened the political parties. Candidates are now selected by primaries, rather than by party caucuses or conventions. This has created a condition in which candidates may win on their own promises or record and owe little subsequent allegiance to their party. In recent years, limits on campaign spending have also increased the relative powers of the incumbents. Over a long period, the progressive substitution of civil service employees for party appointments has increased the proportion of voters who have an interest in larger government and has reduced the proportion who have an employment interest in which party wins. These several developments are still broadly supported, but the consequences should be realized. The individual legislator is now more responsive to local interests and less responsive to the party leaders. The administration must now deal with many individual legislators rather than through the party leaders. The consequence is a proliferation of special interest programs and an increasing difficulty of building a consensus on national issues. A serious review of those changes in our political system that have weakened the political parties deserves high priority.

Fiscal Conditions Contributing to Budget Growth. For a century, orthodox public finance has focused on the characteristics of a revenue system that minimize the aggregate "excess burden" of a given level of government spending. Our professional community has been slow to recognize that the level of government spending may be a function of the characteristics of the revenue system. The analytic framework to address this latter issue has recently been developed in an important new book by Professors Brennan and Buchanan, *The Power to Tax.* I urge you all to read this seminal book which, in my judgment, is the most important contribution to public finance in our generation. For this paper, however, it is sufficient to summarize their conclusions that the level of government spending is likely to increase as a function of the extent of the tax base; the relative reliance on taxes with nonprogressive rates, taxes on capital, deficit financing, and money creation; and the relative share of revenues raised by the central government. It is useful to explore whether the relative growth of government spending in the United States since 1965 has been associated with changes in the characteristics of the revenue system.

The Composition of Tax Revenues. The growth of real government spending since 1965 was *not* broadly consistent with the changes in the composition of tax revenues that Brennan and Buchanan expect would contribute to such growth. Real revenues from the personal income tax, a progressive tax with substantial exemptions and deductions, increased at a 5.5 percent annual rate. Real revenues from the taxation of capital increased at a 1.9 percent annual rate. Real revenues from various commodity taxes increased at a 3.6 percent annual rate. In each of these three cases, the growth rates are contrary to that which might be expected to contribute to a relative growth of government spending. Real revenues from the social security tax, however, increased at a 7.8 percent annual rate. This tax is a broad based, flat rate tax on earnings up to a limit which, for high earning employees, is a lump sum tax. The rapid growth of the social security tax is the one major change in our tax system that may have contributed to the relative increase in government spending. At this time, however, it does not appear that one should rely on a fiscal constitution that limits the structure of taxation to provide an effective limit on total government spending.

Other Revenue Sources. Some part of the growth of government spending since 1965 is probably attributable to the increasing use of debt financing and money creation. During this period, the total government budget had a surplus in only three years, the federal budget had a surplus in only one year, and the proportion of spending financed by debt generally increased. The federal debt held by the public increased at an 8.3 percent annual rate, the central bank purchased about 16 percent of this additional debt, and currency increased at an 8.5 percent annual rate. Although there is no significant short-term relation between the deficit and money creation, a reduction of the deficit is likely to contribute to both reduced spending growth and reduced inflation.

The Federal Share of Government Finances. Some part of the growth of government spending since 1965 is also probably attributable to the increased centralization of government finance. During this period, real federal spending increased at a 4.6 percent annual rate, and real state and local spending financed from their own tax sources increased at a 4.0 percent annual rate. A reduction of federal grants to state and local governments is likely to reduce total government spending.

Summary. We still have only the most rudimentary understanding of the conditions that have led to the rapid growth of government spending. My summary of the conditions that may explain the growth of government spending in the United States may have led to more questions than answers. In any case, I encourage you to address the reasons for government spending growth in your own country in the hope that we can all learn from each other.

III. The Growth of the Economy

The Recent U.S. Experience

The rate of growth of real output in the United States declined in each successive cycle since 1965. The rate of growth of output per unit of input increased somewhat in the 1969–1973 cycle but declined sharply from 1973 to 1979. The decline in the growth rate during the 1969–1973 cycle reflects the combination of a substantial decline in the growth of factor inputs and a small increase in the growth of productivity. The subsequent decline in the growth rate during the 1973–1979 cycle reflects the combination of substantial increase in the growth of factor inputs and a large reduction in the growth of productivity. The rate of growth of the potential work force, as measured by the population age 16 and over, was roughly constant over the whole period since 1965.

Table 2

Annual Rates of Growth of Real Output in the United States: 1965–1979

	1965–1969	*1969–1973*	*1973–1979*
Real Net National Product	3.9%	3.5%	2.7%
Per Unit of			
Population, 16 and over	2.2%	1.8%	1.0%
Hours Worked	2.2%	2.4%	0.8%
Total Factor Input	1.4%	1.7%	0.3%*

*Projected from 1973–1976 data.

Accounting for Slower Economic Growth

The most careful study of economic growth in the United States is reported in a 1979 book by Edward Denison, *Accounting For Slower Economic Growth.* This study attributes the changes in real national income per person employed to identifiable changes in the level and composition of inputs and to identifiable conditions that affect the allocation of resources. Denison does not attempt to explain the number of persons employed. His detailed analysis is based on data only through 1976, but he concludes that the fundamental conditions reflected in the pattern of growth since 1973 have continued through at least 1978.

For this paper, it is sufficient to summarize Denison's estimates of the reasons for the 0.6 percent annual rate decline in real national income per person employed in the period from 1973 through 1976.

Changes in Labor Characteristics. A reduction in hours worked per employee reduced productivity per employee at a 0.5 percent annual rate. An increase in the proportion of young and female workers reduced productivity at a 0.3 percent annual rate. An increase in the average education of the labor force, however, increased productivity at a 0.9 percent annual rate. The net effect of the changes in labor characteristics, thus, increased productivity at a 0.1 percent annual rate.

Changes in Capital Per Employee. An increase in business structures and equipment per employee increased productivity at a 0.2 percent annual rate. Combined with negligible changes in the inventories and land per employee, the net effect of increases in capital increased productivity at a 0.2 percent annual rate. The combination of an increase in business investment for environmental and safety measures plus the increase in crime is estimated to have reduced measured productivity at a 0.4 percent annual rate. The net effect of these changes reduced productivity at a 0.2 percent annual rate.

Unexplained Conditions. The sum of these identifiable conditions is estimated to have increased productivity at a 0.1 percent annual rate. In fact, productivity declined at a 0.6 percent annual rate during this period. The unaccounted residual, thus, was a negative 0.7 percent annual rate—larger than the observed decline in productivity. Moreover, this unaccounted residual declined from a positive 1.4 percent annual rate in the 1948–1973 period to the negative 0.7 percent annual rate in the later period. Denison acknowledges that, "What happened is, to be blunt, a mystery." A recognition of our ignorance is often the beginning of wisdom. We should all be prepared to recognize that we have only the most rudimentary understanding of the recent decline in economic growth.

The Fiscal Effects on Economic Growth

Denison addresses the possible fiscal effects on economic growth in a concluding chapter on "The Unexplained Portion . . ." He observes that the government share of output increased more rapidly in earlier years and concludes that ". . . the general size of government budgets has not had a substantial adverse effect on growth and productivity." Maybe so, but I doubt this conclusion. We should not be too quick to dismiss the effects of increases in the marginal tax and transfer rates or of the increased regulation and paperwork that has been associated with the growth of government spending. Moreover, the allocation effects of the growth of government are a function of the return on economic activity *minus* the marginal tax and transfer rates, so the proportionate effects of a specific increase in these rates increases as a function of their level. The aggregate effects of the growth of government on the growth of the economy have proved difficult to identify, but a developing body of recent studies has provided much improved estimates of the affects of taxes and transfers on the major conditions contributing to economic growth.

The Supply and Allocation of Labor. A major contribution to improved understanding of the labor supply effects of taxes and transfers has been made recently by Jerry Hausman, using cross-section samples and an innovative econometric technique. For husbands, age 25 to 55, he estimates that federal income and social security taxes reduce hours worked by about 8 percent. The deadweight loss is about 22 percent of the tax revenues for a worker with an average wage and increases sharply with the wage level. For wives and single women, the effects on hours worked are substantially higher. Other studies suggest that the effects of taxes and transfers on younger and older males are also higher.

One dimension of the supply of labor for which we have no significant evidence is the effect of taxes and transfers on the allocation of labor by skills, work conditions, and location. The taxation of money wages should be expected to lead to reduced personal investment in training and a reduced supply of labor to occupations and in regions where conditions are less desirable. The observations that wage rates in construction have increased relative to that in services and that employment in the Northeast has declined relative to other regions are consistent with the consequences of higher tax rates on money income, but we do not have good estimates of the magnitude of these effects. These several effects of taxes on the allocation of the labor force may be more important than the effects on hours worked.

The Supply and Allocation of Capital. Gross private saving in cyclical peak years has been a roughly constant proportion of national output in the United States for nearly a century. The negative relation between household and corporate savings implies that households "pierce the corporate veil" in making their own saving decisions. A recent study by George von Furstenberg, however, finds that the composition of saving is strongly affected by the composition of government spending and taxes. Changes in transfers or personal taxes appear to have little affect on total saving. Increases in government purchases of goods and services, however, appear to have a strong negative effect on total saving. The general body of such studies implies that it is very difficult to increase total saving, except temporarily, by fiscal policy, but substantially more research is necessary for a satisfactory understanding of this relation.

Changes in tax rates, however, appear to have a more substantial effect on the allocation of investment among different uses. A recent study by Patric Henderson and Sheng-Cheng Hu indicates that the purchases of new business equipment are significantly dependent on the pretax cost of capital and concludes that a 50 percent reduction in the tax service life would increase the desired stock of equipment by about 14 percent. Their corresponding study of business investment in structures did not lead to satisfactory results. A recent study by Frank de Leeuw and Larry Ozanne indicates that the special tax provisions affecting housing significantly increases the price of housing, and this effect increases with inflation. Both the decline in the growth of real business investment and the increased relative price of housing in recent years are probably the result of the combined effect of the tax system and increasing inflation.

The combination of these studies suggest that tax policy may not significantly change gross private savings but that it may increase business investment at a cost of lower investment in other uses. In addition, with open international capital markets, an increase in the demand for business investment in the United States is likely to increase the total flow of savings available in the United States for all uses.

Summary. Again, we have only the most rudimentary understanding of the decline in real growth of the economy in recent years and the contribution of government spending and taxes to this condition. Given the problems of the U.S. economy, however, our political officials cannot wait for more definitive results from the research community. President Reagan has initiated a program to reduce the real growth of federal spending, to reduce personal and business tax rates, to reduce regulation, and to reduce monetary growth. This program reflects a profound conviction about the values of the American community and how the economy works, a conviction that I share. We do not yet have a sufficient body of objective research, however, to estimate many of the effects of this program. In that sense, the Reagan program is an experiment. We will continue to incorporate the contributions of the public finance community in development of the subsequent details of this program. For the present, however, our program is based more on our shared convictions than on the available analysis.

References

Brennan, Geoffrey and Buchanan, James, *The Power To Tax*, Cambridge University Press, 1980.

Denison, Edward, *Accounting for Slower Economic Growth*, The Brookings Institution, 1979.

Hausman, Jerry, "Labor Supply" in *How Taxes Affect Economic Behavior*, The Brookings Institution, 1981.

Henderson, Patric and Hu, Sheng-Cheng, "Investment in Producers Equipment," in *How Taxes Affect Economic Behavior*, The Brookings Institution, 1981.

von Furstenberg, George M., "Saving" in *How Taxes Affect Economic Behavior,* The Brookings Institution, 1981.

de Leeuw, Frank and Ozanne, Larry, "Housing" in *How Taxes Affect Economic Behavior,* The Brookings Institution, 1981.

Résumé

Cet article récapitule quelle a été la croissance de l'intervention publique et de l'économie aux Etats-Unis depuis 1965 et critique les différentes explications données.

La croissance des dépenses publiques pour une période donnée doit s'expliquer en terme de conditions spécifiques à la période et non en terme de conditions générales susceptibles d'influencer les décisions relatives aux dépenses publiques. Des conditions objectives paraissent expliquer la majeure partie de la croissance des dépenses réelles pour des services publics et environ 70% de la croissance des dépenses globales. On considère plusieurs explications politiques et fiscales concernant la croissance inhabituelle des transferts et subventions fédérales. La conclusion générale est que nous n'appréhendons que de façon imparfaite les raisons de la croissance des dépenses publiques.

Le taux de la croissance économique aux Etats-Unis a décliné avec chaque cycle successif depuis 1965. Les conditions objectives ne semblent expliquer qu'une faible part du déclin de la croissance de la productivité pour cette période. La relation entre la croissance de la productivité, la croissance des dépenses publiques globales et la fiscalité n'est pas claire non plus. Néanmoins, plusieurs études récentes améliorent notre compréhension de l'effet des taux fiscaux marginaux sur l'activité économique. En conclusion, nous n'appréhendons que de façon très imparfaite le déclin de ces dernières années de l'influence des dépenses et des recettes publiques sur la croissance réelle de l'économie.

Public Choice and Growth: Barriers to Trade, Factor Mobility, and Growth*

Mancur Olson

I

This paper takes for granted, among other things, the conclusions of my book on *The Logic of Collective Action*, [Olson (1965)].[1] That book argued that not only governments, but also many nongovernmental or private associations produce public or collective goods. The benefits of lobbying organizations that win favorable legislation or regulations for those in some industry, occupation, or other group usually go automatically to everyone in the relevant category; the higher price or wage obtained by any cartelistic organization similarly goes to every seller. Such benefits are then public goods in the sense that they go to everyone in some group if they go to anyone in the group, even though the special-interest legislation or cartel price may of course be harmful to society as a whole. It follows from this that, at least if a group is large, it will not act to serve its *common* interests, which are collective goods to it, by voluntary or market action. If a typical individual in a group of, say, a million makes a contribution to the provision of a collective good for his group, he bears the whole cost of that contribution but gets on average one millionth of the benefit. The typical individual's voluntary participation in or contribution to any organization seeking to serve his group's interest will accordingly be strikingly less than what would be required for "group optimality" (Pareto-optimality for the group), if indeed there is any participation or contribution at all.

If follows that large groups that succeed in organizing to serve their collective interests must use "selective incentives," or individual

*Parts of this paper have appeared in other publications.

Public Finance and Economic Growth. Proceedings of the 37th Congress of the International Institute of Public Finance. Tokyo, 1981, pp. 15–40

punishments or rewards that distinguish between those members of the group that do contribute to the collective effort from those who do not. The coercive power of a "union shop" with a dues check-off and a picket line that is dangerous to cross on this interpretation is analogous to compulsory taxation by governments that provide collective goods to an entire society. The coercion in both cases provides a *selective* incentive because only those who not pay dues or taxes are punished. In subtle ways that are usually not widely understood, a great many associations use various legal advantages and complementarities between the collective action and the provision of assorted private goods to reward the individuals who contribute to the collective action, i.e., use positive selective incentives. *The Logic of Collective Action* claims to show that, for the United States in the mid nineteen-sixties at least, all large associations with either political or cartelistic power owed their membership to selective incentives rather than to the value of the collective good they provided for their members.

Naturally, selective incentives are hard to come by—coercion is difficult to organize and is resisted, and it is often even more difficult to obtain the considerable resources needed to supply the positive selective incentives needed to get a large group organized. For most large groups with common interests, such as consumers, taxpayers, the poor, and the unemployed, no selective incentives are available. These groups are, for example, too scattered to be subject to picket lines. In no society are most of the people in these categories organized. Even for those groups for which selective incentives are in principle obtainable, it requires fortunate circumstances and rare qualities of political entrepreneurship to create a large scale organization. Collective action, then, is difficult and problematical for those groups for which it is possible, and for some large groups with important common interests it is impossible.

"Small" groups, by contrast, can organize with less difficulty and often without selective incentives. If two identical individuals share a common interest or collective good, each will get half of the benefit of any action in their common interest and so, even with Cournot-type behavior, will have an incentive to make substantial contributions to the common interest. Since the action of each noticeably affects the well-being of the other, they also have an incentive to bargain with one another until they have maximized their joint gains. As groups get larger the share of the total benefit that an individual obtains from any effort he makes to obtain a collective good for his group inevitably gets smaller. In other words, the "externality" to the group of individual action to provide some amount of a collective good for the group rises with the number of members in the group, so the extent to which the individuals in the group have an incentive to act in the group interest diminishes as the group gets larger, the large groups fall farther short of providing themselves with group-optimal amounts of collective goods. This point is argued in a less casual way in *The Logic*, and it is crucial to the argument in the present paper.

II

If the logic that has been impressionistically described is correct, and if we combine it in certain cases with conventional propositions from microeconomic theory and a few other assumptions that will probably not be controversial, a number of further implications follow. The connections to these further implications are set out with some care in my book on *The Rise and Decline of Nations*, [Olson (1982)][2] but some may prefer a briefer and more casual discussion, so this paper will attempt to make each of the implications intuitively plausible in a few sentences.

Implication I is that no society can attain symmetrical or complete organization of group interests, so that it is and will be impossible for leaders of all groups to bargain together to obtain a "core" or Pareto-efficient allocation of resources. This follows trivially from the fact that some large groups do not have access to selective incentives. Implication II is that stable societies with unchanged boundaries will accumulate more organizations and collusions for collective action over time. The reason for this is that as time goes on more of those groups that can organize will have enjoyed the fortunate circumstances and able political entrepeneurship that is needed for organization, whereas the interest of organizational leaders in maintaining their position insures that organizations with selective incentives will not disappear unless destroyed by upheaval or war. Implication III is that "small" groups have disproportionate organizational power in all societies, but since they are not as slow to organize as large groups this disproportion is greater in societies that have lately suffered instability. This follows directly from the logic referred to above.

The fourth implication arises from the fact that, if the associations or collusions for collective action are small in relation to the society of which they are a part, they will gain little from trying to make their societies more efficient, because their members get only a minute fraction of the gains from a more efficient society (they are in a position akin to that of an individual in a large group). Similarly, they will gain from obtaining a larger share of the social output for their members, even if the social loss from the redistribution is a substantial multiple of the amount distributed to them. Thus, with some exceptions, associations for collective action are coalitions which engage in distributional struggle rather than in efforts to increase social efficiency. There are compelling reasons set out elsewhere for believing that most of the efforts of distributional coalitions have excess burdens that are large in relation to the amount they win in distributional struggle. Implication IV is therefore that special-interest organizations and collusions are largely distributional coalitions which on balance reduce the efficiency and income of the societies in which they are located. Implication V is that associations that encompass a large part of the societies in which they are located are severly constrained in seeking redistributions toward their own clients because their own members will bear much of the social costs; if an association represents half of the income-earning capacity of the country, its members will on average suffer half of the loss in social efficiency that results from the redistribution, and it will accordingly not seek any redistributions to its members which cost the society more than twice as much as the amount distributed to its members.

Implication VI is that distributional coalitions will make decisions more slowly than the individuals and firms of which they are comprised (because they must make decisions either through by-laws or by unanimous consent bargaining), and will accordingly tend to have crowded agenda and bargaining tables. Implication VII is that distributional coalitions slow down a society's capacity to adopt new technologies and to reallocate resources in response to changing conditions, and thereby reduce the rate of economic growth. Partly this is due to the crowded agenda and slow decision-making and partly to considerations that are not intuitively obvious or susceptible to summary description. Implication VIII is that distributional coalitions are exclusive; if they are cartels there are fewer sales at the cartel price for each member if new members enter, and if they seek redistributions politically the members will gain from having a minimum winning coalition. Finally, Implication IX is that the accumulation of distributional coalitions increases the complexity of regulation and the role of government, partly for reasons that are not immediately obvious nor capable of brief description.

The Rise and Decline of Nations argued that the preceding considerations help to explain the rapid growth of Japan and West Germany after World War II. The totalitarian governments that had controlled these countries had destroyed most of the organizations for collective action, and certainly all of those on the left, and the occupying powers subsequently eliminated any that collaborated. As a result these countries have had relatively few distributional coalitions, and those they do have are, sometimes because of promotion by occupation authorities, usually relatively encompassing. By the same token, if the argument adumbrated above is correct, the slow economic growth of Great Britain is partly explained by the fact that its uniquely long record of stability and immunity from invasion have given it more time to accumulate special-interest organization and collusion than other countries. Similarly, the relatively rapid growth of the West and South of the United States and the relatively slow growth of the Northeast and older Middle West are also consistent with the argument. The West because of recent settlement and the South because of the Civil War and its aftermath have had relatively little time to accumulate distributional coalitions, whereas the Northeast and the older Middle West have had a considerable time to accumulate such coalitions.

The countries and regions that have just been mentioned constitute important anomalies, but the theory is called into question if it cannot explain other cases as well. The world is complex and multicausal, so no theory should be expected to explain everything, but a theory's claim to credence still rises if the range of its explanatory power can be increased without complicating it or introducing new variables. Thus the pages that follow endeavor to explain the growth of a number of other countries and historical periods.[3]

III

As we can see from Table 1, the original six members of the European Economic community have grown relatively rapidly since World War II, particularly in comparison with Australia, New Zealand, the United Kingdom, and the United States. For some of the member countries the growth was fastest in the nineteen sixties when the Common Market was going into effect. Though I have offered some explanation of the most anomalous or puzzling case of rapid growth in Germany there has been no analysis of the rapid growth of the other four members of the Six. As it turns out, the analysis of the Common Market will also show why New Zealand's postwar growth performance has been as bad as that of the United Kingdom, and why Australia, despite its good fortune in discovering rich deposits of natural resources, has nonetheless grown relatively slowly.

Looking at the timing of the growth of most of the Six, it is tempting to conclude, as many casual observers have, that the Common Market was responsible. This is *post hoc ergo propter hoc* reasoning and we obviously cannot rely on it, especially in view of the

Table 1

Average Annual Rates of Growth of Per Capita Gross Domestic Product at Constant Prices (in percent)

	1950 to 1960	*1960 to 1970*	*1970 to 1977*
Australia	2.0[1]	3.9[2]	2.5[3]
Austria	5.7	3.9	3.8
Belgium	2.0[4]	4.1	3.4
Canada	1.2	3.7	3.4
Denmark	2.5	3.9	2.4
Finland	3.3	4.2	2.9
France	3.5	4.6	3.2
Germany, Fed. Rep. of	6.6	3.3	2.3
Ireland	1.8	3.8	2.2
Italy	4.9[5]	4.6	2.1
Japan	6.8[6]	9.4	3.9[7]
Netherlands	3.3	4.1	2.2
New Zealand	1.7[8]	2.2[9]	
Norway	2.7	4.0	3.9
Sweden	2.9	3.6	1.3
Switzerland	2.9	2.8	−0.1
United Kingdom	2.3	2.3	1.7
United States	1.2	3.0	1.9

Data are from *Yearpaper(s) of National Account Statistics* for 1969 and 1978, Statistical Office of the United Nations, U.N., New York, published in 1970 and 1979, respectively.

[1]1952–1960
[2]1965–1970
[3]1970–1975
[4]1953–1960
[5]1951–1960
[6]1952–1960
[7]1970–1976
[8]1954–1960
[9]1960–1968

fact that most if not all of the careful quantitative studies indicate that the gains from the Common Market were very small in relation to the increases in income that the members enjoyed. The quantitative studies of the gains from freer trade, like those of the losses from monopoly, usually show far smaller effects than economists anticipated, and the calculations of the gains from the Common Market fit the normal pattern. The studies of Edwin Truman and Mordechai Kreinin, for example, while arguing that trade creation overwhelmed any trade diversion, imply that the Common Market added two percent or less to EEC manufacturing consumption. [Truman (1969), Kreinin (1974, Ch. 3, 25–55), Williamson and Battrill (1973)][4] Bela Balassa, moreover, argues that, taking economies of scale as well as other sources of gain from the Common Market into account, there was a "0.3 percentage point rise in the ratio of the annual increment of trade to that of GNP" which was probably "accompanied by a one-tenth of one percentage point increase in the growth rate. By 1965 the cumulative effect of the Common Market's establishment on the Gross National Product of the member countries would thus have reached one-half of one percent of GNP." [Balassa (1967)][5] Careful studies by other skilled economists also suggest that the intuitive judgment that large customs unions can bring about really substantial increases in the rate of growth is not supported by economists' typical comparative-static calculations.

IV

There is a hint that there is more to the matter in some of the more remarkable instances of economic growth in historical times. The United States became the world's leading economy in the century or so after the adoption of its constitution. Germany similarly advanced from its status as a poor area in the first half of the nineteenth century to the point where it was by the start of World War I overtaking Britain, and this occurred after the Zollverein or customs union of most German-speaking areas and the political unification of Germany. These two situations, I shall argue, were similar to the Common Market in three crucial ways. The similarities are sometimes overlooked because the conventional nomenclature calls attention to the differences between the formation of governments and of customs unions.

One of the crucial features of the Common Market was, of course, that it created a large area within which there was something approaching free trade. A second was that it allowed relatively unrestricted movement of labor, capital, and firms within this larger area. A third was that it shifted the authority for decisions about tariffs and certain other matters from the capitals of each of the Six nations to the European Economic Community as a whole. When we think about these features, we immediately realize that the creation of a new or larger country out of many smaller jurisdictions also includes each of these three fundamental features.

As has often been pointed out before, the establishment of the United States of America out of the thirteen independent ex-colonies also involved the creation of an area of free trade and factor mobility, as well as a shift in the institutions which made certain decisions. The adoption of the Constitution did in fact negate tariffs that New York had established against certain imports from Connecticut and New Jersey. Similarly, not only the Zollverein, but also the creation of the German Reich itself included the same essential features. Most of the

German-speaking area of Europe until well into the nineteenth century were separate principalities or city-states or other small jurisdictions with their own tariffs, barriers to mobility, and economic policies, but an expanding common market, as well as a shift of many governmental powers, resulted from the Zollverein and even more from the formation of the German state that was complete by 1871.

There was also a much earlier development elsewhere in Europe that created vastly larger markets, established far wider domains for factor mobility, and shifted the locus of governmental decision-making. The centralizing monarchs of England and France in the late fifteenth and sixteenth centuries tried to create nation-states out of the existing mosaic of parochial feudal fiefdoms; there had been nominal national kingdoms before, but as the textbooks tell us, the real power normally rested with lords of various fiefs or sometimes with virtually self-governing walled towns. Each of these mini-governments tended to have its own tolls and tariffs; a boat trip along the Rhine, with its toll-collecting castles sometimes only about a kilometer apart, is sufficient to remind one how numerous local tolls in Medieval Europe were. The nationalizing monarchs with their mercantilistic policies usually strove to eliminate these local authorities and their restrictions, and in turn imposed highly protectionist policies at the national level. In France a significant proportion of the feudal tolls and restrictions to trade and factor mobility were not removed until the French Revolution, but in Britain the creation of nationwide markets took place more rapidly. Interestingly, creation of effective national jurisdictions in Western Europe was followed by the commercial revolution and in Britain ultimately by the industrial revolution, and in a more general sense by the "rise of the West."

In many respects, and possibly the most important ones, the creation of meaningful national governments is very different from the creation of customs unions, however effective the customs union might be. Nonetheless, in all of the cases we have considered, a much wider area of relatively free trade was established, a similarly wide area of relatively free movement of factors of production was created, and the power to make at least some important decisions about economic policy was shifted to a new institution in a new location. There was in each case at least a considerable measure of what I shall here call "jurisdictional integration." It would be much better if we could avoid coining a new phrase, especially such a ponderous one, but the familiar labels obscure the common features that concern us here.

Since there are several cases of jurisdictional integration followed by relatively rapid economic progress, it is now even more tempting than it was when we looked at the Common Market alone to posit a causal connection. But that would still be at least premature. For one thing, we should have some idea just how jurisdictional integration would bring about rapid growth, and statistical studies such as those cited above for the Common Market suggest that the gains from the freer trade are not nearly large enough to explain substantial economic growth. For another, the number of cases of jurisdictional integration is still not large enough to allow confident generalization. We must therefore look at the specific *patterns* of growth *within* jurisdictions as well as across them to see if they provide corroborating evidence, and in addition present a theoretical model that could explain why jurisdictional integration should have the observed effects.

V

One of the most remarkable and consistent patterns in the advancing economies of the West in the early modern period was the relative (and often absolute) decline of most of what had been the major cities. This decline of many of the major cities is paradoxical, for the single most important development moving the West ahead was surely the *industrial* revolution and Western society today is probably more urbanized than any society in history. The commercial and industrial revolutions created *new* cities, or made great cities out of mere villages, rather than building upon the base of the existing larger medieval and early modern cities. Major capitals like London and Paris grew, of course, as administrative centers and as consumers of part of the new wealth, but they were by no means the sources of the growth. As the famous French historian Fernand Braudel puts it, "The towns were an example of deep-seated disequilibrium, asymmetrical growth, and irrational and unproductive investment on a nationwide scale. . . . These enormous urban formations are more linked to the past, to accomplished evolutions, faults and weaknesses of the societies and economies of the Ancien Regime, than to preparations for the future. . . . The obvious fact was that the capital cities would be present at the forthcoming industrial revolution in the role of spectators. Not London, but Manchester, Leeds, Glasgow, and innumerable small proletarian towns launched the new era." [Braudel (1973) pp. 439–440].[6]

M. J. Daunton shows that, at least for Great Britain during the Industrial Revolution, Braudel was right. Of the six cities that are deemed to be the largest in England in 1600, only Bristol and of course London, were among the top six in 1801. Manchester, Liverpool, Birmingham, and Leeds completed the list in 1801. York, the

3rd largest city in 1600, was the 17th largest in 1801; Newcastle, the 5th largest city in 1600, was 14th largest in 1801, as will be seen from Table 2 [Daunton (1978) p. 247].[7]

Even in the years before 1601 there was a concern among contemporaries about the "desolation of cytes and tounes." Charles Pythian-Adams' essay on "Urban Decay in Late Medieval England" argues from a mass of detailed if scattered figures and contemporary comments that the population and income of many English cities had begun to decline before the Black Death. Though Pythian-Adams finds that the decline of certain cities may be offset by the expansion of others, we are left wondering why so many towns decline while others grow. During the late 15th and early 16th centuries, and especially between 1520 and 1570, Pythian-Adams finds most of more impotant towns were "under pressure," if not in an "acute urban crisis" often involving significant loss of economic activity and population. [Pythian-Adams (1978)][8]

On the Continent towns were not so often partially autonomous institutions operating within relatively stable national boundaries. Partly because of this, and partly because the Continent did not experience the rapid changes of the Industrial Revolution until later, the situation there is not so easily summarized. Nonetheless, there were many similar replacements of older urban centers with newer towns or rural industry. One example is the shift of some of the medieval woolen industry from the cities of Flanders to nearby Brabant and the decline of Flemish woolen production generally in relation to that of the North Italian cities, which in their turn declined as well. Another is the decline of Naples, which on the eve of the French Revolution was probably Europe's fourth largest city. One classic case is the decline of

Table 2

1600		*1801*	
Rank	*Population*	*Rank*	*Population*
1. London	250,000	1. London	960,000
2. Norwich	15,000	2. Manchester	84,000
3. York	12,000	3. Liverpool	78,000
4. Bristol	12,000	4. Birmingham	74,000
5. Newcastle	10,000	5. Bristol	64,000
6. Exeter	9,000	6. Leeds	53,000
		....	....
		8. Norwich	37,000
		14. Newcastle	28,000
		15. Exeter	17,000
		17. York	16,000

the central city of Aachen, and the shift of industry to the suburbs, which Herbert Kisch has chronicled in detailed. [Kisch (1964), Dillard (1967), Pirenne (1936)][9] The expansion of the suburbs at the expense of the old city was a commonplace. [Braudel (1973) pp. 404–405][10]

VI

Medieval towns and cities were normally small by modern standards. Their boundaries were usually precisely defined by city walls and they often had a substantial degree of autonomy (and in some cases were independent of any larger government). Within these small jurisdictions there would naturally be only a few merchants in any one line of commerce and only a limited number of skilled craftsmen in any one specialized craft, even if the population of the town was in the thousands. The primitive methods of transportation in medieval times and the absence of safe and passable national road systems also tended to segment markets, so that a handful of merchants or skilled craftsmen could more easily secure a monopoly if they could cartelize local production. When the merchants in a given line of commerce had more wealth than the townspeople generally, it seem likely that they would interact with one another more often than with those of slender means. To some extent, this would often happen also among those who shared the same skilled craft.

The logic of collective action implies that small groups have far greater opportunities to organize for collective action than large ones, and suggests that if other things are equal there will be relatively more organization in small jurisdictions than in large ones. The logic also implies that small and homogeneous groups that interact socially also have the further advantage that social selective incentives will help them organize for collective action. These considerations entailed Implication Three, that small groups were better and sooner organized than large ones. If the logic referred to earlier was correct, it follows that the merchants in a given line of commerce and practitioners of particular skilled crafts in a medieval city would be especially well placed to organize collective action. If the city contained even a few thousands of people, it is not likely that the population as a whole could organize to counter such combinations, though in tiny villages the population would be small enough for this to occur.

VII

The result of these relatively favorable conditions for collective cartelistic action was of course the guilds. The guilds naturally endeavored to augment the advantages of their small numbers and social homogeneity with the coercive civic power as well, and many of them did indeed influence if not control the towns in which they operated. This outcome was particularly likely in England, where the national monarchies found it expedient to grant towns a substantial degree of autonomy. In what is now Germany guilds would more often confront small principalities more jealous of their power and would need to work out symbiotic relationships with territorial rulers and the nobility. Often in France, for example, the guild would be one of the few ways in which the government could successfully collect taxes, given its administrative limitations, so guilds would sometimes be given monopoly privileges in return for tax payments. The city-states of North Italy extended well beyond the walls of the town, and in these cases the guilds would have a wider sphere of control if they shared power, but at the same time were thereby exposed to instabilities in the North Italian environment which must often have interrupted their development or curtailed their powers. In spite of all the variation from region to region, it is notable that guilds of merchants and master craftsmen, and occasionally also guilds of journeymen, became commonplace from Byzantium in the East to Britain in the West, and from at least the Hanseatic cities in the North to Italy in the South.

The guilds both strengthened themselves and served a useful function in providing social insurance for those of their numbers who fell upon misfortune. They possibly also provided some degree of quality control, much as modern professional associations do, though it is doubtful that the levels of quality they stipulated were optimal for their customers.

Overwhelmingly the guilds were nonetheless distributive coalitions which used monopoly power and sometimes also political power to serve their interests. And, as Implications IV and VII predict, they reduced economic efficiency and delayed technological innovation. The fact that apprenticeship was used to control entry is demonstrated conclusively by the requirement in some guilds that a journeyman could become a master only upon the payment of a fee, by the rule in some guilds that apprentices and journeymen could not marry, and by the stipulation in other guilds that the son of a master need *not* serve the apprenticeship that was normally required. The myriad rules that were intended to keep one master from advancing significantly at the expense of his fellows surely limited innovation.

VIII

What should be expected when there is jurisdictional integration in an environment of relatively autonomous cities with a dense network of guilds? Implication II indicated that the accumulation of special-interest organization occurs gradually in stable societies with *unchanged* borders. If the area over which trade can occur without tolls or restrictions is made vastly larger, a guild or any similar cartel will find that it monopolizes only a small part of the total market. A monopoly of a small part of an integrated market is, of course, not a monopoly at all: no one will pay a monopoly price to a guild member if they can buy at a lower price from those outside the guild. With jurisdictional integration there is also free movement of the factors of production within the integrated jurisdiction, so there may also be an incentive for sellers to move into any community in the jurisdiction in which cartelization has brought higher prices. Jurisdictional integration also means that the political decisions are now made by different people in a different institutional setting at a location that is probably now quite some distance away. The amount of political influence that is required to change the policy of the integrated jurisdiction will also be vastly larger than the amount that was needed in the relatively parochial jurisdiction that previously prevailed. Thus guilds usually lost both their monopoly power and their political influence when integrated nation-wide jurisdictions replaced local jurisdictions.

The level of transportation costs is also significant. If transportation costs are too high to make it worthwhile to transport a given product from one town to another, the jurisdictional integration should be less significant, though there would still be a tendency for competing sellers to migrate to the cartelized locations in the integrated jurisdiction. The time of the commercial revolution was also a time of improved transportation, especially over water, which led to the development of new routes to Asia and the discovery of the New World. The growth in the power of central government also reduced the danger of travel from community to community by gradually eliminating the anarchic conflict among feudal lords and the extent of lawlessness in rural areas, and even lead to more road building and (later) to the construction of canals. If the countryside is relatively safe from violence, transportation is not only cheaper but production may also take place wherever costs are lowest.

When jurisdictional integration occurs, new distributive coalitions matching the scale of the larger jurisdiction will not immediately spring up because, as we know from Implication II, such coalitions emerge only gradually in stable situations. It will not, however, take small groups as long to organize as large ones (Implication III). Thus the great merchants involved in larger scale trade, often over greater distances, were among the first groups to organize or collude on a national scale. They were often also extremely successful—as Adam Smith pointed out, the influence of the "merchants" gave the great governments of Europe the policy of "mercantilism," which favored influential merchants and their allies at the expense of the rest of the nation. Often this involved severely protectionist policies which protected the influential merchants form foreign competitors—mercantilism is to this day used practicially as a synomym for protectionism.

It might seem, then, that the gains from jurisdictional integration in early modern Europe were brief and unimportant, since the mercantilist policies followed close on the heels of the decaying guilds in the towns. Not so. The reason is that tariffs and restrictions around a sizeable nation are less serious than tariffs and restrictions around each town or fiefdom. Much of the trade will be *intra*national whether the nation has tariffs at its borders or not, because of transport costs and the natural diversity of any large country. Trade restrictions at national borders do not have any direct effect on this trade, whereas trade restrictions around each town and fiefdom do reduce or eliminate most of it. Morever, as Adam Smith pointed out, "the division of labor is limited by the extent of the market," and thus the widening markets of the period of jurisdictional integration also made it possible to take advantage of economies of scale and specialization. Another way of thinking of the matter involves noting that the shift of trade restrictions from a community level to a national level reduces the number of miles of tariff barriers by a vast multiple. I believe that the greatest reductions of trade restrictions in history have come from reducing the mileage rather than the height of trade restrictions.

IX

Since the commercial and the industrial revolutions took place during and after the extraordinary reduction in trade barriers and in other guild restrictions, and occurred overwhelmingly in new cities and suburbs relatively free of guilds, there appears to have been a causal connection. Yet both the timing of growth and the fact that guilds were regularly at the locations where the growth was obstructed could conceivably have been coincidences. Happily, there are additional aspects of the pattern of growth which suggest that this was not the case.

One of these is the "putting out system" in the textile industry, which was then the most important "manufacturing" industry. Under this remarkable system, merchants would travel all over the countryside to "put out" to individual families material that was to be spun or woven, and then return at a later time to pick up the yarn or cloth.

Clearly such a system required a lot of time, travel, and transactions costs. There was the question of exactly how much material had been left with each family and of how much yarn or cloth could be made from it, so that there were innumerable occasions for haggling and disputes. The merchant also had the risk that the material he had put out would be stolen. Given the obvious disadvantages, we must ask why this strange system was used. The answer from any number of accounts is that this system despite its disadvantages was cheaper than production in towns controlled by guilds. There may have been some advantages of production scattered throughout the countryside, such as cheaper food for the workers, but this could not explain the tendency at the same time for production to expand in suburbs around the towns controlled by guilds. (Adam Smith said that "if you would have your work tolerably executed, it must be done in the suburbs, where the workmen have no exclusive privilege, having nothing but their character to depend upon, and you must then smuggle it into town as well as you can" [Smith (1976) p. 146)].[11] Neither can any possible inherent advantages of manufacturing in scattered rural sites explain the objections of guilds to the production in the countryside; Flemish guilds, for example, even sent expenditions into the countryside to destroy the equipment of those to whom materials had been put out.

There was also a tendency for economic growth to occur in parts of Europe in which jurisdictional integrations and political upheaval had undermined distributional coalitions of various kinds. A centralized national government came relatively early to England, perhaps in part because it was an island nation. The commercial revolution by all accounts was also relatively strong in that country. In the seventeenth century, and even to an extent in the very early eighteenth century, Britain suffered from civil war and political instability (see, for example, Christopher Hill, [1961][12] and J. H. Plumb, [1967]).[13] Undoubtedly the instability brought some destruction and waste and in addition discouraged long run investment. But within a few decades after it became clear that stable and nationwide government had been re-established in Britain the Industrial Revolution was underway. It's also generally accepted that there was much less restriction of enterprise and trade in mid-eighteenth century Britain than in most of the Continent.

Similarly, the remarkable growth in Holland took place just after that country (or part of it) won independence from Spain. There was also economic progress in France, though less than in England and Holland. There was considerable integration of a relatively large jurisdiction in early modern France, but no upheaval sufficient to destroy many distributional coalitions involving the nobility and the guilds until the French revolution. French kings short of money for wars and other dissipations also often gave legal status to various cartels in return for special taxes. The German-speaking and Italian-speaking parts of Europe did not experience jurisdictional integration until the second half of the nineteenth century and they did not enjoy their share of Europe's advancing prosperity until then either. Of course, thousands of other factors were also important in explaining the varying fortunes of the different parts of Europe, and it would be preposterous to offer the present argument as a monocausal explanation. In view of the importance of the other factors involved, it is nonetheless remarkable how well the theory fits the pattern and timing of growth in Europe.

In the case of the United States, there was not only the Constitutional provision mentioned earlier that prohibited separate states from imposing barriers to trade and factor mobility, but also over a century of westward expansion. Any cartel or lobby in the United States before the present century had to face the fact that substantial new areas were regularly being added to the country. Competition could always come from these new areas, notwithstanding the high tariffs at the national level, and the new areas also increased the size of the polity, so that ever larger coalitions would be needed either for cartelization or lobbying. Vast immigration also worked against cartelization of the labor market. In addition, the United States, like all frontier areas, could begin without a legacy of distributional coalitions and rigid social classes. In view of all this, the extraordinary achievement of the U.S. economy for a century and more after the adoption of the Constitution is not surprising.

X

The case with which we began, the rapid growth in the sixties of the Six nations that created the Common Market, also fits the pattern. The three largest of these countries, France, Germany, and Italy, had suffered a great deal of instability and invasion. This implied that they had relatively less special-interest organization than they would otherwise have had, and often also more encompassing organizations. In France and Italy the labor unions did not have the resources or strength for sustained industrial action; in Germany the union structure growing out of the occupation was highly encompassing.

As Implication III tells us, small groups can organize more quickly and thoroughly than large groups, so even in the countries that had suffered the most turbulence those industries that had small numbers of large firms were likely to be organized. In Italy the Allied occupation had not been so thorough and some industries remained organized from Fascist times. In all of the countries, organizations of substantial firms, which were often manufacturing firms, would frequently have an incentive to seek protection through tariffs, quotas, or other controls for their industry, and in at least some of these countries they were very likely to get it. Once imports could be excluded the home market could also be profitably cartelized. If foreign firms should seek to enter the country to compete with the domestic firms the latter could play upon nationalistic sentiments to obtain exclusionary or discriminatory legislation against the multinationals. At times in some countries, such as in postwar Germany at the time of Erhard, there would because of economic ideology or the interests of exporters be some determined resistance to protectionist pressures, but in other countries like France and Italy in the years just before the creation of the Common Market the capacity or the inclination to resist these pressures was lacking.

In France and Italy and to some extent in most of the other countries, the coalitional structure and government policy insured that tariffs, quotas, exchange controls, and restrictions on foreign firms were possibly the principal threat to economic efficiency. In France, for example, as Jean-Francois Hennart argues in "The Political Economy of Comparative Growth Rates: The Case of France," [Mueller (1983)][14] exchange controls, quotas, and licenses had nearly closed off the French market from foreign competition; raw materials were often allocated by trade associations, and trade and professional associations fixed prices and allocated production in many important sectors. In such situations the losses from protectionism and the cartelization it facilitates could hardly be small. If a Common Market could put the power to determine the level of protection and to set the rules about factor mobility and entry of foreign firms into the market out of the reach of each nation's colluding firms, the economies in question could be relatively efficient. The smaller nations among the Six were different in several respects, but they would also gain greatly from freer trade, in part because their small size made protectionist policies more costly for them. Most of the founding members of the European Community, then, were countries with coalitional structures, protectionist policies, or small sizes that made the Common Market especially useful to them. This would not have so clearly been the case if the Common Market had chosen very high tariff levels against the outside world, but the important Kennedy Round of tariff cuts insured that that didn't happen.

It doesn't follow that every country that joins any institution called a common market will enjoy gains comparable to those obtained by most of the Six. Whether a nation gains from a customs union depends on many factors, including its prior levels of protection and (to a lesser extent) those of the customs union it joins. In the case of France and Italy, for example, the Common Market almost certainly meant more liberal policies for trade and factor mobility than these countries would otherwise have had. In the case of Great Britain, where the interests of organized exporters and the international financial community in the City of London have long been significant, the level of protection was not so high, and it isn't obvious that joining the Common Market on balance liberalized British trade. When many high-tariff jurisdictions merge there is normally a great reduction in tariff barriers, even if the integrated jurisdiction has equally high tariffs, but a country with low tariffs already is getting most of the attainable gains from trade. The coalitional structure of a society also makes a difference. In Britain the professions, government employees, and many firms (such as "High Street" or downtown retail merchants) that would have no foreign competition in any case, are well organized; joining the Common Market could not significantly undermine their organizations. More foreign competition for manufacturing firms can reduce the power of unions, since manufacturers whose labor costs are far out of line must either cut back production or hold out for lower labor costs, but even here the influence is indirect and presumably not as significant as when imports directly undermine a cartel of manufacturing firms. Common markets have been even tried or proposed for developing countries with comparative advantage in the same goods and thus little reason to trade with one another, but this cannot promote growth. For these and other reasons, it isn't possible to say whether a customs union will be good or bad for a country's growth. One has to look at the prior level of protectionism, the coalitional structure, the potential gains from trade among the members, and still other factors in each individual case.

XI

The postwar growth rates of Australia and New Zealand, we recall, are not impressive. They have had rather long histories of stability and immunity from invasion, but not nearly as a long a period of stability as Britain. Though they enjoy exceptional endowments of natural resources in relation to population, their levels of per capita income have lately fallen behind those of many crowded and resource-poor countries in Western Europe. Some calculations of average tariff levels for these two countries, in combination with the foregoing analysis of jurisdictional integration, immediately suggest an explanation for their poor growth performance. Table 3 presents alternative calculations of average industrial tariff levels for a number of countries that were prepared by the Office of the President's Special Representative for Foreign Trade. The two columns at the extreme right of the table probably offer the best measures (because in those columns the weight or relative importance attributed to each tariffs on each commodity is given by the average imports of that commodity by all of the countries considered), but the other measures and calculations by other bodies produce broadly similar results. Nontariff barriers may often be more important than tariffs, but they are both generated by the same organizational and political forces and almost certainly vary across countries in somewhat the same way. The table shows that Australia and New Zealand, and especially New Zealand, have far higher tariffs than any of the other countries described. Their levels of protection are two to three times the level in the EEC and the United States, and four to five times as high as those of Sweden and especially Switzerland. As might be expected from the level of its tariffs, quotas on imports are also unusually important in New Zealand. The impact of protection levels that are uniquely high by the standards of the developed democracies is made even greater by the small size of Australian and New Zealand economies; a large integrated jurisdiction like the EEC or the United States would not lose nearly as much per capita from the same level of protection as Australia and New Zealand do.

The theory offered in this paper suggests that manufacturing firms and urban interests in Australia and New Zealand would have organized to seek protection. When this protection was attained they would sometimes have been able to engage in oligopolistic or cartelistic practices that would not have been feasible with free trade. With high tariffs and limitations on domestic competition firms could survive even if they paid more than competitive wages, so there was more scope for labor unions and greater gains from monopolizing labor than otherwise. Restrictions on Asian immigration would further facilitate cartelization of labor. Stability and immunity from invasion would insure that few special-interest organizations would be eliminated, but more would accumulate (Implication II) as time went on. The result would be that the frontier initially free of cartels and lobbies would eventually become highly organized, and economies that initially had exceptionally high per capita incomes would eventually fall behind the income levels of European countries with incomparably lower ratios of natural resources to population.

Table 3

	No Trade Weighting: Simple Average		*Own-country Import: Weighting*		*World Weights: Simple BTN Average*		*World Weights: Import Weighted BTN Average*	
	1976 Ave.	*Final Ave.*	*1976 Ave.*	*Final Ave.*	*1976 Ave.*	*Final Ave.*	*1976 Ave.*	*Final Ave.*
AUSTRALIA								
Dutiable	28.8	28.0	29.1	28.1	27.8	26.7	26.4	25.2
Total	16.9	16.5	15.4	15.1	13.3	12.8	13.0	12.6
NEW ZEALAND								
Dutiable	31.4	28.3	28.6	25.5	33.0	30.4	30.2	27.5
Total	24.3	21.9	19.7	17.6	20.5	18.7	18.0	16.3
UNITED STATES								
Dutiable	15.6	9.2	8.3	5.7	9.2	5.5	7.6	4.8
Total	14.8	8.8	6.2	4.3	7.1	4.1	5.6	3.5
CANADA								
Appl. Dutiable	13.7	7.8	13.1	8.9	12.0	7.3	12.9	8.3
Appl. Total	12.0	6.8	10.1	6.8	8.9	5.5	9.4	6.1
JAPAN								
Appl. Dutiable	8.1	6.2	6.9	4.9	8.0	5.7	7.9	5.5
Appl. Total	7.3	5.6	3.2	2.3	6.1	4.4	5.8	4.1
EEC								
Dutiable	8.8	6.0	9.8	7.2	9.5	7.0	9.6	7.1
Total	8.0	5.5	6.3	4.6	7.0	5.2	6.9	5.1
AUSTRIA								
Dutiable	14.2	9.8	18.8	14.5	15.9	12.0	17.0	13.3
Total	11.6	8.1	14.5	11.2	10.5	7.9	10.9	8.5
FINLAND								
Dutiable	17.0	14.6	11.6	9.2	11.2	9.0	11.5	9.1
Total	14.3	12.3	8.2	6.5	6.7	5.3	6.7	5.3
NORWAY								
Dutiable	11.1	8.2	10.5	8.0	10.2	7.4	10.0	7.5
Total	8.5	6.3	6.4	4.9	5.8	4.3	5.8	4.4
SWEDEN								
Dutiable	7.8	6.1	7.7	5.9	7.4	5.3	7.1	5.2
Total	6.2	4.9	6.3	4.8	4.6	3.3	4.5	3.3
SWITZERLAND								
Dutiable	3.7	2.7	4.1	3.3	4.2	3.1	4.0	3.1
Total	3.7	2.7	4.0	3.2	3.3	2.4	3.2	2.4
TOTAL								
Dutiable	15.2	11.0	10.6	7.6	11.7	11.1	10.6	7.6
Total	12.9	9.8	7.2	5.2	10.1	7.6	7.2	5.2

There is a need for detailed studies of the histories of Australia and New Zealand from this theoretical perspective. The histories of these countries, like those of others, are undoubtedly complicated and no monocausal explanation will do. Any final judgment should wait for the specialized research. But preliminary investigation of Australia and New Zealand suggests that these countries fit the theory like a pair of gloves.

XII

The paradox arising from the association between freer trade (whether obtained through jurisdictional integration or by cutting tariff levels) and faster growth, and the skillful calculations suggesting that the gains from trade creation are relatively small, remains. Indeed, since we now have a wider array of cases where freer trade is associated with more rapid growth, and several aspects of the pattern of growth suggest that the freer trade is connected with the growth, the paradox is heightened. If freer trade leads to more rapid growth, why doesn't it show up in the measures of the gains from the transactions that the trade liberalization allows to take place?

The reason is that there is a further advantage of freer trade that escapes the usual comparative-static measurements. It escapes these measurements because these gains are *not* direct gains of those who take part in the international transactions that the liberalization permitted, but *other* gains from increases in efficiency in the importing country, which increases are distinct from and additional to any that arise because of comparative advantage.

We know that *differences in costs of production* drive the case for free trade because of comparative advantage. These differences are conventionally assumed to be due to differences in endowments of natural resources among countries, to the different proportions of other productive factors such as labor and capital in different economies, or to the economies of scale that sometimes result when different economies specialize in producing different products. If there is free trade among economies and transport costs are neglected, producers in each country will not produce a product if foreigners with their different endowments of resources can produce it at lower cost. If each country produces only those goods which it can produce at costs as low or lower than those of other countries, there will be more production from the world's resources. A country that protects domestic producers from the competition of imports gives its consumers an incentive to buy from more costly domestic producers, and more resources are used up by these producers. These resources could, in general, yield more valued output for the country if they were devoted to activities in which the country had a comparative advantage and the proceeds were used to buy imports, so normally with freer trade a country could have more of all goods, or at least more of some without less of any others.

The argument offered here is different from the conventional argument for comparative advantage, though consistent and resonant with that argument. To demonstrate that there are gains from freer trade that do not rest on comparative advantage or differences in cost of production, let's look first at the case of a country that has comparative advantage in the production of a good and exports that good, but is also subject to the evolution of distributional coalitions described in Implication II. Let's suppose the exporters who produce the good in question succeed in creating an organization with the power to lobby and to cartelize. It might seem that the exporters would have no interest in getting a tariff on the commodity they export, since their comparative advantage insures that there won't be lower cost imports from abroad in any case. In fact, exporters often don't seek tariffs. To illuminate the logic of the matter, and also to cover an important if untypical class of cases, we must note that they might gain from a tariff. With a tariff they may be able to sell what they sell on the home market at a higher price by shifting more of their output to the world market (where the elasticity of demand is usually greater) because they don't affect the world price that much (in other words, the organized exporters engage in "price discrimination" and thereby get more revenue than before). Even though the country had and by assumption continues to have comparative advantage in producing the good in question, eliminating the tariff will still increase efficiency. The reason is that the tariff is necessary to the socially inefficient two-price system that the organized exporters have arranged. This example is sufficient to show gains from freer trade that do not flow from the theory of comparative advantage or differences in costs across countries, but rather from the constraints that free trade and factor mobility impose on distributive coalitions.

To get at a far more important aspect of this matter, assume that a number of countries have comparative advantage in the same types of production. Their natural resources and relative factor endowments are by stipulation *exactly* the same and there are by assumption no economies of scale. Suppose that these countries for any reason had high levels of protection and that they had been stable for a long time. Then, by Implication II, they would have accumulated a dense network of coalitions. These coalitions would, by Implication IV, have an incentive to try to redistribute income to their clients rather than to increase the efficiency of the society. Because of Implications VI, VII, VIII, and IX they will make their societies have slower decision-making, less mobility of resources, higher class barriers, more regulation, and slower growth.

Now suppose the tariffs between these identical countries are eliminated. Let's suppose, in order to insure that we can handle the toughest conceivable case, that even the extent of distributional coalitions was identical in each of these countries, so there is no case for trade even on grounds of what I call "institutional comparative advantage." Even on these most difficult assumptions, however, the freeing of trade can make a vast contribution. We know from *The Logic of Collective Action* and Implication III that it is more difficult to organize large groups than small ones. When there are no tariffs, the only effective cartels must include all the firms in all the countries in which production could take place (unless transport costs provide natural tariffs). Thus more firms or workers are needed to have an effective cartel. Differences of language and culture may also make international cartels more difficult to establish. With free trade among independent countries there is also no way the coercive power of government can be used to enforce the output restriction cartels require. There is also no way to get special-interest legislation over the whole set of countries because there is no government over them all. Individual governments may still pass inefficient legislation for particular countries, but even this will be constrained if there is free movement of population and resources as well as free trade, since capital and labor will eventually move to jurisdictions with greater efficiency and higher incomes.

Given the difficulties of international cartelization, then, there will be, at least for some time after the freeing of trade and factor mobility, an opportunity for firms in each country to make a profit by selling in *other* countries at the high cartelized prices prevailing there. As firms, even if they continue to follow the cartel rules in their own country, undercut foreign cartels, all cartels fall. With the elimination of cartelization the problems growing out of Implications IV, VI, VII, VIII, and IX diminish, efficiency improves, and the growth rate increases.

Economic theory, I have argued elsewhere, is more like Newton's mechanics than Darwin's biology, and there is a need to add an evolutionary and historical approach. This is also true of that part of economic theory called the theory of international trade. The traditional expositions of the theory of international trade that focus on the theory of comparative advantage are profound and valuable. The world would be a better place if they were more widely read. They also must be supplemented by a theory of change over time of the kind that is presented in *The Rise and Decline of Nations.* The failure of the comparative-static calculations inspired by conventional theory to capture the increases in growth associated with freer trade is evidence that this is so.

Notes

[1]*The Logic of Collective Action* (Cambridge, Mass.: Harvard University Press, 1965).

[2]New Haven: Yale University Press, 1982.

[3]The pages pertain to a paper that was prepared and delivered at the meetings of the International Institute of Public Finance nearly a year before *The Rise and Decline of Nations* went to press, but because of vastly different publication delays some readers may already have read the complete version of the argument that appears in that book. It is hoped that this shorter version of some crucial aspects of the theory in that book will be of use to those readers that are not interested in a book-length treatment.

[4]Edwin M. Truman, "The European Economic Community: Trade Creation and Trade Diversion," *Yale Economic Essays* 9 (Spring 1969), 201–251; Mordechai Kreinin, *Trade Relations of the EEC: An Empirical Investigation* (New York: Praeger, 1974), Ch. 3, 25–55. See also John Williamson and Anthony Battrill, "The Impact of Customs Unions on Trade in Manufacturers," in *The Economics of Integration*, ed. by Melvyn G. Krause (London: George Allen & Unwin, 1973).

[5]Bela Balassa, "Trade Creation and Trade Diversion in the European Common Market," *Economic Journal*, 77 (March 1967), 1–21.

[6]Fernand Braudel, *Capitalism and Material Life*, translated by Miriam Kohan (New York: Harper and Row; London: George Weidenfeld and Nicholson, 1973), 439–40. Published in France as *Civilisation Materiel et Capitalism*.

[7]M. J. Daunton, "Towns and Economic Growth in Eighteenth-Century England," in *Towns and Societies*, Phillip Abrams and F. A. Wrigley, Eds., 247.

[8]Charles Pythian-Adams, "Urban Decay in Late Medieval England" in *Towns and Societies*, op. cit. 159–185.

[9]Herbert Kisch, "Growth Deterrents of a Medieval Heritage: The Aachen Area Woolen Trades Before 1790," *Journal of Economic History*, Vol. 24 (Dec. 1964), pp. 517–537. On these matters see also Dudley Dillard, *Economic Development of the North Atlantic Community* (Englewood Cliffs, New Jersey: Prentice Hall, 1967) and Henri Pirenne, *Economic and Social History of Medieval Europe* (London: Routledge and Kegan Paul, 1936).

[10]Braudel, op. cit., 404–405.

[11]Adam Smith, *An Inquiry Into the Nature and Causes of the Wealth of Nations*, Book I, Chapter X, Part Two, Eds. R. H. Campbell, A. S. Skinner, and W. B. Todd (Oxford: Clarendon Press, 1976), p. 146.

[12]New York: W. W. Norton, 1961.

[13]Boston: Houghton Mufflin, 1967.

[14]In Dennis Mueller, ed., *The Political Economy of Growth* (New Haven: Yale University Press, 1983).

References

Bela Balassa, "Trade Creation and Trade Diversion in the European Common Market," *Economic Journal*, 77 (March 1967), 1–21.

Fernand Braudel, *Capitalism and Material Life,* translated by Miriam Kohan (New York: Harper and Row; London: George Weidenfeld and Nicholson, 1973), 439–40. Published in France as *Civilisation Materiel et Capitalism.*

M. J. Daunton, "Towns and Economic Growth in Eighteenth-Century England," in *Towns and Societies,* Phillip Abrams and F. A. Wrigley, Eds., 247.

Dudley Dillard, *Economic Development of the North Atlantic Community* (Englewood Cliffs, New Jersey. Prentice Hall, 1967).

Christopher Hill, *The Century of Revolution, 1603–1704,* New York, W. W. Norton, 1961.

Herbert Kisch, "Growth Deterrents of a Medieval Heritage: The Aachen Area Woolen Trades Before 1790," *Journal of Economic History,* Vol. 24 (Dec. 1964), pp. 517–537.

Mordechai Kreinin, *Trade Relations of the EEC: An Empirical Investigation* (New York: Praeger, 1974).

Dennis Mueller, ed., *The Political Economy of Growth* (New Haven: Yale University Press, 1983).

Mancur Olson, *The Logic of Collective Action* (Cambridge, Mass.: Harvard University Press, 1965).

Mancur Olson, *The Rise and Decline of Nations* (New Haven: Yale University Press, 1982).

Henri Pirenne, *Economic and Social History of Medieval Europe* (London: Routledge and Kegan Paul, 1936).

J. H. Plumbs, *The Origins of Political Stability in England, 1675–1725,* Boston: Houghton Mifflin, 1967.

Charles Pythian-Adams, "Urban Decay in Late Medieval England" in *Towns and Societies,* op. cit. 159–185.

Adam Smith, *An Inquiry Into the Nature and Causes of the Wealth of Nations,* Book I, Chapter X, Part Two, Eds. R. H. Campbell, A. S. Skinner, and W. B. Todd (Oxford: Clarendon Press, 1976), p. 146.

Edwin M. Truman, "The European Economic Community: Trade Creation and Trade Diversion," *Yale Economic Eassays* 9 (Spring 1969), 201–251.

John Williamson and Authony Battrill, "The Impact of Customs Unions on Trade in Manufactures," in *The Economics of Integration,* ed. by Melvyn G. Krause (London: George Allen & Unwin, 1973).

Résumé

Beaucoup des épisodes les plus notables de croissance économique se sont produits dans la période qui a suivi une réunification nationale ou la création d'une communauté douanière. Les progrès de l'Allemagne après la création du "Zollverein" et la réunification nationale, des Etats-Unis après l'adoption de la constitution nationale, des six membres du marché commun après le traité de Rome et de l'Angleterre après la révolution industrielle et commerciale résultèrent de la création d'un marché plus vaste dans lequel des relations commerciales libres prévalurent et un transfert partiel du pouvoir d'influencer la politique économique s'effectua au profit d'institutions plus haut placées. D'une part les marchés plus vastes réduisirent l'influence des corporations et autres organizations tels que les cartels, d'autre part les décisions concernant la politique économique émanant désormais d'organisations gouvernementales plus centralisées et plus importantes la pression des groupes particuliers fut moins effective et en conséquence la croissance économique fut favorisée.

The Tax System as Social Overhead Capital: A Constitutional Perspective on Fiscal Norms

Geoffrey Brennan
James Buchanan

I. Introduction

The object of concern in this paper is the tax system.

This is, of course, a totally conventional preoccupation—some might say, the *central* preoccupation—of the public finance specialist. However, although our subject matter is orthodox, our perspective is not. We shall not be concerned with the question of what particular tax system is the "ideal" one. Nor shall we deal with the effects of particular tax changes on economic growth, an issue which for many doubtless represents the main focus of this Congress.

Our concerns are in a way more basic. Our aim is to bring to bear on the tax system a particular *perspective*—a perspective that is rather different from that implied by the reigning orthodoxy. For, within orthodox public finance, the tax system is conceived as a set of instruments by means of which "government" pursues certain policy objectives. Within our alternative, "constitutional" perspective, the tax system is instead viewed as a *set of rules* under which the individuals who make up a polity pursue *their own* objectives, both those that are implemented collectively and those implemented privately. This perspective not only provides a rather different conception of what the tax system really *is*. It also directs attention to some implications that the tax structure, and changes in it, have for economic growth—implications that are both significant and too often ignored.

Our central point is that the tax system, whatever its precise nature, represents *social capital*. It does so in the sense that a workable tax system is both costly to accumulate, and costly to destroy. These

Public Finance and Economic Growth. Proceedings of the 37th Congress of the International Institute of Public Finance. Tokyo, 1981, pp. 41–54

costs arise primarily because tax law, like virtually all law, depends for its value on its predictability and its constancy. Frequent changes in the tax law destroy much of what it is that the tax law ought properly to provide. In other words, the tax system is to be viewed as having a *quasi-constitutional* status. That is, it represents not merely an *outcome* of the political process, but more particularly an important part of the *context* within which political and market decisions are made. In part, this "contextual" role derives from the fact that a whole range of private market decisions—what and when to consume, whether or not to take risks, how much to save and how to hold one's savings—are all crucially dependent on the manner in which the tax structure is organized. Less obvious, but no less critical, the tax system also determines the *cost-sharing arrangements* for collectively provided goods and services, and thus the "price" that each voter-taxpayer faces in "buying" such goods and services through the political mechanism. In this sense, the tax structure is a more basic element in the social framework than are many other aspects of political reality which *derive from* the tax system rather than being determined along with it.

Once the quasi-constitutional status of the tax system is recognized, it seems natural to regard that status as something which it is the special role of the public finance expert to protect. At the very least, one ought to require of the would-be fiscal reformer a certain sensitivity to the nature of that which he seeks to reform, and a certain attentiveness to the costs of change. Such sensitivity does not emerge so readily from a conception of the tax system as a "set of policy instruments for particular government objectives": rather, tax policy takes its place in the line-up along with subsidy policy, regulation, expenditure policy, wage policy, etc., as just another weapon in the policy armory—the special status of tax matters tends to be lost.

At the "policy" level, our general argument might be conceived as commending some set of rules or institutional arrangements that place limits on the frequency, and perhaps the extent of tax law changes. But our central object is not so much to generate policy conclusions as it is to hold up an alternative conception of what the tax system really is. Our fundamental conviction is that some sort of "*constitutional understanding*" is imperative in public finance; and that some form of *fiscal constitution* is a crucial ingredient in generating long-term sustainable economic growth.

It is useful to present our argument initially in the most general terms. In section II, we set out some of the language and conceptual apparatus that is preliminary to the main argument. In section III, by appeal to some simple game theory examples, we set out the case for a durable constitution, and then apply this to the fiscal context (sections IV and V) to spell out the implications for tax reform and tax change. Section VI offers some brief concluding remarks.

II. Some Preliminaries

When we talk of a "constitution" in this setting, we will mean the set of rules which determine the ways in which individuals interact in the social structure. The standard analogy is with the rules of some parlor game (poker, chess, or bridge), which lay down such things as what plays are legitimate, how the winner is determined, and perhaps limits on stakes. Such rules do not, of course, represent a total description of any particular play of the game, still less of all possible plays: they simply describe the rules within which all *legitimate* plays must take place. Just as we can distinguish between the rules of bridge and the play of a particular hand so we distinguish between the 'constitution' of a society (or *rules* for interaction) and the particular political and economic outcomes that might emerge from the *actual* interactions among persons and groups within that set of rules (or 'constitution').

In its most general form, the constitution of a society can be depicted in terms of a number of central elements, which would include (following [2]):

(i) a set of "rights," to both person and property;
(ii) a structure for enforcing such rights against other individuals;
(iii) a set of rules relating to how those rights might be exchanged;
(iv) a set of rules concerning how collective decisions shall be made;
(v) a set of rules defining the range over which such collective decisions shall be applied.

Any particular such constitution need not, of course, be written or explicitly codified: it may simply reflect an emergent and consensual understanding of "how things are done,"—an understanding that individuals generally abide by, and which is enforced by appeals to attitudes widely shared (see [6]). In many cases, however, it will be important to have the constitution, or elements of it, rendered *explicitly*, and enforced via institutions that are created as an integral part of the constitutional order itself.

In this paper, we shall focus on aspects of any constitutional structure that bear directly on tax matters. In this connection, we shall define the "*fiscal* constitution" as those rules of the socio-economic game that describe the tax and expenditure structure of the public sector (broadly defined). In a sense, the fiscal constitution is one aspect of those rules which set out what individuals, acting *collectively*, may and may not do to one another [a subset of (iv) and (v) above]. A restriction on the *taking* of property, for example, would be an element in the fiscal constitution, thus defined. Requirements for *uniformity* of taxation, specifications of what can (and cannot) be subject to tax, and any limits on rates that can be applied would be other examples. So would restrictions on the *domain* of government spending and on public budgeting *procedures* (including restrictions on the direct diversion of tax revenues for the private uses of politicians, administrators, or bureaucrats).

We should note that all these are examples of *rules* of the "fiscal game," and are not particular plays within such a "game." Under any such set of fiscal rules, a wide range of particular outcomes is possible, depending on the "plays" of the various actors in the political processes through which collective decisions are actually reached.

Orthodox public finance, in its normative variants, has been largely concerned with what these particular outcomes "ought to be," in terms of the familiar criteria of "efficiency," "equity," "employment," "economic growth," or some weighted combination of these. By contrast, the profession has not paid very much attention to the "*rules*" under which such outcomes emerge. The constitutional approach focuses exclusively on these rules. Such a focus suggests that anyone who is to play the political game, including the would-be economic advisor, ought to pay attention to its rules, and have some sense of why such rules are important. It also suggests that the primary scope for better outcomes lies in the changing of the rules, and not in preaching to the players.

III. The Significance of Rules

Why are *rules* so important? Why indeed is a *constitution* necessary at all?

In public-finance (or indeed in economics and the social sciences generally), the subject matter for analysis is the interaction of persons within a framework of social order. The observed patterns of outcomes are generated by the separate actions of many individual actors. Outcomes *emerge*, as it were. They are not produced as if by the action of a single agent. For any one person who acts in such a process, his own preferred course of action depends on what he predicts other persons will do, and *vice versa*. Within some limits, the individual must remain uncertain as to how others will act, but chaos rather than order would surely be present if persons were required to act in total ignorance as to the behavior of others. Predictability is provided by *rules* for behavior which, taken as a set, provide a shell or setting within which the separately acting persons generate "social" results that are properly characterized as embodying meaningful order. For the individual actor, rules set limits on the uncertainties about the behavior of others: rules establish boundaries. And, by so doing, they greatly facilitate "social efficiency."

The elementary principles of what might be called a "normative theory of rules" or of "constitutions" can best be demonstrated through the use of a series of some highly simplified two-person, two-strategy interaction illustrations, or "games," presented in the subsections below.

Symmetrical Self-Enforcing Rule.

Two trains have just pulled into adjacent platforms at the station. Mr. A is on one train, and he wishes to change quickly to the other before it departs. Mr. B is on the other train, and wishes to change to the train that A is quitting. Connecting the two platforms is an overhead bridge, just wide enough for two people to pass safely provided that each person takes a different side of the bridge. Within the time limits, there is no time for A (or B) to communicate by word or action which side of the bridge he is intending to use. Clearly, in this case, if there is a well-established rule that both A and B observe and expect the other to know and observe, each can catch his train successfully. If no such rule exists, or if one or other party is ill-informed, there is, let us say, an even chance that A and B will collide and both miss their trains.

We can depict this simple interaction in terms of the noncooperative game matrix of Figure 1. Each "player" has two strategies—left or right. The pay-offs to each outcome are indicated in the cells of the matrix, in which the first number is the return to A and the second number is the return to B.

Figure 1

		B's action	
		right	left
A's action	right	[10, 10]	[0, 0]
	left	[0, 0]	[10, 10]

The crucial feature of the interaction illustrated in Figure 1, and of those to be discussed below, is that the set of rules has value because it provides *information*—information that would be more costly to provide in other ways. The information thus provided depends partly on the *durability* of the rule. Consider, for example, the situation in Figure 1 if the rule should be determined, not once-and-for-all, but by a coin toss each morning—heads means left, tails right. The chances that A and B will know the prevailing rule seem slight, and the virtues of having a rule at all are almost entirely lost.

Note that, in this case, it does not matter to either player what the particular rule of action is—whether to keep to the right, or to keep to the left. All that matters is that there *be* a rule. There is, for this reason, no enforcement problem in ensuring that each individual will "play by the rules": once A believes that B will keep to the left, so will he. Neither individual can benefit from breaking the rule in any way.

Non-Symmetrical Rules

The sorts of rules that are of most interest to the public finance specialist are *not* self-enforcing: they are ones that require the coercive power of the state to enforce. One example of an interaction in which such rules are required is the familiar prisoners' dilemma interaction, which underlies much of the modern theory of market failure. For our purposes here, however, it is not useful to rehearse the familiar analysis: we direct attention instead to a variant of the interaction in Figure 1, one that is we believe particularly relevant to the question of tax rules.

To do so, let us alter our initial example slightly. Let A and B now be the drivers of cars heading towards a one-lane bridge. Mr. A is travelling from north to south; Mr. B from south to north. They arrive at the bridge simultaneously: one must give way or they will crash. But this time A and B are *not* indifferent as to who gives way. Nor are they necessarily indifferent as to the rule that ultimately pre-

Figure 2

		B's action	
		give way	proceed
A's action	give way	[−1, −1]	[−1, 15]
	proceed	[10, −1]	[−10, −10]

vails: each may *care* whether the "give way" sign is planted at the north or south end of the bridge. The nature of the interaction here can be depicted in the matrix shown in Figure 2.

As in game 1 there is no unique "equilibrium" outcome in this game: each individual needs to know what action the other will take before he can make his own "best" choice. And as in game 1, there are definite social advantages in having *some* rule—the miserable [−10, −10] outcome can then be avoided entirely. Here, however, it is not clear that it is possible to secure agreement on any *particular* rule, because the opportunity cost of agreeing to any given rule, for the *relatively* disadvantaged player, is the forgone possibility of securing the rule much more advantageous to himself. For example, the cost to A of the rule that requires that he give way is the additional eleven utils/dollars that he might have received from the reverse rule that requires B to give way. Consequently, while both A and B might agree to the desirability of some rule *in principle* they may not agree on any particular rule: an institutional procedure under which the rule to be imposed is determined, say, *at random* might secure unanimous endorsement, even though no *particular* rule could be agreed upon unanimously.[1]

Suppose that, somehow, the rule that emerges is the one that requires A to give way. Note that A has an incentive to break the rule if he thinks he can get away with it. If, for example, in a particular instance there is a *fifty-fifty* chance that B will reach the bridge after A does and hence that B will stop to avoid collision, then we can show that A will rationally violate the give-way rule and proceed. To see this, note that the expected return to A of violating the rule in this case is:

$$E_A = \text{probability of collision} \times \text{cost of provision} + \text{probability of proceeding safely} \times \text{benefit to proceeding safely.}$$

By assumption, the relevant probabilities are 50 percent, and the relevant pay-offs can be read off from the lower row of Figure 2. Thus,

$$E_A = \frac{1}{2}(-10) + \frac{1}{2}(10) = 0,$$

But the return to giving way is (−1), which is less than E_A. Consequently, if there is a fifty-fifty chance (or better) that A will not crash if he disobeys the give-way rule, he will proceed. The give way rule will therefore have to be enforced if it is to act as a rule at all.

There is then a case for some enforcement agency being operative in this game, just as in the prisoners' dilemma case. But though individuals in the prisoners' dilemma case may seek to *break* the law there is never a benefit to either party in *abolishing* the rule or inhibiting enforcement generally. Nor, in the conventional case, is there any advantage to be gained to either party from a *change* in the law.

In our example here, by contrast, order is precarious for a reason over and beyond the familiar free-rider incentive problem in the standard prisoners' dilemma. In Game 2, individuals have an incentive not merely to break the law unilaterally but to *subvert the rule of law* itself. One or another player (whichever one happens to be the relatively disadvantaged in payoffs) may expect to gain from a total breakdown of law followed by a return to the state of nature, from which he might expect a new recontracting to occur. If, in such recontracting, he expects that there is some positive probability that a *different* rule will emerge—this time more favorable to him—the subversion of the originally prevailing law may seem a fully rational course of action.[2]

Equivalently, although both parties recognize the importance of the rule's *stability* in serving the desired information-providing role, the relatively disadvantaged party will always seek to have the rule changed—even though this involves a "period of adjustment" in which there will be necessary uncertainty over the prevailing set of rules. Over this adjustment period, there will be expected net damage to *all* parties: cell 4 in Figure 2 will prevail more than otherwise.

Our discussion is not intended to show that changes in the law or the rules are never desirable. What the analysis does indicate is the logical coherence of the "conservative" view that there is a presumptive case against changing the rules, except where such change is no more than an accommodation to widely established practice. Such a case springs naturally out of a recognition of the "information-creating" role that law plays in human interactions. The law is a form of public capital: it depends in part on its durability for its value.

What the discussion also indicates is that we can expect continual pressure to "reform" the law, even when everyone would agree *ex ante* that law should be stable and even where the prevailing law is no worse than any alternative. Furthermore, even where law reform may possibly involve a change in rules that represents a genuine improvement on the *status quo*, the change may still not be desirable once it is recognized that change itself destroys a capital value. It is as if the individual recognizes, after a time, that the house he has built on his estate is not the best house that he might have built with the money—but this recognition is not sufficient generally to induce him to knock down the existing house and start again. Likewise, the recognition that the prevailing law is not the "best" is not sufficient grounds for law reform.

IV. The Tax Law

The general "principles" that emerge from an understanding of rules (from a constitutional perspective) can be captured in a few simple propositions:

1. rules provide for regularity in actors' behavior, regularity that has value because of the information that it conveys;
2. changes in rules violate that regularity and are hence inherently costly;
3. although the presence of some rule has value, there may be no one *particular* rule regarded as best by all actors—hence, many actors may want a change in rules though they cannot agree as to what change they want;
4. even where there *is* a single "best rule," it will not be costless to achieve a change from some "inferior" rule—hence, an "inferior" rule may in fact be best if it happens to be what prevails.

All these propositions seem to us to be totally valid in the particular application to tax law. Consider each proposition in turn.

Tax Law and Certainty

It has long been recognized that the entire structure of the modern economic system—depending as it does on accumulation, investment and complex exchange—requires the existence of well-defined and well-protected property rights. In the absence of such rights, life would indeed be "solitary, poore, nasty, brutish and short," as Thomas Hobbes reminded us. The justification for the powers of the state lay, in Hobbes' view, precisely in the need to create and defend recognizable rights to property and person. Yet, the protection of individuals and their property from the ravages of others will not ensure the security from which accumulation and complex exchange might spring, if those private rights remain at risk from the ravages of the *state* itself. Limits must be set on the power of the state to *interfere* with the property rights the state is supposed to protect. Such limits involve restrictions on the state's power to *take.* They may also incorporate restrictions on the state's power to tax *in toto,* and on the ability of the state to adjust its taxing arrangements with excessive frequency. Effective limits may, of course, be embodied in the operative rules concerning collective decision-making. It may be argued that electoral competition under simple majority rule may be sufficient to constrain outcomes within tolerable bounds. Whether this is so or not, (see [1] ch. 2) it seems clear that a tolerable social order requires secure property rights—property rights secure *both* from private predation and theft, *and* from the whimsies of an arbitrary state.

The Costs of Tax Change

To illustrate the significance of all this in the tax law context, consider two possible regimes. In the first, the tax system is liable to "reform" annually: a lump-sum poll tax one year gives way to a tax on profits the next, which in turn is replaced by a beer and spirits excise and then a wages tax and so on. In this regime, the citizen can never know what the tax rate on any activity that he undertakes will be; he knows only that there is some non-negligible chance that he will lose virtually the entire value of anything he accumulates, that the particular industry in which he seeks to invest will be obliterated and so on. In the second regime, by contrast, any tax system decided on must prevail for two decades: the individual can plan his economic future over a twenty year time horizon in full knowledge of what tax arrangements he will face. It seems difficult to imagine that accumulation, entrepreneurship and consequent growth would be higher in the first of these societies than the second, almost irrespective of what the particular tax chosen in the second regime happens to be.

The Pressure for Tax Change

It almost goes without saying that the tax system is always vulnerable to the workings of special interests. Virtually every citizen would like a tax break in his own favor—and as anyone who has been involved in any tax reform exercise will no doubt testify there is never any shortage of special pleading for concessional tax treatment from almost every quarter.

What is a more germane consideration for the profession, however, is the pressure for tax reform that arises from the "tax reform specialists"—members of the revered profession of public finance experts whose training and interests equip them so well for the tax reform exercise. Nor is the pressure for tax reform among this group solely to be explained in terms of income maximization (though that helps). Every good public finance man worthy of his salt would surely like to feel that he has had "an influence" on the tax structure—to bequeath to society a sample of his fiscal creativity. These are, after all, the terms in which we justify our existence to ourselves.

Yet it does seem at times as if tastes for alternative tax systems among the cognoscenti are a little like tastes in hats. One man likes accruals taxation of capital gains, another the integrated company income tax, another the exemption of mortgage interest, another the inclusion of imputed rent. Some are pure Haig-Simons men; others extol the consumption/expenditure tax. And so on and so on.

Now, it can be queried whether our record in terms of effective reforms implemented as a profession, is particularly distinguished. But the question our discussion here poses, is whether, if we had had much more influence, it would have mattered much to anyone but ourselves. The simple truth is probably that a certain amount of what we urge so forcefully is pure self-indulgence. Certainly it is difficult to find within the profession any widespread sympathy for the idea of leaving well enough alone. There seems to have been relatively little basic understanding of the point that the tax system *is* a piece of social capital, and that changing it involves *destroying* social capital.

To be sure, any tax policy advocate will talk *as if* the particular "reforms" that *he* is proposing will be the last ever to be effected—that *his* system will prevail for the foreseeable future. But any change in the tax law implies that the tax law is *susceptible* to change—and the pressure for reform necessarily implies a shift towards more change rather than less. On balance, the profession has, possibly implicitly, stood for more change: the ancient wisdom to the effect that ". . . an old tax is a good tax" seems to have been pretty much forgotten.

V. Tax Change and the Fiscal Constitution

Whether or not the costs of excessive change in the tax law are recognized by the tax policy experts, they do seem to be recognized in the rules and procedures of prevailing tax reform arrangements. For in most countries, tax reform is accorded a quasi-constitutional status. In the English-dominated part of the world, for example, tax reform is largely entrusted to specially assigned "Royal Commissions" or Committees of Enquiry (the Carter Commission in Canada and the Asprey and Mathews Committees in Australia exemplify). Such committees operate explicitly *outside* the arena of regular parliamentary politics. Neither politicians, nor professional bureaucrats, are (typically) members of such bodies.

Apparently it is recognized that the determination of relative tax burdens and the structure of the tax system more generally are not matters that should be dealt with simply in the context of annual budgetary deliberations. Moreover, although a "call for submissions" from interested parties and "public hearings" are part of the normal tax reform committee's procedures, it is clear that the committee's task is not simply that of weighing up a whole array of special pleas and deciding which should prevail. The task is rather to provide recommendations as to which tax system is best for the community in the light of abstract normative criteria—often enough laid down in the terms of reference. In that sense, the standard normative framework for orthodox tax analysis could be viewed as providing a set of *constitutional* rules by which tax systems can be evaluated. The notions of "horizontal and vertical equity," "neutrality," and "simplicity" take on, in this view, status as elements of a fiscal constitution (as in [3]).

More important for our purposes, however, is the implication that the tax system should not be decided merely as a part of regular political processes—that effective "limits" on both the nature and frequency of tax reform are required, over and above limits embodied in majoritarian electoral constraints. And it is the limits on the *frequency*, rather than the *nature*, of tax changes that deserve particular emphasis here, precisely because it is the frequency aspects that the profession seems not to have emphasized.[3]

None of this is, of course, to deny the necessity of occasional tax reform exercises: tax systems do tend to decay somewhat over time, partly in response to parliamentary/Congressional "fiddling" and partly in response to the creative responses of imaginative taxpayers and their advisers who exploit ambiguities and omissions in the tax law. There may even be changes in common notions of what fiscal justice requires, and genuine advances in professional understandings of the workings of alternative tax regimes.

Nor is it to deny the importance of doing the occasional tax reform "properly"—of getting the tax system reasonably efficient and tolerably fair. In this connection, it should perhaps be noted that fairness may not only have an intrinsic value; it also seems likely that tax systems that are patently unfair are unlikely to survive for long periods—at least without potentially costly enforcement and/or social unrest. In that sense, tax systems that are widely regarded as inequitable are themselves likely to be less than optimally "durable"; and to the extent that they encourage taxpayer dishonesty, tend to breed a disrespect for the law in general that can enormously depreciate the overall social fabric.

Nevertheless, it can hardly be denied that the public finance profession has been one of the most consistent and vocal lobbies for tax reform over the last thirty years or so in almost every country. And this has no doubt given the impression to the public at large that the "experts" believe that tax reform is necessarily and desirably a continuous on-going process. Nor is such an impression entirely unjustified. Orthodox analysis cultivates a view of the tax system as a set of "policy instruments," through which "governments" can pursue their various objectives; as those objectives change, so ought the tax instruments through which their achievement is sought.

Indeed, in tax advocacy rhetoric, reformist zeal often seems to imply the view that the current situation is so bad that *any* change would be a change for the better. It needs to be stated categorically therefore that precisely the opposite presumption is the appropriate one. Unless we can be sure that the tax system finally emerging from the tax reform process will be distinctly better than what we have—and maybe not even then—it may be best to do nothing.

Notes

[1]In our illustrative example, we assume that side-payments or compensations, in money or other goods, are not possible. To the extent that such payments are possible, *A* and *B* might, of course, agree on one of the nonsymmetrical rules. Side-payments in effect convert the nonsymmetrical payoff structure into one that is, at least potentially, symmetrical. For purposes of our generalized analysis, we want to remain within the nonsymmetrical payoff example.

[2]Something of this sort seems to have underlain Hobbes' anxiety about the fragility of the rule of law. In this sense, to conceive of the Hobbesian analysis of political order as an application of the prisoners' dilemma interaction and of "free-rider" problems as traditionally posed in public goods theory seems somewhat misconceived.

[3]In the third volume of Law, Legislation, and Liberty [4] Professor F. A. Hayek recognizes the constitutional nature of the tax-share structure. His reform proposals include the assignment of the authority to determine tax-share allocation to a "senior" special representative assembly devoted to making "laws," that would, once chosen, be expected to remain in being for relatively long periods. The "lower" representative assembly would "govern" in the standard way, and would be empowered to set budgetary levels, and hence, tax rates, within the determined tax-share structure.

References

[1] Brennan, Geoffrey and Buchanan, James: *The Power To Tax* (New York, Cambridge University Press, 1980).

[2] Buchanan, James: *The Limits of Liberty* (Chicago, University of Chicago Press, 1975).

[3] ———: "Taxation In Fiscal Exchange" *Journal of Public Economics*, Vol. 6 (March 1976), pp. 17–29.

[4] Hayek, F. A.: *Law, Legislation and Liberty (Vol. III) The Political Economy of a Free People* (Chicago, University of Chicago Press, 1979).

[5] Head, J. G.: "Issues In Australian Tax Policy For The Eighties" Anzaas Conference Paper, Brisbane 1981 (mimeo).

[6] Hunt, Lester: "Some Advantages of Social Control: An Individualist Defense" *Public Choice* 36, No. 1 (March 1981), pp. 3–16.

Résumé

Selon le point de vue orthodoxe des finances publiques, le système fiscal est considéré comme l'un ou (plus) "des moyens d'action politique" dont dispose le gouvernement dans la poursuite de ses objectifs. Cet article présente un point de vue différent sur le système fiscal—ce que j'appelle "un point de vue constitutionnel"—selon lequel le système fiscal est entendu comme *un ensemble de règles*, à l'intérieur duquel les individus poursuivent leurs propres objectifs à la fois de façon privée sur les marchés et à la fois de façon collective par l'intermédiaire de processus politiques.

La fonction première pour de telles règles est de fournir des *renseignements* à chaque individu sur ce que chacun peut anticiper que les autres feront: les règles fiscales établissent en effet "les termes de l'échange" pour chaque individu lorsqu'il agit de façon collective. Cette valeur d'information dépend à son tour, pour partie, de *la durée* de cet ensemble de règles fiscales établi. Pour cette raison, le système fiscal représente une pièce importante du capital social; il est coûteux de remplacer un système fiscal qui marche, car changer le système fiscal revient à détruire les renseignements accumulés sur les règles du jeu politique.

Cet article analyse quelques cas qui illustrent l'importance de règles stables et aussi la pression qui existe pour changer les règles même lorsque tous les individus préféreraient vivre selon un ordre stable. Nous soutenons que, bien que le statut quasi-constitutionnel du système fiscal n'ait pas été suffisamment souligné et défendu par les spécialistes de finances publiques, les modifications institutionnelles qui l'emportent en ce qui concerne la réforme fiscale, dans bien des pays, reflètent une prise de conscience de besoins particuliers pour la durabilité des aménagements fiscaux.

Collective Goods and Population Growth[1]

Carl S. Shoup

I. Introduction

The aim of the present paper is to bring together two familiar phenomena and note some of the possibilities they suggest when thus juxtaposed. One phenomenon is the collective-use good, or simply collective good: the good is such that the cost of serving one more user is zero. The other is population growth.

Once the two are viewed in relation to each other, some implications are obvious. Rapid population growth need not be feared in so far as consumption or business use is purely collective. No further input is needed to give each of the newcomers as much as each of those in the initial group has been using. In certain other instances some additional input is required if additional users are to be served, but the input increment is a smaller percentage of the initial input than the additional users are of the initial users. The good is then "imperfectly collective," or "quasi-collective."

A collective good can be termed "joint over users," in contrast to, say, mutton and wool, where the production process is joint over the goods, and the output consists of multiple commodity products (Shoup, 1966, pp. 615–16).

The relevant questions then are: What kinds of goods are collective? Quasi-collective? To what extent can they be substituted for non-collective goods, that is, individual goods?[2] These are the questions to which the present paper is addressed, with emphasis on the purely collective goods.

Although all agree that the world's population will increase substantially over the next few decades, some observers have concluded that this increase is no cause for alarm. They believe that it will itself lead to so much more output that output per capita will rise, or at

Public Finance and Economic Growth. Proceedings of the 37th Congress of the International Institute of Public Finance. Tokyo, 1981, pp. 55–68

least not fall appreciably (Simon, Chs. 1, 2, 23). For example, the larger the population, the greater is the number of fruitful ideas that will be generated for technological advances. Other observers are less optimistic: the recent *Global 2000 Report* to the President of the United States forsees only a modest, if any, global increase in human welfare by the year 2000, with a risk that welfare will have fallen by then, in some countries, and that "biological capabilities to meet basic needs" may be undermined by early in the next century (United States, Council on Environmental Quality, Vol. Two, p. viii). The Worldwatch Institute (Brown) is somewhat more pessimistic. They conclude that forests, grasslands, crop lands and fisheries are already being utilized in some places at rates higher than can be sustained.

In any event, the danger seems real enough to warrant exploration of the possibilities of meeting a larger share of human needs through collective goods.

II. Population Estimates

The United States Bureau of the Census gives three estimates, in *Global 2000* (Volume Two, pp. 10, 12), of the world population in the year 2000 (in millions): 5,922; 6,351; and 6,798. Of the middle estimate, the "more developed regions" will account for 1,323 million persons (1975: 1,131 million) and the "less developed regions," 5,028 million (1975: 2,959 million). Clearly, the projected growth of population presents a problem, or an opportunity, for less developed countries.

A second set of projections, by the Community and Family Study Center (*Global 2000,* p. 24) give 5,883 million persons as a medium estimate for 2000, as against the 6,351 million estimate by the Census Bureau.

These totals depend largely on what is assumed to happen in two countries: China and India. China is estimated to have a 1980 population of close to one billion (Environmental Fund, and *Global 2000,* Volume Two, pp. 21 and 29); India, not far short of 700 million. Together, China and India account for about 37 percent of the global population as of 1980. Projections for the year 2000, medium-range estimates, are 1,329 million for China and 1,021 million for India (U.S. Census), or 1,125 million and 947 million, respectively (CFSC).

Adding the United States (228 million) and the U.S.S.R. (266 million) yields a total, for these four most populous countries, of virtually half (48.8 percent) of the world's population in 1980.

The annual growth rates of population in China and India are only

1.7 and 1.9 percent, respectively. In contrast, in Indonesia, the fifth most populous country in the world, population is estimated to be increasing at an annual rate of 2.5 percent, implying, if continued, a doubling in 28 years, from the 1980 total of 153 million to 306 million. Japan is more like the other industrialized countries: an annual increase of only 0.9 percent (1980 population, 117 million).

In Africa (478 million, growth rate 2.8 percent), the rates for the two most populous countries, Nigeria and Egypt, are 3.0 and 2.7 percent, respectively, implying, if continued, a doubling of Nigeria's 86 million by the year 2003, and of Egypt's 42 million by the year 2006. Africa as a whole is growing at 2.8 percent a year.

So too is Latin America as a whole, and its most populous country, Brazil, has the same rate of population growth (2.8 percent). As to the second most populous, Mexico, there is some difference of opinion, the Environmental Fund estimate being only 1.5 percent instead of the 3.6 percent estimated in official data.

Population growth rates are far lower in Europe and North America excluding Mexico. Only four of the countries in these regions show a rate of 1 percent or higher (Hungary, Iceland, Ireland, Poland). At the rate for Europe as a whole, 0.4 percent, it would take about 150 years for the population to double. The growth rate is slightly negative in Austria, the Federal Republic of Germany [West Germany], and Luxembourg. The U.S.S.R. (not included in the figures for Europe) and the United States have almost identical, and low, growth rates: 0.8 and 0.7 percent respectively, except that when allowance is made for illegal immigration the natural rate for the United States rises to 1.2 percent (Environmental Fund, 1980, notes 18a and 18b).

Looking much farther ahead, one observer estimates that the world population will level off at about 11 billion in the third quarter of the next century (Ibrahim, 1980).[3]

The 1980 rates of population growth may drop before long in many countries. From interviews with some 400,000 women in the Third World it has been estimated that a high percentage of such women want no more children (*New York Times,* August 10, 1979, reporting on the World Fertility Study). China is reported to have committed itself to achieving zero population growth between 1985 and 2000 (Sterra).[4]

The age distribution of a given population will affect the ease with which collective goods can be substituted for individual goods. If it turns out that the older age group can substitute collective goods more readily, this fact will mitigate the difficulties seen ahead: "How to support the retired population may well prove to be one of the most widespread social questions in the early twenty-first century"

(Perlman, p. 14). Even developing countries will encounter this problem; from 1950 to 1975 such countries experienced increases in life expectancy of 9 to 15 years (Perlman, p. 5). Presumably a part of this increase reflected a longer life after retirement from the labor force.

III. Degrees of Collective Use

Collective goods are usually services rather than commodities: for example, a weather forecast, and certain public health measures, and, within narrow spatial limits, a theatre performance. They are commonly called public goods, but this is misleading, since collective goods may or may not be dispensed outside the price system (Shoup, 1974, pp. 37–38). If exclusion of would-be users by price is feasible, the private sector can distribute the good, although perhaps less efficiently than can the government. Only if exclusion by price is not feasible must the government dispense the good, and cover the cost by taxation.

Accordingly, an increase in collective goods does not necessarily imply growth of the government's share in total output. It does so only if the new collective goods are not price-excludable, hence not suited for sale on a market.

Within the general category of collective goods there may be distinguished three types: the super-collective good, the pure collective good, and the quasi-collective good.

The super-collective good is such that an addition to the number of users actually decreases the total cost of maintaining a certain level of service; the marginal cost per person is negative. These goods are rare, and not of much importance. Warmth in a theatre or other public place may be such a good: heat radiating from the additional bodies allows some decrease in total input of fuel, while maintaining the initial degree of warmth (Shoup, 1976, pp. 192–93, 195–97).

The pure collective good is such that the marginal cost of servicing persons is zero. Total cost neither increases nor decreases with an increase in the number of persons served a given level or amount of the good.

The quasi-collective good is one such that total cost increases as the number of persons served increases, but in a proportion less than the increase of persons. This concept is to be distinguished from increasing returns to factors, which has to do with increasing the unit amount or level of the good. Here, that amount or level is held constant while the number of users increases (for some conjectures on marginal cost per person served, for each of the chief governmental services, see Shoup, 1969, p. 143). These quasi-collective goods are of two types, with respect to their rising total cost as users increase.

One type is such that when the zero-marginal-cost point has been passed, and before inputs are increased, further users can be accommodated only by inconveniencing the initial users. The quality or level of the service to the initial users declines. The prevailing level can be maintained for those users, and be supplied to the new users, only by an increase in total cost. Such a good may be called a congestion good. Congestion caused by the new users increases the marginal cost, for all users, of maintaining the initial level of service.

The second type of quasi-collective good is such that, if additional users are to be satisfied, total cost must rise because the new users are farther away, and cost of the good rises with distance from input. An example is television or radio broadcasting. If additional users can be found only at greater distances, more power must be applied. If this is not done, the initial users do not suffer an inconvenience, as in the congestion case; the would-be new recipients are simply excluded by insufficient input. If greater power is applied, the initial users may even benefit from the stronger signals. Let us term this good a dispersion good. Dispersion of the additional users is responsible for a positive cost per additional user.

A pure collective good exhibits constant returns to users and may also show increasing returns to population.

Constant returns to users means that as the number of users of the good is increased by a certain proportion the product, measured in user-units, increases by that same proportion. For example, let 100 users each use 10 units of a pure collective good. The product consists of 1,000 user-units. Let 100 more users appear, each using the same 10 units. There is no increase at all in factor input. User-units now total 2,000, twice as many as before; the product has doubled as the users have doubled. In this sense there are constant returns to users. To be distinguished from this, as noted above, is the concept of constant returns to factors; if the input of every factor is, say, doubled, output measured in terms of units alone doubles, and the number of users is immaterial.

A certain good may of course exemplify both types of constant returns: to users, and to scale (of factors). In the illustration above, let the number of units double when all inputs double; each user now gets 20 units instead of 10 units. Further, let the number of users double, without impairing the use of the units by the initial 100 users. Now, with 200 users using each 20 units, the total of user-units is 4000. Product has quadrupled while input and users both have doubled.

Increasing returns to population may or may not occur in the presence of a collective good. They will occur under the following circumstances. First, the population increase causes an increase in the number of those who use one or more collective goods, so that the number of user-units increases. Second, the population increment consists partly of workers, so that total input increases, and with it, total output of units, hence also of user-units. Let the sum of these two increases in user-units yield an increase that is greater in proportion to the initial product than is the increment of population to the initial population. Increasing returns to population then obtain.

IV. Substitution of Collective Goods for Individual Goods

The present inquiry is limited to those collective goods that are usually dispensed by government rather than the private market. Each of the major goods of this category will be examined briefly to ascertain whether and to what degree they can be increased and used as substitutes for certain individual goods. If such substitution is important quantitatively, the threat of economic hardship that may be implicit in further population growth will be correspondingly reduced.

Public Health Measures as Substitutes for Future Medical Costs

Increased expenditure on public health will commonly reduce the need for medical care in future years. Public health measures are usually collective goods, though sometimes only imperfectly so. Medical care is commonly an individual good, though of course overhead costs represent a certain jointness over users if current total use is below capacity.

As an example, let us consider mosquito control as a substitute for care of malaria patients. The amount of expenditure needed to reduce the mosquito population by a given amount is more or less independent of the population of humans that will reap the benefits. It is at least more independent than is the amount of expenditure needed to give an equivalent level of relief through medical care after the disease has struck. Admittedly, the concept of an "equivalent" level is somewhat vague, but surely the preventive measures are more joint over users than are the corrective measures. The practical difficulty here is that the total amount now being spent on corrective or relief measures (medical care) is so low in some developing countries that a small amount of substitution would leave little or nothing to be given up to finance the substitute further. Still, it seems worthwhile for each country to reexamine its present use of health resources, to ask if a part might be transferred from medical care to public health.

This shift would probably call for increased governmental activity and less private-sector production, since the jointness over users of public health measures is coupled, usually, with lack of price-excludability. Public health measures might be funded from outside sources until the need for medical care declined.

The continuing concentration in urban areas may make it more feasible for governments to deliver certain public health outputs and, where necessary, enforce the use of them.

Medical care also yields benefits to others than the patient. There are relatives, friends and others who might feel obliged to help cover the sick person's medical bills. Probably everyone is benefitted by living in a society of persons who are relatively free of illness and are unhandicapped by injuries. On this score, medical care is as much a collective good as are public health measures.

Crime Prevention

A somewhat more doubtful case for extensive substitution is that of crime prevention. Perhaps in many developing countries there is too little to be gained by spending more on police activity of a kind that would be a substitute for individual goods, e.g., locks, guns, private safes and the like.

Some police activity in some countries is viewed by the "beneficiaries" as being chiefly a means of keeping them under the control of a government they fear or distrust.

In general, the marginal cost of crime prevention is probably positive and rising and may exceed average cost, as population increases.

Nevertheless, there seems to be enough promise in this substitution to warrant surveys of the possibilities in most developing countries.

Education

The cost of educating one more person is virtually zero when classes are of less than optimum size. In general, however, and over substantial increases in enrollment, education as currently dispensed is almost an individual good: if the number to be educated doubles, total cost almost doubles, and indeed may even more than double. Are there, then, other modes of education that can be substituted, in part, the cost functions of which would approximate that of the collective good?

In some developing countries the answer may well be yes. In many such countries illiteracy is so widespread that the immediate task is to teach reading and writing. In India, for example, the illiteracy rate is said to be 64 percent; ten years ago it was 70 percent; in absolute amount, however, more are illiterate now than then, because of population growth ("India's Population Growth . . .," *New York Times*, March 19, 1980). Perhaps expanded use of radio and television, to note but one possibility, could be a partial substitute for classroom teaching. The marginal cost per pupil would then be greatly reduced. The technical task of substituting collective modes for part of the prevailing modes of education must be left to the professional educator, but the need for such a substitution is pressing.

Another product of education is already being dispensed as a collective good: the benefit that comes to all from living in a society of literate, knowledgeable persons.

Fire Protection

Fire protection is an activity in which both collective goods and individual goods simultaneously contribute to the product, fire-damage limitation, which at its extreme of effectiveness becomes fire prevention.

Urbanization increases the demand for this good, so it will probably increase more in importance in developing countries, where urbanization is proceeding rapidly. As more dwellings or business buildings arise within a given area, an unchanging level of service, however measured, cannot be maintained without some increase in fire-fighting equipment and personnel. The incremental cost for users may well be less than that incurred by purchasing individual goods: fire-resistant building materials, fire warning systems, and the like.

Studies could be made of representative urban business and dwelling areas in developing countries, to find out more precisely what the factors are that bear on a decision whether to reduce expenditures on individual goods, devoting the saving to increasing the amount spent on collective goods.

Contract Enforcement

Better contract enforcement by government courts might reduce private costs enough to be worthwhile. Such enforcement is not completely a collective good; more users means more courts, more judicial manpower. Once enforcement reaches a high level, however, the attitude of the entire community toward fulfillment of obligations may be so changed for the better that an increase in population by that time will not bring with it a need for expansion of the governmental service or at least not for an expansion greater or as great, in proportion to the population increase.

Here, too, movement into urban areas makes this collective-good option more practicable.

Sewerage, and Garbage and Refuse Removal

These activities are only to a small degree collective. Whether the service is dispensed by the government or by private firms, the addition of one more user increases total cost almost proportionately, if not by more than that. In the short run, of course, if the system is not fully utilized, new users may be connected to a sewer system at little cost.

One aspect of sewerage, that of promoting public health, can be discussed under that heading.

Some types of garbage and refuse also pose dangers to health. By and large, however, there seems to be little opportunity to employ collective techniques in dispensing these services. Total cost therefore rises as fast as, if not faster than, population increases.

Cultural and Recreational Facilities

Much the same is true of cultural and recreational facilities: the collective element is small.

Streets, Highways, Bridges

Up to this point congestion has not been a major factor to consider. Indeed, fire protection and crime prevention are, in general, dispersion goods, not congestion goods. On highways, bridges and streets, however, congestion soon appears. To maintain a given level of the service as the number served increases, total cost must increase. Meanwhile, congestion causes a decline in the level of service.

In the present context, highways, streets and bridges are of limited interest, since there is no individual good for which these facilities are good substitutes.

Railroads, Port Facilities

Railroads, port facilities and other types of large-unit infrastructure are so important to economic growth in developing countries that they may be built in initial sizes that leave an almost zero marginal cost per user for a time. A country may then treat infrastructure as a collective good over an initial period of time. Of course the collective-use aspect disappears when the infrastructure comes to be used to the point of congestion, but up to that point the collective-use aspect may be significant (see Biehl, pp. 54–55). How long the short period is depends on the degree to which the infrastructure has deliberately been overbuilt in order to economize over the long run.

Military Services

As already indicated, for some of the services rendered by government there are no close substitutes at all in the individual-good mode, hence no chance to save expense, when population increases, by substituting collective goods for individual goods. Prime examples of this are the services rendered by the military, and exploration of space.

The services rendered by the military, often grouped euphemistically under the term "defense," are five: nuclear deterrence, conventional deterrence, damage limitation in the event of war ("damage" to persons as well as property), conquest, and internal control (Shoup, 1969, pp. 102–104, 143). It may be conjectured that marginal cost per person served is zero for deterrence and perhaps conquest, positive but unchanging for damage limitation, and positive and increasing for internal control. Only the two types of deterrence and perhaps conquest are pure collective goods, but damage limitation may qualify as a quasi-collective good, since marginal cost is probably below average cost, per user. In any event, these five services are all open to use by anyone in the community, indeed must be used if offered, and so cannot be distributed in the price-exclusion mode. Internal control might be an exception; it refers to the military's using their power to control the country themselves directly, or through some representative. This is of course a good that is not dispensed to everyone in the community.

Exploration of Space

The benefits of space exploration, at least in its present stage, are collective goods. One more beneficiary adds nothing to total cost.

V. Summary

Opportunities for substituting modes that involve more of the collective element are not great, in governmental activities, save for public health. In that one field, however, they are so marked as to warrant intensive study. Education, too, may prove to offer some cost lowering per person if more of present output is dispensed in a collective mode.

The private sector has not been studied here, as to possibilities of substituting, within that sector, collective modes of dispensing for individual modes. Initially, substitutions by government seem the more urgent, if only because it may be assumed, tentatively, that competition in the private market would already have dictated the use of the preferable mode, aside from externalities.

Notes

[1]I am indebted to Professors Richard M. Bird and John B. Burbidge for comments on an earlier draft of this paper.

[2]The term "individual good" is used here instead of "private good" because the latter term does not distinguish between a collective good and a non-collective good; it merely designates a good that is obtained in the private enterprise sector. A term is needed that denotes simply the absence of any collective feature, whether the good is supplied by private enterprise or by the government: the cost of supplying one more user with a unit of the good is just the cost of producing one more unit. "Individual good" is used here, therefore, to denote the absence of any collective feature. Such a good may be conceptually either price-excludable or non-price-excludable, though in fact there are few real-life combinations of non-collectiveness and non-price-excludability. Professor Head gives as an example an oil field that can be tapped at no charge by wells drilled on the land outside the owner's boundaries (Head, 1962, p. 210, or 1974, p. 175). Taking into account the pricing aspect, four cases are formed, as follows.

Let *C* stand for collective, *c* for non-collective, *P* for price-excludable, *p* for non-price-excludable. The four combinations are: *CP*, collective but price-excludable (theatre at less than capacity); *Cp*, collective and non-price-excludable (space exploration); *cP*, non-collective and price-excludable (apples); *cp*, non-collective and non-price-excludable (oil, in example above). Collective goods, accordingly, are those, and only those, in groups *CP* and *Cp*. Individual goods are those, and only those, in groups *cP* and *cp*.

[3]A recent report from the United Nations (1981) estimates that world population will level off at 10.5 billion by the year 2110, but adds that, depending on the degree of success of campaigns to limit population growth, the stabilized figure could be as small as 8 billion or as large as 14 billion.

[4]In contrast, a recent news item reports that the U.S.S.R. has decided to give cash bonuses totalling $12.1 billion by 1985 in an effort to reverse a falling birth rate. *Wall Street Journal,* June 4, 1981, p. 1.

Note

Studies of relative efficiency in the public sector and private sector seem to have made no reference, even in passing, to the decrease in average cost of a user-unit in government's output of collective goods as population increases. To take but one example, the often-cited article by Professor Baumol (1967) and the comments on it by seven economists (see under Baumol) and Baumol's two rejoinders: the concept of zero marginal cost per user is referred to only by Dean A. Worcester, Jr. He mentions marginal cost pricing, apparently in terms of marginal cost over users, as possibly implying zero price, but only in the context of a change in the area distribution of population, not an increase in population over time (see Shoup, 1976, p. 208). Professor Julian M. Simon (1981) has suggested that 20 percent of United States taxes (not specified whether federal only or also state and local taxes) "finance activities that are little affected by population size . . . .." Neither in his book (1977) nor in reviews of that book by Boulier, Moreland, and Leibenstein, is it pointed out that goods joint over users mitigate the economic problems raised by population growth.

Similarly, Government officials and committees forecasting levels of welfare in an expanding world do not consider the role of collective goods, which convert population growth from a danger to a positive benefit (e.g., United States Congress, 1980).

References

Baumol, William J., "Macroeconomics of Unbalanced Growth: The Anatomy of Urban Crisis," *American Economic Review* 57 (June, 1967): 415–26; and, in the same journal, September 1968, Vol. 58, Carolyn Shaw Bell, pp. 877–84; L. K. Lynch and E. L. Redman, pp. 884–86; Dean A. Worcester, Jr., pp. 886–9[illegible]; J. W. Birch and C. A. Cramer, pp. 893–96; and William J. Baumol, pp. 896–97—all under the caption, "Macroeconomics of Unbalanced Growth: Comment," and, again in the same journal, September, 1969, Vol. 59, Joan Robinson, "Macroeconomics of Unbalanced Growth: A Belated Comment," and William J. Baumol, "Comment on this Comment," p. 632 (both).

Biehl, Dieter, "Determinants of Regional Disparities and the Role of Public Finance," Festschrift, Paul Senf, *Public Finance*, Vol. XXXV, No. 1, 1980, pp. 44–71.

Brown, Lester R., *The Twenty-Ninth Day*. A Worldwatch Institute Book. New York: Norton, 1978.

Boulier, Bryan L., Review of Simon (1977), *Journal of Political Economy*, Volume 87, No. 4, August, 1979, pp. 910–12.

Environmental Fund, 1980, Washington, D.C. *World Population Estimates, 1980*.

Head, John G., "Public Goods and Public Policy," *Public Finance*, Vol. 17, No. 3, 1962, pp. 197–219.

Head, John G., *Public Goods and Public Welfare*. Durham, N.C.: Duke University Press, 1974.

Ibrahim, Youssef M., "World Fertility in Rapid Decline . . .," *New York Times*, June 15, 1980.

Leibenstein, Harvey, review of Simon (1977), *Journal of Economic Literature*, March, 1979, Vol. XVII, No. 1, pp. 147–49.

Moreland, R. Scott, review of Simon (1977), *Economic Journal*, December, 1978, Vol. 88, No. 352, pp. 873–74.

New York Times, March 19, 1981. "India's Population Growth . . ."

Perlman, Mark, "Human Resources and Population Growth," International Economic Association Conference Paper, Preliminary Draft, 1980 (typescript).

Ramsberger, Boyce, "Expert Says U.S. Population . . .." *New York Times*, December 3, 1978, quoting Dr. Charles F. Westoff, Director of Princeton University's Office of Population Research, in the December, 1978 issue of *Scientific American*.

Russell, Clifford S. and Norman K. Nicholson, eds., *Public Choice and Rural Development*. Washington, D.C.: Resources for the Future: RFF Research Paper R-21, 1981.

Shoup, Carl S. "Public Goods and Joint Production," in Tullio Bagiotti, ed., *Essays in Honour of Marco Fanno*, University of Padua: Padua: Cedam, 1966, pp. 612–22.

Shoup, Carl S. *Public Finance*. Chicago: Aldine, 1969.

Shoup, Carl S., "Non-Zero Marginal Cost per Consumer, with Non-Excludability," in Warren L. Smith and John M. Culbertson, eds., *Public Finance and Stabilization Policy*, Essays in Honor of Richard A. Musgrave. Amsterdam: North-Holland Publishing Co., 1974, pp. 37–38.

Shoup, Carl S. "Collective Consumption and Relative Size of the Government Sector," in Ronald Grieson, ed., *Public and Urban Economics*, Essays in Honor of William S. Vickrey. Lexington: Heath, 1976, pp. 191–212.

Simon, Julian L., *The Economics of Population Growth*. Princeton: Princeton University Press, 1977.

Simon, Julian L., "Adding Up the Costs of Our New Immigrants," *Wall Street Journal*, February 26, 1981.

Sterra, James P., "Chinese Will Try . . .," *New York Times*, August 13, 1979.

United Nations and United States Agency for International Development, *World Fertility Study*. Baltimore: Johns Hopkins Press, 1979. Extracts reprinted in *New York Times*, August 10, 1979.

United Nations, Fund for Population Activities, *Report*, cited in *New York Times*, June 15, 1981.

United States Council on Environmental Quality, and United States, State Department, *The Global 2000 Report*. Three Volumes: I, "Entering the Twenty-First Century"; II, "The Technical Report"; III, "Documentation on the Government's Global Sectoral Models: The Government's 'Global Model.'" Washington, D.C.,

United States Government Printing Office, 1980.
United States Congress, Joint Economic Committee, *Hearing on the Global 2000 Report.* Washington, D.C., United States Government Printing Office, 1980.

Résumé

Puisque le coût marginal que représente la fourniture d'un bien collectif à un seul usager supplémentaire est égal à zéro, la croissance de la population loin d'agir sur les ressources, abaisse le coût moyen par unité d'utilisation pour de tels biens. Cet article essaye de voir dans quelle mesure on peut satisfaire une plus grande proportion de besoins humains par des biens collectifs dans le secteur public et pose la question "Qu'est-ce-que des biens collectifs?" dans quelle mesure peuvent-ils se substituer à des biens non-collectifs?—la même chose pour des biens semi-collectifs? Les activités prises en considération ici sont la santé publique, l'éducation, la protection contre l'incendie, le respect des contrats, le tout à l'égout et l'enlèvement des ordures, des programmes culturels et de loisirs, la construction et l'entretien d'équipement pour les routes, les ports, les rues, les autoroutes, les ponts, le service militaire et l'exploration de l'espace. En général, il existe dans le secteur public, des possibilités de substitution, mais elles ne sont pas grandes sauf en ce qui concerne la santé publique et certains aspects de l'éducation.

De telles substitutions n'entraînent pas nécessairement une augmentation de l'activité publique; certains biens collectifs peuvent être fournis par le secteur privé dans la mesure où ils peuvent avoir un prix.

Optimal Fiscal and Monetary Policies in Neoclassical Dynamic Models

*Christophe Chamley**

1. Introduction

The neoclassical method in economics rests on two principles: consumers choose their preferred actions in their opportunity set, and producers choose among the available technologies to maximize profit. The fundamental theorem of welfare economics is that under proper assumptions about consumer preferences and production technologies, a competitive equilibrium, with complete markets, is a Pareto optimum. With the introduction of future markets and contingent markets, the analytical tools of this method can be applied to the study of the optimal intertemporal allocation of resources.

In this framework, the role of the government is twofold: first, when the conditions of the fundamental theorem of welfare economics are not satisfied, public intervention may be necessary to bring the economy to its Pareto frontier, and to improve its *efficiency*. Second, society may prefer an allocation of resources (even non-Pareto optimal) which is different from the competitive allocation, for *equity* reasons.

Public intervention takes the form of taxes, expenditures, and trading rules. Because of the space constraints in this paper, I will discuss only some problems in the relations between taxation, government deficits, and the economic *intertemporal* allocation of resources. This analysis will rely on stylized models which do not pretend to be good descriptions of real economics, but provide a framework to develop clearly the implications of some basic assumptions. More-

*I am very grateful to Drs. Augusztinovics and Wainshal for their insightful comments, which were helpful for the revision of this paper.

Public Finance and Economic Growth. Proceedings of the 37th Congress of the International Institute of Public Finance. Tokyo, 1981, pp. 69–87

over, these models are often used as metaphors in the current policy debate on U.S. tax reform.

A crucial element of an intertemporal model is the horizon envisioned by agents in their optimization plans. This has been considered in relation to the problem of the national debt since Ricardo, and its importance has grown recently with the development of various public and private retirement programs. Two different views have been proposed.

According to the first, the horizons of private individuals and society are identical. During his finite lifetime, an individual takes into account in his actions, the welfare of his immediate descendants with whom he is able to interact (through bequests, etc.). Since the welfare of his descendants depends on their own descendants, by an inductive argument, one can show that individuals will internalize the welfare of all future generations. The private sector is then represented by families with a horizon which can be considered to be infinite (Barro, 1974).

The opposite view which originates in the work of Brumberg and Modigliani (1954), assumes that individuals behave privately towards their descendants with the same selfishness that they display in their behavior towards their unrelated contemporaries. Individuals in their *private* decisions are selfish, and limit their planning horizon to their own lifetime. However, they may be concerned about the income distribution between generations or in the same generation. This income distribution has the properties of a public good and has to be enforced by public institutions.[1]

The implications of these two views for fiscal and monetary policies are presented in the next two sections. The problem of time consistency is also considered. These sections are followed by a brief discussion on the empirical evidence for each model.

Section 5 is addressed to the problem of uncertainty with incomplete markets. Most intertemporal decisions are taken under uncertainty (and reciprocally). The existence of complete contingent markets would support an efficient allocation of resources (Arrow, 1964). However, this requirement may not be satisfied if the state of nature is not observable (moral hazard), or when organization costs prevent the creation of a large number of markets. Indeed, Keynes emphasized the role of expectations in investment decisions when complete markets do not exist (1936, chapters 12 and 16). In section 5, this problem is illustrated by an example where the competitive allocation of resources is not Pareto optimal, and can be improved upon by public intervention.

2. Models with Infinite Horizon

Fiscal Policy

In an economy with complete markets, and where agents have perfect foresight, the problem of optimal intertemporal fiscal policy (taxation and debt) is very similar to the standard problem of optimal taxation investigated initially by Ramsey (1927), and analyzed recently by numerous authors:[2] the private sector is represented by a large number of consuming families (with identical ordinal preferences), and producers who behave competitively. The role of the policymaker is to devise a set of taxes which minimizes the distortions created by tax rates between net consumer prices, and satisfies a tax revenues constraint.

Some of the problems peculiar to the intertemporal setting can be illustrated by considering a one-good model where agents optimize between labor and leisure, and between the levels of consumption at different dates. Assume that the fiscal instruments are the tax rates on the incomes of labor and capital respectively, on consumption, and the possibility of budget deficits or surpluses.

A first best policy for the government is to raise an initial capital levy by an amount equal to the present discounted value of future public consumption. This capital generates a stream of revenues which finances public expenditures. In a given year the government budget may be in deficit or surplus, but the budget constraint over time is satisfied. Since no tax is necessary, there is no distortion.

As in the standard problem of optimal taxation, when this lump sum tax solution is not feasible,[3] a combination of tax rates should be devised which minimizes choice distortions. Consider first a permanent increase of the *ad valorem* tax rate on consumption goods. It is equivalent to say that the consumption tax lowers the value of leisure and of capital, in terms of consumption. This can be decomposed into two effects: the first is equivalent to a labor income tax and distorts the labor-leisure choice; the second is equivalent to a capital levy. The consumption tax is equivalent to a combination of a payroll tax and a capital levy, and is therefore always more efficient than the labor income tax for an equal amount of revenues.[4]

Note also that the distortion introduced in the labor-leisure choice could be offset by a labor subsidy. Indeed, a capital levy is equivalent to a combination of a tax on consumption, and a subsidy on labor at the same rate, constant over time.

Let us now consider the taxes on the incomes of capital and labor. A tax on capital income has very different effects in the short-run and the long-run: in the very short-run the capital stock is fixed, and the tax is equivalent to a capital levy; in the long-run, it distorts the savings rates. The latter effect arises only because the tax is expected, and is independent of the actual implementation of the tax. This raises the problem of time consistency of an optimal policy, which is considered below. When the tax rates are free to adjust, we can expect a large tax on capital in the short-run with a budget surplus, and a low tax rate in the long-run.

More precise results on the relative efficiency properties of the taxes on capital and labor, respectively, depend on the structure of preferences, and on the production technology (as we expect from standard results in public finance). There is, for example, no general argument in favor of a payroll tax, or against an income tax. However, it is instructive to consider two special cases.

Assume first that in the production technology, the capital-labor ratio is fixed. In this case the taxes on the incomes from capital and labor, respectively, are equivalent. For the same amount of revenues, they imply the same efficiency cost. This cost is independent of the respective tax rates on capital and labor, and depends only on the amount of tax revenues and on the structure of preferences. In the special case where the labor supply is inelastic, capital and labor are fixed; the efficiency cost of taxation is nil.

For the second example, let us consider the class of utility functions which are additively separable between periods, and stationary. These functions are very popular in the literature on optimal growth[5] because they generate sequential decisions, and under reasonable assumptions, intertemporal programs with a turnpike property.[6] As we expect from the previous discussion, the optimal tax rate on capital is very large in the short-run, and equal to zero after some date.[7] The tax rate on labor income tends to a limit value in the long run.

The use of deficits or surpluses allows to smooth the variations of the tax rates on labor income over time and reduces the intertemporal distortions.[8] The efficiency cost of a tax program is an increasing function of the initial level of the public debt (positive or negative, if the government owns some capital). A higher initial level of the debt (or lower public wealth) implies higher tax rates and greater distortions. Some economists have called for a reduction of this debt through a temporary budget surplus (Ricardo, 1964, p. 162, Meade, 1958). This policy is efficient only insofar as its burden falls directly or indirectly on accumulated private assets. In this case, the quicker the debt is reduced, the better. When there are some institutional restrictions on the level of the wealth tax,[9] the optimal level of the public wealth (the opposite of the debt) in the long-run is smaller than the present value of public expenditures; additional revenues are raised by the payroll tax. In the limiting case where there is no restriction on the tax of wealth, we find again that a lump-sum wealth levy is optimal and first-best.

An optimal policy may not be achievable either because the parameters of the model are not known precisely, or because the timing of different tax changes may be too complicated. For this reason, it is useful to consider the efficiency cost of fiscal policies with tax rates on capital and labor incomes, constant over time.[10] This efficiency cost is positively related to the elasticities of substitution between consumption and leisure, and between consumption of different dates, and it increases with the elasticity of substitution between capital and labor in the production technology. Different estimates have been proposed for this latter parameter. They are in general smaller than 1.5, which is considerably smaller than infinity (the partial equilibrium case of fixed factor prices). This implies as can be expected from the discussion of the first example above, that the efficiency cost of taxation is not too sensitive to the ratio between the tax rates on capital and labor incomes respectively,[11] and also that the efficiency gain of tax reform (for example, from an income tax to an optimal tax) are moderate.

The method we have followed here is to measure the efficiency cost of taxation in welfare cost (or in income equivalent). Some studies rely on a tax incidence method. I believe that this latter method produces misleading results. For example, in the case of additive utility functions, the net rate of return is fixed in the long-run and equal to the rate of time preference. A lowering of the tax rate on capital income lowers the gross rate of return, increases the capital-labor ratio and the level of output. This description of events does not take into account the lower level of consumption during part of the transition period, and grossly overestimates the benefits of tax reform.[12]

Monetary Policy

The previous results about fiscal policy can be immediately extended to a monetary economy. Money is here outside money, and is held as a medium of exchange (an explicit demand equation can be derived for example by the inventory model (Tobin, 1956)). When individuals have perfect foresight and markets adjust instantaneously to equilibrium, there is complete equivalence between the creation of money (which results in inflation) and an effective tax on money.[13] In this case, the optimal monetary policy is derived as an application of the optimal taxation problem.[14] To simplify the argument, consider the steady state. Denote by m, g, π, r the level of real balances, the real growth rate of the economy, the inflation rate, and the real interest rate respectively. The demand for money depends on its opportunity cost, the nominal interest rate $r + \pi$. The revenues raised through money issuance (or a tax on money) are equal to $(\pi + g)m$. The government is also assumed to raise revenues by a combination of other taxes: the marginal efficiency cost of one unit of revenues raised by this latter source is denoted by e (for the marginal dollar of tax revenues, the private sector's welfare is reduced by an equivalent of $1 + e$ dollars).

The inflation tax reduces the amount of real balances and the services provided by money. Since at the equilibrium, the services of the marginal unit of money are valued at the nominal interest rate, the welfare cost of a reduction dm is equal to $(r + \pi)dm$. The optimal inflation rate is found when the marginal efficiency costs of the inflation tax and other taxes are equal:

$$\frac{(r + \pi)\dfrac{dm}{d\pi}}{\dfrac{d}{d\pi}[(\pi + g)m]} = -e$$

which is equivalent to

$$\epsilon = -\frac{r + \pi}{m}\frac{dm}{d(r + \pi)} = \frac{e}{1 + e\left(\dfrac{g + \pi}{r + \pi}\right)},$$

where ϵ is equal to the interest elasticity of the demand for money (r is assumed to be fixed).

When taxes are not distortionary, the marginal efficiency cost e, is equal to zero. We find $r + \pi = 0$. The optimal inflation rate is equal to minus the real rate of return as suggested by Friedman (1969).

When the efficiency cost of taxation is very large, and r is equal to g, revenues of the inflation tax should be maximized:

$$\epsilon = 1$$

This is the rule proposed by Bailey (1956).

The above argument relies on a steady state analysis with fixed factor prices. It would be more rigorous to use a model of intertemporal optimization with endogenous factor prices, as in the previous section. However, the results obtained by this latter method are not very different.[15] When the marginal efficiency cost is not too large, the rule $\epsilon = e$ gives a first order approximation of the optimal inflation rate even on the transition to the steady state.[16] (The approximation overstates the exact value when ϵ increases with π.)

These results can be extended to economies with imperfect information and costly market adjustments. In these cases, the issuance of money is no longer equivalent to a direct tax on money balances. Four examples can be considered: inflation expectations are adaptive; the demand for money adjusts with a lag to the expected inflation rate; there is a short-term Phillips relation between inflation and output; the welfare cost of inflation is greater than the reduction of services provided by cash balances.[17] The first three effects should increase the optimal value of the long-run permanent inflation rate. The last effect decreases the optimal value.

As a final note, we should observe that in real economies the ratio between outside money and wealth is fairly small. Usually the amount of revenues which can be raised by the inflation tax is small, at least in economies with a fully developed banking system. However, for some countries where the cost of tax collection is high, the inflation tax may not be irrelevant.[18]

The Problem of Time-Consistency

As we have seen in Section 1.1, the optimal tax rates on capital differ sharply in the short and in the long-run. The anticipation of a tax on capital at a given date distorts the relative prices of consumption between the period from the present to the date of the tax, and the period following the tax. When the first period is short, this distortion is small. Therefore, the optimal tax is larger in the short-run than in the long-run. However, as time goes by, the long-run becomes the short-run. It may have been optimal to announce no tax on capital at some (future) date. But when that date becomes the present, the past is fixed, and the no-tax policy is no longer optimal. If the government can revise its policy in an unexpected way, the optimal policy is not time-consistent.[19] The government can lower the efficiency cost of the tax only if the private sector can be consistently deceived. But you cannot fool all the people all the time. A repeated use of capital levies would certainly increase the expected probability of more levies in the future and distort the private intertemporal choices. The previous empirical results (no capital income tax in the long-run) seem to indicate that the gains of this type of policy may not be large. Also the ability of the government to deceive systematically private individuals is dubious in democratic institutions.

The same problem of time consistency arises in the determination of an optimal monetary policy. A permanent inflation generates a total amount of revenues equal to the present value of the flow of monetary expansions. But the government can do better: at the beginning of the policy horizon it can declare void the money which has been previously issued, and sell to private individuals a new currency; the present value of revenues (a stock) is increased by the amount of money individuals want to hold. In other terms, the optimal inflation rate is initially infinite. Because it is not infinite for any future date, the optimal policy is time inconsistent. Auernheimer (1974) has proposed that an honest government would honor past commitments as follows: at each instant the price of money should be taken as given. The results of the previous section are valid when this constraint is taken into account. Also, this type of constraint could be applied to the problem of an optimal fiscal policy. (The government would not alter unexpectedly the value of capital in terms of consumption.)

Finally, the restriction of the policy choice to the class of constant tax rates over time is not sufficient to produce a time consistent policy. However, the previous results indicate that in this class of policies, the possible benefits of a strategy of deceit are small (Chamley, 1981c).

3. The Life-cycle Models

Let us first summarize the fundamental mechanism of life-cycle models: assume that the level of the capital stock is given. Given the production technology and the tax system, this level determines the net interest and wage rate and, therefore, the lifetime budget constraints of individuals. The individuals who behave competitively optimize their labor supply and consumption in each period. Because of retirement they, by and large, save first during the working years, dissave in the later years, and *leave no bequest.* The total capital stock is equal to the sum of the accumulated savings of all individuals living at the same time. A stationary equilibrium is obtained when this latter value of the capital stock is equal to the initial value that was taken as given.[20]

The taste for consumption during retirement has important effects in the redistribution of wealth between generations; a stronger taste in that direction generates a larger capital stock owned by old people; this capital generates a higher wage rate earned by the young generations. We assume that individuals care about the welfare of the future generations as a public good, although they cannot alter the intergenerational distribution individually, since a personal bequest is like a drop in the ocean.

The diversity of criteria used in studies of income distribution reflects a certain lack of understanding of these problems. Like others, I will use here an additive social welfare function which enables us to treat the steady state aggregate consumption and the maximin criteria as special cases. Since I consider only the problem of intergenerational income distribution, I will assume that each generation is composed of a large number of identical individuals.[21]

The main difference between the class of life-cycle models and the models with infinite horizon is that in the former the competitive equilibrium is not a social optimum. Since the capital stock is generated by an individual need to carry wealth into the retirement period, there is no reason why the level of capital should be optimal with respect to future generations. Therefore, the government may use fiscal and monetary policy to improve social welfare, even if there is no public expenditure to finance. The following discussion will be simplified by assuming that there is one good in the economy and unless specified otherwise, individuals live two periods, work (a variable amount) in the first and retire entirely in the second; they consume in both periods.

Fiscal Policy

In life-cycle models of overlapping generations, an important fact is the timing difference between the streams of labor income and of consumption. The same applies to taxes. The tax on labor income is paid by young individuals during the first period of their life, and the capital income tax is paid on income earned in the second period. The consumption tax is paid in both periods. Through a proper use of these instruments the government can redistribute wealth between generations. For example, the level of capital transmitted from generation to generation can be increased by a subsidy on labor income and a tax on capital income or on consumption. Wealth is transmitted to the young by the subsidy, and taken away for the next generation by the tax levied when they become old.

An important consequence is that the optimal values of the tax rates are not determined by the Ramsey rules.[22] Indeed, some surprising results may occur: consider an economy where individuals have a weak taste for consumption in the retirement period. They do not save much and the level of capital is low. Some economists would propose to improve the "incentives for saving," i.e., lower the tax on capital or subsidize savings. In fact, the opposite policy should be applied. In such economies, the marginal utility of old people (in their second period) is low, and the marginal utility of young people is high. The competitive equilibrium is improved upon from a social point of view, by a redistribution from the old to the young, i.e., a tax on capital and a subsidy to labor.

In life-cycle models, the role of the government debt is particularly important. As in Section 2, the government balances its budget over time, and bonds are paid by future taxes. These taxes are anticipated by individuals. However, since individuals have a life-cycle horizon which is shorter than the infinite horizon of the government, these bonds have a positive wealth for their holders. As a consequence, the public debt lowers the capital stock. This is the main argument against Social Security. A related result is that contrary to the situation in Section 2, the optimal long-run level of the public debt is fixed and independent of initial conditions. In fact, if possible, the government should adjust this level such that the *gross* rate of return is equal to the social rate of time preference.

Furthermore, in this case, the "wealth carrying" effect of taxation does not apply anymore since this is done by public ownership. The optimal tax rates are determined by the Ramsey rules.[23]

Monetary Policy

As in Section 2, and under the same assumptions about market adjustments, monetary policy is simply defined by a tax levied on money (either directly or implicitly through a monetary expansion which induces an increase of the price level). Money is outside money; it is used as a store of value (like capital or government debt) and provides additional transaction services. Optimal monetary policies can be determined by a straightforward application of the public finance methods used in the previous section. It is important to emphasize that the optimal monetary policy depends in a crucial manner on the fiscal policy. (The point has sometimes been overlooked.)

We have seen in Section 3 that an important fiscal instrument is the public debt. When the government can adjust the level of the debt (and own some capital if the optimal level is negative), the standard results of optimal taxation apply (Section 2); the optimal inflation rate is greater than (equal to) minus the rate of return, when the efficiency cost of taxation is positive (equal to zero).

When the level of the debt cannot be adjusted optimally, a tax on money can be used to shift private savings from money to capital. The social bequest to the following generations is achieved through an increase of the wage rate.[24] One could argue that a lowering of the labor tax would lead to the same result. In fact, in a two period model with taxes on old and young individuals (at different rates respectively), the equivalent of the optimal debt policy is realized, and monetary policy is useless for capital accumulation.

The seminal study on the problem of money and growth (Tobin, 1965), followed by others, used a savings function expressed in terms of a fraction of income. This formulation, because of its ad hoc nature, overlooks the importance of the choice of fiscal policy and intergenerational transfers, in the incidence of inflation on capital accumulation.

To illustrate this, consider the following argument: in a life-cycle model where individuals have homothetic preferences, the level of wealth per capita is proportional to the net wage rate, and it is also a function of the net rate of return. Assume first that the elasticity of wealth with respect to the rate of return is equal to zero. Consider now an increase of the inflation rate to stimulate capital accumulation. The additional government revenues are used to lower the tax on capital (if the money-wealth ratio is the same for all individuals, this policy is "fair" to wealth holders). Assuming a Cobb-Douglas technology with a capital income share α, the change of the capital per head dk, is related to the change of real balances dm, by the relation[25] $dk = -dm/(1 - \alpha)$. The change of the consumption level in the steady state dc, is equal to $dc = (r - g)dk$, where r and g denote the gross rate of return and the growth rate, respectively. We have to add to this term the net change of the money services valued at $(r + \pi)dm$, where π is the inflation rate. The total change of *effective* consumption dz, is then measured by: $dz = (r - g)dk + (r + \pi)dm$. Using the first relation, we find $dz = ((r - g)/(1 - \alpha) - (r + \pi))(-dm)$. An increase of π reduces monetary balances and increases consumption if $r - g > (1 - \alpha)(r + \pi)$; the optimal inflation rate is equal to $(\alpha r - g)/(1 - \alpha)$. A realistic number for α is $1/4$. As long as the gross rate of return is less than four times the growth rate, the optimal inflation rate is negative.

Assume now that the elasticity of accumulated wealth with respect to the net rate of return is positive. The increase of capital (induced by substitution from money), lowers the net rate of return and therefore tends to choke the first effect described above; the argument applies *a fortiori* (the case of a negative interest elasticity is unlikely to occur). It seems that the benefits of inflation for long-term capital accumulation have been exaggerated. (Also as Summers pointed out, inflation may increase significantly the effective tax rate on capital income in a nonindexed tax system.)

4. Bequest or No Bequest?

The growing importance of the public debt and retirement programs has stimulated numerous empirical studies of the two models used in the previous sections. Two types of tests have been used: the first relies on aggregate time series. Following the pioneering work of Ando and Modigliani (1964), a consumption function is estimated which depends on income, wealth and other variables like Social Security wealth (future benefits minus contributions). The coefficients of wealth should be predicted by the life-cycle theory; also if this theory is valid, the coefficients of real wealth and of net Social Security wealth should be identical.[26] Such tests do not have a proper treatment of expectations, and they depend too much on the particular properties of the business cycle. They produce mixed results. The reader can sometimes suspect that the author of the study, after numerous experimentations, presents only the regressions which suit him best. Indeed, Auerbach and Kotlikoff (1980) have shown with synthetic data generated by a simulation model, that by choosing a proper estimation interval during a transition period of the Social Security program, it is possible to obtain any regression coefficient.

The second type of study uses microeconomic data and tests the relation between the accumulated savings of an individual with various variables such as labor income, Social Security savings, pensions, etc. In a life-cycle model one would expect a dollar-for-dollar substitution between private savings and Social Security taxes (except for additional problems created by the earning test, the difference between the rate of return on Social Security and the market rate, etc.). Again, the evidence is mixed.[27] It seems that the net public debt reduces to some extent the level of capital but the substitution is not perfect.

The life-cycle theory also does not explain why the U.S. net savings rate has decreased only slightly despite the huge increase of the Social Security program.

Finally, it should be pointed out that the accumulated savings of some individuals in the past, at the moment of retirement, has been abnormally low (Diamond, 1977). To some extent, retirement programs have been introduced to protect individuals against their own myopia. Far from leaving bequests to coming generations, some people do not leave a bequest to themselves for their old days. On the other hand, other (possibly richer) individuals obviously do not accumulate wealth only for lifetime consumption. It is possible that an integration of the two-models will be found in a framework taking into account the diversity of endowments and tastes.

5. Uncertainty and Incomplete Markets

The problem of uncertainty is important in intertemporal decisions, and was not addressed in the previous sections. In an economy with uncertainty, money is not only held for transaction services, but also for its portfolio properties (Tobin 1958). It is often argued that the government can, by altering the composition of its portfolio of liabilities (money, bonds), change the desired level of capital, and the real variables in the economy (Tobin 1980).

The validity of this result rests on the assumption that markets are imperfect or that government liabilities provide real services (for example, liquidity) in addition to being a store of value in a portfolio. When these capital markets are perfect[28] and government liabilities do not bring real services, the composition of the government debt does not matter, as the composition of the corporate debt does not matter in the Modigliani-Miller theorem. Open-market operations do not have an effect on the real allocation of resources (Chamley and Polemarchakis, 1981).

An important shortcoming of the neoclassical model with uncertainty can be found in the fact that even among individuals living at the same time, the number of future contingent markets is extremely small. For investment decisions which depend on the marginal efficiency of capital even a few years ahead, there is no future market. The capital markets cannot be used to convey information or future demand at specific dates.

Keynes emphasized that in these conditions, "there is no clear evidence from experience that the investment policy which is socially advantageous coincides with that which is most profitable" (1936, p. 157).

As an illustration, consider the following example which contains the three essential elements of the problem: investors and consumers are different individuals; the profitability of investment today depends on the consumption tomorrow; there is no future market today.

Assume that there is a large number of investors and consumers who behave competitively and live two periods. There are two goods in the economy, *A* and *B*. Consumers are endowed with a fixed quantity of good *A* in the second period (for example, leisure or a consumption good which can be produced by giving up leisure). Their utility is concave and additively separable in the consumption levels of goods *A* and *B* in the *second* period. The good *B* is produced during the *first* period by the capitalists. Their utility increases with their consumption of *A* (for simplicity they do not consume *B*), and it decreases with the quantity of good *B* produced (because of the production cost).

The marginal utility of consumption of *B* (for the consumers) is random and revealed to the capitalists only in the second period. The only market is the market between the two goods in the second period. The competitive equilibrium is, in general, not an *ex ante* Pareto optimum: the consumption of good *A* by capitalists depends, in general, on the state of nature in the second period. This is not the case in an *ex ante* Pareto optimum. The uncertainty on the rewards of investment for capitalists is socially inefficient since consumers' taste is revealed only in the second period when investment has already taken place. In this simple example, a policy which restricts the fluctuations of aggregate consumption is socially beneficial.[29]

Keynes argued that the state should intervene to reconcile the private social benefits of investments through decentralization, "partly through its scheme of taxation quotas, partly by fixing the rate of interest, and partly perhaps, in other ways" (Keynes, 1936, p. 378).

Public intervention can be justified by a careful theoretical and empirical analysis of the shortcomings of some assumptions often used in the neoclassical framework. Of course, these shortcomings do not deprive the method of its usefulness. Quite the contrary, the determination of a proper set of incentives (for example, "the rate of reward to those who own the instruments of production") should be established by the neoclassical principles. To conclude with Keynes (1936, p. 378):

> Our criticism of the accepted classical theory of economics has consisted not so much in finding logical flaws in its analysis as in pointing out that its tacit assumptions are seldom or never satisfied, with the result that it cannot solve the economic problems of the actual world. But if our central controls succeed in establishing an aggregate volume of output corresponding to full employment as nearly as its practicable, the classical theory comes into its own again from this point onward.

Notes

[1]Also the competitive equilibrium may not be Pareto optimal in this framework; for example, the capital stock may be greater than the Golden Rule value, or the rate of money inflation may not be optimal.

[2]For an introduction, see Sandmo (1976). The classical reference is Diamond and Mirrlees (1971). See also Atkinson and Stiglitz (1980, lecture 12).

[3]Under the assumption of a large number of identical families, it is not clear why the lump sum solution is not feasible. This nonfeasibility is more realistic when the population is composed of families with identical ordinal preferences, but different endowments which are not observable.

[4]The existence of an initial capital stock in the dynamic case corresponds to the existence of pure profits in the static case. It is always efficient to tax first pure profits (Munk, 1978). It should be emphasized that capital income is not a "pure profit" in the intertemporal framework.

[5]The first example has been analyzed by Ramsey (1928). For a clear exposition, see Arrow and Kurz (1970).

[6]A more general set of sufficient assumptions for the turnpike property has been proposed by Koopmans (1960) and analyzed by Iwai (1972). Utility functions generating intertemporal programs which do not satisfy the turnpike property should, in my view, be rejected for empiriral applications. More work on intertemporal preferences would certainly be useful.

[7]Auerbach (1979), has shown that the steady state tax rate on capital income is equal to zero in the infinite horizon model, with a discount rate equal to the growth rate. For a general study see Chamley (1982).

[8]The requirement of a balanced budget policy in each period is treated in the same way, with an additional constraint for each period.

[9]For example, this tax may take the form of a tax on wealth income with a rate smaller than 100 percent.

[10]See Chamley (1981a) for a detailed analysis of the capital income tax, and Chamley (1981c) for an extension to the payroll tax, or the consumption tax.

[11]Assume for example, a discount rate of 4%, a growth rate of 2%, a capital income share of .2 in a Cobb-Douglas production function, and an initial uniform tax structure on the incomes of capital and labor at the 20% rate. A reform towards the optimal ratio between the interest tax and the wage tax generates an efficiency gain not greater than 0.5% of the consumption level for most realistic parameters of the utility function (Chamley 1981b).

[12]In fact, the long-run effect is of the first order, whereas we know that at least for small tax rates, the efficiency gain of tax reform is of the second order. (For an example of this method, see Summers, 1981b.)

[13]Consider, for example, the steady state situation where the government raises revenues by letting the money supply grow at the rate n. If g is the rate of growth of the economy, the inflation rate π is equal to $\pi = n - g$. The government would raise the same amount of revenues by a tax on money at the rate $\pi + g$ (the inflation rate would be $-g$ in this case).

[14]The results are fairly obscure when money is considered as a consumption good in the utility function (Phelps, 1973, Siegel, 1978). The analysis is somewhat simpler and has an immediate interpretation when money is considered as a productive input. This is the approach followed in the text.

[15]See Chamley (1981b). There is also a minor technical problem about the optimal inflation in the beginning of the planning horizon (see Section 1.3).

[16]When the budget deficit is optimal the efficiency cost e is constant over time.

[17]For a discussion of the welfare cost of inflation, see Fisher (1980c).

[18]Fisher (1980b) discusses in detail the empirical relevance of inflationary financing. On average, industrial countries raised 6% of their revenues by printing money

(between 1960 and 1975). This ratio was higher for some countries as Chile (18%), Uruguay (28%), or Argentina (46%).

[19]For other examples, see Calvo (1978), Kydland and Prescott (1980), and Fisher (1980a). When the elasticity of substitution between capital and labor is finite, the wage tax has some incidence on capital in the short-run; the optimal tax on labor income is also time inconsistent. Because of this, the optimal intratemporal tax structure in the long-run is not identical with the standard result obtained with fixed factor prices; this difference may be small however (Chamley 1982).

[20]Diamond (1965) in his classical work, discusses the dynamics and the stability of the model.

[21]The problem of intra-generational distribution is also important in a growing economy (savings may be a luxury good) but cannot be considered in this paper. See, however, Hamada (1972) Ordover and Phelps (1975), and Ordover (1976).

[22]See Pestieau (1974), Chamley (1977), Atkinson and Sandmo (1980).

[23]They may be different from zero if government expenditures are nil, because of the deficit or surplus generated by the public debt.

[24]Weiss (1980) considers a two period model with random labor endowment in the first period. The Friedman rule is not optimal for a criterion of expected utility in the steady state (it is still Pareto optimal). A contingent monetary policy alters the rate of return between periods and provides partial insurance across generations.

[25]By the homotheticity assumption, $da/a = dw/w$, where a and w denote the level of assets per capita ($a = k + m$), and the gross wage rate respectively. By the production function $dw/w = \alpha\, dk/k$. Using $da = dk + dm$, we find $dk = -dm/(1 - \alpha/(1 - R))$, where $R = m/a$. This ratio is usually very small (less than 1/20) and $1 - R$ is not very different from one.

[26]The classical reference is Feldstein (1974). See also Buiter and Tobin (1979).

[27]See Kotlikoff (1979), Gultekin and Logue (1979).

[28]It is convenient to take the following assumptions (which are too restrictive and can be partially relaxed): short-sales are allowed, and individuals have complete information about the fundamentals, (i.e., the real shocks in the economy). Markets do *not* have to be complete.

[29]The Pareto optimal allocation, as described here, could also be decentralized by a contingent fiscal policy which would determine the relative price of A and B (or as a non-linear function of consumption). Instead of taste uncertainty, we could also imagine a labor productivity uncertainty in the second period.

References

Ando, A. and F. Modigliani, (1963). "The 'Life Cycle' Hypothesis of Saving: Aggregate Implications and Tests," *American Economic Review*, 53, pp. 55–84.

Arrow, K. J., (1964). "The Role of Securities in the Optimal Allocation of Risk Bearing," *Review of Economic Studies*, 31, pp. 91–96.

Arrow, K. J. and M. Kurz, (1970). *Public Investment, the Rate of Return and Optimal Fiscal Policy*, Baltimore: Johns Hopkins Press.

Atkinson, A. B. and A. Sandmo, (1980). "Welfare Implications of the Taxation of Savings," *Economic Journal*, 90, pp. 529–547.

Atkinson, A. B. and Joseph E. Stiglitz, (1980). *Lectures on Public Economics*, New York: McGraw-Hill Co.

Auerbach, A., (1979). "The Optimal Taxation of Heterogenous Capital," *Quarterly Journal of Economics*, November, pp. 589–612.

Auerbach, A. and L. Kotlikoff, (1980). "An Examination of the Empirical Tests on Social Security and Savings," Mimeo, Yale University, New Haven, CT.

Auernheimer, L., (1974). "The Honest Government's Guide to the Revenue from the Creation of Money," *Journal of Political Economy*, 82, 3, 598–606.

Bailey, M., (1956). "The Welfare Cost of Inflationary Finance," *Journal of Political Economy,* 64, 93–110.

Barro, R. J., (1974). "Are Government Bonds Net Wealth?" *Journal of Political Economy,* 82, 1035–1117.

Brumberg, R. and F. Modigliani, (1954). "Utility Analysis and the Consumption Function: An Interpretation of Cross Section Data," in *Post-Keynesian Economics,* K. Kurihara (ed.), New Brunswick: Rutgers University Press, 388–436.

Buiter, W. H. and J. Tobin, (1979). "Debt Neutrality: A Brief Review of Doctrine and Evidence," in *Capital Investment and Saving,* G. M. Von Furstenberg (ed.), Cambridge: Ballinger Publishing Co.

Calvo, G., (1978). "On the Time Consistency of Optimal Policy in a Monetary Economy," *Econometrica,* 46, 1411–1428.

Chamley, C., (1977), "Aggregate Capital Accumulation, Taxation, and the Public Debt," Ph.D. Dissertation, Harvard University, Cambridge, MA.

———, (1981a). "The Welfare Cost of the Capital Income Tax in a Growing Economy," *Journal of Political Economy,* 89, 468–496.

———, (1981b). "On the Infinite Welfare Cost of Inflation and Other Second Order Effects," Cowles Foundation Discussion Paper No. 598, Yale University, New Haven, CT.

———, (1981c). "Efficient Tax Reform in a Dynamic Model of General Equilibrium," Mimeo, December, Cowles Foundation, Yale University, New Haven, CT.

——— and H. M. Polemarchakis, (1981). "Asset Markets, General Equilibrium and the Neutrality of Money," Mimeo, September, Cowles Foundation, Yale University, New Haven, CT.

Chamley, C. (1982). "On Efficient Taxation in Intertemporal General Equilibrium," Mimeo, January, Cowles Foundation, Yale University, New Haven, CT.

Dasgupta, P. S. and J. E. Stiglitz, (1972). "On Optimal Taxation and Public Production," *Review of Economic Studies,* 39, 87–103.

Diamond, P. A., (1965). "National Debt in a Neoclassical Growth Model," *American Economic Review,* 55, 1125–1150.

——— and J. Mirrlees, (1971). "Optimal Taxation and Public Production I: Production Efficiency" and "II: Tax Rules," *American Economic Review,* 61, 8–27, and 261–278.

Diamond, P. A., (1977). "A Framework for Social Security Analysis," *Journal of Public Economics.*

Feldstein, M. S., (1974). "Social Security, Induced Retirement and Capital Accumulation," *Journal of Political Economy,* 82, 905–926.

Fisher, S., (1974). "Money and the Production Function," *Economic Inquiry,* 12, 517–533.

———, (1980a). "Dynamic Inconsistency, Cooperation and the Benevolent Dissembling Government," *Journal of Economic Dynamics and Control,* 93–105.

———, (1980b). "Seignorage and the Case for a National Money," Mimeo, Massachusetts Institute of Technology, Cambridge, MA, July.

———, (1980c). "Towards an Understanding of the Costs of Inflation," Mimeo, Massachusetts Institute of Technology, Cambridge, MA, October.

Friedman, M., (1969). "The Optimum Quantity of Money," in *The Optimum Quantity of Money and Other Essays,* Chicago: Aldine Publishing Co.

Fullerton, D. and R. H. Gordon, (1981). "A Reexamination of Tax Distortions in General Equilibrium Models," Mimeo, National Bureau of Economic Research, No. 673.

Gultekin, N. B. and D. E. Logue, (1979). "Social Security and Personal Saving: Survey and New Evidence," in *Capital Investment and Saving,* G. M. Von Furstenberg, (ed.), Cambridge: Ballinger Publishing Co.

Hamada, K., (1972), "Lifetime Equity and Dynamic Efficiency on the Balanced Growth Path," *Journal of Public Economics,* 1, 379–396.

Iwai, K. (1972). "Optimal Growth and Stationary Ordinal Utility: A Fisherian Approach," *Journal of Economic Theory,* 5, 121–151.

Keynes, J. M., (1936). *The General Theory of Employment, Interest and Money*, New York: Harcourt, Brace & World, Inc., Herbing edition, 1964.
Koopmans, T. C., (1960). "Stationary Ordinal Utility and Impatience," *Econometrica*, 78, 287–309.
Kotlikoff, L., (1979), "Testing the Theory of Social Security and Life Cycle Accumulation," *American Economic Review*, 69, 396–410.
Kydland, F. E. and E. C. Prescott, (1980). "Dynamic Optimal Taxation, Rational Expectations and Optimal Control," *Journal of Economic Dynamics and Control*, 2, 79–91.
Meade, J. E., (1958). "Is the National Debt a Burden?" *Oxford Economic Papers*, 10, 163–183.
Munk, K. J., (1978). "Optimal Taxation and Pure Profits," *Scandinavian Journal of Economics*, 80, 1–19.
Ordover, J. A. and E. S. Phelps, (1975). "Linear Taxation of Wealth and Wages for Intragenerational Lifetime Justice: Some Steady-State Cases," *American Economic Review*, 65, 660–673.
Ordover, J. A., (1976). "Distributive Justice and Optimal Taxation of Wages and Interest in a Growing Economy," *Journal of Public Economics*, 5, 139–160.
Pestieau, P. M., (1974). "Optimal Taxation and Discount Rate for Public Investment in a Growth Setting," *Journal of Public Economics*, 3, 217–235.
Phelps, E., (1973). "Inflation in the Theory of Public Finance," *Swedish Journal of Economics*, 75, 67–82.
Ramsey, F. P., (1927). "A Contribution to the Theory of Taxation," *Economic Journal*, 37, 47–61.
Ramsey, F. P., (1928). "A Mathematical Theory of Saving," *Economic Journal*, 38, 543–559.
Ricardo, David, (1965). *The Principles of Political Economy and Taxation*, J. M. Dent & Sons, Aldin House, London.
Sandmo, A., (1976). "Optimal Taxation: An Introduction to the Literature," *Journal of Public Economics*, 6, 37–54.
Shoven, J. B., (1976). "The Incidence and Efficiency Effects of Taxes on Income from Capital," *Journal of Political Economy*, 84, 1261–1283.
Siegel, J., (1978). "Notes on Optimal Taxation and the Optimal Rate of Inflation," *Journal of Monetary Economics*, 4, 297–305.
Summers, L. H., (1981a). "Optimal Inflation Policy," *Journal of Monetary Economics*, 7, 2, 179–194.
———, (1981b). "Capital Taxation and Accumulation in a Life Cycle Growth Model," *American Economic Review*, September, 74: 533–544.
Tobin, J., (1956). "The Interest Elasticity of the Demand for Cash," *Review of Economics and Statistics*, 38, 241–247.
———, (1958). "Liquidity Preference as Behavior Towards Risk," *Review of Economic Studies*, Vol. 25, 67, 65–86.
Tobin, J., (1965). "Money and Economic Growth," *Econometrica*, 33, 671–684.
———, (1980). *Asset Accumulation and Economic Activity*, Basil Backwell.
Weiss, L., (1980). "The Effects of Money Supply on Economic Welfare in the Steady State," *Econometrica*, 48, 565–576.

Résumé

Cet article présente une analyse critique de quelques problèmes de la pensée économique relatifs à des politiques fiscales et monétaires efficaces dans des économies dynamiques selon la théorie des choix du second rang. Ces politiques sont analysées dans le cadre d'une taxation efficace avec deux modèles types d'équilibre général (avec ou sans transfert entre les générations).

En général, les politiques efficaces n'ont pas de cohérence dans le temps: pour des prix de facteur endogènes, une fraction au moins de l'incidence d'un impôt, (choisi arbitrairement) retombe sur le capital accumulé; ceci produit un effet partiel de taxation forfaitaire ce qui pourrait porter un gouvernement irresponsable à augmenter les impôts à l'improviste et à accumuler un surplus, afin de réduire le coût d'efficacité de l'imposition.

Pour chacun des deux modèles, on analyse des politiques efficaces concernant le taux de croissance de l'argent (ou taux d'inflation). L'article étudie aussi l'amplitude de l'effet causé par l'inflation sur une consommation de type régulier qui se produit dans le cadre du cycle-vie du fait que l'on substitue le capital à l'argent.

On étudie aussi des politiques appliquées à une économie offrant des caractères d'incertitude. En l'absence de marchés futurs pour la consommation, une politique fiscale qui limite les fluctuations de la consommation globale peut être bénéfique du point de vue social.

Monetary-Fiscal Policy for Promoting Growth: The Merits and Shortcomings of the Keynesian Approach

David I. Fand

I. Introduction

The American economy is suffering from stagflation. In 1980, for the first time in our history, we had experienced an unbelievable combination of interest rates of 20 percent and inflation rates reaching almost 18 percent. We also experienced negative productivity growth for several quarters, large budget deficits, large trade deficits, a weak dollar, financial assets shrinking in value, and considerable speculation in gold, silver, jewelry, tangibles, and other collectibles.

I shall argue that these indicators of our poor economic health are the consequences of inappropriate policies; more specifically, of policies that the Carter administration followed in the United States—which produced high inflation and high interest rates. Some support for this view is that changes introduced by the Reagan administration seem to correct some of these problems.

My thesis is that the American economy was not then, and is not now, suffering from degenerative diseases and dying slowly of old age, but rather was suffering then from following hyperactivist policies that have not worked. I further argue that if we slow down, and reverse, these super-Keynesian policies—as the Reagan administration is attempting—the American economy will regain its former prowess and strength.[1]

Policies that were appropriate and desirable in the 1930s, 1940s, and 1950s are not appropriate in the conditions of the 1970s and in the 1980s. My criticism of the 1977–79 expansionist policies followed in the United States is not therefore intended to imply that Keynesian

Public Finance and Economic Growth. Proceedings of the 37th Congress of the International Institute of Public Finance. Tokyo, 1981, pp. 89–100

aggregate demand policy is necessarily inappropriate in many circumstances. I am rather criticizing the super-Keynesian redistributionist policies which have led us astray.

In this paper I shall try to explain why the super-Keynesian policies damaged the American economy and why we have to move in a different direction to meet the challenges of the 1980s. Each section of the paper will focus on some doctrine or policy that caused problems for the United States in the post-World War II period.

II. Managed Money and Discretionary Monetary Policy

We live in a world of central banking and managed money, and this has enabled activists to favor policies that set the stage for many of the problems that the American economy is now experiencing.

Monetary policy in the United States is decided by a committee, the Federal Open Market Committee (FOMC), that meets regularly to assess the economic situation and to determine policy. And this world of central banking, paper money, and discretionary monetary policy contrasts sharply with the kind of automaticity that was associated in earlier periods with the gold standard.

Starting with the creation of the Federal Reserve System and with renewed emphasis on the post-World War II period, discretionary monetary policy in the United States has sought to achieve varying domestic policy goals. At times, the focus of policy was to achieve stable prices; at other times, reducing unemployment. In some periods, monetary policy was used to protect the balance of payments; at other times, to protect the exchange value of the dollar. These goals vary over time; they are dependent on objective conditions, the international monetary system (fixed or flexible exchange rates), the severity of the domestic problems, and the members of the FOMC who make the decisions. Until very recently, monetary control measures targeted interest rates and credit conditions; since 1979, the FOMC has set as its targets the monetary aggregates and money growth rates.

Before the Federal Reserve and before the evolution of modern discretionary central banking, the world operated under some variant of the gold standard. In such a system, domestic monetary policy is determined, more or less, by the balance of payments, depending on the degree to which countries are playing by the rules of the gold standard regime. Surpluses in the balance of payments are supposed to lead to domestic monetary expansion; and deficits, to domestic monetary contraction. There is no role, or very little role, for discretionary policy under an automatic international monetary system linked to gold.

In a regime of managed money and discretionary central banking, policy makers such as the FOMC have typically sought to mediate among alternative policies. Monetary policy is no longer a relatively automatic and straightforward response to the balance of payments or to changes in price levels, interest rates, and exchange rate movements. Moreover, since monetary policy may often provide the wherewithal for intervention, it is not surprising that this policy area is one that has received so much of the attention of the activists. And as it is currently constituted, monetary policy is rather a fairly intricate decision-making process that may involve adjudication among sharply conflicting policies, goals, and objectives.

At the end of World War I, many people assumed that discretionary monetary policy-managed money should do better than an automatic gold standard. It was widely believed that prices and wages were not sufficiently flexible on the downward wide to permit the cost structure in many countries to adjust readily to the vicissitudes of the balance of payments. A substantial consensus emerged that central banking and managed money, coupled perhaps with some degree of policy activism, would do better than an automatic gold standard.

There was probably a common view at the end of World War I. Yet, as we look around at the high inflation, the seemingly high unemployment, the low productivity, and diminished economic growth—the universal stagflation—that have afflicted most of the industrial countries in the last decade or two, one may wonder whether the post-World War I consensus on the advantages of a discretionary system may not have oversimplified the problem to a considerable degree.[2]

There has been renewed interest in recent years on developing monetary control procedures that will give us more stable growth of money. There has also been some renewed interest in some versions of the gold standard because of the fear that central banking, paper money, and discretion cum fine tuning lead to excessive monetary growth. In the United States now, Congress has appointed a gold commission to look into the possibility of using some kind of gold backing for our currency. And the Federal Reserve has been required by law to report on the intended policy with respect to the monetary aggregates. There appears to be a much greater emphasis on the behavior of the monetary aggregates and on stable monetary growth in the foreseeable future, and this tendency will be greatly strengthened by any successes of the Reagan economic program.

III. Money and Wealth

The changing relation between nominal money, which can be printed, and real wealth or capital, which must be produced, is another factor that has created policy difficulties in the past two or three decades.

The relation between money and wealth is analytically difficult and has many facets. There is a sense in which money is wealth. It is true for an individual; for the more money he has, the wealthier he is. But it is not necessarily true for the society as a whole; for if each of us has more money, it does not follow that we all have more wealth; perhaps all that will happen is that prices will rise proportionately to the increase in money.

The creation of additional money can add to wealth in particular circumstances. These circumstances were clearly recognized by Lord Keynes, whose general theory will undoubtedly rank with the great contributions of Adam Smith, David Ricardo, Alfred Marshall, and others. He spelled out some conditions in which the printing of additional money could be transformed into additional wealth for a society.

Unfortunately, these conditions are far from general. While fiscal expansion and money creation in the 1930s and early 1940s could have, and did, increase the wealth of the American society, the speed-up in money growth in the 1960s did not increase our wealth, income, or output. Indeed, the high, and accelerating, rates of monetary growth in the 1960s may have reduced wealth.

This brings us to a second aspect of the relation between money and wealth—that faster money growth can, at times, also reduce wealth. Indeed, this may characterize the period since the mid-1960s, and this negative relation between money and wealth seems to characterize many of the industrial countries, all of whom appear to be suffering from stagflation.

The key to the puzzle relating money and wealth is that when prices have been stable and are expected to remain stable, the printing of nominal money is equivalent to the printing of real wealth and capital because the additional nominal money, in a regime of stable prices, constitutes additional real wealth. On the other hand, when the creation of additional money raises inflationary expectations sufficiently, it reduces the real value of the existing monetary balances and thus contributes to a reduction in real wealth.

The link between government actions and inflationary expectations is thus crucial. If there is excess capacity, and expectations are that prices will be stable and not rise, the government can create new money and, in effect, print real wealth and capital. But when capacity utilization is high and inflationary expectations emerge in response to government action, the printing of money easily becomes counterproductive. As the government creates new money, it is literally destroying private wealth by raising inflationary expectations.

IV. The Paradox of Thrift

Another doctrine which created a climate of opinion favorable to fiscal expansion, large deficits, a speed-up in money growth, and hyperactivism followed from the Keynesian idea of the paradox of thrift. This idea generated a presumption that there were inadequate investment outlets and that social spending of many kinds was probably in the public interest.

One of Keynes' great contributions was to go behind the savings and investment processes and to explain what he called the paradox of thrift. He argued that an attempt by the public to save in the conditions of the 1930s would not increase investment, the capital stock, and economic growth, but would, paradoxically, lead to a reduction in output.

The paradox of thrift was that as more people attempted to save in order to invest, to increase the capital stock, and to facilitate economic growth, they would, in fact, succeed in reducing economic output. In other words, the desire to save more leads to less employment, output, and income.

Keynes called this the paradox of thrift because we normally associate more thrift with more investment and output; in contrast, when the paradox holds, additional thrift will lead to a decline in output. Note that additional spending by the government here leads to additional private output. Thus, it is possible to have both more social spending and more private spending simultaneously when the paradox applies. This possibility of having more of both, which seems to violate the law of conservation of matter, is thus a direct consequence of the paradox.

In the past two decades we have learned that the paradox of thrift is not a general condition, that budget deficits are not always productive, and that more social spending does not always lead to more private output. It is not always true that additional savings lead to less output and that larger deficits lead to greater output. The paradox of thrift may have been a characteristic of the 1930s when Keynes wrote his general theory. It clearly has not been operative in the last two decades.

Unfortunately, many of our policies in the past decade seem to assume that one could have both more public spending and more private spending and that increases in the public sector will not require reductions in the private sector.

The paradox of thrift is a convenient paradigm for political leaders who seek to satisfy the competing demands of different constituencies. There are always conflicting demands, and the easy way to deal with these demands is to opt for additional government expenditures and deficits. But it is difficult to argue today, in light of the stagflation and high interest rates of the past decade, either that larger deficits will lead to greater output, or that increased public spending will lead to increased private spending.[3]

V. Fiscal Drag and Fiscal Mortgage

Fiscal drag—the notion that our tax structure serves as a drag on the American economy and prevented it from achieving a robust rate of growth—gained a wide audience in the 1950s.

In the early 1960s an influential analysis of why the United States seemed not to be growing as much as expected—or believed possible—was attributed to fiscal drag. This doctrine asserted that recoveries in the United States economy were being choked off because our progressive tax structure was pulling too much out of the private economy—thereby preventing a robust recovery. Kennedy's Council of Economic Advisors, in its first Economic Report, sought to rationalize the incomplete recoveries of the 1950s, primarily in terms of the restrictive effects of fiscal drag. The concept of the full employment surplus was developed as one way to measure and highlight the phenomenon of fiscal drag.

The obvious solution to fiscal drag was to cut taxes as first recommended by the Kennedy Council. But as time went on, some activists highlighted the alternative of increasing expenditures as a better way to overcome the debilitating effects of fiscal drag.

Many of the expenditure programs that were set up initially in the 1960s were not screened as carefully as they might have been, but were justified implicitly because the additional public spending was viewed as necessary to overcome fiscal drag.

The acceleration of government spending and the deficits since 1965 are unbelievably large. They were rationalized—at least in the initial period—by this philosophical notion that some of these expenditures were essential not so much for their specific and stated purposes but to overcome the depressing effects of fiscal drag. It is not entirely surprising that what first appeared as a problem of fiscal drag in the early 1960s soon emerged as a problem of fiscal mortgage at the end of the decade.

The summary of expenditures, revenues, and deficits for a few selected years shown in Table 1 illustrates the emergence of the fiscal mortgage.

As expenditures exploded, the government increased revenues by direct measures through taxation and indirectly through inflation-bracket creep. In the 1970s, expenditures, revenues, and deficits were accelerating, causing the private sector to shrink relative to the public sector.[4] The Reagan three-year tax reduction is motivated in part by a desire to redress this shrinkage of the private sector.

VI. The Inflation-Unemployment Trade-off

The concept and interpretation of a negatively inclined Phillips Curve is another doctrine which may have generated a climate of opinion that was more accepting of fiscal deficits, high rates of monetary growth, and inflation. The slope of the long-run curve relating unemployment and inflation was assumed to be negatively inclined. This gave rise to the notion of a trade-off—that by accepting additional inflation, we could permanently lower unemployment.

The negatively inclined curve seemed to predict that a little bit of inflation could yield desirable public policy aspects, and this may

Table 1

Federal Budget Receipts, Outlays, and Deficits for Selected Fiscal Years (in billions of dollars)

Year	*Receipts*	*Outlays*	*Surplus or Deficit (−)*
1960	$ 92.5	$ 92.2	$ 0.3
1965	116.8	118.4	−1.6
1970	192.8	195.7	−2.8
1975	279.1	324.2	−45.2
1980	517.1	576.7	−59.6
1982	626.8	725.3	−98.6

These data are for the uniform budget. The corresponding numbers for federal government receipts and expenditures in the national income and products account for fiscal 1982 are:

Receipts	$ 641.0
Expenditures	741.4
Deficits	−100.4

have led the public to be a little more tolerant and positive of what would otherwise have been viewed as an inflationary policy. For two decades, policies in many industrial nations have been implicitly or explicitly based on this notion that a country can achieve a permanent reduction in unemployment if it is willing to accept some additional increases in the inflation rate.

The trade-off notion was taken to mean that if a society is willing to accept a little more inflation, it would thereby gain more output and employment.

While the Phillips Curve was an immensely popular idea in the 1960s, the late 1960s and 1970s experience certainly seems to belie its relevance. What we have seen in the 1970s is that more inflation is associated with more recorded unemployment and less output, in sharp contrast to the trade-off idea that more inflation leads to more output and less (recorded) unemployment.

The trade-off idea assumes some degree of money illusion—that people somehow confuse money wages and real wages. Critics of the Phillips Curve have always questioned whether people will fail to see through the mirage of inflation, especially if it continues for some time. The decade of the 1970s suggests that people ultimately do see through the money illusion, and while the Phillips Curve trade-off may have worked in the early 1960s, its alleged benefits could not be realized in the 1970s.

We can sum it up by saying that even if the Phillips Curve was negatively inclined in the early 1960s—so that it was literally possible to trade off more inflation for more output and less unemployment—it appears to be positively inclined in the 1970s.[5] In our current situation, higher levels of inflation appear to be associated with higher (recorded) levels of unemployment.

VII. The Dollar—Domestic and International Aspects

We have discussed a number of post-Keynesian ideas: discretionary money policy; money and wealth; the paradox of thrift; fiscal drag; and the inflation-unemployment trade-off. Taken together, these doctrines all seemed to suggest that political leaders could create more income and more wealth domestically by actively pursuing policies of monetary and fiscal expansion. Interestingly enough, these doctrines also seemed to suggest that monetary and fiscal activism would increase our international wealth and power. The dollar was an international money that was widely respected. No one questioned its authority. The United States government could exert extraordinary influences on world affairs because it could, seemingly, solve many problems by making dollars available.

Up until the mid-1960s, America exerted unique and far-reaching influence in world affairs because the dollar was the most respected international currency. The dollar was, in fact, the center of the international monetary system. And we could supply these dollars to foreigners without causing inflation to accelerate domestically because dollars were not only widely used as a means of payment but also widely respected as a store of value.

The United States was then in the condition that De Gaulle referred to as "deficits without tears." The United States could run deficits, obtain resources from other countries, and pay for these resources by supplying foreigners with dollars. And so long as foreigners were willing to hold additional dollars, this was a relatively painless way to increase American influence, power, resources, and hegemony.

But this age could not go on indefinitely, and it has come to an end because we have saturated the world with dollars. The dollar is no longer the desired currency it was in the early post-war period. The post-Reagan dramatic rise of the dollar reminds us that wealth and power may be inversely correlated with activism.[6]

VIII. Activism and Expansionary Policy

We have just summarized a number of post-Keynesian ideas that create a climate in which activism and stimulatory policies appear to result in more wealth, more output, more employment, more power, and more hegemony. In the early part of the post-war period, stimulatory policies probably did lead to more wealth and output. Unfortunately, in the latter part of the period, and especially in the last decade or so, stimulatory policies and expansionism probably led to less output and less wealth.

The merits and the shortcomings of the Keynesian approach can thus be viewed in terms of the post-war period. In the early part of the period, especially during the phase when we were recovering from the Great Depression, Keynesianism had a very constructive role to play. It suggested a number of policies which would lead to an economy of high employment, high output, and relatively stable prices. Unfortunately, toward the latter part of the period, the earlier moderate Keynesianism was somehow transformed into super-Keynesianism, hyperactivism, and redistributionism, and we ended up with high inflation and stagnation, with less wealth, less output, and less employment.

We can state our views another way. In the appropriate circumstances of an under-employed economy, Keynesian ideas and policies have an important role to play in stabilizing non-inflationary growth of aggregate demand. On the other hand, Keynesian ideas used to excess easily become hyperactivist and redistributionist policies and do not give the hoped for results. Indeed, instead of more output and employment we get less. In chronological terms, the Keynesian approach shows up best if we look at the period from, say, 1950 to 1965. The deficiencies and the shortcomings of the Keynesian approach show up most clearly if we take the period from, say, 1965 to 1980. It is unfortunate that the year 1965 is also the year of the Vietnam escalation. The stagnation and high interest rates that we are suffering from now is not really related to the Vietnam war, but to the super-expansionary monetary and fiscal policies and redistributionist policies that we followed in the latter part of the 1970s.

As already noted, this criticism of the hyperactivist-expansionist-redistributionist policies followed by the Carter administration is not intended to suggest that the Keynesian concern with aggregate demand, especially if it is used in moderation, is inappropriate in many circumstances.

In sum, the merits of the Keynesian approach relate to its concern and emphasis on aggregate demand and high employment; its shortcomings relate to its relative benign neglect of the inflationary dangers and its transformation into a paradigm of super-Keynesianism, hyperactivism, and redistributionism as evidenced in the Carter administration.

Notes

[1]The terms I have used, super-Keynesianism, hyperactivism, and redistributionism all need to be defined precisely, but I shall not attempt it here. By super-Keynesianism, I have in mind a tendency to follow expansionary policies even though there are some serious risks of causing inflation to accelerate. By hyperactivism I mean a tendency to act and introduce policy changes at a time when many others would wait to gain a better understanding of the problem. By redistributionism I mean a tendency to favor policies to redistribute income with relative neglect of whether these policies may limit the growth of, or even reduce, output. Why all three tendencies came together in the Carter administration is an interesting problem that would require another paper.

[2]They were rightly concerned with the deflationary aspects of a gold standard and also with the fact that under a gold standard there can be considerable short-run fluctuations in the price level. But they probably overlooked, or had no way of foreseeing, the kind of inflationary momentum that could develop in a system of managed money.

[3]Some of the errors in the Johnson and Carter administrations were, in my opinion, intimately related to the paradox of thrift. Johnson's belief that he could undertake the Vietnam escalation without giving up any of his Great Society goals—that he

could have both guns and butter—appear to be related to this paradox. Similarly, some of the expansionary policies followed by the Carter administration assumed that additional social spending would generate more private spending and, in this way, may also be related to the paradox of thrift. See *Economic Report of the President, 1980*.

The link between Keynesianism, and especially of super-Keynesianism, and the kind of redistributionist policies that emerged in the latter part of the 1970s may, I believe, be traced to the paradox of thrift.

[4]The shrinkage of the private sector is, of course, related to the stagnation and the negative productivity that we have been experiencing in some recent years.

[5]The experience in the 1970s would seem to suggest that the negative relationship between inflation and unemployment no longer holds even if it held in the 1960s. Indeed, there may even be a positive relation between inflation and unemployment. See the discussion in Lucas (9).

[6]The dollar has strengthened very considerably—almost unbelievably—under the Reagan administration. The usual explanation relates the strength of the dollar to the high interest rates in the United States. However, the dollar may be strengthening for other reasons—to wit, the increased military expenditures and the emphasis on defense in the United States.

References

Economic Report of the President, 1980.

Economic Report of the President, 1982.

Fand, David I. "Keynesian Monetary Theories, Stabilization Policy, and the Recent Inflation," *The Journal of Money, Credit, and Banking*, August, 1969.

———. "Some Issues in Monetary Economics," *Banca Nazionale del Lavoro Quarterly Review*, September, 1969. Also in the *Review of Federal Reserve of St. Louis*, January, 1970.

Friedman, Milton and Schwartz, Anna. *A Monetary History of the United States, 1867–1960*. Princeton University Press, 1963.

Friedman, Milton. "The Role of Monetary Policy," *American Economic Review*, May, 1968.

———. *The Optimum Quantity of Money*. Aldine Press, 1969.

———. "Nobel Lecture: Inflation and Unemployment," *Journal of Political Economics*, June, 1977.

Lucas, Robert E., Jr. "Tobin and Monetarism: A Review Article," *Journal of Economic Literature*, June, 1981.

Tobin, James. *Essays in Economics*. Markham Press, 1971.

———. *The New Economics One Decade Older*. Princeton University Press, 1974.

———. *Asset Accumulation and Economic Activity*. University of Chicago Press, 1980.

Résumé

Nous avons passé en revue un grand nombre d'idées keynésiennes et post-keynésiennes suggérant que activisme et politiques expansionnistes apporteraient davantage de richesses, de production et d'emploi. Dans la première partie de la période d'après-guerre, de la fin de la Deuxième Guerre Mondiale jusqu'au début des années 60, des politiques de stimulation ont pu conduire à davantage de richesses et de production. Malheureusement, dans la deuxième partie de cette période et surtout dans la dernière décade environ, des politiques expansionnistes ont probablement résulté en moins de production et moins de richesse.

On peut donc examiner les mérites et les défauts de la perspective keynésienne par rapport à la période d'après-guerre. Au début de cette période, le Keynésianisme a eu un rôle constructif à jouer en suggérant et mettant l'accent sur des politiques qui conduiraient à une économie de fort emploi et de forte production, et on l'espérait, de prix stables. Malheureusement, à la fin de cette période la politique keynésienne modérée du début fut transformée en une prise de position politique différente qui mit l'accent sur des politiques expansionnistes en négligeant les coûts potentiels.

En somme, les mérites de la perspective keynésienne tiennent à son souci de la demande globale et du plein emploi. Ses défauts tiennent à sa négligence relativement bénigne des dangers inflationnistes et de sa transformation dans les années 70 en un paroxysme de super-keynésianisme, hyperactivisme et redistributionisme.

Politique Monétaire et Politique Budgétaire dans un Modèle Dynamique Synthétique d'une Economie en Croissance

Claude Vedel

L'objet de cet article est d'étudier les politiques monétaire et budgétaire et leurs effets sur l'activité économique, le taux d'inflation et le taux d'intérêt, dans le cadre d'un modèle dynamique synthétique qui puisse être considéré comme une représentation unitaire des théories keynésienne et néo-classique.

Le modèle proposé prend en effet la forme, à court terme, lorsque les anticipations inflationnistes et le niveau général des prix sont donnés, d'un modèle IS-LM à prix fixe qui constitue l'une des bases de l'analyse macro-économique depuis qu'il a été mis en lumière par HICKS [8]. On y retrouve, en considérant l'équilibre du marché des produits et l'équilibre du marché de la monnaie, les conclusions habituelles quant à l'efficacité à court terme des politiques de stabilisation tant monétaire que budgétaire.

Les enchaînements des équilibres temporaires sont assurés d'une part par un réajustement des anticipations inflationnistes qui prend ici la forme d'anticipations adaptatives du type proposé par CAGAN [2], d'autre part par une évolution du niveau général des prix déterminée par une équation de Phillips liant le taux d'inflation effectif au taux d'inflation anticipé et à une variable d'écart de l'activité économique par rapport à sa valeur sur le sentier de croissance normal. La courbe de PHILLIPS [12] utilisée ici est du type de celle avancée par PHELPS [11], compatible avec la théorie du taux de chômage naturel de FRIEDMAN [4]. Elle joue ainsi le rôle de l'équation manquante signalée par FRIEDMAN [5], [6], permettant de déterminer les grandeurs nominales, à côté des grandeurs réelles (niveau d'activité et taux d'intérêt) fournies par les équations d'équilibre temporaire.

Public Finance and Economic Growth. Proceedings of the 37th Congress of the International Institute of Public Finance. Tokyo, 1981, pp. 101–126

Le modèle comporte un équilibre de long terme néo-classique où sur un sentier de croissance normal de l'activité économique, correspondant au taux de chômage naturel, on retrouve la validité de la théorie quantitative et la neutralité de la monnaie.

Par ailleurs l'analyse présentée ici constitue une combinaison des conceptions keynésienne, wicksellienne et fishérienne du taux d'intérêt. En effet si sur le sentier de croissance normal de long terme le taux d'intérêt réel est à son niveau naturel, à court terme on peut, comme chez WICKSELL [16], associer à un taux d'intérêt effectif inférieur au taux d'intérêt naturel un taux d'inflation plus élevé que l'inflation de long terme (et symétriquement si le taux d'intérêt est supérieur au taux d'intérêt naturel). Conjointement on distingue à la suite de FISHER [3], taux d'intérêt nominaux et taux d'intérêt réels, un taux d'intérêt nominal étant égal à la somme du taux d'intérêt réel et du taux d'inflation anticipé.

Le problème de l'étude simultanée des variations de l'activité économique et du taux d'inflation a déjà été abordé dans des modèles de manière plus ou moins partielle par des auteurs comme LAIDLER [10] ou TAYLOR [14], entre autres. Le premier utilise un modèle dynamique en temps discret qui, en considérant uniquement le marché de la monnaie et la version néo-classique de la courbe de Phillips, permet de présenter une théorie monétariste des fluctuations de l'activité économique autour d'un sentier de croissance exogène; les taux d'intérêt sont absents de l'analyse. Le second développe un modèle IS-LM dynamique en temps continu intégrant des éléments repris ici, mais la formulation des fonctions de demande de produits et de monnaie est laissée de côté et il ne s'intéresse qu'aux effets de la politique monétaire sur l'activité économique par rapport à un niveau stationnaire du revenu national. Le modèle présenté ici envisage aussi les effets de la politique budgétaire. En outre comme le modèle de LAIDLER [10] il traite des fluctuations de l'activité économique par rapport à un sentier de croissance à long terme.

Les principaux résultats en matière de politique économique sont les suivants: A court terme la politique monétaire et la politique budgétaire stimulent toutes deux l'activité économique au-dessus du sentier de croissance normal. Mais à long terme un accroissement une fois pour toutes du taux de croissance de la masse monétaire ou une augmentation de son niveau initial de même qu'un accroissement de la part des dépenses publiques dans le revenu national n'ont plus d'effets sur l'activité économique. Il faut pour que ces effets soient maintenus durablement que le taux de croissance de la masse monétaire soit continuellement accru, provoquant ainsi une inflation explosive, ou que la part des dépenses publiques dans le revenu national augmente sans cesse. Ces résultats traduisent des phénomènes d'instabilité instrumentale au sens de HOLBROOK [9]. Si on cherche à contrôler le taux d'inflation, seule la politique monétaire, en convergeant vers une valeur finie du taux de croissance de la masse monétaire, peut permettre d'atteindre l'objectif de manière stable; la politique budgétaire nécessite une diminution continuelle de la part des dépenses publiques dans le revenu national.

Par contre on peut trouver une politique budgétaire stable, associée à une certaine part des dépenses publiques dans la dépense globale, qui permette de maintenir constant le taux d'intérêt nominal; aucune politique monétaire stable ne permet d'y parvenir.

1. Le modèle

Le modèle comporte deux formes: la forme d'un modèle statique conduisant à un équilibre temporaire à un instant t lorsque les anticipations inflationnistes et le niveau général des prix sont donnés, ou la forme d'un modèle dynamique, en temps continu, lorsqu'on introduit un mode d'ajustement des anticipations inflationnistes et du niveau des prix.

Dans le premier cas les variables endogènes sont le niveau du produit national, le taux d'intérêt réel et le taux d'intérêt nominal. Dans le second cas les inconnues sont une mesure de l'écart entre l'activité effective et l'activité normale sur le sentier de croissance à long terme, le taux d'inflation effectif, le taux d'inflation anticipé et les taux d'intérêt.

Les équations seront donc présentées sous des formes alternatives appropriées.

L'originalité essentielle du modèle tient à ce que les fonctions de demande de monnaie et de produits sont des fonctions explicites des taux d'intérêt (nominal ou réel) et d'une variable de ressources qui est une moyenne géométrique du revenu national courant Y et du revenu national normal $\bar{Y}$.

L'économie est une économie à trois marchés: produits, monnaie et titres. Ce dernier n'est pas envisagé explicitement (Id. de Walras).

Le marché des produits

La demande privée de produits est envisagée de manière agrégée sans distinguer une demande de biens d'investissements et une demande de biens de consommation. Elle dépend de manière exponentielle du taux d'intérêt réel r et d'une moyenne géométrique à coefficients h et $1 - h$ des revenus courant et normal. A la demande privée s'ajoutent les dépenses publiques G. On peut ainsi écrire la condition d'équilibre du marché des produits:

$$Y = Y^h \bar{Y}^{1-h} \cdot e^{a-ur} + G, \quad 0 < h < 1, \quad a > 0, \quad u > 0 \tag{1}$$

La demande privée de produits est proportionnelle au revenu moyen $Y^h \bar{Y}^{l-h}$, manifestant ainsi une inertie des dépenses au revenu normal anticipé $\bar{Y}$ qui croît à un taux exogène n. L'inertie, ou le retard d'anticipation, est d'autant plus grande que h est proche de 0. e est la base des logarithmes naturels; h, a et u sont des paramètres.

Si on désigne par $z = 1 + (G/Y^h \bar{Y}^{1-h} \cdot e^{a-ur})$ et $b = \text{Log } z$, $z = e^b$, z et b sont des paramètres de politique budgétaire qui varient dans le même sens que le rapport entre dépenses publiques et dépenses privées $G/Y^h \bar{Y}^{1-h} \cdot e^{a-ur}$, ou que la part des dépenses publiques dans le produit national; z varie entre 1 et $+\infty$, b entre 0 et $+\infty$ lorsque les dépenses publiques augmentent, toutes choses égales par ailleurs. La constance de b (ou de z) implique une évolution des dépenses publiques au même rythme que les dépenses privées et que le produit national.

Dans ces conditions l'équation (l) peut être réécrite sous la forme:

$$Y = Y^h \bar{Y}^{1-h} \cdot e^{a-ur} \cdot z \tag{1a}$$

ou

$$Y = Y^h \bar{Y}^{1-h} \cdot e^{a+b-ur}. \tag{1b}$$

Si on appelle $\hat{r} = (a + b)/u$, le taux d'intérêt naturel, (1b) devient:

$$Y = Y^h \bar{Y}^{1-h} \cdot e^{u(\hat{r}-r)} \tag{1c}$$

et sous forme logarithmique:

$$\begin{aligned} \text{Log } Y &= \text{Log } \bar{Y} + (u/1 - h)(\hat{r} - r) \\ &= \text{Log } \bar{Y} + (a + b - ur)/(1 - h) \end{aligned} \tag{1d}$$

ou encore

$$(1 - h)x = u(\hat{r} - r) = a + b - ur \tag{1'}$$

si on désigne par $x = \text{Log } (Y/\bar{Y}) = \text{Log } Y - \text{Log } \bar{Y}$, une mesure de l'écart entre le revenu national effectif et son niveau normal, une mesure de la composante transitoire du produit national, avec:

$$x \gtreqless 0 \quad \text{suivant que} \quad Y \gtreqless \bar{Y}.$$

C'est cette mesure de l'activité économique qui sera utilisée dans le modèle dynamique où l'équation (1′) remplacera l'équation (1).

Notons que le taux d'intérêt naturel $\hat{r}$ dépend de la part des dépenses publiques dans le revenu national et croît avec elle. Cela peut s'expliquer par le fait que pour financer ses dépenses l'Etat doit avoir recours à l'emprunt (1). Ce modèle ne comportant pas de contrainte budgétaire de l'Etat, cette question ne peut pas être complètement explicitée (2).

On a par ailleurs supposé $h \neq 1$, c'est-à-dire que la demande privée de produits n'est pas proportionnelle au revenu courant seul et qu'il existe un effet d'inertie, pour éviter que le taux d'intérêt soit toujours égal au taux naturel. Dans ces conditions $x \gtreqless 0$ si et seulement si $r \lesseqgtr \hat{r}$. Lorsque le taux d'intérêt réel est inférieur au taux d'intérêt naturel, la demande de produits est stimulée par rapport à son niveau sur le sentier de croissance normal (au taux n) et inversement quand le taux d'intérêt est supérieur au taux naturel. Le taux d'intérêt naturel est le taux d'intérêt réel associé au sentier de croissance normal ou de long terme.

On voit ainsi apparaître un phénomène de type wicksellien. Il ne s'explique pas comme chez STEIN [13] par un déséquilibre du marché des produits avec retard d'ajustement, mais par un retard d'anticipation au niveau de la demande de produits qui dépend non seulement du revenu courant mais aussi du revenu normal $\bar{Y}$. L'augmentation du taux d'inflation consécutive à la faiblesse du taux d'intérêt effectif par rapport au taux d'intérêt naturel ne proviendra pas d'un excès de la demande sur l'offre de produits comme chez l'auteur précité, mais sera déterminé par la relation de Phillips, une surchauffe de l'activité économique et un déséquilibre implicite du marché du travail.

Le marché de la monnaie

La demande de monnaie en termes réels dépend de manière exponentielle du taux d'intérêt nominal i, qui représente le coût d'opportunité de la détention d'encaisses monétaires. Elle est d'autre part, comme la demande de produits, proportionnelle à une moyenne géométrique à coefficients g et $1 - g$ du revenu effectif Y et du revenu normal $\bar{Y}$. L'équilibre du marché de la monnaie s'écrit donc:

$$M/P = k \cdot Y^g \bar{Y}^{1-g} \cdot e^{-li}, \quad k > 0, \quad 0 < g < 1, \quad l > 0 \tag{2}$$

ou sous forme logarithmique:

$$\text{Log}\, M - \text{Log}\, P = \text{Log}\, k + g\, \text{Log}\, Y + (1-g)\, \text{Log}\, \bar{Y} - li \tag{2a}$$

M représente la quantité nominale de monnaie, supposée exogène; P est le niveau général des prix; e la base des logarithmes naturels; k, g et l sont des paramètres positifs. En dérivant (2a) par rapport au temps et en notant D l'opérateur d/dt, on obtient:

$$D\, \text{Log}\, M - D\, \text{Log}\, P = g(D\, \text{Log}\, Y - D\, \text{Log}\, \bar{Y}) + D\, \text{Log}\, \bar{Y} - lDi$$

ou encore, en tenant compte de la définition de $x = \text{Log}\, Y - \text{Log}\, \bar{Y}$, de celle de $n = D\, \text{Log}\, \bar{Y}$, le taux de croissance exogène du revenu normal, et en notant $m = D\, \text{Log}\, M$, le taux de croissance de l'offre nominale de monnaie, $p = D\, \text{Log}\, P$, le taux de croissance du niveau général des prix ou taux d'inflation effectif

$$m - p = gDx + n - lDi. \tag{2'}$$

L'équation (2a) sera utilisée pour déterminer l'équilibre temporaire, l'équation (2'), qui est une équation différentielle, interviendra dans le modèle dynamique.

Remarquons au passage que le taux de croissance du revenu réel est égal à $n + Dx$, et le taux de croissance du revenu nominal PY à $p + n + Dx$; leurs évolutions pourraient être déterminées.

La relation de FISHER

Nous adopterons la conception usuelle depuis FISHER [3] suivant laquelle le taux d'intérêt nominal est égal à la somme du taux d'intérêt réel et du taux d'inflation anticipé:

$$i = r + p^e \tag{3}$$

où p^e est le taux de croissance du niveau général des prix anticipé à un moment donné pour tout le futur. Cette relation est une expression de la cohérence du taux d'intérêt nominal qui s'établit sur le marché des titres avec le taux d'intérêt réel qui explique le comportement de demande de produits, compte tenu des anticipations inflationnistes.

A côté du taux d'intérêt réel ex ante on pourrait définir un taux d'intérêt réel ex post $R = i - p = r - (p - p^e)$. On a supposé que c'était le taux d'intérêt réel ex ante qui influençait la demande privée de produits. Le taux d'intérêt réel ex post est inférieur (supérieur) au taux d'intérêt réel ex ante lorsque le taux d'inflation effectif est supérieur (inférieur) au taux d'inflation anticipé.

La relation de PHILLIPS

Les équations (1), (2) et (3) permettent de déterminer le niveau d'activité effectif Y, les taux d'intérêt réel et nominal, r et i, étant donné à un instant t le niveau du revenu normal, le niveau général des prix P, le taux d'inflation anticipé p^e et la politique économique suivie (caractérisée par M et G). A partir de là un ajustement est supposé se produire qui affecte le niveau des prix et le taux d'inflation anticipé. L'ajustement des prix dépendra du taux d'inflation effectif, lui-même déterminé par une relation de PHILLIPS. En effet on considèrera que l'existence d'un excédent du revenu national effectif sur le revenu normal est inflationniste et symétriquement qu'un déficit du revenu effectif par rapport au revenu normal est déflationniste. Mais par ailleurs un biais inflationniste de l'économie est introduit dans la mesure où le taux d'inflation anticipé génère une inflation effective avec un coefficient égal à l'unité conformément à la version néo-classique de la relation de PHILLIPS:

$$p = cx + p^e \quad c > 0 \tag{4}$$

où c est un paramètre positif.

L'influence du différentiel d'activité x sur le taux d'inflation effectif peut s'expliquer en considérant le marché du travail et la notion de taux de chômage naturel. Implicitement l'économie est au niveau du taux de chômage naturel sur le sentier de croissance normal, lorsque $Y = \bar{Y}$, $x = 0$. Lorsqu'on s'écarte de ce sentier pour une raison quelconque, par exemple lorsqu'on se situe au-dessus ($x > 0$), le taux de chômage est réduit par rapport au taux de chômage naturel. Une pression à la hausse du taux de croissance du salaire nominal s'ajoute alors à l'effet du taux d'inflation anticipé. Si le salaire réel est égal à la productivité marginale du travail ou si la part des salaires dans le revenu national est constante on sait que cette augmentation du taux de croissance du salaire nominal conduit à une augmentation du taux d'inflation. Un phénomène symétrique se déroule lorsque le taux de chômage est supérieur au taux de chômage naturel ($x < 0$), il réduit dans ce cas l'inflation par rapport à l'inflation anticipée.

Le comportement d'anticipations inflationnistes

A court terme les anticipations inflationnistes seront considérées comme données (p^e = constante) mais au niveau de l'analyse dynamique on doit envisager un ajustement de celles-ci. Le mode de formation des anticipations inflationnistes retenu ici est celui correspondant à l'analyse de CAGAN [2] des anticipations adaptatives:

$$Dp^e = d(p - p^e) \quad d > 0 \tag{5}$$

où d est un paramètre positif qui s'interprête comme la vitesse d'ajustement des anticipations inflationnistes aux réalisations.

On peut également introduire dans ce modèle des anticipations rationnelles, faisant dépendre le taux d'inflation anticipé de la différence entre le taux de croissance attendu de la masse monétaire et le taux de croissance normal des variables réelles n. Les agents économiques sont ainsi supposés appliquer la théorie quantitative de la monnaie pour former leurs prévisions de hausse des prix sans adapter passivement celles-ci au taux d'inflation constaté comme ici. L'erreur d'anticipation porte sur le taux de croissance de la masse monétaire qui est ajusté en fonction des constatations.

2. L'équilibre temporaire

On peut maintenant s'intéresser à la manière dont sont déterminés à un instant t quelconque les niveaux du revenu national et des taux d'intérêt. Nous supposerons comme c'est habituel dans les analyses d'équilibre temporaire que le taux d'inflation anticipé est une donnée à l'instant t. En outre le niveau du revenu normal $\bar{Y}$ est connu et les variables de politique économique M ou Log M et G ou plutôt b, l'indicateur du rapport dépenses publiques-dépenses privées (3), sont des données exogènes. Il suffit pour pouvoir déterminer le niveau d'activité effectif de supposer que le niveau général des prix est rigide à court terme, c'est-à-dire que les quantités sont plus flexibles que les prix à court terme; cette hypothèse est naturellement de type keynésien. On peut alors présenter un modèle très proche d'un modèle IS-LM qui permet d'étudier, en statique comparative, les effets à court terme des politiques monétaire et budgétaire.

L'équilibre de court terme

L'équilibre temporaire est déterminé par les équations (1), (2) et (3):

$$Y = Y^h \bar{Y}^{1-h} \cdot e^{a-ur} + G$$
$$M/P = k \cdot Y^g \bar{Y}^{1-g} \cdot e^{-li}$$
$$i = r + p^e$$

ou encore (1d), (2a) et (3):

$$\text{Log}\, Y = \text{Log}\, \bar{Y} + (a + b - ur)/(1 - h)$$
$$\text{Log}\, M - \text{Log}\, P = \text{Log}\, k + g\, \text{Log}\, Y + (1 - g)\, \text{Log}\, \bar{Y} - li$$
$$i = r + p^e$$

où les inconnues sont Log Y ou $x = \text{Log}\,(Y/\bar{Y})$, r et i, et les variables exogènes: Log P, p^e, Log $\bar{Y}$, b et Log M. Le système peut être réécrit de manière équivalente:

$$x = (a + b - ur)/(1 - h)$$
$$\text{Log}\, M - \text{Log}\, P = \text{Log}\, k + gx + \text{Log}\, \bar{Y} - li$$
$$i = r + p^e$$

ou si on élimine le taux d'intérêt réel r à l'aide de la dernière équation:

$$i = p^e + \frac{a + b}{u} - \frac{1 - h}{u} x \tag{6}$$

$$i = \frac{g}{l} x - \frac{1}{l} \text{Log}\,(M/kP\bar{Y}) \tag{7}$$

qui sont les équations des droites IS et LM dans le plan (x, i), (figure 1). On en déduit les valeurs d'équilibre à court terme, x^* et i^*, du différentiel d'activité et du taux d'intérêt nominal:

$$x^* = \frac{up^e + a + b + (u/l)\,\text{Log}\,(M/kP\bar{Y})}{1 - h + (u/l)g} \tag{8}$$

$$i^* = \frac{(u/l)gp^e + (g/l)(a + b) - (1 - h/l)\,\text{Log}\,(M/kP\bar{Y})}{1 - h + (u/l)g} \tag{9}$$

La statique comparative

On déduit des équations (8) et (9) des résultats en matière de politique économique analogues aux résultats habituels avec cette

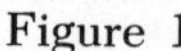

Figure 1

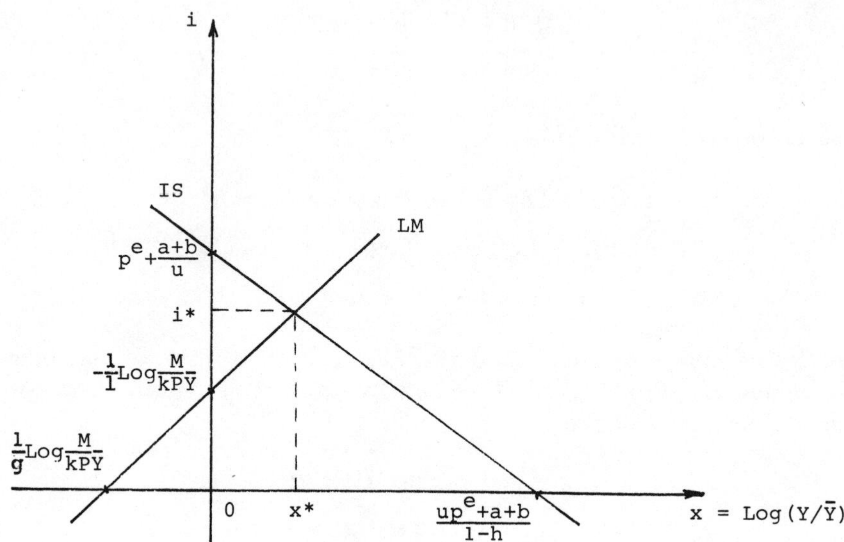

L'équilibre temporaire

différence qu'ils concernent ici des variations de variables logarithmiques:

$$\frac{\Delta x}{\Delta \operatorname{Log} M} = \frac{u/l}{1 - h + (u/l)g} > 0$$

$$\frac{\Delta x}{\Delta b} = \frac{l}{1 - h + (u/l)g} > 0$$

La politique monétaire et la politique budgétaire sont toutes deux efficaces pour stimuler l'activité économique à court terme. De même les effets sur le taux d'intérêt nominal (mais aussi sur le taux d'intérêt réel puisque p^e est exogène) sont les effets traditionnels:

$$\frac{\Delta i}{\Delta \operatorname{Log} M} = \frac{-(1 - h/l)}{1 - h + (u/l)g} < 0$$

$$\frac{\Delta i}{\Delta b} = \frac{g/l}{1 - h + (u/l)g} > 0$$

La politique monétaire réduit le taux d'intérêt, la politique budgétaire l'augmente.

On pourrait également avec le même modèle retrouver une explication du paradoxe de GIBSON, suivant lequel l'inflation n' est pas complètement incorporée dans le taux d'intérêt nominal, même lorsqu'elle est anticipée. Il suffirait d'étudier les effets d'une variation du taux d'inflation anticipé sur le taux d'intérêt nominal et sur le taux d'intérêt réel; le taux d'intérêt nominal étant accru par l'augmentation des anticipations inflationnistes mais moins que proportionnellement par suite d'une baisse du taux d'intérêt réel.

Une variation du niveau des prix a, quant à elle, le même effet qu'une variation en sens inverse de la masse monétaire; elle intervient en effet uniquement en affectant les encaisses réelles. Enfin on pourrait étudier l'influence d'une variation exogène du revenu normal (représentant par exemple des chocs extérieurs).

3. L'équilibre de long terme et sa stabilité

Le système dynamique constitué par les équations (1′), (2′), (3), (4) et (5) introduit les processus de réajustement des prix et des anticipations inflationnistes. Il permet ainsi d'étudier les enchaînements des équilibres temporaires entre eux lorsqu'on s'écarte de la solution d'équilibre de long terme. Celle-ci correspond à la solution: $\hat{p} = m - n$, $\hat{x} = 0$, $\hat{r} = (a + b)/u$, $\hat{p}^e = m - n$, $\hat{\imath} = \hat{r} + m - n$.

La politique économique va à court terme perturber cet équilibre; mais si le système est stable et si on ne change plus le taux de croissance de la masse monétaire et le rapport dépenses publiques-dépenses privées, le réajustement des prix et des anticipations inflationnistes provoquera un retour à l'équilibre de long terme.

Pour simplifier l'étude du modèle qui comporte initialement cinq équations, on le ramènera à un système de trois équations en (p, x, i). On peut alors montrer que l'équilibre de long terme est stable si et seulement si la condition de CAGAN [2] est vérifiée ($ld < 1$). Pour établir les équations différentielles qui déterminent les évolutions du taux d'inflation, du différentiel d'activité par rapport au sentier de croissance normal et du taux d'intérêt nominal, nous traiterons à la suite de ALLEN [1] l'opérateur D comme un scalaire et appliquerons la règle de calcul matriciel de CRAMER.

Résolution du système dynamique

Après élimination de r et p^e, on obtient le système de trois équations en (p, x, i):

$$p + gDx - lDi = m - n \tag{10}$$

$$-up + (1 - h + uc)x + ui = a + b \tag{11}$$

$$Dp - c(d + D)x = 0 \tag{12}$$

ou sous forme matricielle, en traitant D comme un scalaire:

$$\begin{pmatrix} 1 & gD & -ld \\ -u & 1 - h + uc & u \\ D & -c(d + D) & 0 \end{pmatrix} \begin{pmatrix} p \\ x \\ i \end{pmatrix} = \begin{pmatrix} m - n \\ a + b \\ 0 \end{pmatrix}$$

Le déterminant de la matrice est égal à:

$$[gu + (1 - h)l]D^2 + uc(1 - ld)D + ucd.$$

Lorsqu'on l'annule on obtient l'équation caractéristique du système dynamique:

$$[gu + (1 - h)l]D^2 + uc(1 - ld)D + ucd = 0$$

La méthode de CRAMER nécessite le calcul des co-facteurs associés à chaque variable endogène; on les désignera par C_p, C_x et C_i.

$$C_p = \begin{vmatrix} m - n & gD & -ld \\ a + b & 1 - h + uc & u \\ 0 & -c(d + D) & 0 \end{vmatrix}$$

$$= (m - n)ucd + ucDm + lcD^2b + lcdDb$$

$$C_x = \begin{vmatrix} 1 & m - n & -ld \\ -u & a + b & u \\ D & 0 & 0 \end{vmatrix} = uDm + lD^2b$$

$$C_i = \begin{vmatrix} 1 & gD & m - n \\ -u & 1 - h + uc & a + b \\ D & -c(d + D) & 0 \end{vmatrix}$$

$$= cd(a + b - un + um) - (1 - h)Dm + cDb + gD^2b$$

En multipliant chaque variable endogène par le déterminant et en égalisant avec le co-facteur associé on obtient les trois équations différentielles permettant de déterminer les trajectoires de $p(t)$, $x(t)$ et $i(t)$:

$$[[gu + (1 - h)l]D^2 + uc(1 - ld)D + ucd]\,p(t) = -nucd + ucdm(t) + ucDm(t) + lcD^2b(t) + lcdDb(t) \tag{13}$$

$$[[gu + (1 - h)l]D^2 + uc(1 - ld)D + ucd]\,x(t) = uDm(t) + lD^2b(t) \tag{14}$$

$$[[gu + (1 - h)l]D^2 + uc(1 - ld)D + ucd]\,i(t) = acd - ucdn + ucdm(t) - (1 - h)Dm(t) + cdb(t) + cDb(t) + gD^2b(t) \tag{15}$$

On a considéré dans ces expressions que les paramètres g, u, l, h, d, a et n étaient constants; mais le taux de croissance de la masse monétaire et la part des dépenses publiques dans la dépense globale sont susceptibles de varier de manière continue dans le temps.

Ces équations différentielles sont du second ordre avec second membre (non homogènes); l'étude de leurs solutions d'équilibre et de la stabilité ne pose pas de problème.

La stabilité de la solution de long terme

On peut vérifier aisément en posant $Dm(t) = Db(t) = D^2b(t) = 0$ et $Dp(t) = D^2p(t) = Dx(t) = D^2x(t) = Di(t) = D^2i(t) = 0$ que la solution d'équilibre de long terme est bien:

$$\hat{p} = \hat{p}^e = m - n, \quad \hat{x} = 0, \quad \hat{r} = (a + b)/u, \quad \hat{\imath} = \hat{r} + m - n.$$

D'autre part une condition nécessaire et suffisante pour que des équations différentielles du second ordre aient des solutions stables, convergeant vers la solution d'équilibre, est que l'équation caractéristique ait des coefficients tous positifs. Cela impose ici la condition: $1 - ld > 0$. Cette condition est identique à celle du modèle de CAGAN [2]; pour qu'elle soit vérifiée il faut que la vitesse d'ajustement des anticipations inflationnistes d ne soit pas trop élevée ou que la demande réelle de monnaie ne soit pas trop sensible aux variations du taux d'intérêt nominal ou du taux d'inflation anticipé.

Comme chez CAGAN le système peut devenir explosif si le phénomène de fuite devant la monnaie devient trop prononcé lorsque le taux d'inflation augmente, soit parce que les prévisions inflationnistes s'adaptent très vite, soit parce que la demande de monnaie est fortement sensible au taux d'inflation anticipé (4).

On pourrait obtenir une condition de stabilité moins restrictive que celle de CAGAN en introduisant un ajustement du revenu normal anticipé $\bar{Y}$. Par exemple du type:

$$D \text{ Log } \bar{Y} = n + f(\text{Log } Y - \text{Log } \bar{Y}) \quad f > 0$$

Dans ce cas la condition de stabilité devient:

$$uc(1 - ld) + fu > 0$$

Dans toute la suite de l'article nous supposerons que la condition de CAGAN est satisfaite et donc que le système dynamique est stable.

Cette stabilité de la solution d'équilibre de long terme peut se réaliser à la suite d'un choc exogène soit par une convergence monotone des variables endogènes soit à travers des oscillations lorsque le discriminant de l'équation caractéristique est négatif, c'est-à-dire lorsque la condition suivante est vérifiée:

$$uc(1 - ld)^2 < 4\, gu + l(1 - h)$$

Dans l'hypothèse inverse le système est monotone.

4. Les effets de la politique économique

Dans le cadre de ce modèle dynamique où la production en moyenne augmente et où il existe un biais inflationniste, la variable normale de politique monétaire est le taux de croissance de l'offre nominale de monnaie. De même, du fait de la croissance des dépenses publiques et privées, la variable de politique budgétaire adaptée au problème est le rapport de ces deux types de dépenses ou un indicateur qui varie dans le même sens que ce rapport (*ici b*). Mais en ce qui concerne la politique monétaire on doit également considérer les conséquences d'une variation à un moment donné de la quantité de monnaie sans changement du taux de croissance courant m.

Nous allons donc envisager, d'un point de vue dynamique, d'une part les effets d'un accroissement du taux de croissance de la masse monétaire et ceux d'une augmentation exceptionnelle de la quantité de monnaie à un instant sans modification permanente du taux de croissance, d'autre part les conséquences d'une augmentation de la part des dépenses publiques dans la dépense globale. Ces diverses opérations seront par commodité effectuées au temps $t = 0$.

Pour étudier ces questions et leurs effets sur l'ensemble des variables endogènes de notre système nous utiliserons des diagrammes de phases dans l'espace différentiel d'activité—taux d'inflation (x, p); la simplicité du modèle permet en effet de donner une représentation de l'évolution de toutes les variables dans un espace à deux dimensions (système dynamique du deuxième ordre).

Les équations de phases

Le modèle dynamique peut être réduit à un système de deux équations différentielles en p et x; à partir des relations (10), (11) et (12) on obtient en effet:

$$Dx = \frac{1}{g + \frac{l}{u}(1 - h)} (m - n - p + lcdx) \qquad (16)$$

$$Dp = cd\left[1 + \left(\frac{lc}{g + \frac{l}{u}(1 - h)}\right)\right]x + \frac{c}{g + \frac{l}{u}(1 - h)}(m - n - p) \qquad (17)$$

et par conséquent:

$$Dx \gtreqless 0 \quad \text{si et seulement si:} \quad p \lesseqgtr m - n + lcdx$$

$$Dp \gtreqless 0 \quad \text{si et seulement si:} \quad p \lesseqgtr m - n + d\left[g + (1 - h)\frac{l}{u} + lc\right]x$$

Les deux équations précédentes permettent de sectoriser le plan (x, p) et de définir dans chaque secteur les forces d'évolution qui agissent sur x et sur p par l'intermédiaire de Dx et Dp.

En outre dans le même espace on peut représenter des familles de droites de même pente sur lesquelles la valeur des autres variables endogènes est constante. En effet, d'après l'équation (4) de la courbe de Phillips:

$$p = p^e + cx$$

et donc le taux d'inflation anticipé est constant sur les droites de pente c, quelles que soient les valeurs de x et p et en particulier pour celles qui sont solutions du système dynamique. Il en va de même pour le taux d'intérêt nominal i, qui d'après l'équation (11) est constant sur les droites d'équation:

$$p = i - \frac{a+b}{u} + \left(\frac{1-h}{u} + c\right)x$$

et donc de pente $1 - h/u + c$. Enfin le taux d'intérêt réel varie en sens inverse du différentiel d'activité x d'après l'équation (1'):

$$x = (a + b - ur)/(1 - h)$$

Il est donc constant sur des droites de pente ∞ dans le même espace.

Les indications présentées ci-dessus sont à la base de la construction des diagrammes de phases des figures 2, 3 et 4 (5).

Dans les trois cas la politique économique modifie la situation d'équilibre ou les conditions initiales par un choc exogène, déséquilibrant ainsi le système. Les diagrammes de phases montrent comment s'opère le retour à l'équilibre.

Les effets de la politique monétaire

Le cas d'un accroissement du taux de croissance de la masse monétaire. Initialement l'économie est en situation d'équilibre de long terme: $p_0 = m_0 - n = p_0^e$, $x_0 = 0$, $r_0 = (a + b_0)/u$, $i_0 = r_0 + m_0 - n$. Au temps $t = 0$, le taux de croissance de la masse monétaire passe de m_0 à $m > m_0$, ce qui déplace l'équilibre en: $\hat{p} = m - n = \hat{p}^e$, $\hat{\imath} = r_0 + m - n$; les niveaux d'équilibre de x et r restant inchangés. Un processus dynamique de rééquilibrage va alors se dérouler. Comme le montre la figure 2 au début le taux d'intérêt nominal baisse ainsi que le taux d'intérêt réel; le taux d'inflation effectif, le taux d'inflation anticipé et l'activité économique augmentent. Ces phénomènes se comprennent aisément à partir de l'analyse de l'équilibre temporaire: l'augmentation supplémentaire de la masse monétaire (bien que marginale) stimule l'activité économique et fait baisser les taux d'intérêt, conformément à l'analyse keynésienne habituelle. L'activité accrue par rapport à son niveau normal augmente le taux d'inflation au-dessus du niveau d'équilibre antérieur qui correspondait aux anticipations. Ces anticipations inflationnistes s'adaptent, bien qu'avec retard. Le taux d'intérêt nominal est la première variable dont l'évolution se renverse, traduisant ainsi un phénomène friedmanien bien connu: il se met à augmenter après une première phase de baisse, le renversement s'expliquant par le réajustement des anticipations inflationnistes d'une part

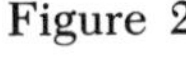

Figure 2

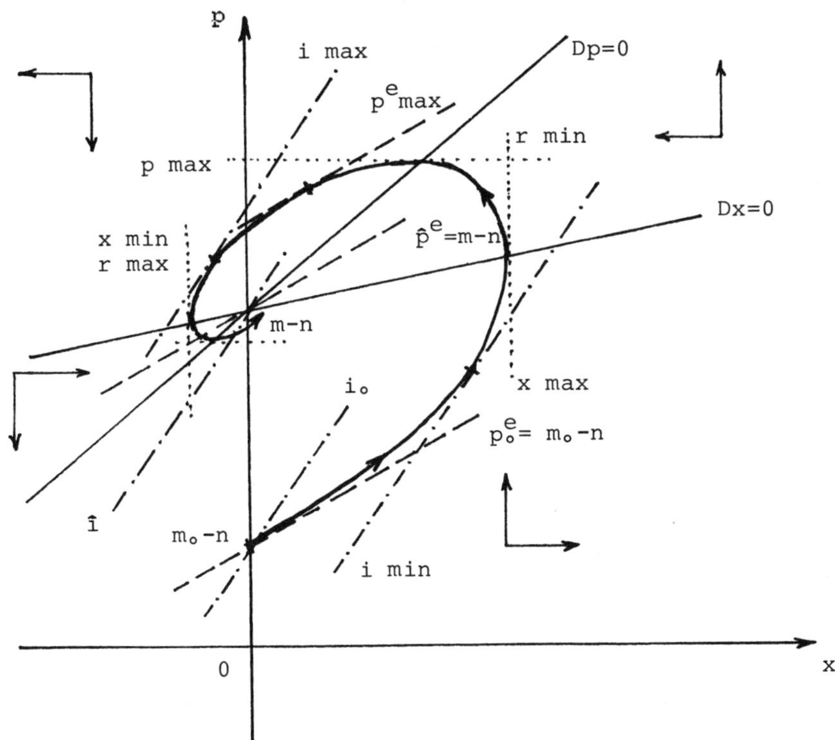

Effets d'une augmentation du taux de croissance de l'offre de monnaie

et par la réduction des encaisses monétaires provoquée par l'augmentation du taux d'inflation effectif d'autre part. Le phénomène inflationniste s'amplifie au-delà du nouveau niveau d'équilibre mais provoque au passage un retournement de l'activité économique (plus précisément de la variable d'écart x) et du taux d'intérêt réel. L'explication essentielle se situe au niveau de l'équilibre du marché de la monnaie où l'offre réelle de monnaie est plus affectée par l'inflation que la demande, en particulier à cause du retard des anticipations inflationnistes et malgré un réajustement partiel du taux d'intérêt nominal. La baisse d'activité et l'augmentation du taux d'intérêt réel conjointes se poursuivent jusqu'à provoquer un retournement du taux d'inflation effectif tout d'abord, puis du taux d'inflation anticipé ensuite. L'ajustement dynamique se poursuit jusqu'au nouvel équilibre avec éventuellement des oscillations autour de celui-ci. Finalement le taux d'inflation effectif (et anticipé) et le taux d'intérêt nominal ont été les seules variables affectées par l'accroissement du taux de croissance de la masse monétaire. Malgré une efficacité initiale et à court terme de cette politique monétaire, on retrouve à long terme la neutralité de la monnaie et la validité de la théorie quantitative.

Le cas d'une augmentation exceptionnelle de la quantité de monnaie. Au lieu d'agir sur le rythme d'accroissement permanent de la masse monétaire, la politique monétaire peut prendre la forme d'une augmentation exceptionnelle de la quantité de monnaie, l'évolution ultérieure s'effectuant au même rythme de croissance qu'auparavant. En d'autres termes l'opération consiste à changer de sentier de croissance d'offre de monnaie; on passe après un saut sur un sentier de croissance parallèle (dans un espace semi-logarithmique). Le taux de croissance de la masse monétaire devient infini pour un instant avant de retrouver son niveau antérieur m_0. Nous supposerons que cela s'effectue au temps $t = 0$, l'économie étant initialement en situation d'équilibre de long terme.

Cet accroissement de M (et donc de Log M) va provoquer des sauts de dimension finie du différentiel d'activité x et des taux d'intérêt, sauts correspondants à ceux établis lors de l'étude de l'équilibre temporaire: $\Delta x > 0$, $\Delta i = \Delta r < 0$. Deux phases vont ainsi intervenir. Dans un premier temps l'activité économique est stimulée et les taux d'intérêt baissent, conformément à l'analyse keynésienne usuelle; cela implique également d'après la relation de Phillips un saut du taux d'inflation effectif: $\Delta p = c \cdot \Delta x$. Puis, comme le montre la figure 3, il va se produire un réajustement dynamique avec éventuellement (c'est le case envisagé dans la figure) poursuite durant un certain temps de l'accroissement du taux d'inflation du fait du relèvement des anticipations inflationnistes, mais surtout une baisse du différentiel d'activité x et une hausse des taux d'intérêt réel et nominal. Le processus conduit au retour vers l'équilibre de long terme initial avec ou sans oscillations autour de celui-ci, après un retournement du taux d'inflation effectif et du taux d'inflation anticipé qui suit avec retard.

Comme dans le cas précédent l'explication fondamentale du retour à l'équilibre de long terme est l'effet de l'inflation sur la valeur réelle de l'offre de monnaie, combinée avec un retard des anticipations inflationnistes. Mais maintenant les effets stimulants de la politique monétaire sur l'activité économique et son effet dépressif sur les taux d'intérêt se produisent à l'instant initial seulement.

Les effets de la politique budgétaire

On part du même équilibre initial de long terme: $p_0 = m_0 - n = p^e_0$, $x_0 = 0$, $r_0 = (a + b_0)/u = \hat{r}_0$, $i_0 = \hat{r}_0 + m_0 - n$. Au temps

Figure 3

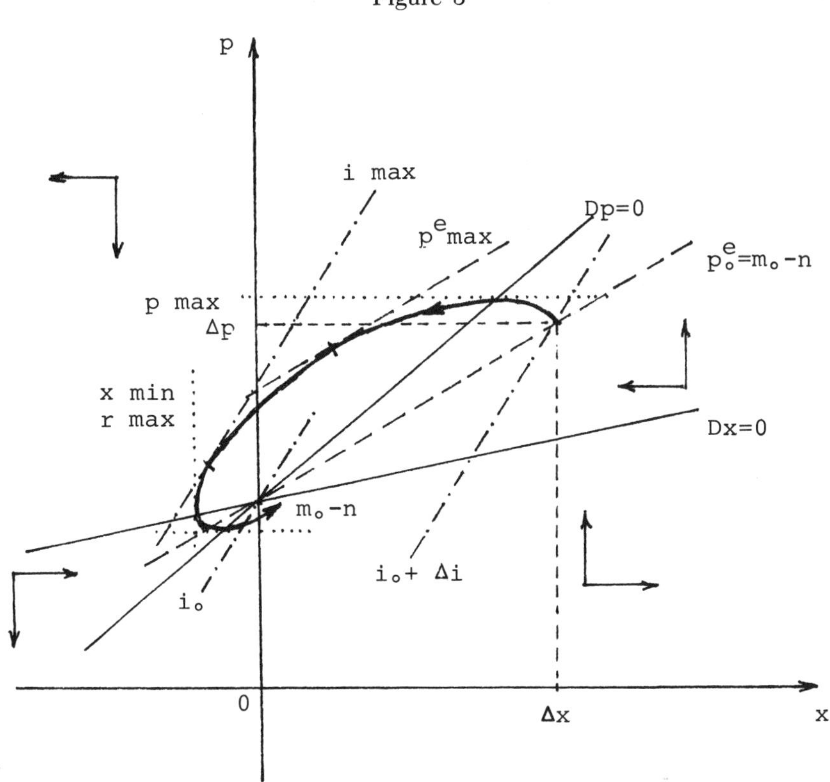

Effets d'une augmentation de la quantité de monnaie (m_0 = *cte*, $\Delta x > 0$, $\Delta i < 0$, $\Delta p > 0$)

$t = 0$, l'indicateur de la part des dépenses publiques dans la dépense globale augmente par suite de l'augmentation des dépenses publiques et passe de b_0 à b. Au niveau de l'équilibre final de long terme cela modifie seulement les taux d'intérêt réel et nominal (6) qui deviennent respectivement $\hat{r} = (a + b)/u$ et $\hat{\imath} = \hat{r} + m_0 - n$. Mais comme dans la situation précédente les conditions initiales sont modifiées par cet accroissement du rapport dépenses publiques-dépenses privées. En effet comme nous l'avons vu en étudiant l'équilibre temporaire (section 2) et comme il est habituel, la politique budgétaire accroît à la fois l'activité économique et les taux d'intérêt. Par conséquent au temps $t = 0$ des sauts dans les conditions initiales se manifestent: $\Delta x > 0$, $\Delta i = \Delta r > 0$. On peut vérifier aisément que l'effet initial sur les taux d'intérêt est inférieur à l'effet final à long terme: $\hat{\imath} - i_0 = \hat{r} - r_0 = (b - b_0)/u < \Delta i$ (7) ce qui permettra une hausse ultérieure des taux d'intérêt. Par ailleurs, l'activité économique étant accrue au-dessus du sentier de croissance normal, le taux d'inflation est lui aussi stimulé et saute ($\Delta p > 0$). Seul le taux d'inflation anticipé n'est pas au départ affecté. Les effets initiaux de la politique budgétaire sont suivis comme dans le cas précédent d'une phase dynamique de réajustement (figure 4). Ce réajustement vers l'équilibre de long terme est tout à fait du même type que le précédent à cette seule différence que l'augmentation des taux d'intérêt vise à atteindre un niveau d'équilibre plus élevé alors qu'auparavant il s'agissait de compenser une baisse initiale.

L'inflation supplémentaire engendrée par la stimulation de l'activité économique annihile à long terme l'effet initial sur l'activité provoqué par l'augmentation permanente du rapport dépenses publiques-dépenses privées. Elle manifeste ses effets par une contraction de l'offre

Figure 4

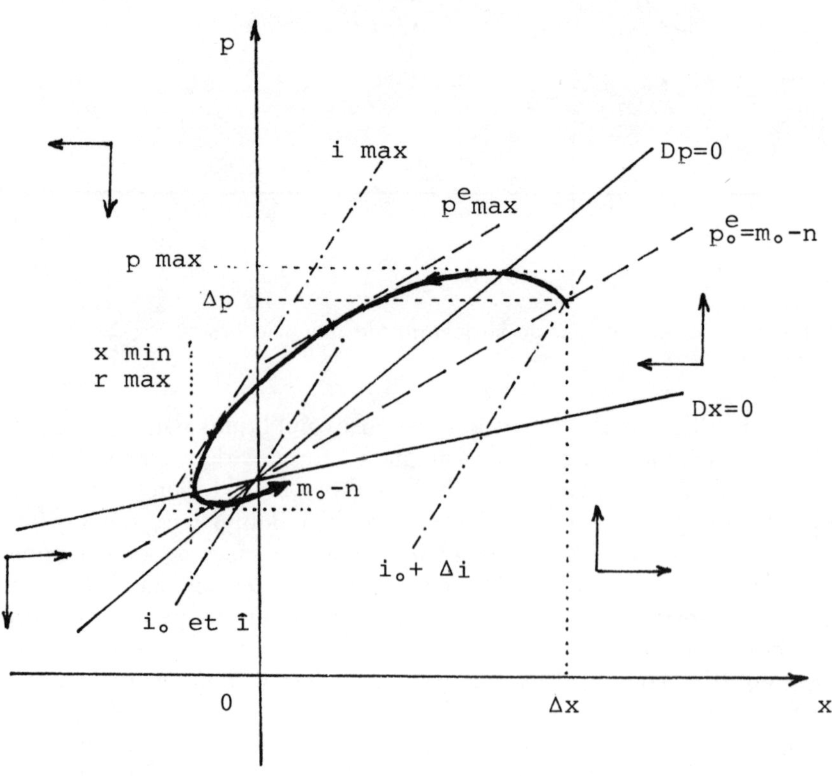

Effets d'un accroissement de la part des dépenses publiques dans la dépense globale. ($\Delta x > 0$, $\Delta i > 0$, $\Delta p > 0$)

réelle de monnaie et du fait de son caractère excédentaire par rapport à l'inflation d'équilibre.

Ce modèle permet ainsi de montrer comment la politique budgétaire, même si elle prend la forme d'un accroissement permanent de la part des dépenses publiques dans le revenu national, n'a que des effets stimulants transitoires.

On rejoint ainsi les conclusions néo-classiques, tout en partant d'un cadre d'équilibre temporaire très proche des modèles keynésiens habituels. Ni la politique monétaire, lorsqu'elle est pratiquée sous la forme d'un accroissement exceptionnel de la masse monétaire ou par un changement de pallier de son taux de croissance, ni la politique budgétaire considérée sous l'aspect d'une augmentation donnée de la part des dépenses publiques dans la dépense globale, n'ont d'effet permanent sur l'activité et la croissance économique.

Cette conclusion est toutefois fortement dépendante de l'hypothèse de stabilité du système qui peut être battue en brèche lorsqu'on considère que les anticipations sont de type adaptatif; il en irait différemment avec des anticipations rationnelles.

D'autre part on peut se demander si d'autres schémas d'évolution temporelle des variables de politique économique que ceux considérés jusqu'à présent permettent d'atteindre des niveaux d'activité situés de manière permanente au-dessus du sentier de croissance normal. Nous allons voir que la réponse est positive mais au prix d'une instabilité instrumentale.

5. Politique économique et stabilité instrumentale

Jusqu'à présent le modèle dynamique a été considéré comme un modèle explicatif qui détermine les évolutions du taux d'inflation, effectif et anticipé, des taux d'intérêt et de l'écart de l'activité économique par rapport au sentier de croissance normal, en fonction des variables de politique économique b et m. Il est possible également de le considérer comme un modèle de politique économique où le niveau d'une variable précédemment endogène est pris comme objectif et à l'aide duquel on cherche à déterminer le sentier d'évolution de l'un des instruments de politique économique permettant de maintenir cet objectif au cours du temps. On peut ainsi s'efforcer de maintenir constant soit le différentiel d'activité par rapport au sentier de croissance normal, soit le taux d'inflation, soit le taux d'intérêt nominal.

La solution de ce type de problème peut soit être stable soit être instable. Elle est stable quand le paramètre de politique économique qui est affecté à l'objectif converge vers une valeur finie au cours du temps. On parle à la suite de HOLBROOK [9] d'instabilité instrumentale lorsque l'instrument de politique économique doit tendre vers une valeur infinie pour satisfaire de manière permanente l'objectif fixé au cours du temps.

Il est possible de traiter aisément ces questions à l'aide des équations différentielles (13), (14) et (15) et on peut mettre en lumière des résultats intéressants:

Il n'existe pas de politique économique stable permettant de maintenir durablement la croissance économique au-dessus du sentier de croissance normal.

La politique monétaire, plus précisément le taux de croissance de la masse monétaire, est un instrument stable de contrôle du taux d'inflation, mais pas la variable de politique budgétaire b. Par contre ce dernier instrument converge vers une valeur stable quand on s'efforce de maintenir constant le taux d'intérêt nominal; ce n'est pas le cas du taux de croissance de la masse monétaire.

Le contrôle de l'activité économique

Si on se donne comme objectif le maintien de l'activité économique au-dessus du sentier de croissance normal en s'imposant par exemple $x = \bar{x} > 0$, l'équation différentielle (14) devient:

$$ucd \cdot \bar{x} = uDm(t) + lD^2b(t)$$

Le maintien de cet objectif par la politique monétaire impose que $m(t)$ satisfasse:

$$Dm(t) = cd \cdot \bar{x}$$

ou encore:

$$m(t) = m_0 + cd \cdot \bar{x} \cdot t$$

On peut donc bien stimuler de maniére permanente l'activité économique mais cela implique une augmentation continuelle du taux de croissance de la masse monétaire qui tend vers l'infini quand t tend vers l'infini. L'accroissement continuel du taux d'inflation qui en résulte est difficilement admissible.

Le maintien de l'objectif par la politique budgétaire nécessite que $b(t)$ réalise:

$$D^2b(t) = (ucd/l) \cdot \bar{x}$$

et donc:

$$b(t) = \frac{ucd}{2l} \cdot \bar{x} \cdot t^2 + H_1 t + H_2$$

La politique budgétaire nécessaire pour maintenir $\bar{x}$ est encore plus instable que la politique monétaire. Pour maintenir l'activité économique de manière durable au-dessus du sentier de croissance normal, il faut augmenter de manière assez rapide et perpétuellement la part des dépenses publiques dans les dépenses globales.

Aucun des deux instruments de politique économique n'est satisfaisant pour atteindre un objectif d'activité.

Le contrôle du taux d'inflation

Fixons comme objectif de croissance du niveau général des prix la valeur $p = \bar{p}$, constante au cours du temps. Dans ces conditions l'équation différentielle (13) devient:

$$ucd \cdot \bar{p} = -nucd + ucdm(t) + ucDm(t) + lcD^2b(t) + lcdDb(t)$$

Si on cherche à maintenir l'objectif à l'aide de la politique monétaire, l'équation différentielle suivante en $m(t)$ doit être satisfaite:

$$Dm(t) + dm(t) = d(\bar{p} + n)$$

Si m_0 est le taux de croissance initial de la masse monétaire, la solution de cette équation est:

$$m(t) = \bar{p} + n + (m_0 - \bar{p} - n) \cdot e^{-dt}$$

Elle converge vers $m = \bar{p} - n$ quand t tend vers l'infini; la politique monétaire est donc un instrument stable pour contrôler le taux d'inflation.

Si par contre on cherche à contrôler le taux d'inflation avec la politique budgétaire, $b(t)$ doit satisfaire l'équation différentielle:

$$D^2b(t) + dDb(t) = (ud/l)(\bar{p} + n - m_0)$$

dont la solution est:

$$b(t) = (u/l)(\bar{p} + n - m_0) \cdot t + K_1 e^{-dt} + K_2$$

où K_1 et K_2 sont des constantes qui dépendent des valeurs initiales de b.

Quand t tend vers l'infini, b doit tendre vers plus ou moins l'infini suivant que $m_0 \lesseqgtr \bar{p} - n$. L'instrument budgétaire est instable; par ailleurs il ne permet pas d'atteindre durablement l'objectif si $m_0 > \bar{p} - n$, car b est borné inférieurement par 0.

Ainsi seule la politique monétaire est un instrument approprié pour contrôler le taux d'inflation.

Le contrôle du taux d'intérêt nominal

Le contrôle du taux d'intérêt nominal $i = \bar{\imath}$ impose la satisfaction de l'équation:

$$ucd \cdot \bar{\imath} = acd - ucdn + ucdm(t) - (1 - h)Dm(t) + cdb(t) + cDb(t) + gD^2 b(t)$$

tirée de l'équation différentielle (15).

Si on cherche à maintenir ce taux d'intérêt nominal par une politique monétaire, elle doit être telle que:

$$-Dm(t) + \frac{ucd}{1-h} \cdot m(t) = \frac{ucd}{1-h} (\bar{\imath} - \hat{r} + n)$$

d'où:

$$m(t) = \bar{\imath} + n - \hat{r} + (m_0 - \bar{\imath} - n + \hat{r}) \cdot e^{(ucd/1-h)t}$$

$m(t)$ tend vers $\pm\infty$ suivant que $\bar{\imath} \lesseqgtr \hat{r} + m_0 - n$ quand t tend vers $+\infty$. La politique monétaire est instable. On retrouve ici un phénomène wicksellien. En effet si on cherche à maintenir le taux d'intérêt nominal en dessous de $\hat{r} + m_0 - n$ cela implique une augmentation continuelle du taux de croissance de la masse monétaire et un processus cumulatif d'inflation.

Par contre l'objectif peut être atteint par une politique budgétaire stable. En effet celle-ci doit satisfaire:

$$D^2 b(t) + (c/g)Db(t) + (cd/g)b(t) = (cd/g)\, u(\bar{\imath} + n - m_0) - a$$

Les coefficients de l'équation caractéristique sont positifs et donc $b(t)$ converge vers $u(\bar{\imath} + n - m_0) - a$.

Contrairement à l'opinion courante si on veut stabiliser le taux d'intérêt nominal, il est préférable de pratiquer une politique budgétaire plutôt qu'une politique monétaire (8).

Notes

[1]On peut montrer que si les dépenses publiques nouvelles sont financées par l'impôt il est possible que cela ne stimule pas la demande globale lorsque les agents privés anticipent l'augmentation du taux de prélèvement fiscal. Une politique budgétaire indépendante de la politique monétaire et qui soit efficace à court terme implique donc, dans ce modèle, un financement par l'emprunt.

[2]A propos de l'introduction d'une contrainte budgétaire de l'Etat voir notre article [15]. Ce type de contrainte n'étant pas linéaire en logarithmes ne peut être introduite ici de manière simple. Le problème de l'incidence du moyen de financement des dépenses publiques nous semble être un problème secondaire dans la mesure où ce qui importe ici est l'utilisation d'un paramètre structurel de politique budgétaire, efficace à court terme.

[3]On suppose, par homogénéité avec le modèle dynamique, que l'Etat détermine non pas le niveau absolu des dépenses publiques G mais le rapport entre dépenses publiques et dépenses privées.

[4]Si on avait envisagé des anticipations rationnelles du type de celles indiquées avant, en considérant que le taux d'inflation anticipé est déterminé par les prévisions en matière de croissance de la masse monétaire avec ajustement de celles-ci suivant les réalisations, on aurait pu montrer que le système était toujours stable.

[5]En particulier on a tenu compte des relations qui existent entre les pentes des diverses droites dans le plan (x, p).

[6]L'une des hypothèses implicites du modèle est que l'accroissement de la part des dépenses publiques dans le produit national n'a pas d'effet sur le taux de croissance du revenu normal de long terme. Des arguments pouvant être avancés dans le sens d'un effet négatif ou d'un effet positif cette hypothèse semble raisonnable dans le cadre d'un modèle agrégé aussi simple.

[7] $\frac{\Delta i}{\Delta b} = \frac{1}{u + (1-h)g/l} < \frac{1}{u} = \frac{\hat{\imath} - i_0}{b - b_0}$

[8]Notons toutefois que ce résultat n'est pas maintenu avec des anticipations rationnelles.

References

[1] ALLEN R. G. D., *Macro-economic theory*, Londres, Macmillan, 1967.

[2] CAGAN P., "The monetary dynamics of hyperinflation" dans FRIEDMAN M., éd., *Studies in the quantity theory of money*, Chicago, Chicago University Press, 1956.

[3] FISHER I., *The theory of interest*, New York, Reprints of economic classics, Augustus M. Kelley, 1961; première éd. 1930.

[4] FRIEDMAN M., "The role of monetary policy," *American Economic Review*, vol. 58, mars 1968, pp. 1 à 17.

[5] FRIEDMAN M., "A theoretical framework for monetary analysis," *Journal of Political Economy*, vol. 78, mars-avril 1970, pp. 193 à 238.

[6] FRIEDMAN M., "A monetary theory of nominal income," *Journal of Political Economy*, vol. 79, mars-avril 1971, pp. 323 à 337.

[7] FRIEDMAN M., "Nobel lecture: Inflation and unemployment," *Journal of Political Economy*, vol. 85, juin 1977, pp. 451 à 472.
[8] HICKS J. R., "Mr. Keynes and the "Classics": A suggested interpretation," *Econometrica*, vol. 5, 1937, pp. 147 à 159.
[9] HOLBROOK R. S., "Optimal economic policy and the problem of instrument instability," *American Economic Review*, vol. 62, mars 1972, pp. 57 à 65.
[10] LAIDLER D., "The influence of money on real income and inflation. A simple model with some empirical evidence for the United States, 1963–72," *Manchester School*, vol. 41, décembre 1973, repris dans LAIDLER D., *Essays on money and inflation*, Manchester, Manchester University Press, 1975.
[11] PHELPS E. S. et al., *Microeconomic foundations of employment and inflation*, New York, Norton, 1970.
[12] PHILLIPS A. W., "The relationship between unemployment and the rate of change of money wage rates in the United Kingdom, 1861–1957," *Economica*, vol. 25, novembre 1958, pp. 283–299.
[13] STEIN J., *Money and capacity growth*, New York, Columbia University Press, 1971.
[14] TAYLOR D., "A simple model of monetary dynamics," *Journal of Money, Credit and Banking*, vol. 9, février 1977, pp. 107–111.
[15] VEDEL C., "La contrainte budgétaire de l'Etat et les politiques économiques de stabilisation," Université de Nantes, 1971.
[16] WICKSELL K., *Interest and prices*, Londres, Macmillan, 1936; première éd. en allemand 1898.

Summary

The purpose of the paper is to present a simple model which provides a synthesis of Keynesian and neoclassical analyses. With its help it is possible to study the effects of monetary and fiscal policies.

In the short run the temporary fix-price equilibrium is the same as that of the IS-LM model. In the long run, after price adjustments occurred, a neoclassical equilibrium is restored. To treat economic activity and price level and interest rate variations in a growing economy, a second order dynamic model is used. A special form of the demand for goods and the demand for money functions, as well as the use of a neoclassical Phillips relationship, allows to overcome the problem of Friedman's missing equation. Inflationary expectations are of the adaptive Cagan type.

At the policy level the model generates several well-known results: short run efficiency of stabilization policies, long run neutrality of a constant rate monetary policy, etc. With respect to instrumental stability only monetary policy (the rate of growth of the quantity of money) is stable and able to control the rate of inflation. Fiscal policy (the ratio of public to private expenditures) is a stable instrument to control the interest rate. None of these is stable to control economic activity. The latter points to problems with short run efficiency of stabilization policies.

Fiscal and Monetary Policy in the Context of Development: A Schumpeterian Approach*

Wolfgang F. Stolper

Introduction: Limitations of the Topic

An exhaustive technical analysis of even the major aspects of the subject matter is obviously impossible within the confines of an article. Besides, actual developments vary in place and time, and would thus require attention to institutional detail and historic developments. Yet economic theory is, as we should have learned from Schumpeter, the analysis of how institutions work in their historic context, and if institutions require change and perhaps also births and deaths, we have learned from Tinbergen [Tinbergen, (1952) and later] to see theory and economic policy as mirror images of each other.

I will limit the topic as follows: Parts I and II sketch out a Schumpeterian view of development as applied to Less Developed Countries (LDC's). In Parts I and II it is argued that the crucial target variable, the reaching of which makes all else possible, should be the improvement in productivity. It is argued that micro-economic signals and policies become the more important the less well the market works, and that successful government policy requires attention to micro-economic quantities. It is argued that "equilibrating" tendencies tending to preserve the status quo and thus preventing development are perhaps even stronger in LDC's than in MDC's because of the enlarged

*My colleagues Harvey Brazer, Richard C. Porter and Sue Ranney have criticized the first draft of this paper. A later version was critically read by Professor R. Richter of the University of the Saarland and Professor D. Biehl of Frankfurt. I have taken all of their suggestions to heart and wish to thank them for their service of friendship. I am, of course, solely responsible for the views expressed.

Public Finance and Economic Growth. Proceedings of the 37th Congress of the International Institute of Public Finance. Tokyo, 1981, pp. 127–147

role LDC's give to government. It is argued that, nevertheless, insistence of market-type signals in no way presupposes a political preference for a "free-market economy", though it is, of course, not argued that different political decisions affect the same people or groups of people in the same way.

In Parts III and IV, I sketch how the classical Musgrave analysis has to be adapted to the institutional and historic requirements of LDC's, and how monetary policy might be seen as an instrument of raising productivity. Throughout I shall minimize actual examples, although it would be easy to give them from the dozen or so countries in which I have actually worked, and from the rest of the less developed world which has been analyzed in the literature.

I. Schumpeterian Ideas: The Relevance of Equilibrium Economics to Growth

Economic development will be defined as a continuous improvement in the productive apparatus of an economy allowing it to make ever better decisions about how to meet the needs of its people. Measuring successful development by growth in per capita income seems to me justifiable *provided* measurement of that growth is in prices that reflect in a consistent manner the scarcities of factors of production as well as the preferences of consumers or planners. [Little et. al. (1970), Krueger (1978), Bhagwati (1978)]. It has been shown that growth and income distribution are *in reality* not inconsistent. [Chenery and Ahluwalia (1974), Stolper (1980), den Tuinder (1978)]. It seems to me also more important to improve the lot of the poorest than to distribute a miserable income more evenly.

Economic development involves the mobilization and allocation of resources. I refer, of course, to *real* developments. This involves, as far as I am concerned, a Schumpeterian view of the process of development which, like the Marxist view is essentially historical—institutional, yet differs radically from it in crucial respects. Most important in the present context is that, while the Schumpeterian view gives a most important role to the government and to money, it nevertheless puts *micro*-economic considerations into the center of its analysis while much (most?) of growth economics and much of monetary and public finance theory remain in the realm of macro economics. To quote Schumpeter: "[The] analysis of the economic phenomena of any given period must proceed from the economic facts that produce them and not from the monetary aggregates that result from them." [Schumpeter (1946), p.3]. This quotation might have served as the motto of this paper.

The major purpose of economic development must be, in my opinion, the improvement in productive capacity without which the achievement of more humane targets becomes impossible. That is, I would put major emphasis on changes in production functions, on improvement of the input-output relationships and not on full employment (which in any case is a questionable concept in LDC's), or on the "better" distribution of a miserable income. [Turnham and Jaeger (1971)]. Increasing productivity requires, however, concentration on micro-economic problems in the economy. The Schumpeterian view puts the micro-economic relationships into the center of its analysis, and builds up the macro-economic relationships from them. I believe—following in this both Schumpeter and Tinbergen—that fiscal policies also have to concentrate on the micro-economic variables.

To develop these points, I must first discuss how the Schumpeterian view applies in LDC's and elsewhere. There are two aspects to this Schumpeterian view of development: (i) Prices have a function, and general equilibrium economics deals with perfectly real phenomena (i.e., it is important to get prices right). (ii) Development involves discontinuous changes in production functions and hence in the price system, i.e., development involves the periodic destruction of this equilibrium.[1]

Many of the troubles of LDC's are the consequence of the neglect of *equilibrium* economics. This fact makes macro-economic policies no less important, but they are no substitute for the micro-economic signals of an undistorted market. Nor is the argument a plea for an unfettered market without regulation or government interference in any shape or form. It is *not* ideological, but the simple recognition that factors are scarce and must therefore by economically allocated, and that if they are not, there will be repercussions of an unexpected and undesired kind, such as unexpected shortfalls in outputs, or unexpected and undesired budgetary behavior.

The practical implication for LDC's planning is the central importance of project analysis at "correct" prices. Despite all its difficulties and short-comings, cost-benefit analysis is central. The importance of a (reasonably) correct exchange rate is by now well established. The theory of the second best as applied to the protection of industries suggests that tariffs or quotas can be third best methods at best to achieve the aims of protection. [Lipsey and Lancaster (1956/57); Bhagwati and Ramaswahmi (1963), Bhagwati (1968)]. As long as labor must eat, shadow rates of wages cannot be zero. [Little and Mirrlees (1968); Dasgupta, Marglin, Sen (1972); Squire and van der Tak (1975)].

Whatever shadow rate of interest is decided upon will depend not only on the marginal productivity of capital whatever this may be but on some very real and difficult political decisions as to how much austerity can be imposed upon the people.

These comments all imply something about the dynamics of a situation. Shadow wages cannot be zero because lost savings rather than lost output are the proper measure. There is a direct connection here to the budget and/or to economic policies. Labor cannot in fact be paid zero wages; therefore decisions made with a zero wage rate will lead to subsidies which burden the budget where they compete with desired savings.

But this links with the second and more important aspect of Schumpeterian development: the changes in production functions. There is *no* way in which macro-economic policies, whether of the Keynesian or monetarist type can by themselves lead to development which is self sustaining. They cannot lead to a steady increase in productivity beyond what is possible by steady capital accumulation which leads to a steady increase in the capital-labor ratio.

The periodic destruction of the equilibrium is the chief characteristic of the Schumpeterian process. When and how to destroy the existing equilibrium—Chakravarty's "structural break" [Chakravarty (1959)]—is precisely what underlies the problem of introducing the new investments which are supposed to transform an economy.[2] It should be obvious, however, (though it is not in reality), that no project has a chance of transforming an economy if it does not pay off at proper prices.

It is the constant search for very specific investment projects which will *in fact* increase the productive capacity of an economy which must be central to economic policy.[3] Investments consist of input streams for a number of years which after varying lags produce output streams. To decide upon an investment project requires that the decision-makers make the best guesses what are, at the moment when the investments are being decided upon, the best prices of the inputs; whether these input prices are likely to change drastically; and what in all likelihood will be the output prices when the inputs finally produce outputs. This simply reflects that the world is a most uncertain environment; it also states that the long run is a sequence of short runs, and that whatever the opportunity cost of an input may be five years hence, its present cost is its opportunity cost now.

The importance of the Schumpeterian ideas in this context is twofold: there must be new ways of doing things which lead to the elimination of older methods, Schumpeter's "creative destruction." These new ways can only be achieved in the context of an existing situation.

Equilibrium economics and its periodic destruction through changing production functions, which is the essence of Schumpeterian dynamics, are necessarily and inextricably linked.

II. Schumpeterian Ideas: The Need to Stimulate Change

The central Schumpeterian vision of development is the periodic destruction of an equilibrium which has strong tendencies to maintain and to assert itself. In fact it does not only require toughness and single-mindedness to break out of this equilibrium but also considerable imagination. Even an LDC which ideologically gives the central role to government planners cannot escape the problem of what to do, when and how. Decisions must change the economy in specific and feasible ways. General policies have limited usefulness. Moreover, the very fact that markets in LDC's do not exist or are very imperfect make giving attention to micro-economic signals and policies all the more important. The function of monetary and fiscal policies in the context of development must be to aid in the allocation of resources, to assure the best possible timing of the "structural break," to guarantee the best arrangement in the collection of resources for development.

All LDC's wish to increase savings and investments, say, by fiscal policy. Austerity is therefore advocated. Now cost-benefit analysis requires that the government give the planners an idea of the social discount rate, i.e., of the degree of austerity considered feasible and desirable at a political level. But surely the politically acceptable and economically desirable degree of austerity is not independent of the uses to which the collected funds are put. This remains true whether we adopt the formulations of the World Bank, using public income as the *numéraire* for the evaluation of projects or if we opt for the Little-Mirrlees formulation of public income at world market prices. There are always useful things to do in LDC's (and not only there) like schools or dispensaries which require resources but unfortunately do not generate any benefits even within a reasonably long time planning horizon.

Moreover, while you can save for general purposes, investments must be specific. And it is all too frequently not so clear that specific investments are productive, that they generate net benefits. They can be made "economic" for example, by foreign trade policy measures. Observe that in this case the micro-economic signals are adjusted in such a way that they justify the macro-economic policy *ex post.* But if the micro-economic signals do not reflect the true scarcities and preferences, the result must be unexpected repercussions in the economy. If the fiscal policy leads to tax erosion, government savings will be reduced. There will be spillovers into the balance of payments as cost of production rise because of inefficient investments. There simply is no way to hide inefficiencies in allocation in the economy at large.

Micro-economic processes have, in my opinion, logical priority. They provide the *rationale* for the necessary macro-economic policies. In LDC's monetary and fiscal policies must be made to serve the purposes of the proper allocation of resources for growth.

The case for not trusting market signals rests upon the actual (or alleged) presence of market imperfections, the existence of public goods, the (possible) existence of Musgrave's "merit wants," and the existence of technological externalities. None of this is, of course, denied nor is it further discussed. The real question is what should be put in its place. The common answer: "the market will not work efficiently, therefore Government must act," will not do in *this* form. The reason is not only that market imperfections could easily be matched by Government inefficiencies. There is indeed a *prima facie* case for policy intervention in all such instances. But the real issue then becomes the *precise* manner and extent of that intervention. This follows from the general theory of the second best.

In any case, a particular policy prescription must be defended not only on the basis that it will produce certain results, but that it will do so better than other alternatives. Therefore, the case made here is not one against government intervention. It is rather a case for government policies adapted to specific situations and taking cognizance of the limitations under which government must make decisions and execute them. If superior civil servants are scarce they should not waste their time on trivial problems.[4] There is therefore a strong case to be made for decentralization and using indirect methods—as socialist countries discover when they are really interested in raising the standard of living of the poor rather than cementing the position of the powerful. The case for using the price mechanism to the fullest possible extent is strengthened by the existence of corruption which necessarily becomes endemic with a poorly paid and inefficient civil service and a multitude of administrative rules.[5]

I return to the central point of the Schumpeterian vision, the discontinuous change in production functions leading to a process of "creative destruction." The idea seems as important for LDC's as for MDC's. But *who* is likely to introduce the change in the production function? In MDC's the problem relates to the question who the entrepreneur is likely to be, and how competition works. In this context, Schumpeter is—correctly—quoted as singing the praises of big business, even of monopolies, as the source of new ideas and as institutions which are capable of financing the innovations. [e.g., Samuelson (1981)]. There is an almost exact analogy here to the claims made in the case of LDC's that in the absence of a capital market and of adequate private savings, the government through its budget must substitute for it: bigness and centralization are said to be needed to produce the ideas, and to be able to finance and to execute them. The issue is of considerable policy interests also in LDC's for the following reasons.

First, the implication of Schumpeter's statement is not really that monopolies are good, but rather that the real competition in a dynamic economy does not come primarily from the entry of "imitators" who compete excess profits away, but from the erosion of the monopoly position through innovators whose activities result in the "creative destruction" of the old equilibrium, i.e., the elimination of the old positions.

This leads, secondly, to the very important question as to what are the chances of the process of "creative destruction" occurring without an active competitive policy. In new, rapidly growing industries, it is very likely that monopolies in the capitalist world will not be able to keep the process from working. But where past investments are large, vested interests in existing technology and against innovation can build up, which, given the proper institutional environment, either prevent innovation or seek to change the institutional environment in such a manner as to prevent the erosion of one's position. "Voluntary" textile export quotas, attempts to limit "voluntarily" Japanese automobile exports to the U.S., trigger prices, are important MDC examples of the catastrophic import substitution policies of LDC's.[6]

The import substitution policies in LDC's are in fact supplemented by a whole host of industrialization policies; many of these are in turn supplemented by monetary and fiscal policies, which actually strengthen the position of existing inefficiencies and prevent new industries from arising. The discrimination against small industries through subsidized development banks, the monopoly position created through "pioneer" certificates and special tax exemptions are examples.

The *World Development Report 1981* of the World Bank documents in some detail what should be *a priori* obvious: that countries which have pursued import substitution policies did not only do worse than countries that allowed themselves to be part of the world economy, but that the latter, and not the former, adapted more easily to the oil shocks of the seventies.

The point—in all parts of the world—is precisely that government policy should be designed to allow innovation *and* "creative destruction." The characteristic policies of the successful LDC's—starting with our host country Japan,[7] including South Korea, Taiwan, or Hong Kong and Singapore, and perhaps gradually Brazil—are precisely policies which not only have stimulated investments but facilitated change. The case for using the market does *not* contrast with a case against government. It is a case for a particular kind of government policy.[8]

The arguments presented are just as applicable to socialist economies as to our kind of LDC's and MDC's. In all economies there are built-in resistances to change, which try, if possible, to use government power and economic policies to preserve the status quo. LDC's try to give government factories monopoly positions, the demands of the so-called New International Economic Order—which in my opinion are harmful to LDC's—the propositions for regional trading blocs, all have the characteristics of Kindleberger's *Aging Economy*, even when they are old before their time.

III. Fiscal Policy: The Budget as a Substitute for the Capital Market

Sections I and II have discussed the process of development, the process of change, the manner in which productivity could be raised, the fundamental importance of micro-economic policies. This is the context in which I would like to put monetary and fiscal policies. Like all LDC's, I should like to see monetary and fiscal policies used to help an economy produce a higher standard of living primarily for the poor. It can do so only if it aids in increasing productivity, and it can do this only if it aids in a continuous change of productive methods. It should help to stimulate savings up to the point where these savings can be productively used. Now it should be obvious that monetary and fiscal policies cannot do everything. Sections III and IV argue that traditional policies may be more applicable to LDC's than Keynesian policies.[9] This should not be too surprising since classical policies were developed at a time in which present MDC's were also "less developed." However, my argument is not that Keynesian policies are wrong as that the functions given to government are different in LDC's than in MDC's and therefore require a different mix of policies. I should like to discuss here a number of important points relating to shadow pricing, the interaction of fiscal and monetary policies, and who should do what.

To start with a general point, I have argued that the "correct" factor prices are essential for the decision of how much and specifically which investments should be undertaken. I am now arguing that it is dangerous to use the budget as a means of changing the "wrong" into "right" prices. The method, originally suggested by Tinbergen has dangers for LDC's which it has not in the context of MDC's for which Tinbergen originally developed it. This is so because the budget has in LDC's functions additional to those it has in MDC's, and the importance of the individual functions it shares in LDC's and MDC's varies in the different contexts. My point is that Musgrave, writing on the threefold function of the public household in the context of MDC's can take it for granted that a market exists and works [Musgrave (1959)]. His problem is therefore essentially to improve the working of the market mechanism, where that mechanism is applicable; to promote public goods; and to "adjust" for "merit wants."

But this does not exhaust the problem in LDC's. First, few LDC's have a budgetary system which could be used to achieve an internally consistent policy. Even fewer have a comprehensive view of the public sector [Stolper (1971), (1973)]. Second, in many LDCs the government itself tries to do the allocation work proper of the market. Factories which are elsewhere in the (private) market nexus are built with public funds. The whole question of the size of the budget looks different when it includes the question of how big total investments ought to be.

This question is related as to what the "social discount rate" ought to be. At least since Pigou, it has been a classical function of the government to promote capital formation and economic growth but *not* to provide savings. This saving function is in MDC's totally subordinate to the stabilization function.[10] In many LDC's it is of primary importance. I conclude (a) that the allocation function[11] of the budget becomes dominant, and (b) that budgetary policies must be judged also by the manner in which they affect the savings function.

This means that all policies and all investments must be judged by how they affect both future taxable capacities and future expenditure patterns. The former is particularly relevant to directly productive investments which are both on the supply and the demand side in the market nexus. The budget will quickly reveal whether individual investment decisions have just been made to look "economic" by adjustments of prices or cost, or whether they really contribute to growth. The (recurrent) budget is particularly relevant to investments in the social sectors whose effects on taxable capacity are at best much delayed, but whose effects on current expenditures can be devastating.

To avoid misunderstanding: it is, I believe, useful to present the budget in two parts as a recurrent and a capital or development budget, because it is important to have an institutional set-up that forces the budget makers to reveal the effects of present investment decisions on future savings. But this does *not* mean that the unitary nature of the total budget should be forgotten, or that the idea is advocated that the recurrent budget should be balanced by taxes while it is right to borrow for capital expenditures; or, even worse, that the recurrent budget should be kept as small and the capital budget as large as possible. All such conclusions would be devastatingly wrong.

In either case, inadequate growth of taxable capacity or excessive growth of recurrent expenditures reduces savings. Since there are very few aims in this world that can be reached without economic means, the provision of these means must be of prime importance. In this sense, the budget, not the plan is the really important document for economic policy [Stolper (1966), (1971)].

Hence, economic policies other than tax and expenditure policies become central. Assume, for example, that shadow wages should be lower than the wages actually paid. To use budgetary subsidies to convert market into shadow wages would immediately cut into savings and thus raise shadow interest rates and reduce investments, which would have created employment and increased taxable capacity. And the higher wages actually paid would necessarily cut into savings. (See Section II.) Wage policy becomes, thus, central.

The same point can be made with respect to interest rates or price policies. To illustrate with two real examples of LDC's:

(a) In one country long term interest rates are below short term rates. The (publicly owned) banks, therefore, prefer to lend on short term. To stimulate medium and long term investments, the banks get budgetary funds for long term lending. To generate the funds the government must raise taxes or get into (foreign) debt. If the long term lending finances efficient investments, the banks will be repaid, the repayments can be relent, and taxable capacity will increase; if not, the banks have simply been paid to act as a transmission belt for budgetary funds and the programs will peter out unless tax and/or foreign indebtedness are increased [Stolper (1978)]. This is not only a clear-cut and particularly simple case illustrating the interrelationship of monetary (interest rate), and fiscal (tax) and debt policies; it also brings out in crude nakedness the importance of making sure that the investments actually financed will pay off at "honest" prices.

(b) And, price policies become more, not less, important if the budget is to finance development. In another country, the textile industry is largely public. It's prices are kept low "for social reasons." The industry is not overly efficient to start with—and why should it be if it has access to the budget? The result of the price policy is, however, that the industry is not only unable to generate funds for expansion[12] but cannot even generate funds for its own maintenance. This in turn means that the financing of maintenance and expansion requires budgetary funds, and hence increased taxation of the same people in whose supposed interest textile prices were kept low in the first place. This problem cannot be side-stepped by arguing that certain subsidies are "politically necessary" or "socially justified."

The examples—which could be multiplied almost *ad libitum*—illustrate the points I wish to stress: if the budget is to get a central role in achieving growth of the economy, its savings as well as its allocation (in a micro-economic sense) function assumes enormous importance and limits its ability to achieve the allocative ends through subsidies and taxes in a manner that is taken for granted in MDC's. Economic policies not directly involving the budget become essential for converting actual into desired prices. And it becomes of central importance that the investments to be financed do in fact raise output and productivity at prices which reflect true scarcities.

Attempts to improve budgetary procedures in order to make the budget a versatile instrument of economic policy are old and essential. Program budgeting is but the latest of these attempts. The idea is important even if the execution has fallen far short of expectations. For lack of space, I will not deal with it, except to say that it is one instance where perfectionism has ruined the application of a perfectly good and important idea.

However, I would like to make some comments about the aims of budgetary policy. The attention given to the stabilization function has so dominated thinking in the MDC's that the "classical" rules of budgeting are dismissed as primitive, among them the idea that tax revenues should be resistant to cyclical changes. We desire built-in stabilizers that move counter-cyclically. But if the budget is to substitute for the non-existent capital market and to finance developments over the longer term, a fairly stable source of income is precisely what you want. In fact, the idea of a stable income over the cycle is not dead, but is shifted to the balance of payments where compensatory finance is to make up for losses from fluctuating commodity prices. "Built-in stabilizers" in LDC's may require less rather than more fluctuations in budgetary receipts because budgetary expenditures are intended to grow at a more or less stable rate in any case.[13]

To determine the demand for productive capital requires therefore a strict adherence to the principle that only those projects meeting strict economic criteria should be undertaken. To do this properly and to take care of those essential projects which have no clear market demand (like health and education) budgetary projections particularly of the recurrent cost must be made for the purpose of ensuring that the projects are really feasible in the particular sense that the budgetary savings implied in the chosen social discount rate will actually be forthcoming. In that sense as much as possible—at the social discount rate—should be used to raise productive and hence taxable capacity, and as much as possible should be invested in schools and hospitals—meaning "without interference with the savings function of the budget."[14] Clearly, the budget and budgetary policy become absolutely central for the development process but in a quite different manner from MDC's. The budget and budgetary policy must be integrated with the micro-economic decisions which have logical priority and which certainly require economic policies other than budgetary (or monetary) policies to work.[15]

IV. Monetary Policy and the Incentive System

I limit my remarks to two problems: the monetization of subsistence production and the limits to inflationary policies in achieving the Schumpeterian "forced savings" to finance growth.

(i) In most LDC's, modernization of the economies and growth requires that the very large number of producers somehow are drawn into the money nexus. In the more developed countries, including socialist developed economies, recent monetarist theory and policy has proposed that the money supply however defined be increased by x% per year. The purpose of this policy prescription is obviously the control of inflation, and as Mr. Fredman has recently pointed out in a popular form "Monetarism is a new form for an old empirical generalization known as the quantity theory of money . . .. In [a] scientific sense, Karl Marx was a monetarist and so are the bankers in Russia and China today" [Friedman (1982)]. Indeed inflation in a socialist economy rather than underfulfilment of the Plan is the real sign of failure. Obviously, if the prescription is to increase the money supply by 3% p.a. it is implied that real output will rise by 3% p.a. How *that* is to be achieved is left to the market.

In LDC's there is an equivalent suggestion that monetization of subsistence production requires or permits that the money supply be increased. The trouble in LDC's is that markets are imperfect and must be created, and that central banks which can increase (and control) the money supply do not yet exist or lack the proper instruments to make monetary policy work.

The process of monetization itself requires the development of financial instruments which allow the Central Bank to pursue a more effective monetary policy, such as the creation of newly issued commercial papers for crop financing which in turn can aid in creating a bills portfolio of varying maturities upon which the banking system can operate. The technical details are of no interest here [Stolper (1966) Ch. VI]. The process requires the making of crop estimates, expected prices, expected imports resulting from the increased farm income. I.e. we are back at the correct micro-economic signals without which unforseen budgetary and balance of payments problems will certainly arise.

The implications of this approach are first of all that farmers will change their behavior and produce surplusses for the domestic or foreign market and in turn buy not only products they used to make themselves and buy additional products from newly created industries; they must also be convinced that this will make them better off than they were before. As a rule, farmers have no money illusion. This in turn means on the one hand that they receive sufficiently high prices for their crops, on the other hand that they can buy the things they want at sufficiently low prices: income is, after all, income only when it can be spent.

In many LDC's Marketing Boards (Caisses de Stabilisation) which were originally set up to stabilize prices have been used as instruments of taxation. If farm gate prices are lowered too much farmers will not produce for the market. Ghana, perhaps Burma, provide examples of excessive taxation which backfired, the Ivory Coast an example of successful taxation. At the same time, the terms of trade are also moved against the rural sector by protectionistic policies which have been documented again and again in the literature on effective protection in LDC's. Farmers cannot in fact buy the goods of the protected industries. The case is even worse. Essential imports, such as spray pumps to fight cocoa diseases, or trucks and spare parts to bring the crops to the market have been kept out of N'Krumah's Ghana by faulty designs of the tariff structure. The point of Little and Associates [1970] is not that free trade is the best of all policies. It is rather that even free trade would have done substantially better than what governments actually did. The implication is that successful monetization requires careful attention to price policy including tariff policy in general, not just to farm price policy.

Finally, if it is desired to raise farm incomes, it is essential to make life on the farms bearable: rural roads, piped water even if it means only a few standpipes in the villages, electricity, a movie, as well as the availability of kerosene lamps or transistor radios are essential. This means that successful monetization implies also certain requirements for investment policy and provides a strong argument for the provision of *some* social investments which—see the preceding section—need *not* be subsidized.

(ii) The case for inflationary finance of developmental investments is essentially the Schumpeterian case of forced savings. This case is made with special forcefulness in the Latin American context, although inflation is presented less as "beneficial" than as inevitable. Prebisch (1961), Sears (1962) or Dorrance (1963) have pointed out a long time ago, that inflation is no bed of roses and that there is no necessary or factual relation between inflation and growth. And indeed there should be none, because there is no way to control what happens to the new money beyond the first round of spending, and what will happen depends precisely on how the new money is spent.

The Schumpeterian case of forced saving rests on a number of premises which are relevant also to LDC's. One is that insufficient savings are forthcoming to finance the desired "structural break." [Chakravarty (1959)]. In the Schumpeterian case the reason is that at the old parameters savings are optimally allocated. In LDC's this is certainly not the major reason. Secondly, for the process to work relatively smoothly—it can never work painlessly—the economy must have sufficient flexibility to allow the shifting of factors of production from their previous uses to the execution of innovations. This is certainly not the case in LDC's. It is the very rigidity of their economic structures which makes inflation inevitable in the eyes of the structuralists. Thirdly, and most important, the inflationary financing must *in fact* lead to an increase in productive capacity and after a lag to an increase in output which allows bank credit to be repaid and thus ends the inflationary process.

The last point is the true link with micro-economic considerations. It requires a linkage with cost-benefit considerations of specific projects. The Schumpeterian entrepreneur must be convinced that, at the existing and expected prices—both undistorted—he must be able to compete successfully and he must convince his financial backers of the realism of his plans. This is, of course, difficult, particularly if the same people who expect the profits from the innovations are also threatened with the losses from the "creative destruction" involved. In LDC's, with planners trying to take the place of the (supposedly or really) missing entrepreneurs, the planners must show directly that at undistorted existing and expected prices the expenditures of resources are justified because they will lead to the creation of more resources. In either case, the micro-economic signals and considerations must dominate the willingness to finance investments. If the signals are (approximately) right and taken seriously the inflationary process will have improved the productive structure; if not, stagflation is likely to follow.

Now this is different from both the Keynesian or monetarist approaches. Even in a sophisticated Keynesian approach the economic nature of the investment is assumed rather than specifically built into the theory. Innovations seem peculiarly harmless. The more primitive monetarist approach which suggests that the money supply be increased at a constant rate is theoretically quite difficult to accept even if we could define money in a unique way once and for all because there is *no* direct controllable and traceable link between the newly created money and what happens in the economy after the initial use of the newly created money to finance an innovation. Again investments are assumed to be economic and innovations peculiarly harmless. Pragmatically the monetarist prescription may nevertheless not be a bad policy prescription, particularly in highly inflationary situations.

There is another reason to reject the structuralist solution. The theory of the second best points out that the first best policy measures attempt to eliminate the existing distortions. If this is not possible, it is necessary to devise *specific* policy measures which will fulfill their purpose of improving the situation. If it is desired to break bottlenecks it may be best to do so directly. The case of the Federal German Republic between 1952–1954 is a famous and successful example in this respect. The problem was precisely of the kind that is used by structuralists to defend inflationary policies: inadequate savings and bottlenecks in the economy. Between 1952 and 1954, under the Investment Aid Law of 1952, 132,000 firms in all sectors of the economy were forced to buy about DM 1 bil. of bonds which were channeled to 187 enterprises in the bottlenecks sectors [Stolper and Roskamp (1979)]. In other words, when faced with precisely the "structuralist" problem, the Germans rejected the inflationary solution, and pragmatically used monetary, fiscal and very direct interventionist policies to solve the problems. The alternative to inflation is not necessarily "orthodoxy."

The funds generated by monetary means must *really* break the bottlenecks, and they must be supplemented by other appropriate policies. They cannot do this if they simply finance government consumption, or if they are offset by rising money wages, or lead to inefficient production. In the German case, wages were kept low—by unemployment and the export of unemployment from East to West

Germany which prevented an aggressive wage policy—savings were stimulated by fiscal measures, and government proper as well as the social security system had very substantial surplusses.[17]

Finally, notice that, superficially, I seem to be reverting to a version of the banking theory of money. However, unlike the banking theory I am not arguing that if the newly created money is spent on productive investments there can be no inflation. Quite the contrary: there *will* be an inflationary effect which, indeed, is the essence of the process of development. Only, in the Schumpeterian case it will be self-limiting. All I am arguing is that in the first round, the newly created money should allow productive people to get hold of the resources needed to execute their plans. This is after all hardly news to investment bankers. That there remain enormous uncertainties goes without saying, two of them being the future policies of the central bank and of the ministry of finance. The MDC equivalent of what I have been discussing is that fiscal policies may lead to a "crowding out" of private investments—a factual, not a theoretical question—and that monetary policy may or may not let interest rates rise. But to pursue this line of thought further and in particular to apply Schumpeterian ideas to the policies of the present American Administration would lead too far afield.[18]

Thus to make monetary policy effective (including possible inflationary finance) requires paying substantial attention to micro-economic policies, and the proper fiscal policies. The failure of inflationary policies are the failures of paying attention to productivity, and the—frequently deliberate—distortions of prices, something which is by now amply documented in the literature on trade policy.

Notes

[1]I repeat: advocacy of the serious use of the price system carries *no* ideological commitment of any kind. The justification for taking world market prices as the proper guide even within the Soviet Bloc should indicate how little ideology there is in the insistence on factor prices reflecting true scarcities. The "Marxist" insistence on "socially necessary labor" is generalized to socially necessary inputs, and the reference to world market prices is essentially the idea that they are more competitive and hence reflect more truly what is "socially necessary." It seems more satisfactory to start with a modern theory in the first place.

[2]Whether this is done privately or by government is in principle irrelevant though it makes politically a great deal, and as I have argued, a very harmful, difference, if it is governmental without stringent safeguards [Stolper (1971)].

[3]The following qualifications should be kept in mind which I state "in desparate brevity," to use a favorite phrase of Schumpeter. (a) Cost-benefit analysis can only be guess work, but it should be the best guesses that can be made. It is an aid in en-

suring that one has thought through what one proposes to do. (b) Cost-benefit analysis is, as far as I am concerned, applicable only to decisions which are both on the supply and the demand side within the market nexus. (c) The statement made in the text in no way underestimates the importance of such aims as improving the health or education of the people. The (partly political) establishment of a social discount rate and, as will be argued below, the budgetary repercussions of all decisions imply how much should be spent on changing the productive structure and how much elsewhere. [See Stolper (1966), (1971).]

[4]The following real example will illustrate the point. In Nigeria, bottles are used on the average nine times before they break, and bottles are imported. There also was a bottle deposit to ensure that the bottles would be returned after use. At one time, junior civil servants decided that the bottle deposit amounted to an interest-free loan by consumers to beer brewers and soft drink bottlers (which was true) and should be abolished. Unfortunately, this lead, among other things, to the export of bottles to neighboring countries where they brought a price somewhat higher than the bottle deposit. It led to a domestic shortage of bottles, hence to a shortage of beer and soft drinks. The (excellent) top civil servants had to spend their time to undo the nonsense created by inexperienced juniors instead of worrying about the very real problems confronting their country in the aftermath of the civil war. Such examples could undoubtedly be duplicated in virtually every country.

[5]G. Myrdal (1968) discusses some of these problems under the general heading of "the soft state." Given the tasks allocated to the government and the inability to cope with them, the wonder is not that corruption exists, but that it is not still greater. Of course, in socialist countries, information becomes available only in periods of crisis, as is the case at present in Poland.

[6]Charles P. Kindleberger (1978) has beautifully analyzed this problem of reduced adaptability in developed economies. It is just as applicable to LDC's.

[7]It may seem surprising that Japan should be considered an LDC before the Second World War. Obviously it was not in the same sense in which, for example, India is considered and considers itself an LDC. The following considerations may resolve any puzzlement. In the first place, being an LDC implies mainly being poor, and in no way suggests that the country could not be a leader in cultural achievements. By no stretch of imagination can India, or Japan, or China be considered anything but countries at the highest level of civilization. However, secondly, such a wise scholar as Simon Kuznets has shown that Japan is really the only presently developed country which at the "beginning of [its] modern growth" had a per capita income comparable to that of present day LDC's. All others were already fairly developed countries (by modern LDC standards) when their "modern" development started. Thus Kuznets estimates Japanese per capita income in the quinquennium 1874–1879 to have been $74 of 1965 purchasing power. This compares with $77 for India for the period 1952–1958. (Kuznets, (1971), The Japanese figure is found in Table 2, p. 24; the Indian figure in Table 3, p. 31.)

[8]I can appeal both to real historical developments (reform in Hungary and elsewhere in the Soviet bloc, contrasted with the monstrosities of the Pol Pot regime in Cambodia) and to theoretical points. To quote Schumpeter in two different aspects, in his *Crisis of the Tax State* (1954), Schumpeter makes the case that precisely and only in an individualistic society does the State have a function as a counterpart to the individual. This conclusion is based essentially on what nowadays is referred to as failures of the market mechanism, public goods and, perhaps, merit wants. More interesting in the present context are Schumpeter's arguments which today we would probably classify as being based upon the theory of the second-best. For example, after pointing out where monopolies might do better than "pure" competition, Schumpeter points out that "it ain't necessarily so." "It is certainly conceivable that an all-pervading cartel system might sabotage all progress as it is that it might realize, with smaller social and real costs, all that perfect competition is supposed to realize. This is why our argument does not amount to a case against state regulation . . .. Rational . . . regulation by public authority turns out to be an extremely delicate problem

which not every government agency . . . can be trusted to solve." [Schumpeter (1942) p. 91]

[9] I have a dark memory that the late Oskar Lange argued that Ricardian rather than Keynesian policies are applicable to LDC's which in the 1940's, were deemed to include eastern and southeastern Europe. I have, however, been unable to find a reference. I would in any case substitute "Schumpeterian" for "Ricardian," and would not be prepared to write off Keynesian policies completely: it is, after all, also important to get the totals right.

[10] This is generally true. However, in the 1950's the government of the Federal German Republic did provide more savings than individual savers and occasionally even more than business, and for the same reason given in LDC's: the absence of a well-working capital market. [W. F. Stolper and K. W. Roskamp, (1979), p. 389, Table 4.]

[11] Although I use, in paying my respects to R. A. Musgrave, his terminology, I really mean by the "allocation function" the micro-economic aspects of the budget, and not the relative size of the public and the private sectors.

[12] Even if planners should decide that the industry should not expand, it would still be important in a socialist country, which the country in question claims to be, that the industry make profits to contribute to the budget.

[13] Since this was written, I have read Mr. Wolfson's book, in which the same ideas are expounded. Dirk J. Wolfson, (1979), particularly Ch. 9.

[14] Professor (now President) Harold T. Shapiro has assured me that my suggested procedure for deciding upon the two types of investment is equivalent to equating their returns at the margin. I believe this to be true but have been unable to give a formal proof.

[15] Since this was written I have given some more thought to the implications of budgetary policies and their relationships to micro-economic policies (deregulation, foreign trade policies, specific tax policies such as all-savers certificates, or rules for depreciation) and while the specific form of budgetary policies is certainly much different in MDC's and LDC's, I am now certain that the problems discussed in the context of LDC's are just as important as in the context of developed countries.

[16] The growth of the socalled underground economies in inflation plagued countries shows that here, too, LDC's and MDC's are not all that different.

[17] Stolper and Roskamp (1979), p. 389, for figures for the years 1949–1960. Even in 1960, government contributed DM 18.1 bil. of net savings, compared to DM 17.4 bil contributed by business, DM 14.8 bil. by households, and DM 3.3 bil. by social insurance funds.

[18] I cannot resist one more comment. In the 19th century there raged the famous "Methodenstreit" about induction vs. deduction. Schumpeter's comments on that controversy were that it never made any sense and that the actual development of economics as a science just ignored it and went its own logical way. I suspect that something similar will be said in the future about the controversy between Keynesians and monetarists. As far as demand pull inflation is concerned, there is total agreement that the two approaches are equivalent as an explanation of what happens. When it comes to cost-push inflation, there is also agreement that the difference between the two is really a question of fact: whether there is or is not crowding out.

References

J. Bhagwati, *The Theory and Practice of Commercial Policy: Departures from Unified Exchange Rates*, (1968), Special Papers in International Economics No. 8, Princeton.

———. *Anatomy and Consequences of Exchange Control Regimes,* (1978), National Bureau of Economic Research, Ballinger Publishing Company, Cambridge, Massachusetts.

——— and V. K. Ramaswami, "Domestic Distortions, Tariffs, and the Theory of the Optimum Subsidy," (1963), *Journal of Political Economy,* Vol. LXXI, February, 1963.

S. Chakravarty, *The Logic of Investment Planning,* (1959), North Holland, Amsterdam.

H. C. Chenery, M. S. Ahluwalia, et al., *Redistribution with Growth,* (1974), Oxford University Press, for the World Bank.

P. Dasgupta, S. Marglin, A. K. Sen, *Guidelines for Project Evaluation,* (1972), for UNIDO, United Nations, New York.

Milton Friedmann, "Defining Monetarism" *Newsweek* July 12, 1982.

G. S. Dorrance, "Economic Development and Monetary Stability: The False Dilemma," (1963), IMF, *Staff Papers,* Vol. X, No. 1.

C. P. Kindleberger, "The Aging Economy," (1978), *Weltwirtschaftliches Archiv,* Vol. 114, No. 3.

J. G. Kleve and W. F. Stolper, *Tunisia—Changes in Income Distribution, 1961–1971,* (1975), Center for Research on Economic Development, The University of Michigan, Ann Arbor, Michigan.

A. O. Krueger, *Liberalization Attempts and Consequences,* (1978), National Bureau of Economic Research, Ballinger Publishing Company, Cambridge, Massachusetts.

S. Kuznets, *The Economic Growth of Nations. Total Output and Production Structure,* (1971), Harvard University Press, Cambridge, Massachusetts.

R. G. Lipsey and K. Lancaster, "The General Theory of the Second Best," (1956/57), *The Review of Economic Studies,* Vol. 24.

I. Little and J. Mirrlees, *Manual of Project Analysis in Developing Countries,* (1968), OECD, Paris (3 Vols.).

I. Little, T. Scitovsky, M. Scott, *Industry and Trade in Some Developing Countries,* (1970), Oxford University Press (for OECD), London.

R. A. Musgrave, *The Theory of Public Finance* (1959), McGraw-Hill, New York.

G. Myrdal, *Asian Drama: An Inquiry into the Poverty of Nations,* (1968), Twentieth Century Fund.

R. Prebisch, "Economic Development and Monetary Stability: The False Dilemma," (1961), *Economic Bulletin for Latin America,* Vol. VI, No. 1, March.

P. A. Samuelson, *Economics,* (1980), 11th ed., McGraw-Hill, New York.

J. A. Schumpeter, *Capitalism, Socialism, and Democracy,* (1942), Harper and Brothers, New York and London.

———. The Decade of the Twenties," (1946), *American Economic Review,* Vol. XXXVI, No. 2, May.

———. "The Crisis of the Tax State," (1954), *International Economic Papers,* Macmillan, London. (Translated from *Die Krise des Steuerstaates* (1918) by W. F. Stolper and R. A. Musgrave).

D. Seers, "A Theory of Inflation and Growth in Underdeveloped Economies Based on the Experience of Latin America," (1962), *Oxford Economic Papers,* N.S. Vol. 14, June, pp. 173–195.

Lyn Squire and H. G. van der Tak, *Economic Analysis of Projects,* (1975), The Johns Hopkins Press (for the World Bank), Baltimore and London.

W. F. Stolper, *Planning without Facts,* (1966), Harvard University Press, Cambridge, Massachusetts.

———. *Budget, Economic Policy, and Economic Performance in Underdeveloped Countries,* (1971), Kieler Vorträge, N. F. No. 69, J. C. B. Mohr (Paul Siebeck), Tübingen.

———. "Some Problems in Adapting the Ideas of Budgeting and Planning to Underdeveloped Countries," in H. Haller, G. Hauser, H. Schelbert-Syfrig (eds.), *Sozialwissenschaften im Dienste der Wirtschaftspolitik* (Festschrift Bickel), (1973), J. C. B. Mohr (Paul Siebeck), Tübingen.

———. "Development in the Large and in the Small: The Case of Tunisia, 1961–

1971," (1978), *Weltwirtschaftliches Archiv*, Vol. 114, No. 3 (French Translation in Annales Economiques).

———. *Income Distribution and Economic Policies: The Case of Two African Countries*, (1980), Kieler Vorträge, NF no. 92, J. C. B. Mohr (Paul Siebeck), Tübingen.

W. F. Stolper and K. W. Roskamp, "*Planning a Free Economy—Germany 1945–1960*," (1979), *Zeitschrift für die Gesamte Staatswissenschaft*, Vol. 135, No. 3.

J. Tinbergen, *On the Theory of Economic Policy*, (1952), North Holland, Amsterdam.

B. A. den Tuinder, (co-ordinating author), *Ivory Coast—The Challenge of Success*, (1978), The Johns Hopkins University Press (for the World Bank), Baltimore and London.

D. Turnham, assisted by Annelies Jaeger, *The Employment Problem in Less Developed Countries*, (1971), OECD, Paris.

D. J. Wolfson, *Public Finance and Development Strategy*, (1979), The Johns Hopkins University Press, Baltimore and London.

World Development Report, 1981, (August, 1981), The World Bank, Washington, D.C.

Résumé

Cet article essaye d'appliquer les idées Schumpeteriennes de développement à l'application de politiques fiscales et monétaires dans les pays sous-développés.

La première partie montre l'importance des ideés d'équilibre économique. Nous soutenons que le principal objectif à atteindre devrait être d'accroître la productivité. Ceci demande de prêter attention aux prix, à la fois ceux en cours et ceux prévisibles, tous deux sans distorsions. Ceci souligne l'importance cruciale des analyses provisionnelles.

La deuxième partie soutient que ce qui se passera en réalité dépend moins de politiques macro-économiques que d'indicateurs micro-économiques. L'article montre que l'équilibre résiste au changement. On fait référence à la théorie des choix de second rang pour justifier l'accent mis sur des politiques compétitives spécifiques. Des prix, qui ne sont pas justes, ont à coup sûr des conséquences budgétaires considérables.

La troisième partie considére les implications sur la politique budgétaire. Dans les pays sous-développés, on attend du budget qu'il fournisse de l'épargne, c'est-à-dire qu'il se substitue au marché du capital qui fait défaut. Ceci limite sévèrement la politique fiscale au sens que l'on donne à ce terme dans les pays plus développés. Subventions et déficits sont des menaces directes pour l'épargne, l'accumulation du capital et les changements structurels. Les canons classiques de la politique budgétaire ont parfaitement leur place bien que les raisons qui les justifient diffèrent de celles données au 19ème siècle. Une politique des prix et des salaires rend la politique budgétaire possible.

La quatrième partie considère brièvement le rapport des indicateurs micro-économiques avec les politiques monétaires. En fait, il n'existe pas de relation direct et unique entre l'inflation et la croissance. Une telle relation est impossible. Car ce qui va se passer dépend d'abord de la façon dont précisément on dépense l'argent supplémentaire, c'est-à-dire dépend des décisions micro-économiques. Les problèmes "structuralistes" demandent vraiment des politiques spécifiques, comme le suggère la théorie des seconds choix. Pour que la monétisation d'une production de subsistance réussisse, il faut des indicateurs micro-économiques adéquats.

Que l'inflation mène ou non à une épargne forcée dépend aussi de la façon exacte dont l'argent est dépensé.

Effective Monetary and Fiscal Policy to Promote Economic Growth—A Socialist Approach

*Béla Csikós-Nagy and Otto Gadó**

1

The socialist state wants to achieve economic growth—and if possible, smooth growth—within a system of a planned economy, because only such growth can provide a steady and continuous increase in the standard of living of the population.

Given the present state of the world economy, however, and the varying sensitivities to foreign trade of different economies, growth ceases to be a comparatively simple quantitative matter. It inevitably will be affected by the requirement of international equilibrium, i.e., it is subject to a balance of trade constraint. Such an equilibrium can be achieved only by expanding exports, if growth is to be maintained at the same time. Import restrictions without affecting exports can only affect the structure of imports. Only export orientation truly reflects mutually advantageous international economic relations since it also insures a market for imports from other countries. But export orientation requires that an appropriate structure of production be brought about which can supply internationally competitive exportable goods.

Questions related to this problem are now of primary interest to Hungary. Hungary is one of the countries most affected by changes in world market prices. The first oil price explosion of 1973 cost Hun-

*The authors are State Secretary, President of the National Office for Prices and Materials, titular professor, Karl Marx University of Economics, Budapest, Chairman of the Hungarian Economic Association, member of the Executive Committee of the International Economic Association; and retired Deputy President of the National Planning Office, titular associate professor, Karl Marx University of Economics, Budapest, honorary President of the IIPF, Chairman of the Financial Section of the Hungarian Economic Association, respectively.

Public Finance and Economic Growth. Proceedings of the 37th Congress of the International Institute of Public Finance. Tokyo, 1981, pp. 149–166

gary almost 10 percent of her national income, and the second explosion of 1979/80 almost another 4 percent. These were very heavy blows which even a purposeful economic policy can overcome only within the framework of a ten-year program.

It was a major achievement that the measures to restore the upset international equilibrium worked as desired. By 1980, the balance of payments in convertible currencies was restored, though the Rouble balance remained unbalanced. However, adjustment to the deteriorating terms-of-trade in the latter relation procedes as planned. At the same time, the price of the considerable success in attaining international equilibrium was economic stagnation. Thus we must still cope with the problem of growth.

Already during the implementation of the 1968 reforms it was pointed out that the country had to shift from a production controlled to a demand controlled growth path. Before the reform it had been believed that the expanding path of production could be determined independently of market requirements. It had been an important planning axiom that every year industry had to grow faster than agriculture, and heavy industry more rapidly than light industry. The planners were guided by the interrelations of planned material and commodity balances. This conception of economic development was almost totally divorced from the "external" expectations likely to confront the economy.

A demand-controlled growth path, on the other hand, subjects development policy to the severe test of the market. For the national economy to develop along such a growth path in an optimal manner requires, however that organizations (institutions) have been changed so as to aim at profitable sales of final products, and that investment decisions are controlled by the return on capital measured by international sales.

So far we have only partially succeeded in shifting to a demand-controlled growth path. Again and again production-controlled growth and the policies it implied only worsened the balance of foreign trade deficits, which then required restrictive measures. Investment cycles resulted which simultaneously indicated the "birth throes" of the search for a new growth path. The change in economic policy in 1979 deserves attention from this point of view: it considerably reduced the rate of growth and ensured short-run priority of balance-of-foreign trade equilibrium over growth.

Under Hungarian conditions, the primacy of external equilibrium is subject to the conditions that during the period during which the balance of trade equilibrium is being restored, the goods and services needed to secure currently required domestic consumption needs should remain available and the standard of living and the quality of life of the population should not deteriorate.

Of course, external balance does not require that the international receipts and payments on current account have to be balanced in every year. External equilibrium is quite compatible with such foreign borrowing which, by increasing export capacity, will produce the additional foreign income necessary for amortization and interest payments.

Foreign borrowing has, of course, an upper limit set by an acceptable ratio of debt service (interest and amortization) to export earnings. The increase in the interest burden during these years has been particularly burdensome. All these facts fundamentally affect monetary—and indirectly fiscal—policy. This is all the more true as no free capital flows have so far developed and international agreements such as joint ventures have so far only marginal importance.

The outlined socio-economic objectives determine the tasks of monetary and fiscal policy, i.e., of financial policy.[1] A financial policy may be said to be optimal during a given period if under the economic conditions of the country it promotes economic growth in the best possible manner, subject to the desired external and internal equilibrium conditions. It should, however, be added that we have succeeded neither in an exact empirical or theoretical formulation of this optimum.

It is obvious that economic growth is influenced by many domestic and foreign factors besides financial policy. Nevertheless, if economic growth is disturbed by conditions that correspond to those outlined, monetary and fiscal policy must be blamed, either because the methods were inappropriate, or because they did not react quickly enough or with necessary force to the problems that have arisen in the course of economic development.

2

The theoretical bases of the functioning of a socialist economy were first worked out by Soviet economists who generalized the experiences of the Soviet Union with the implementation of the planned economy. The essence of this system of control and management is the *unity of planning, control and organization.* Planning has primacy shown by the fact that control and management is exercised by breaking down the macro-plans to the micro-level, by using plan indicators thus arrived at. This is complemented by officially fixed systems of prices and wages and is given a legal framework by government measures. Organizationally a system of institutions is developed and maintained which effectively secures

(a) the upward flow of information necessary for working out the plan, the downward flow of detailed informations about the plan, and, simultaneously, the flow of regular information among enterprises which are linked by production;

(b) state control and management relying on the obligatory plan indicators; and, finally,

(c) a continuous check by confronting planned indicators with factual data.

In such a socialist planned economy money can play but a relatively passive role. The primary role belongs to the detailed indicators of the economy-wide plan which are addressed to enterprises. These indicators specify not only the tasks to be implemented, but also the specific means (materials, machinery, labour, etc.) to be used for their implementation. No monetary and fiscal policy giving an active role to money can develop in this model. At best it can play only a very small role. Of course, even in this planning system there is a role for finances: for, financial policy creates and maintains financial relations which contribute to attaining the growth rate defined in the economy-wide plan and to the proper allocation of the means to be used for the implementation of the plan.

It should, however, be added that these first elaborated theoretical bases of the functioning of a socialist economy relied on the experience of that historical period when natural resources did not yet limit the development of the forces of production, and the single country striving to build up socialism could neglect the requirements deriving from the international division of labour.

After World War II a new situation arose when several European countries underwent a socio-economic transformation. The necessity to revise the theorems about the socialist economy did not arise for some time, mainly during the period of extensive economic development. But the inescapable transition to the intensive stage of development, particularly in the wake of the changes in the world economic conditions (i.e., the two oil-price explosions of 1973 and 1980, and the resulting declining business, etc.) inevitably made such revision necessary mainly in the smaller more open countries. We shall, therefore, procede to examine what financial policy can best serve the development of an efficient structure of production as the essential base of economic growth of such smaller countries.

Of course, the specific *external and internal conditions* of the economies differ in the individual socialist countries, depending on the level of development attained, traditions, the size of the country, etc. This is precisely why it is impossible that, given the actual level of development, an economic control and management system should operate in these countries with a uniform role of financial policy. There are, however, necessary common features:

(i) The overwhelming majority of the means of production are socially, i.e., collectively owned by the state or cooperatives. (Agriculture in some countries is an exception.)

(ii) From this follows the necessity of economy-wide planning. The plan determines the main directions of development, the allocation proportions. It accounts for and develops the established social relations.

(iii) The countries make efforts to solve their economic problems in common and to exploit in the course of development and on the basis of mutual advantage the possibilities provided by the functioning of the Council for Mutual Economic Assistance.

3

In 1920, Mises wanted to prove that rational economic calculation was impossible in a socialist economy. The debate started by him ended with the so-called "Lange-Lerner solution." In our days Kantorovich worked out the optimal functioning of a socialist economy based on shadow prices. Thus the basis of an optimal policy is in many respects the *problem of prices.* Substantively, the question is indeed the following: is the law of price[2] at work in socialism, and if so, how does state planning and public ownership modify it?

Two questions arise: can relative scarcities and their continuous changes be expressed in a system of official prices? And, how can the role of prices reflecting the structures of production be changed into one in which prices give the signals for the desired change in that structure.

During the debates of the thirties, Oscar Lange [Lange, (1936, 1937)] still believed that realistic economic calculations could also be expressed in an official system of prices. Some countries (e.g., Bulgaria) have in fact based their solution on this view. They believe that the annual revision of official prices can maintain the link between world market and internal prices. The Hungarian solution on the other hand applied more flexible mechanisms which allowed prices to change widely under the impact of market factors.

In an economy controlled by a system of obligatory plan indicators, price always follows structure. If, on the other hand, the state exercises its control by means of economic instruments, price influences the shaping of structure, and the scope of this price function depends precisely on how the controls are applied.

Thus, in this system function of the prices is linked to an effective financial policy. The Hungarian experience of the rational function of prices in national economic control suggests that control exercised by means of tools formulated in terms of value (price and incomes policy) is better than one formulated in physical terms (production and distribution policy); that control through monetary and fiscal policy is better than value-control; and within financial control, that indirect methods are preferable to direct ones.

We must deal with two problems of the function of prices in detail: producer prices (in the terminology of some countries: wholesale prices) and the consumer (retail) prices.

4

Socialist countries emphasize again and again the necessity to activate commodity (market) and money relationships, which can be understood as a greater freedom, profit-motive, and risk-taking of enterprises. Indeed, the role of financial policy depends on the role of commodity and monetary relations in the control of the economy.

It is, however, obvious that financial policy is part of general economic policy and can exert its effect only within and in mutual interaction with other aspects of it. Its role differs depending on whether financial policy is called upon merely to follow or to influence the national economic processes.

The Hungarian system of control and management defines the tasks of financial policy, or, if you like, the effect of commodity and monetary relations in a double manner. In the process of *economy-wide planning* the impacts and signals of the commodity and monetary relations have to be stated in an iterative manner, their interactions have to be allowed for, the impacts themselves from other policy goals have to be repeatedly controlled and their probable effects have to be projected. Monetary and fiscal policies play an important role in the economic processes which realize the targets of the economy-wide plan.

5

Ever since the introduction of the New Economic Mechanism in 1968, the tools of monetary and fiscal policy have been embodied in the practice of Hungarian economic control and management in the system of economic regulators. This regulatory system has to fulfil both mentioned basic tasks.

Within the system of regulators there are particular centralized government decisions which must be implemented. These refer mainly to the major investment projects and to infrastructural development. But the smooth transaction of commodity turnover necessitates management based on central prescriptions also in the sphere of means of production and consumer articles. This holds first of all for the fulfilment of intergovernmental agreements within the CMEA and for some state orders from national defense and health service organs. In these respects, financial policy has "follow-up" tasks.

The basic tools of the regulatory system are the economic regulators: price, tax, credit, etc. These are elaborated in the process of economy-wide planning. This means that the five-year plan consists not only of the plan itself approved by the National Assembly and obligatory for the government as a whole (but not broken down by ministries and enterprises), but also of comprehensive background material (computations) which underlies the plan though its implementation is not compulsory. The economic regulators are in harmony with the computations. As harmony is achieved through a process of iteration, the impact of finances on national economic planning asserts itself through these iterative processes.

From harmony with the plan there follow several requirements:

The plan indicators quantified in the plan cannot be identified with the targets (much less with the available means for their implementation). The implementation of the indicators approximates the planned optimal development of the economy *only if and insofar as the actual foreign and domestic economic conditions agree with* the assumptions underlying the plan.

This interpretation is unequivocally reflected by the sixth five-year plan of Hungary for 1981–85, which sets considerably fewer quantitative economic targets than in the past, and even these in a manner that leaves the implementation relatively flexible by means of giving ranges "from . . . to . . ." for the indicators.

It follows that whenever the assumptions underlying planning and the working out of the economic regulators change, the original targets have to be flexibly changed within the band (zone) marked out in the plan. In the case of some major deviation even a modification of the economy-wide plan may be initiated by the National Assembly, and/or the regulatory tools have to be adjusted to the new conditions, since otherwise they would disorient the leadership of the economic organizations.

It is one of the most serious problems of economic control and management what procedures to follow with these modifications.

For, the longer adjustment to changed conditions are delayed the longer the losses from disorientation have to be suffered, and the greater the danger that needs for changes will accumulate, which may finally lead to major changes and a break in the economic processes. A relatively flexible handling of the regulators is desirable, but changes must not be too frequent, either, since enterprises must be allowed time to adjust. There exists no uniform "recipe" how these partly contradictory requirements can be best realized although *this is a basic problem of the efficiency of financial policy.* It has, however, become established in Hungarian practice that changes must never be retroactive, although they may affect already concluded but not yet implemented transactions.

6

As far as possible, the control system has to apply *identical criteria towards every sector (enterprise).* But even this stipulation must not be interpreted too rigidly, as economy-wide requirements towards agriculture, manufacturing, or public utilities (postal service, railways) obviously differ. But if, within the same branch, we set stricter financial conditions for the enterprise capable of rapid development and looser ones for those lagging behind, the result will presumably be far from optimal.

Therefore, conditions must not be differentiated by enterprises (or groups of enterprises) as far as possible, nor should it be attempted to bring enterprises into identical position, as in the final analysis this would impair the uniform impact of the commodity and monetary relations.

The requirements tending towards uniformity *differentiate the enterprises in the economic processes.* Depending on the mode of regulations this affects the development possibilities of the firms and, perhaps partly, also the growth of incomes of the employees.

But any economically justified *differentiation also has social limits.* Society does not easily put up with too great a differentiation, particularly not if some of the differences can be traced back to minor or major deficiencies of the regulatory system or to deviations from general principles.

The discussion demonstrates that the formulation of the most appropriate monetary and fiscal policy, the choice of its instruments and their necessary modification or change is one of the most difficult tasks for the economic leadership of the state and one with important repercussions on state finances.

It should finally be added that socialist economic units have to reckon not only with market prognoses, but also with expected reactions of the state control bodies. On the other hand, they may legitimately expect that state control refrains from improvisations, and that its behavior should allow a soundly calculating and weighing enterprise to foresee the control bodies' actions.

7

We will now examine the function of *monetary and fiscal* policy in a socialist planned economy of the Hungarian type.

The task of fiscal policy is to centralize in the system of the state budget[3] those monetary resources which are sufficient to solve the tasks incumbent upon the budget.

The overwhelming majority of budgetary revenues—about 80 per cent—derives from state-owned enterprises and from cooperatives. These revenues are of several kinds:

Indirect taxes built into the price system (e.g., turnover tax) which the enterprise collects and transmits to the budget. (We shall return to the interrelations with consumer price policy.)

Payments related to particular factors of production which increase the costs of enterprise. Examples in Hungarian practice are the social insurance contributions to be paid by the enterprise, and until 1980 also a charge on fixed and circulating assets tied up in production; or the land tax in agriculture.

Obligatory payment of a part of the profit (expressing the performance of the enterprise) in the form of the profit tax. The size of indirect taxes and taxes on factors of production is determined by the price system. The profit tax may apparently be autonomously determined by fiscal policy. However, the payment to be made by the firm must not be so big as to impair its incentives, the cost-sensitivity of the enterprise. The 50–60 per cent applied in Hungarian practice seem to reach the upper limits. And the amount and allocation of the part remaining at the disposal of the enterprises should be in harmony with the computations of the economy-wide plan.

On the *expenditure side,* there are the traditional budgetary items, such as the outlays of the organs responsible for providing defense and social, cultural, health and administrative services, etc. In their totality, they may be assumed to grow faster than GDP.

From the practical point of view social expenditures are total social insurance benefit payments (pension, family allowance, etc.) in excess of the payments by the enterprises and the workers (employees) themselves. It is clear that these payments must be provided by the socialist state from budgetary means irrespective of whether those incomes provide the necessary coverage for them or not.

One of the most important questions of *the harmony of monetary and fiscal policies* is how to finance investment (and part of the increase in circulating assets). For those investments which have been decided upon the basis of pay-off requirements (either centrally or on the enterprise level), financing is justifiably the task of the monetary sphere.

The centrally determined investments, on the other hand, primarily relating to infrastructure have to be partially or entirely financed by the budget. Nor can the budgetary support for certain other investment projects or other targets be excluded. Thus, agriculture in Hungary as elsewhere is supported by the state partly with direct budgetary allocations, partly with price subsidies given to industrial producers of agricultural inputs, (machinery, chemicals).

Our discussion has shown that the role of credits and loans increases in the allocation and reallocation of monetary assets for development. It should also be clear that in a socialist economy the creation of the money necessary for transacting the turnover and its availability to the economy, takes essentially the form of credits. This is true also when the national banking system raises foreign credit to finance the economy. Of course, private, public, or enterprise savings are also available for lending before there is recourse to foreign resources. While the right of disposal of each saver is maintained the mediation of the bank allows them to participate in the financing of the economic processes.

In this context a number of problems are discussed in the Hungarian economic literature:

First, the *tasks* of monetary and fiscal policies frequently intermingle. Even today fiscal policy plays a greater role than the regulating and distributing functions of the market. Such statements can even be found as that the budget takes on more than it can bear or than what would be justified by the equilibrium of the national economy. Related to this is the fact that the state budget has a deficit, which is covered by short term credits from monetary means reducing to the same extent the availability of monetary assets to finance other economic possibilities.

Secondly, the problem of the *capital market,* that is, of the free flow of accumulated enterprise, personal, perhaps public, monetary assets to finance investment and development against the payments of interest or other returns has not yet been solved. Scientific research is looking for ways how certain elements of the diversified practices all over the world could be usefully taken over. The absence of a well working capital market necessarily increases the reallocative role of fiscal policy.

Thirdly, there is also a debate to what extent enterprises should be obliged to finance their *growing inventories* themselves—perhaps with the help of short term credits—from the same monetary assets that are used to finance investment in plant and equipment. Some economists believe that the system of revolving bank credit should be used instead, which would relieve fiscal policy of some of its tasks.

8

In this section we are going to examine the function of prices somewhat more closely.

For a long time, there existed a single method for the *formation of producer prices,* whether officially set or determined by the enterprise itself: price was based on the average cost and the permitted profit. The problems involved were: What should be considered average, and can a particular cost be accepted if the given product is turned out only by a single firm? How often should or could prices be adjusted to changes in average costs? How big should the permissible profit be? Can it be determined by a general item and for some longer period? Should it be changed as costs, or should the equilibrium relations between effective demand and supply change?

Over time these questions were answered differently in different countries. But this cannot hide the fact that differences in profit or profitability[4] among enterprises as the result of prices thus formed, do not reflect differences in the efficiency of production from the standpoint of the economy as a whole.

This recognition has prompted the Hungarian economic leadership to introduce for all groups of products which can be internationally traded, domestic producer prices whose proportions reflect the actual Hungarian relative export and import prices. Agricultural prices are at present excepted. Manufactured products are generally valued at export prices, raw materials and primary energy at import prices. This also means that a producing enterprise can raise its domestic price as a result of increased costs only if, and to the extent that, export prices have risen. It must reduce the price if export prices decline.

Thus, these prices are intended to lead to a profit which allows a wider assertion of commodity and monetary relationships. It is based on the financial interests of the enterprises, and results in the activities of the enterprises becoming differentiated on the basis of world market prices (i.e., in a more objective manner).

In the European socialist countries associated in the Council for Mutual Economic Assistance, however, three markets operate side by side: the domestic, the CMEA and the world market. This leads to particular incentives and regulations.

The CMEA market is characterized by bilateral balancing of commodity trade and by multilateral settlements. Certain tendencies can be observed: bilateral exchange should involve commodity patterns with almost identical capital requirements or labor intensity. The effort to reconcile the interests of the countries also appears in the so-called contract prices set in the CMEA commodities trade. In principle, these contract prices should reflect the average of world market prices over the preceding five years. At the same time changes in the terms of trade of any country should not exceed the extent laid down on a high (state-political) level; therefore, bilaterally fixed export and import prices of some products may temporarily deviate in either direction.

The problem of the commodity pattern is gaining increased importance also with the non-socialist world market. It is easier for the socialist countries to export food, raw materials, and typical semi-finished products to the industrially developed countries than machines and highly processed consumer goods. This is not always a problem of the technical quality of finished goods. It is partly a matter of market organization and, to no small extent, the result of protectionist measures taken against countries outside the area of Western integration.

Thus, the CMEA countries rely essentially on world market-prices. Moreover quantities above those fixed in interstate agreements have to be procured from non-socialist markets or paid for in convertible currencies. This makes it understandable that in conforming to world market prices, Hungarian practice bases itself on non-socialist market prices. In certain cases, the prices used may temporarily deviate from this principle, with supports being paid from the state budget.

But this in turn requires that the fiscal system bring about through taxes and subsidies that the enterprises earn *also in the CMEA trade*—transacted under different conditions—essentially the same incomes which they could realize from domestic sales in domestic prices. Thus the mentioned budgetary instruments are used as complements to the price system to bring about the economic conditions for meeting interstate export-import commitments.

Finally, certain taxes are used to ensure that sales on all three markets at least tend to result in *identical profitabilities,* and that procurement of basic materials, primary energy and some semi-finished products from all three markets should lead to *identical input cost.* (For machinery and finished goods there exists an autonomous tariff system—with gradual reductions coordinated within GATT—which does not apply to imports from the CMEA.)

9

For *consumer prices* the following principles were applied for a long time:

Relative consumer prices may be established autonomously and independently of relative producer prices. They should reflect a social (budgetary) preference for the consumption pattern of low-income strata. They should be kept as stable as possible, even independently of the movement of producer prices. Finally, the prices of consumer staples should, by all means, be set officially.

By 1975–79, when we started to build the higher world market prices of materials and energy into the domestic price system, the application of these principles in Hungary had led to a situation in which the producer price level inclusive of the commercial profit margin had risen above the consumer price level and a so-called "negative two-level price system" had emerged. In addition, relative consumer prices which differed greatly from relative inputs led to irrational individual consumption patterns. Analysis also showed that budgetary price subsidies intended to support low-income strata frequently led to relatively greater advantages for high-income strata because of their pattern and level of consumption.

For these reasons the pricing principle had been formulated that, over a longer period, gradually relative consumer prices should more accurately reflect relative producer prices: This means that the role of fiscal instruments to correct personal incomes through price subsidies has to be limited; that most consumer prices should immediately move together with producer prices, in harmony with the pricing and business policies of the selling firms; and that the scope of official price formation has to be reduced to about 50 percent of the volume of consumption, and even for these prices, any deviation from relative producer prices can be allowed only temporarily and for a shorter period.

Of course, changes in consumer prices, must always be expected to involve important social problems. Hence, social policy must be harmonized with fiscal policies.

10

Among the instruments of monetary policy the *exchange rate* plays an important role.

The *commercial rate of exchange* applied in Hungarian foreign trade is based on the average amount of Forint inputs at domestic prices needed to earn a unit of foreign exchange considering the actual commodity pattern of exports. The actual guidelines define the functions of commercial exchange rate policy as supporting domestic price policy and protecting against inflation, i.e., safeguarding relative price stability; establishing economic and particularly foreign trade equilibrium; improving the export efficiency and the commodity pattern of exports; and harmonizing these aims and any deviating requirements.

In every period, analysis of the actual economic situation and the main objectives of economic policy must determine which of these tasks should be given priority. At present, the primary objective is to moderate imported inflation by a gradual revaluation of the Forint, though this continually raises the efficiency requirements of exporters. Optimal harmonization of these two targets is a task with farreaching consequences for monetary policy at any time.

Changes in the exchange rate may become necessary for two reasons: first, because the average (domestic) valuation of the Forint vis-à-vis foreign currencies changes; and, second, because the relative exchange rates of individual convertible currencies change vis-à-vis each other on international money markets.

To establish the need for and the actual degree of changes in the exchange rate against convertible currencies, computations are made at regular intervals—quarterly or if necessary more frequently—considering the world market price changes of important basic materials and the actual foreign exchange prices of foreign trade deals.

In principle, the income effects of exchange rate measures must not be neutralized by fiscal policy instruments. The changes in exchange rates are not implemented at one stroke, shock-like, but gradually, at shorter intervals.

The convertible currencies and the national currencies of the CMEA member countries[5] have so-called non-commercial rates of exchange which are applied for example, to tourism and to certain payments not related to foreign trade. In May 1981, the commercial exchange rates of convertible currencies were 113.5 percent of the non-commercial rates. The two exchange rates are gradually being unified by revaluing the Forint in the case of the commercial rates and by devaluing it in the case of the non-commercial rates. The aim is to bring about a uniform exchange rate which is one of the pre-conditions for a later, narrowly interpreted, convertibility of the Forint currency.[6]

* * *

We have tried to sketch briefly the role of monetary and fiscal policies in promoting economic growth and to describe equally briefly the instruments applied in Hungarian practice. The substance of the latter is a system of control and management in which economy-wide planning relies on economic regulators and, as regards the instruments actually used, accords priority to the indirect ones.

But the control of the economic processes must not be left simply to some "automatism." In socialist countries, the government must pursue a definite structural policy. It has to determine centrally the ratio of consumption to accumulation, the relative investment shares of industry, agriculture and the tertiary sector. What is more: it is essential that the government should have clear ideas in these respects.

The task of financial policy is to implement these ideas to make the ratios real and to activate the price function—as well as the financial instruments regulating and promoting its operation—in the flexible shaping of the structure of production, in adjusting production to needs and, in general, in raising efficiency. These tasks are also reflected in the sixth five-year plan of the Hungarian People's Republic for 1981–85.

But unforeseeable effects have to be surely reckoned with in the course of plan-implementation, even if it is to be hoped that they will not be as big as the 1973–74 price explosion and the subsequent recession. Therefore, financial policy must be prepared to react to such changes as rapidly as possible, while trying to maintain the original targets and to assert as much as possible the principles of the regulatory system. The individual economic units and possibly even society as a whole must be enabled to adjust as quickly as possible to such changes and their implied requirements. Only thus can financial policy fulfill its tasks to lead the economy to an efficient equilibrium growth path.

Notes

[1]Henceforth we shall use the term "financial policy" as a synonym for "monetary and fiscal policy."

[2]In the terminology of socialist countries: "the law of value."

[3]The Hungarian legal system defines this term as the central budget, the budgets of the local councils, and state financial funds set aside for the solution of certain special tasks.

[4]By profitability the Hungarian practice means the ratio of profit to the value of fixed and circulating assets employed plus the wages expressing the use of live labor.

[5]The transferable rouble has only a commercial rate of exchange, while the national currencies of the CMEA member countries only have non-commercial rates of exchange.

[6]The unification of the commercial and non-commercial rates was carried out as of October 1, 1981. The rates are now quoted once a week to allow the necessary corrections to be carried out more frequently. The Forint was not on the whole revalued during 1982, and by the middle of 1982 it was devalued by about 5%.

References

Mises, L.: "Die Wirtschaftsrechnung im sozialistischen Gemeinwesen." *Archiv für Sozialwissenschaft*, April 1920. See also, F. A. Hayek, ed., *Collectivist Economic Planning. Critical Studies on the Possibility of Socialism* by N. G. Pierson, Ludwig v. Mises, Georg Halm, and Enrico Barone. London: Rutledge & Kegan Paul, Ltd., 1953, reprinted several times), where English translations of the Mises article and of other classical articles are reprinted. See also F. A. Hayek, "Socialist calculation: the competitive solution." *Economics*, May 1940.

Lange, O.: "On the Economic Theory of Socialism." *Review of Economic Studies*, October 1936; February 1937. Lerner, A. P.: "Economic Theory and Socialist Economy." *Review of Economic Studies*, October 1936.

Kantorovich, L. V.: *Ekonomichesky raschot nailuchshego ispolzovaniya resursov*. Moscow, 1959. Translated as *The Best Use of Economic Resources*, Harvard University Press, Cambridge, Mass., 1965. (Translated by P. F. Knightsfield, edited by G. Morton.)

Résumé

A partir d'une analyse de l'économie socialiste planifiée de la Hongrie, le rapport étudie les politiques fiscales, monétaires et financières qui peuvent efficacement contribuer à la croissance économique.

De nos jours, cette croissance est largement affectée par les exigences de l'équilibre économique international qui se traduisent par un bilan déficitaire de la balance des paiements pour un petit pays, pauvre en matières premières, susceptibles aux exportations. Le rapport passe en revue les résultats atteints et les problèmes qui restent à résoudre en Hongrie.

Parmi les méthodes appliquées au début de la planification conçue comme un ensemble de plans sectoriels assortis d'indices obligatoires, l'argent ne pouvait jouer qu'un rôle relativement passif. Le développement a été motivé par les circonstances externes et internes spécifiques du pays. La manière dont on cherche à résoudre le problème des prix sert bien souvent de base à une politique optimale, surtout si on remplace les indices obligatoires par des moyens économiques pour réaliser le plan national. Dans les pays socialistes, on reconnait de plus en plus la nécessité de faire valoir les relations qui existent entre produits, marché et investissement, c'est-à-dire une plus grande autonomie des entreprises, un intéressement plus grand au profit et la volonté de prendre des risques.

Les rapporteurs présentent les méthodes appliquées en Hongrie depuis la réforme de 1968, connue sous le nom de "Nouveau mécanisme économique" et surtout les interdépendances de la planification et de la régulation avec la création de marges de variations pour la réalisation du plan ainsi qu'un système de développement de la formation des prix.

La politique financière et la politique des prix doivent permettre aux entreprises de se développer en fonction de leur efficacité.

Le devoir de la politique fiscale est de centraliser dans le budget les moyens nécessaires, ce qui se fait par le système de la taxation, présenté en détails dans le rapport. Un des problèmes importants touchant à l'harmonisation de la politique fiscale et de la politique monétaire est le mode de financement des investissements. On cherche à élargir le recours au crédit et à assouplir les mouvements de capitaux.

La politique des cours de change joue un rôle important. A ce sujet, il faut remarquer le pas important, fait en Hongrie en 1981, avec l'introduction d'un cours unique pour le commerce et pour le tourisme, soumis à des ajustements fréquents en fonction des variations des marchés monétaires mondiaux.

On ne peut cependant pas laisser la direction des processus économiques à un automatisme quelconque; le Gouvernement joue un rôle important dans l'établissement d'une politique structurelle et la définition des proportions économiques les plus importantes qui servent ensuite de base à une politique financière qui, à son tour, doit s'adapter à des changements imprévus et se préparer à y trouver des solutions.

Tax Policy and Investment

*Robert Eisner**

Should We Encourage Investment?

There is a widespread view that more investment means more rapid growth, that government policy should promote investment, and that tax incentives are an efficient instrument to that end. Each of these propositions leaves room for doubt.

That all investment may safely be assumed to contribute to growth stems from several confusions. First, with positive marginal time preference and perfect information, maximizing agents will only abstain from additional current consumption if the marginal return to waiting is positive. Hence, in a proper Böhm-Bawerkian world, those investments in more round-about production which are undertaken will show a positive net marginal product, adding more to future output than their cost.

But all this follows from the assumptions of positive marginal time preference, correct information and freely maximizing agents. It does not follow that all or any investment not consistent with these assumptions will have a positive net marginal product and thereby contribute to growth. Suppose when every ditchdigger already has one shovel we divert some diggers from digging in order to invest in more shovels, so that each worker remaining in the ditch can have two shovels. We can readily see that net output will be reduced. Even after the initial expansion in the stock of shovels, more of our resources will go to replacing the larger numbers of shovels that rust away each year and less to digging the ditches. Clearly, less earth will be thrown.

*William R. Kenan Professor of Economics at Northwestern University, U.S.A. The author is grateful for the remarks of the discussants, and Ottó Gadó, chairman of the session, when this paper was presented at the Tokyo Congress.

Public Finance and Economic Growth. Proceedings of the 37th Congress of the International Institute of Public Finance. Tokyo, 1981, pp. 167–180

To generalize, given available technology and resources, additional investment may be wasted. This fact has sadly been recognized only belatedly in many nations where ill-conceived investment projects have brought varying degrees of economic disaster.

A second, perhaps more generally appreciated reservation about investment promoting growth is the widespread recognition that, given conventional neo-classical production functions with declining first derivatives (marginal products) for each of the factors and positive cross partial derivatives, devotion of a greater share of output to investment will only temporarily raise the rate of growth. The declining marginal product of capital as the proportion of capital rises, coupled with the need to devote greater and greater proportions of output to replacement and to maintaining any given factor ratio, will result ultimately in stabilization at a new, higher output path but one in which the rate of growth is no higher. And net output, as we have indicated above, may actually prove less.

In a planned economy, planners must make some decision as to how much of output to devote to current consumption and how much to capital accumulation. Investment should be promoted in all directions to the point but only to the point where its marginal product equals the marginal rate of time preference. Of course, utility functions differ and with only limited, feasible redistribution possibilities, planners' decisions may violate individual preferences. Many may not like having their current consumption reduced in order to make possible higher output and consumption later, particularly if the later higher consumption relates to different individuals.

But why should the rate of investment in an unplanned, market economy not be left to market decisions by firms and individuals attempting to maximize their wealth, profits and satisfaction? We may start with a presumption that a free, competitive market will, in the absence of externalities, reach a general Pareto-optimum. This optimum will, in principle, include a rate of investment such that no individual can derive more satisfaction from current *and* future consumption without some other individual deriving less. A government policy to promote investment must then seek its rationale in evidence of substantial failure of market forces to obtain optimality or in a social-welfare dictated choice among income distributions and Pareto-optima. In terms of the latter, there is little that we can say in general other than that, conceptually, we may think of two separate operations. The first of these redistributes wealth in the desired fashion. The second allocates over time the income and consumption flowing from that wealth on the basis of preferences expressed in competitive markets.

Distributional consideration aside, justification for government policy to promote investment may flow from any or all of the following:

A. lack of effectively clearing markets, which would include most conspicuously the case of involuntary unemployment;
B. externalities, such that there are benefits and/or costs to society which do not go into the individual calculus;
C. differences between individual and social risk;
D. elements of imperfect competition, oligopoly and oligopsony in product and factor markets;
E. biases in existing tax and fiscal policy which need correction.

Lack of effectively clearing markets most clearly calls for government action. When there is involuntary unemployment, all bets are off. Particularly where unemployment is due to inadequate aggregate demand, private investment is likely to be depressed. Recessions traditionally bring very sharp declines in business investment, associated with the development of excess capacity and lowered expectations of profits from expansion. It is urged in some quarters that investment should be stimulated in such situations in order to increase aggregate demand and employment. It would seem more appropriate, however, generally to redress the balance between aggregate demand and aggregate supply by measures more neutral to the allocation of resources. Business investment is particularly difficult to raise during a recession, but readily self-sustained in a boom.

The matter of externalities cuts both ways. The very fact that we are not a slave economy externalizes to the firm a good deal of labor costs. Individual firms pay only a small part of the social costs of maintaining workers replaced by machines. Firms may thus invest more on the basis of their own private calculus than is warranted in a total social maximization. But conversely, investment may generate jobs and benefits for entire neighborhoods and other firms which make its value greater than perceived by the original investor.

To the extent, as is generally presumed, that individuals and firms are risk averse, the degree of competition itself may be negatively related to the amount of investment. The larger the enterprise, the more may risks be pooled. In principle then, risks for society as a whole are likely to be less than those faced by individual entrepreneurs. The prospects for investment by individual firms may depend upon the uncertain action of other firms. Each firm may hold back when it would be profitable for all to proceed if they knew they would be operating in tandem. And while greater size of firm may permit reduction of risks, thus encouraging investment, higher degrees of monopoly in particular markets may lead to less than competitive output and hence discourage investment.

Finally, a major case for government intervention to encourage investment is frequently made out of the argument that the existing tax system discourages investment. Here reference is to income taxes in general, which by taxing the return to capital (along with other returns) are alleged to discourage saving. In the United States, the "double taxation" of dividends, it is argued, further reduces the after-tax return to capital and makes it more costly to the firm. But taxation of income with complete loss offset reduces risk and hence may encourage investment, as pointed out by Tobin (1958) and Gordon (1981).

Some claim that inflation has raised the rate of taxation of business income and reduced the after-tax return on investment.[1] These results stem from reduction in the present value of depreciation allowances for tax purposes with the higher interest rates associated with inflation, taxation of swollen profits on inventory which do not reflect current production, and taxation of nominal capital gains which, in a period of inflation, do not correspond to real capital gains. Taxation of nominal gains may then constitute a tax on capital itself.

There are generally a number of existing offsets to these investment-discouraging effects of the tax system, such that current government policy in most countries may on balance encourage business investment. In the United States, these offsets include: the deductibility for tax purposes of swollen nominal interest payments; the exemption of accrued capital gains from taxation until they are realized and then the exclusion of substantial components of even realized gains from taxable income; the exclusion from taxation of saving itself as well as much of the income from saving via private pension funds and nonprofit institutions; repeated accelerations of depreciation for tax purposes over the last quarter century; and the institution of the investment tax credit applying to the bulk of investment in equipment and indeed to considerable amounts of structures (as classified in national income and product accounts), particularly in public utilities. The combination of inflation and debt-financing with accelerated depreciation, the investment tax credit, non-taxation of capital gains and tax-deductibility of interest payments is such that business income taxes can turn into an investment subsidy, as pointed out by Hall (1981) and Chirinko and King (1981).

Aside from specific intervention focused on investment, general government policy has profound effects. First, provision of fiscal and monetary policies that keep the economy at or close to full employment is a major prop to investment. The stability and smoothness of the aggregate demand path will also encourage investment by reducing risk. Inflation, while in some ways encouraging investment in assets which would at least maintain their real value, may discourage investment to the extent that it increases the variance of relative prices and perceived risk. While government taxation may in some instances discourage effort and reduce supply, of labor as well as saving, government expenditures may frequently prove essential in providing the overhead capital, intermediate services, complementary factors and general climate essential for business investment.

The Efficacy of Tax Incentives

If government action to influence the rate of investment in a market economy is deemed desirable, the question remains whether traditional tax policy instruments or any possible tax policy instruments are effective or efficient. The record of existing tax incentives for investment is at best mixed. Presumed incentives have been substantial in the United Kingdom but rates of investment and growth there have been among the lowest in the world among developed countries. In recent work with Robert Chirinko for the Office of Tax Analysis of the United States Treasury, I have suggested that large scale econometric models can correctly show only very limited effectiveness for specific investment tax incentives.[2]

Some basic conceptual issues regarding determinants of investment are not hard to find. First, we must be careful to distinguish among levels of the firm, industry and economy as a whole. While one firm or industry can increase investment at the expense of other firms or industries, in the entire economy more capital accumulation requires less consumption, more output, less output devoted to intermediate product or services, or more net gifts or loans from the rest of the world. More business investment in plant and equipment can also come at the expense of other forms of investment, by government or by individuals in housing. More business investment as defined in the traditional national income and product accounts can come at the expense of investment in human capital, knowledge, and research and development.

Under conditions of less than full employment, there may be substantial opportunities for increases in employment and output which would both stimulate and make room for more investment. Under conditions of full employment, increases in the supply or efficiency of the various factors of production may also increase output and bring about more investment. Beyond this, more investment requires more saving out of existing output, that is, less consumption, or less diversion of resources to intermediate product, among which we may include, for example, national defense and advertising.[3]

It has been widely if not always recognized that the major factors in variation of investment and major opportunities for changing the rate of investment relate to general levels of employment and output and their growth. Gross private domestic investment fell 85 percent in the United States from 1929 to 1933. The recession of 1974–75 caused a drop of some 17 percent in real, nonresidential business investment in plant and equipment. Recessions, whether endogenous or brought on by anti-inflationary government policies, have been major depressants of investment.

Gross private domestic investment, it should also be noted, grew by 155 percent from 1945 to 1946 as resources were released from war production. And Japan, which has had a relatively high proportion of its product devoted to investment, has had a very tiny proportion devoted to military expenditures.

In a full employment economy, with a fixed proportion of resources taken by government, private investment will depend essentially on the proportion of income saved. In traditional terms, this will involve the intersection of schedules of the supply and demand for saving, the latter denoted as investment demand. While some recent work has claimed substantial elasticity in the supply of saving with respect to its rate of return,[4] the traditional and more widely buttressed view is that under conditions of full employment *aggregate* saving is a highly constant ratio of aggregate income.[5] The tax system may channel more or less saving in areas such as residential housing or other assets with opportunities for little taxed or untaxed capital gains, but the aggregate of saving is largely determined by the desire to provide for retirement income and bequests, the growth and age distribution of population and income, and risk and uncertainty, particularly with respect to length of life.

Real rates of interest or rates of return are viewed as having substitution and income or wealth effects which move in different directions. Thus, a higher rate of return will offer a substitution effect in favor of saving but an income or wealth effect in favor of consumption. Most research has shown no clear evidence that either effect dominates. If the supply of saving is inelastic with respect to its rate of return, tax policy focused specifically on investment will have little effect in a full employment economy. As firms respond to the policy by trying to invest more they will, ideally, raise rates of interest and return on saving. But if this higher return does not in fact generate more saving, the higher rates of interest will only serve to cancel the effects of the tax incentive on investment demand.

Less than ideally, the increase in investment demand generated by tax incentives may, if a greater supply of saving is not forthcoming, create excess demand and greater inflation. This could conceivably generate more saving as it reduces the real value of the government debt held by the public. With lesser perceived wealth in the form of this government debt, the public may then endeavor to save more by consuming less.

Gross investment may usefully be viewed as the sum of investment to replace the depreciating stock of existing capital, investment to fit a changing mix of total production including new products and old products in new places, investment to embody technological change and effect new processes of production, investment to increase the durability of capital or the ratio of capital to other factors of production, and investment to provide additional capital stock to produce additional output.

Investment demand is then generated by firms striving to maximize profits or, more rigorously, to maximize their present values, that is the present values of the streams of expected future profits. This maximization must be accomplished subject to the constraints of a production function and expected future production functions relating output to inputs of all factors, current and expected prices or demand and supply curves for output and all inputs, and costs of adjustment in changing factor inputs and outputs over time. Given appropriate information as to all of these, firms decide their paths of capital stocks and hence investment, and alter both as new information dictates.

This formulation indicates, alongside parameters of functions of production, supply, and demand, the critical role of expectations. Investment is a particularly forward looking activity, the justification for which rests heavily upon future developments. Major difficulties in understanding and predicting investment behavior have thus related to the difficulty of knowing even current expectations regarding critical variables, let alone either the future path of expectations or how they will be altered by changes in events or policies.

Attempts to estimate investment functions have involved a variety of necessarily simplified specifications. Many have focused on the acceleration principle, relating investment demand to past or expected changes in the rate of demand for output. A related role of demand has been found in the utilization of existing capacity. Some formulations, in varying degrees, have introduced profits or liquidity, either directly or as a catalyst or felicitator for other determinants of investment.

Most common forms of investment functions have viewed investment as the sum of replacement of capital and the distributed lag response or adjustment of capital to desired or equilibrium levels. Equilibrium capital stocks in turn depend upon expected demand for output, taken explicitly or implicitly as a function of capital and labor inputs, and the relative prices of output and capital or of capital and labor. At a fairly aggregative level, this equilibrium capital stock is then usually written as

$$K^* = f(P,c,Y), \tag{1}$$

where P = the price of output,
c = the rental price or user cost of capital,
and Y = output.

As written, equation (1) abstracts from the role of expectations. Current and expected values of variables are implicitly assumed to be the same. The relation between P and c presumably encompasses the relative price of capital and other factor inputs. Some formulations substitute w, a measure of the cost of labor, for P.[6]

The partial derivatives of K^* are taken to be positive with respect to P and Y, and negative with respect to c. In his original "neoclassical" formulation of the investment function, Jorgenson (1963) assumed, on the basis of a Cobb-Douglas production function and other stipulations, that the demand for capital took the particular form:

$$K^* = \beta(P/c)Y. \tag{2}$$

This formulation generates certain special and strong effects of tax policy on investment. It makes the equilibrium capital stock inversely proportional to its rental price, c (and directly proportional to output, Y). The effects of investment tax policies on the equilibrium capital stock are thus directly proportional to their effects upon the rental price, c. The amount and durability (or depreciation rate) of capital determine replacement investment. The rest of gross investment is determined in a distributed lag adjustment process stemming from changes in P, c, and Y.

A somewhat more general formulation might be built from a more general, CES (constant elasticity of substitution) production function which implies constraints neither of unitary elasticity of substitution nor constant returns to scale.[7] We find then

$$K^* = \beta(P/c)^{\sigma}Y^{r}, \tag{3}$$

where σ is the elasticity of demand for capital with respect to the relative price of output and capital and r is the elasticity of demand for capital with respect to output. (This last elasticity will be more than, equal to, or less than unity as the returns to scale are decreasing, constant, or increasing.)

Often in separate investment studies as well as in the investment equations of large scale macroeconomic econometric models, tax policy enters directly in its effects on c, the rental price of capital, or on profits or liquidity. My analysis with Chirinko of the role of investment tax parameters in major American econometric models concluded that indicated effects "depended overwhelmingly on how these parameters entered the investment equations."[8] The tax parameters were sometimes embodied in liquidity variables or in cost-of-capital terms and elasticities of substitution were assumed large or estimated to be large because they were tied to other variables correlated with investment. Changes in tax parameters then seemed to have large effects on investment.

These models varied significantly, however, in critical specifications and hence in results. We reestimated the investment equations after respecifying them without what we felt to be extreme and arbitrary assumptions. We then found all of the models showing relatively modest effects of the various tax incentives.

We questioned the applicability of any of the models, though, to predicting the effects of changes in tax parameters. All contained the implicit assumption that changes in the cost of capital and other variables in the historical period of estimation were associated with changes in expectations in the same manner as would be changes related to tax parameters.

With this caveat, my own conclusion as to the indicated effects of tax incentives such as acceleration of depreciation or the investment tax credit is that a dollar of tax reduction will generate no more than 40 cents of added investment. This is hardly a cost-effective way of encouraging business investment.

More cost-effective tax measures can certainly be found. These would relate essentially to affecting the relative price of capital at the margin. For one thing, potentialities for intertemporal substitution would be realized. Current investment could be stimulated with no loss of tax revenues, and a future gain, by announcing now future reductions in tax incentives.

But these and other devices could be most effective if they entailed little or no tax benefits for investment that would be undertaken without such benefits but very substantial incentives to induce additional investment. Thus, for example, instead of the 10 percent investment tax credit in the United States on all eligible "equipment" investment, we could have a tax credit or subsidy of 40 percent, concentrated on investment above the average of the previous three years or on investment net of 120 percent of depreciation allowances. And for maximum effectiveness, its duration could be completely uncertain.[9]

Further, to include all firms, it may be important to use a subsidy rather than a tax credit. Large numbers of companies in the United States, and very large proportions of smaller companies, already report no taxable income. Investment tax credits and accelerated depreciation offer no direct advantage to these firms and hence little incentive for more investment.

Conclusion—Evaluation in a Broader Perspective

In a market economy, tax and general fiscal policy can contribute most to investment by maintaining relatively full employment. Investment is sharply less and clearly sub-optimal with depressions, recessions and substantial unemployment.

Specific tax policies for investment in the United States and, possibly in varying degrees in other countries, have not been cost-effective. They have affected the distribution of taxation and after-tax income considerably more than they have affected investment.

Measures can be devised to raise the ratio of added investment to reduction in taxes but they raise certain fundamental questions regarding consequences for productivity and growth. To the extent that these measures are successful, will they not bring about precisely the additional investment which was not deemed sufficiently profitable or productive without special tax benefits? If we want additional investment, is that the additional investment we want?

A 10 percent investment tax credit, for example, may be expected to induce firms to move down their marginal efficiency of investment curve to the point where they are making investment for which the present value of expected future returns aside from the tax advantage is only 90 percent of the cost of investment. A 40 percent marginal tax credit, such as I suggested above, would induce firms to carry investment to the point where the present value of expected non-tax-related returns is only 60 percent of the cost of investment. This is likely to mean that much of our investment will entail a sacrifice of more current consumption than the increase in future consumption it makes possible. This may well be a prescription for reductions in net output, as the depreciation (and replacement requirements) for such investment will exceed its contribution to gross output. This then will contribute not to growth but to an actual reduction in new output.

Recalling the possible justifications for government policies to promote investment, we may question their applicability to business plant and equipment. In general, profit-maximizing firms should ordinarily be expected to acquire the additional plant and equipment which they deem profitable. What appears profitable to firms should be all investment which promises a real rate of return and hence contribution to productivity and growth equal to or in excess of the rate of preference for current over future consumption. While there may well be instances in the case of individual firms, industries or regions where investment in excess of the resultant of individual firm decisions is warranted, the case for general promotion of private business plant and equipment investment has not, in terms of our fundamental criteria, been established.

Capital formation, however, includes far more than what we traditionally measure in business spending for plant and equipment or even, in the somewhat wider but still narrow category, in the United States, of gross private domestic investment. Capital formation properly includes not only business acquisition of plant and equipment and additional inventories but investment in tangible capital by government and government enterprises, households and nonprofit institutions. A new automobile providing additional transportation services may properly be viewed as investment whether it is acquired by business, by government or by households. Government construction of roads or airport runways are as much investment, and in some instances more productive, than acquisition of additional vehicles and aircraft by trucking firms and airlines.

But further, expenditures for research and development and the development of natural resources entail the accumulation of capital, and frequently more productive capital than the acquisition of additional tangible goods. And most important, investment in health and education and the basic capacity and skills of human labor involves some of the most fundamental accumulation of the capital necessary for output and economic growth. In extensive work in developing a "total incomes system of accounts," I have found that narrowly defined business investment in plant and equipment has been no more than some 14 percent of total capital formation in the United States in recent years.[10]

Should tax policy focus on promoting that 14 percent while in varying degrees neglecting the rest? This question is all the more pointed if we recognize that while profit-maximizing private business can be expected to have every interest in adequate investment in its own plant and equipment, there is reason to expect underinvestment in other forms of capital.

Research and development are widely, and I believe correctly, viewed as having substantial externalities. It is not possible for individual firms or enterprises to keep to themselves for long the fruits of research. Without subsidy or socialization of research and development, there is every reason to expect insufficient private investment.

With regard to the mass of human investment, it is not likely to pay private business to invest adequately precisely because, in a nonslave society, capital in human beings cannot generally be bought and sold. In its decisions to train and offer job experience to new workers, a firm must balance costs against probable returns over the period when the worker is likely to stay with the firm. Benefits to the worker and to other firms and society at large cannot be taken into account in the individual firm calculus. This cuts all the more cruelly in decisions regarding jobs for those with less than average skills or with no skills or experience at all: disproportionately youths, women and, in the United States, blacks and other minorities.

And again, precisely because there is no market for human capital, opportunities for individuals to borrow and invest in themselves are greatly limited. Without government or some other form of social support, there is reason to expect chronic underinvestment in human capital and intangible capital generally. It is there that tax policy or other government policy to promote investment can best be directed.

We may close on one final note related to the contrasting properties of the capital invested in business plant and equipment and that in human beings. Tax reductions and incentives to promote business investment will increase the income and wealth of the owners of business capital, generally the richest members of society. One perhaps need not be overly cynical to believe that at least some of the substantial support for such measures among business interests and the relatively wealthy is related to this fact.

Greater investment in human capital, to the contrary, entails additions to income and wealth of broad masses of the population. If it is concentrated among those who have been most lacking in human capital, it will not only add to total output but add most to the incomes of the relatively poor. Tax policies and general fiscal measures not for business investment in plant and equipment but for research and development, basic skills and training of workers and management, and investment in all forms of human capital may properly follow from goals of optimal growth and distribution of economic well-being.

Notes

[1]See Feldstein (1980).

[2]Chirinko and Eisner (1981a and 1981b).

[3]In the official national income and product accounts most of national defense spending, along with all other government expenditures for goods and services, is counted as final product, but current expenditures by business for advertising are not.

[4]See Boskin (1978).

[5]See, for example, Denison (1958) and David and Scadding (1974).

[6]It is not always clear at what level this formulation is intended to apply. At the level of the firm, the assumption of perfect competition would preclude the role of output as an exogenous variable; under perfect competition, the prices of outputs and inputs would be exogenous and the quantities of outputs and inputs would be determined endogenously. At the level of the industry or the economy as a whole, however, neither price of output nor the rental price of capital would be viewed as entirely exogenous.

[7]See Eisner and Nadiri (1968 and 1970) and Eisner (1969).

[8]Chirinko and Eisner (1981a), p. 24.

[9]Assume that firms knew a marginal credit on, say, investment in excess of average investment of the past three years, would continue. Assume further that planned current and future investments were already higher than past investment. Then the incentive to invest currently would be reduced by the consequent expectation of loss of the credit on future investment. Thus, if k were the nominal rate of marginal credit, the effective rate in present value terms would be

$$k* = k[1 - \{(1 + i)^{-1} + (1 + i)^{-2} + (1 + i)^{-3}\}/3]$$

where i = the rate of discount for future losses of the credit.

[10]Eisner (1980), pp. 227–228.

References

Boskin, M. 1978. "Taxation, Saving and the Rate of Interest." *Journal of Political Economy*, Vol. 86, No. 2, Part 2 (April): S3–S27.

Chirinko, R. S. and R. Eisner. 1981a. "The Effects of Tax Policies on Investment in Macroeconometric Models: Full Model Simulations." OTA Paper 46, U.S. Department of the Treasury, Office of Tax Analysis, Washington, D.C. Published in abbreviated version as "Tax Policy and Investment in Major U.S. Macroeconomic Econometric Models," *Journal of Public Economics* 20, No. 2 (March, 1983): 139–66.

———. 1981b. "The Effects of Tax Parameters on the Investment Equations in Macroeconomic Econometric Models." OTA Paper 47. U.S. Department of the Treasury, Office of Tax Analysis, Washington, D.C. Published in Marshall E. Blume, Jean Crockett and Paul Taulman, eds., Economic Activity and Finance (Ballinger, Cambridge, Mass. 1982): 25–83.

——— and S. R. King. 1981. "Inflation and Investment Incentives in Conventional and Extended Neoclassical Models." Northwestern University.

David, P. A. and J. L. Scadding. 1974. "Private Savings: Ultrarationality, Aggregation and 'Dension's Law.'" *Journal of Political Economy* 82, No. 2, Part 1 (March/April): 225–49.

Denison, E. F. 1958. "A Note on Private Saving." *Review of Economics and Statistics* 40 (August): 261–67.

Eisner, R. 1969. "Tax Policy and Investment Behavior: Comment." *American Economic Review* 59 (June): 379–88.

———. 1980. "Total Income, Total Investment, and Growth." *American Economic Review* 70 (May): 225–31.

——— and M. I. Nadiri. 1968. "On Investment Behavior and Neo-Classical Theory." *Review of Economics and Statistics* 50 (August): 369–82.

———. 1970. "Once More on that 'Neoclassical Theory of Investment Behavior.'" *Review of Economics and Statistics* 52 (May): 216–22.

Feldstein, M. 1980. "Inflation, Tax Rules and Investment: Some Econometric Evidence." National Bureau of Economic Research Working Paper No. 577. Cambridge, Mass.

Gordon, R. H. 1981. "Taxation of Corporate Capital Income: Tax Revenues vs. Tax Distortions." Bell Laboratories, Murray Hill, New Jersey.

Hall, R. E. 1981. "Tax Treatment of Depreciation, Capital Gains, and Interest in an Inflationary Economy." Working Papers in Economics No. E-80-6. Domestic Studies Program, Hoover Institution and Stanford University, Stanford, California.

Jorgenson, D. W. 1963. "Capital Theory and Investment Behavior." *American Economic Review* 53 (May): 247–59.

Tobin, J. 1958. "Liquidity Preference as Behavior Towards Risk." *Review of Economic Studies* 25 (February): 65–86.

Résumé

On a cherché une justification à la politique gouvernementale de promotion des investissements sans vraiment la trouver dans le chômage involontaire, les externalités, les différences entre risque social et individuel, une compétition imparfaite, ou des distorsions dans les impôts et la politique fiscale en cours. Les interactions de l'inflation et du système fiscal sont telles que à l'opposé de l'argumentation habituelle on peut dire qu'il est probable que la politique gouvernementale encourage déjà dans bien des pays l'investissement des entreprises. Et qu'accroître l'investissement au-delà des taux déterminés par les forces de marché peut ne pas ajouter à la croissance ou à la production nette.

Des incitations fiscales particulières à l'investissement, y compris aux Etats-Unis, ne semblent pas efficaces. Des pertes majeures dans les revenus fiscaux et des changements dans la distribution du revenu s'effectuent avec un faible accroissement consécutif de l'investissement. Cela peut relever des inélasticités relatives de la demande pour le capital et de l'offre d'épargne.

Ces dernières années l'investissement des entreprises en installations et matériel n'a pas dépassé 14% de la formation totale de capital aux Etats-Unis. On peut argumenter en faveur d'accroissements de cet investissement défini de façon plus large, et qu'y comprend celui de l'état, des ménages et du capital intangible et humain.

Substitution and Technical Progress: A Putty-Clay Model for The Netherlands

S. K. Kuipers
*A. H. van Zon**

1. Introduction

In 1974 Den Hartog and Tjan published their famous paper in which they developed their empirical vintage model of the private sector of the Dutch economy. [Den Hartog and Tjan, 1974]. Their purpose was to show that the rising unemployment in the early seventies was not caused by stagnating aggregate demand but by wages which grew too fast and investments which grew too slow. The model was of the clay-clay variety, which means that neither *ex ante* nor *ex post* capital can be substituted for labour. Capital can be substituted for labour only in an indirect way: an acceleration of real wage growth will induce a faster scrapping of old machinery and hence, given the higher labour productivity of younger vintages due to embodied labour-augmenting technical progress, it will induce a rise in the growth rate of the overall capital intensity.

The Den Hartog-Tjan (1974) paper gave rise to a hearty discussion on the use of empirical vintage models in the Netherlands. In this discussion two main trends can be distinguished. In the first trend Den Hartog's and Tjan's basic approach was accepted, but criticism was levelled at some specific points, as for instance: the estimation method, the surviving fractions assumed, the bias in technical prog-

*University of Groningen, The Netherlands. Part of this research has been made possible by a grant of the Netherlands Organization for the Advancement of Pure Research (ZWO) and the National Programme of Labour Market Research (NPAO). An extended version of this paper is published in *De Economist*, CXXX (1982) under the title, "Output and Employment Growth in the Netherlands in the Postwar Period: A Putty-Clay Approach."

Public Finance and Economic Growth. Proceedings of the 37th Congress of the International Institute of Public Finance. Tokyo, 1981, pp. 181–206

ress, the sensitivity of the model to changes in the parameter values and the scrapping condition. [For instance, Muysken and Van Ardenne (1976); De Klerk, Van der Laan and Thio (1977); Driehuis (1979); Kuipers and Bosch (1976).] The second trend of criticism was directed against the philosophy underlying the vintage approach according to which the production structure of an economy can be described by a vintage model, as well as against the conclusion that the slowdown of employment growth since the late sixties should be attributed to a growth of real wages. [Driehuis and Van der Zwan (1977).]

Den Hartog and Tjan rejected the latter kind of criticism. [Den Hartog and Weitenberg (1977); Den Hartog and Tjan (1980), esp. pp. 129–130.] Some of the former criticism was accepted however. This led to a revised version (Den Hartog and Tjan (1976)), which differed mainly from the 1974 version in that it explicitly accepted the distinction between capacity output and capacity demand for labour on the one hand and actual output and actual employment on the other. This version became the production block in the Dutch medium-term model Vintaf II.[1]

It is somewhat curious that one feature of the Den Hartog-Tjan vintage model has hardly been challenged in so intensive a discussion as has been carried on in the Netherlands in the seventies. This is the assumption of complementarity ex ante.[2] One of the consequences of this assumption is a rather high estimate of embodied labour-augmenting technical progress of about 5 percent a year according to the Den Hartog-Tjan analysis. [See also Sandee (1976), p. 4.] Although the question whether the growth of average labour productivity in the newest vintage is caused by technical progress only or by a combination of both technical progress and substitution is an interesting one in itself, it is also important from the point of view of a right understanding of the observed slowdown of employment growth since the late sixties. If for instance, contrary to what Den Hartog and Tjan assume, ex ante substitution has been a real phenomenon, then, consequent on the moderate real wage rise in the inter war years and in the fifties, average labour productivity in the pre-1960 vintages will be lower than Den Hartog and Tjan estimated. The consequence is an earlier scrapping of the prewar and the early postwar vintages, which may imply a lower capacity demand for labour in the sixties and in the seventies. This tendency is still strengthened by the fast growth of average labour productivity in the post-1960 vintages, consequent on the fast growth of real wages in this period. Scrapping of vintages in the eighties may however show some retardation as the result of this relatively fast growth.

The aim of this paper is to test the assumption of ex ante complementarity by developing a putty-clay vintage model for the Netherlands. The main features of this model are:

(a) an ex ante constant returns to scale CES-technology. In this respect it is more general than other empirical putty-clay models which assume an ex ante Cobb-Douglas technology. [For instance,: Baum, Görzig and Kirner (1971); Mizon (1974); Malcolmson and Prior (1979).] Sandee's model should be mentioned as an exception;
(b) complementarity ex post;
(c) embodied labour—and capital—augmenting technical progress;
(d) a variable life time of oldest equipment. Vintages are scrapped as soon as they no longer yield any rent. This feature is in correspondence with the Dutch vintage literature. It makes this model more general than most other putty-clay models in which the life time of oldest equipment is assumed to be fixed and equal to the planned life time at the moment of the investment decision;[3]
(e) the production technique is chosen in such a way that the net present value over a fixed expected life time is maximized. Although the assumption of a fixed expected life time as such is still rather restrictive, it is more general than the assumption made in other studies in which the expected life time is assumed to be equal to the constant life of (oldest) equipment, [e.g., Baum et al. (1971), Mizon (1974).] or to be one year (myopic foresight). [Sandee (1976).] It would be more satisfactory from a theoretical point of view to assume that the entrepreneurs maximize the net present value of their firms over an infinite time horizon.[4] Such a procedure implies that decisions with respect to present investments are not taken independently from those taken with respect to future generations of equipment. An important characteristic of this procedure is that the optimal expected life time of equipment is determined simultaneously with the optimal production technique. [e.g., Malcolmsom and Prior (1979).] The drawback of this approach however is that it makes high demands upon the nature of the information entrepreneurs have about developments in the remote future. As this information will probably be quite limited and moreover very uncertain, one may question whether entrepreneurs will indeed look so far ahead. As a consequence one may ask oneself whether entrepreneurs will not restrict themselves to the investment under consideration by maximizing the net present value of this investment over an exogenously determined expected life time. These considerations underlie the assumption made in this paper of maximization of the net present value of investments over a fixed expected life time.

In the following sections it will be shown that there is reason to doubt the assumption of ex ante complementarity. The elasticity of substitution also turns out to be substantially lower than unity. A Cobb-Douglas specification must therefore probably be rejected too. However, a rejection of ex ante complementarity does not mean that the Den Hartog-Tjan diagnosis with respect to the slowdown of employment growth since the late sixties is denied. Both analyses lead to the conclusion that this phenomenon must be attributed to too fast a growth of real wages and to too slow a growth of investments. With respect to the sixties there is a difference however: contrary to the Den Hartog-Tjan analysis, this analysis does include merely a few years of structural labour shortage (capital abundance).

The plan of this paper is as follows. In section 2 the model and its estimation procedure are described. The estimation results are presented in section 3. Section 4 is devoted to an interpretation of the postwar growth performance in the light of the estimation results. The consequences of these results for economic policy are discussed in section 5, while some concluding remarks are made in section 6.

2. The Model and Its Estimation

The Model

Production Structure. The ex ante production structure can be described by a constant return to scale CES-production function:

$$X_{\tau\tau} = [A\{(1 + \mu_n)^{\tau} N_{\tau\tau}h_{\tau}^{\delta_1}\}^{-\rho} + B\{(1 + \mu_i)^{\tau} I_{\tau\tau}h_{\tau}^{\delta_2}\}^{-\rho}]^{-1/\rho} \qquad (2.1)$$

The symbols have the following meaning:

$X_{\tau\tau}$ capacity output of vintage τ in period τ;
$N_{\tau\tau}$ capacity demand for labour of vintage τ in period τ;
$I_{\tau\tau}$ gross investments in equipment of vintage τ;
h_{τ} index of working hours in period τ;
μ_n embodied labour-augmenting technical progress;
μ_i embodied capital-augmenting technical progress;
ρ substitution parameter: $\sigma = 1/(1 + \rho)$ (σ is the elasticity of substitution);
A, B, δ_1, δ_2 parameters.

Whereas the entrepreneurs can choose the most profitable production technique ex ante, it is true that, ex post, because the investment decision has been taken, the technical coefficients are fixed. They can only change as the consequence of a change in labour time and equipment-operating time on the one hand and disembodied technical progress on the other. Because clay-clay studies reveal technical progress to be mainly embodied[5] and as an assumption of both embodied and disembodied technical progress will increase the complexity of the estimation of the model considerably, technical progress will be assumed to be only embodied. In this respect one modification will however be made: in order to prevent the possibility that the model is unable to explain economic growth in the early postwar years, whereas explaining it in the other years of the postwar period—an anomaly which is well-known in the Dutch clay-clay literature—it is assumed that in the fifties there was embodied and disembodied technical progress, where the latter is Hicks-neutral.[6]

The production structure ex post can now be described in the following way:

$$\frac{X_{\tau t}}{I_{\tau t}} = \left(\frac{h_t}{h_\tau}\right)^{\delta_2} (1 + \gamma)^{t-\tau} \frac{X_{\tau\tau}}{I_{\tau\tau}} \qquad \tau \in V_t \tag{2.2}$$

$$\frac{X_{\tau t}}{N_{\tau t}} = \left(\frac{h_t}{h_\tau}\right)^{\delta_1} (1 + \gamma)^{t-\tau} \frac{X_{\tau\tau}}{N_{\tau\tau}} \qquad \tau \in V_t \tag{2.3}$$

$$I_{\tau t} = \Omega_{t-\tau} I_{\tau\tau} \qquad \tau \in V_t \tag{2.4}$$

The meaning of the symbols is as follows:

- $X_{\tau t}$ capacity output of vintage τ in period t;
- $N_{\tau t}$ capacity labour demand of vintage τ in period t;
- $I_{\tau t}$ equipment of vintage τ in period t;
- h_t index of working hours in period t;
- V_t set of vintages that yield a non-negative rent in period t;
- $\Omega_{t-\tau}$ technical survival fraction of equipment of vintage τ in period t;
- γ rate of Hicks-neutral disembodied technical progress.

Equation (2.4) defines the value of equipment of vintage τ in period t corrected for technical depreciation. Substitution of equation (2.3) in equation (2.2) yields:

$$\frac{N_{\tau t}}{I_{\tau t}} = \left(\frac{h_t}{h_\tau}\right)^{\delta_2 - \delta_1} \frac{N_{\tau\tau}}{I_{\tau\tau}} \qquad \tau \in V_t \tag{2.5}$$

The equation shows that the capital intensity of vintage τ changes only if the change in the number of operating hours of equipment and the change in working time have different influences on output ($\delta_2 \neq \delta_1$).

From equations (2.2), (2.5) and (2.4) follows:

$$X_{\tau t} = \Omega_{t-\tau} \left(\frac{h_t}{h_\tau}\right)^{\delta_2} (1+\gamma)^{t-\tau} X_{\tau\tau} \quad \tau \in V_t \tag{2.6}$$

$$N_{\tau t} = \Omega_{t-\tau} \left(\frac{h_t}{h_\tau}\right)^{\delta_2-\delta_1} N_{\tau\tau} \quad \tau \in V_t \tag{2.7}$$

Choice of the Production Technique. Entrepreneurs are assumed to choose that production technique which maximizes the net present value of the investments over the expected life time. Net present value (NPV_τ) is defined as:

$$NPV_\tau = \sum_{t=\tau}^{\tau+\theta_1-1} \{(X_{\tau t} - w^e_{\tau t} N_{\tau t})(1+r)^{-(t-\tau)}\} - I_{\tau\tau} \tag{2.8}$$

in which

θ_1 expected life time of equipment;
$w^e_{\tau t}$ in period τ expected real wage rate in period t;
r discount rate.

For the sake of simplicity the expected life time of equipment is assumed to be constant. In a world with imperfect foresight it will generally differ from the actual life time. In this world entrepreneurs are forced to make an independent forecast of the life time. As far as they are risk-averters, they will probably try to prevent an overestimation of the life time. For this reason one may in fact expect the life time to be underestimated. Although it is not the same, the view that an expected life time is independent of the actual life time resembles somewhat the idea originating with empirical investment theory that entrepreneurs judge investment projects according to the pay-off period. In this respect different criteria are possible: entrepreneurs may be assumed to strive for a minimization of the pay-off period, or they may be assumed to decide to invest if the pay-off period does not exceed a critical one.[7] The underpinnings of these hypotheses are exactly the same as those of the assumption that the expected life time is assessed independently of the actual life time, namely the lack of information in an uncertain world. In the following pages the expected life time will also be indicated as the planning period.

Substitution of equations (2.6) and (2.7) in equation (2.8) yields:

$$NPV_\tau = X_{\tau\tau}\Sigma_1 - N_{\tau\tau}\Sigma_2 - I_{\tau\tau}, \tag{2.9}$$

in which:

$$\Sigma_1 = \sum_{t=\tau}^{\tau+\theta_1-1} \Omega_{t-\tau} \left(\frac{h^e_{\tau t}}{h_\tau}\right)^{\delta_2} (1+\gamma)^{t-\tau}(1+r)^{-(t-\tau)} \tag{2.10}$$

$$\Sigma_2 = \sum_{t=\tau}^{\tau+\theta_1-1} \Omega_{t-\tau} \left(\frac{h^e_{\tau t}}{h_\tau}\right)^{\delta_2-\delta_1} w^e_{\tau t}(1+r)^{-(t-\tau)}, \tag{2.11}$$

where $h^e_{\tau t}$ is the expectation of the index of working hours for period t formulated in period τ.

Maximization of (2.9) under the restriction of (2.1) gives for the optimal production technique:

$$\frac{N_{\tau\tau}}{I_{\tau\tau}} = \left\{\frac{B}{A}\left(\frac{1+\mu_i}{1+\mu_n}\right)^{-\rho\tau} h_\tau{}^{-\rho(\delta_2-\delta_1)}\Sigma_2\right\}^{-1/1+\rho} \tag{2.12}$$

The equation (2.12) shows, that the optimal labour intensity not only depends on the technological parameters B, A, μ_i, μ_n, ρ, δ_2 and δ_1, but also Σ_2 and hence, according to (2.11), on the expected real wages, the expected index of working hours, technical depreciation and the discount rate.

Formation of Expectations. Entrepreneurs are assumed to expect constant relative changes in the real wages and in the index of working hours:

$$w^e_{\tau t} = w_\tau(1 + gw^e_\tau)^{t-\tau} \quad t \geqq \tau \tag{2.13}$$

$$h^e_{\tau t} = h_\tau(1 + gh^e_\tau)^{t-\tau} \quad t \geqq \tau, \tag{2.14}$$

where

gw^e_τ the in period τ expected growth rate of real wages;
gh^e_τ the in period τ expected relative change in labour time.

It is further assumed that the expected growth rates are calculated as the averages of the actual growth rates over the last θ_2 years:

$$gw^e_\tau = \frac{1}{\theta_2} \sum_{t=\tau-\theta_2+1}^{\tau} \frac{w_t - w_{t-1}}{w_{t-1}} \tag{2.15}$$

$$gh^e_\tau = \frac{1}{\theta_2} \sum_{t=\tau-\theta_2+1}^{\tau} \frac{h_t - h_{t-1}}{h_{t-1}} \tag{2.16}$$

Scrapping Condition. Equipment of a certain vintage τ is scrapped, if it does no longer yield any rent:[8]

$$X_{\tau T} = w_T N_{\tau T} \tag{2.17}$$

The economic life time is $T - \tau$.[9] It is decisive, if it is smaller than the maximum technical life time S. If $S < T - \tau$, equipment is scrapped on technical grounds. As will become clear in the next section, it is assumed that the depreciation scheme is a compromise between the principles of depreciation by evaporation and depreciation by sudden death.

Total Capacity Output and Total Capacity Demand for Labour. Total capacity demand for labour (N_t) and total capacity output (X_t) can be calculated from:

$$N_t = \sum_{\tau \in V_t} N_{\tau t} \tag{2.18}$$

$$X_t = \sum_{\tau \in V_t} X_{\tau t} \tag{2.19}$$

As the technical depreciation scheme $\Omega_{t-\tau}$ and time series of $I_{\tau\tau}$, w_t and h_t are available, total capacity output and total capacity demand for labour can be calculated by using equations (2.12), (2.11), (2.1), (2.6), (2.7) and (2.13)–(2.19) if the values of r, θ_1, θ_2, ρ, A, B, δ_1, δ_2, μ_i, μ_n and γ are known. However, the parameter values themselves must estimated. A broad description of the estimation procedure is given in section 2.[10]

The Estimation Procedure

Because the model is non-linear both in the variables and parameters, the parameters cannot be estimated by means of a linear estimation method. The non-linear estimation method (*NLEM*) used, is derived from that one developed in Berndt, Hall, Hall and Hausman (1974). The method tries to find, in an iterative way, the set of parameters which minimizes a certain objective function. As objective function the following one is used:[11]

$$F = \sum\left(1 - \frac{1}{q_X}\right)^2 + \sum\left(1 - \frac{1}{q_N}\right)^2, \tag{2.20}$$

where q_x and q_N are defined as:

$$q_X = \frac{X^a}{X}, \tag{2.21}$$

$$q_N = \frac{N^a}{N}, \tag{2.22}$$

where X^a is actual output and N^a is actual employment.

Because the number of parameters to be estimated is too large for F to converge towards a minimum, the number of variables to be estimated by *NLEM* has been reduced in two ways.

(1) The elasticities of capacity output with respect to working hours (δ_1 and δ_2) are fixed to Den Hartog's and Tjan's a priori estimates: $\delta_1 = 0.75$; $\delta_2 = 0.75$.[12] As the discount rate, the average real rate of interest of consols in the period 1921–1939 and 1950–1978 is used: $r = 0.02$.[13]

(2) The parameters θ_1, θ_2, μ_n, μ_i and γ are changed iteratively over the interval:

$6 \leqq \theta_1 \leqq 16$ with step size 1;
$1 \leqq \theta_2 \leqq 5$ with step size 1;
$0.040 \leqq \mu_n \leqq 0.055$ with step size 0.0025;
$0.000 \leqq \mu_i \leqq 0.005$ with step size 0.0025;
$-0.0200 \leqq \gamma \leqq -0.0150$ with step size 0.0025

The number of parameters to be estimated by *NLEM* is therefore reduced to three: A, B and ρ. This made convergence within 30 steps possible for almost all runs. In principle F has to be calculated for every permissible combination θ_1, θ_2, μ_n, μ_i and γ. This yields a grid of F's from which the combination of parameter values with the lowest value of F can be chosen as the optimal parameter set. This procedure is, however, very labour and computer-time consuming. Fortunately, it appeared that the optimal values of μ_n, μ_i and γ were quite insensitive to changes in θ_1 and θ_2. This made it possible to narrow the intervals for μ_n, μ_i and γ and thus to diminish considerably the number of permissible combinations.

Finally, it appeared necessary to add a boundary condition to the decision criterion, minimization of F. This condition involves the net present value of investments being non-negative in every period. It is hard to imagine that entrepreneurs would decide to invest in case of a negative net present value of investment. Hence, the optimal parameter set is the set which minimizes F under condition of a non-negative *NPV*.

3. Estimation

The Estimation Period and the Data Used

The estimation period covers the years 1950–1977. The estimation is performed by means of yearly data on actual output, actual employment, gross investment in equipment, real wages and the number of working hours of the Dutch private sector, excluding the exploitation of natural gas. The output and employment data cover the period 1950–1977. Given a maximum technical life time of 45 years, investment time series for the period 1905–1977 are needed. As investments in 1905 may be based on five-year lagged real wages, time series of real wages back to 1900 are used. Apart from some minor changes, the data of output, employment, investments, nominal wages, output deflator and working hours are taken from Den Hartog and Tjan (1979).[14] The minor changes concern changes in the last years due to changes in the C.P.B. statistics and extrapolations of real wages from 1900 to 1921 by means of the growth rate of real wages in the period 1922–1929.[15] The technical depreciation scheme is taken from Den Hartog-Tjan (1976). According to this scheme, the survival fraction remains unity in the first 6 years of the life of a machine and then decreases gradually to 0.005 at a life time of 45 years. The maximum technical life time is 45 years.

The relative change in average labour productivity in the postwar period was about four times as high as its value in the interbellum. For this reason the rate of embodied technical progress in the pre-1940 period is put at 1/4 of the estimate for the postwar period. The procedure is in accordance with the one used by Den Hartog and Tjan (1976).

Estimation Results

The estimation of the parameters as indicated in section 2 showed the following broad tendencies.

(1) The objective function F is a decreasing function of the length of the planning period θ_1, whereas it is an increasing function of the lag θ_2.
(2) An increasing length of the planning period raises the frequency of negative net present values. The frequency is, however, a decreasing function of θ_2.
(3) Higher values of θ_1 require higher values of μ_n in order not to disturb the boundary condition $NPV \geqq 0$. The optimal values of μ_i and γ turned out to be rather insensitive with respect to θ_1 and θ_2: $\mu_i = 0$ and $-0.0175 \leqq \gamma \leqq -0.015$.

Figure 3.1 shows these tendencies. This figure makes quite clear that the reaction of F on changes in θ_1 and θ_2 points to a unique solution. This solution is actually a boundary solution: the combination that gives the lowest value of F under the condition that NPV is non-negative.[16] The one-to-one correspondence between θ_1 and μ_n and the insensitivity of μ_i and γ for changes in θ_1 and θ_2 also point to a unique solution for μ_n, μ_i and γ. The optimal parameter values are summarized in table 3.1.

The first 8 parameter values are estimates; the values δ_1, δ_2 and r are fixed a priori; the value of F is the value of the objective function for the presented values of the parameters.[17]

From table 3.1 the following can be concluded.

(1) Embodied technical progress appears to be of a purely labour-augmenting nature. During the fifties there is some slight disembodied labour—and capital—diminishing technical progress. An explanation of the latter phenomenon might be found in less overtime,

Table 3.1

The Optimal Parameter Values

Parameter	*Value*	*Parameter*	*Value*	*Parameter*	*Value*
A	0.032	μ_i	0	δ_1	0.75
B	0.257	γ	−0.0175	δ_2	0.75
ρ	2.125	θ_1	13	r	0.02
μ_n	0.0475	θ_2	4	F	0.08102

less work efforts and less shift work. This would occur when the recovery period is advancing and, as a result, the need to work hard and acceptance of overtime are diminishing.[18] Another explanation might be a change in the production structure towards more capital-intensive industries. [See also Den Hartog and Tjan (1975) and (1980).]

(2) The elasticity of substitution in the newest vintage is rather low:

$$\sigma = \frac{1}{1 + \rho} = 0.320$$

This also explains the rather high value of μ_n which is only slightly lower than the Den Hartog-Tjan estimate: $\mu_n = 0.051$. This means that the change in average labour productivity must primarily be attributed to technical progress. Although substitution as such cannot be denied, its effect on average labour productivity is certainly less important than is assumed in putty-clay models based on a Cobb-Douglas technology. This result is also at variance with that obtained by Sandee, who finds a value of 0.9. [Sandee (1976), p. 25.] The explanation of this value may be that Sandee assumes embodied Hicks-neutral technical progress, which according to the results of this study may imply a specification error. [Sandee (1976), p.7.]

(3) The planning period appears to be 13 years. To put it differently, entrepreneurs use an expected life time of 13 years in calculating the net present value of their investment projects. This is comparable to some of the results obtained in the Malcolmson-Prior study.[19] The entrepreneurs are clearly much less myopic than Sandee supposes.[20] In section 4 it will appear that the actual life time of equipment is decreasing from 45 years in the early-fifties to about 15 years in the mid-seventies. This means that the expected life time is indeed somewhat smaller than actual life time. This confirms our guess in section 2. It may also explain the difference with respect to the Mizon study in which expected life time is assumed to be equal to actual life time. Mizon finds a life time of about 25 years. [Mizon (1974), pp. 363, 364.]

Forecasting Results

In order to test the forecasting performance of the model the following employment model has been estimated:

Figure 3.1

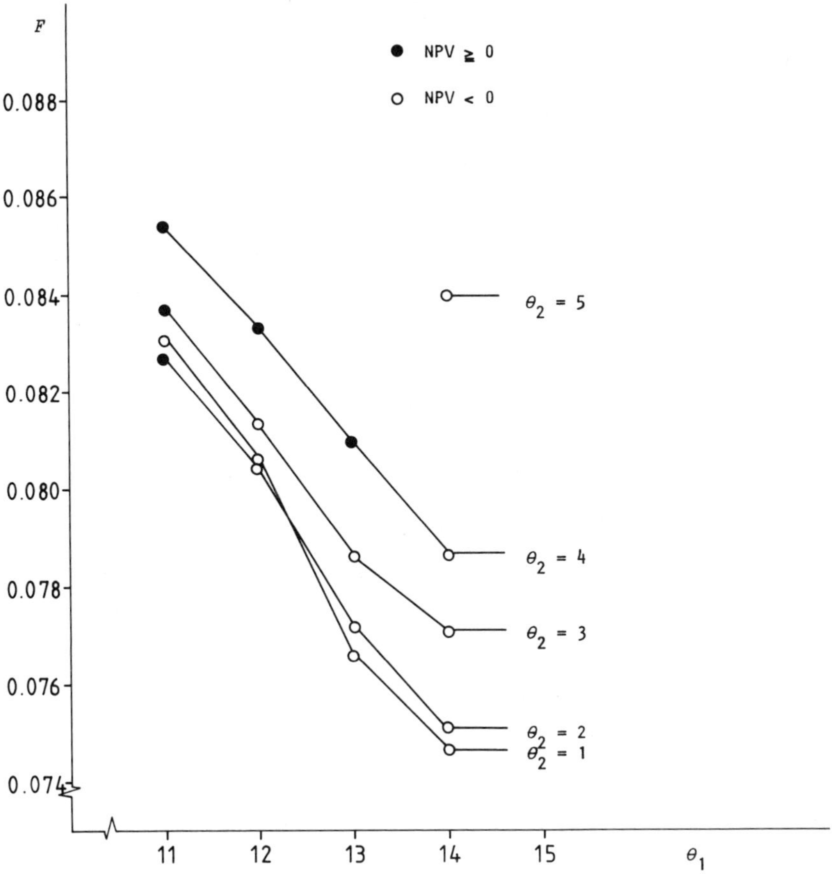

The influence of θ_1 and θ_2 on F ($\mu_n = 0.0475$, $\mu_i = 0$ for $\theta_1 \geq 11$, while $\gamma = -0.015$ for $\theta_1 \leq 12$ and $\gamma = -0.0175$ for $\theta_1 \geq 13$).

$$N_t^a - N_{t-1}^a = \theta(N_t^* - N_{t-1}^a) \quad 0 < \theta < 1 \tag{3.1}$$

$$N_t^* = \beta q_{X,t} N_t \quad \beta > 0 \tag{3.2}$$

where

N_t^a	actual employment;
N_t^*	desired employment;
N_t	capacity demand for labour;
$q_{X,t}$	capacity utilization rate.

Equation (3.1) is the stock adjustment equation, well-known from investment theory. According to equation (3.2) the desired utilization rate with respect to capacity labour demand is proportional with the capacity utilization rate.

From equations (3.1) and (3.2) follows:

$$N_t^a = \theta\beta q_{X,t}N_t + (1 - \theta)N_{t-1}^a \tag{3.3}$$

Maximum likelyhood estimation for regression with autocorrelated errors by means of time series of N^a and time series of N and q, estimated by means of the vintage model, yields for the period 1951–1977:[21]

$$\begin{array}{llll} N_t^a = 0.199\ q_{X,t}N_t + 0.806\ N_{t-1}^a & R^2 = 0.999 \\ \quad\ (4.016) \qquad\qquad (16.186) & DW = 1.946 \end{array} \tag{3.4}$$

Equation (3.4) shows that the fit is remarkably good. It further shows that the adjustment of actual to desired employment is rather slow: in one year not more than 20 percent of the difference between N_t^* and N_{t-1}^a has been eliminated. This result is in correspondence with that obtained by Den Hartog and Tjan for a similar specification.[22] The coefficient β appears to be not significantly different from unity. Hence, the desired utilization rate with respect to capacity demand for labour equals the utilization rate with respect to capacity output. Differences between N^a/N and X^a/X are only due to a slow adjustment of actual to desired employment.

By means of actual data of real wages, working hours and investments in equipment the model can generate time series X_t and N_t, which may be used—together with the time series of actual output which is needed to construct a time series q_x—to obtain forecasts of N_t^a for the years 1978–1980. In table 3.2 the predictions of N_t^a are shown together with the actual values.

Table 3.2 shows that the model slightly underestimates employ-

Table 3.2

Comparison of Predictions of N_t^a with Actual Values, in Thousands of Man Years

Year	*Predictions*	*Actual Values*	*Difference*
1978	3981	3999	−18
1979	3994	4029	−35
1980	4026	4025	+1

ment. The deviations are not so large however as to exclude confidence in the forecasting performance of the putty-clay model.[23]

4. Interpretation of Postwar Output and Employment Growth

In order to acquire some insight into the postwar Dutch growth performance, the time series of the quantities which are most revealing in this respect have been presented in table 4.1. These quantities are:

(1) the life time of oldest equipment $(T - \tau)$;
(2) capacity output (X);
(3) capacity demand for labour (N)
(4) the stock of capital (K);
(5) the increase and decrease in capacity demand for labour due to investment on the one hand and technical depreciation and obsolescence on the other $(+\Delta N$ and $-\Delta N$, respectively);
(6) the utilization rates with respect to capacity output and capacity demand for labour $(q_X$ and q_N, respectively);
(7) the capital intensity of the youngest vintage $(k_{\tau\tau})$;
(8) the aggregate capital-output ratio (χ).

One of the most striking features of table 4.1 is the strong fall in the life time of oldest equipment from 45 years in the mid-fifties to about 15 years in the mid-sixties. Although the clay-clay studies also show this tendency, they differ with respect to the speed of the decline as well as with respect to the year in which the decline begins. According to these studies the decline begins not earlier than the early-sixties while it is maintained until the end of the seventies. [For instance, Den Hartog and Tjan (1976) and Kuipers, Muysken and Van Sinderen (1979).]

The consequence of the strong fall in the life time of oldest equipment is that the scrapping of equipment happens at an increasing rate. What this actually means becomes clear when one realizes that in the span of only 5 years (1955–1960) all the prewar vintages were scrapped. This does not only imply a strong rejuvenation of the stock of equipment, but also high growth rates of average labour productivity and a slowly growing or even declining capacity demand for labour. Table 4.1 shows that the last phenomena indeed occurred in the second half of the fifties. Figure 4.1—in which the time paths of capacity labour demand, actual employment and labour supply (corrected for a frictional unemployment of 50 thousand man years) are

Table 4.1

Time Series of Some Characteristic Quantities

Year	$T\text{-}\tau$	X^1	q_X	N^2	q_N	$-\Delta N^3$	$+\Delta N^4$	K^5	$k^6_{\tau\tau}$	χ^7
1950	45	21737	1.076	3195	1.058	—	—	26702	11.4	1.23
1951	45	22786	1.039	3305	1.032	109	219	28403	11.3	1.25
1952	45	23686	1.005	3192	0.993	109	196	29882	11.5	1.26
1953	45	24769	1.051	3487	0.977	109	205	31657	12.5	1.28
1954	45	26342	1.056	3617	0.962	115	245	34064	13.2	1.30
1955	44	28228	1.059	3749	0.946	146	277	36921	14.1	1.31
1956	39	30295	1.040	3857	0.934	194	303	40072	15.1	1.32
1957	35	32122	1.009	3895	0.929	268	305	42857	15.6	1.34
1958	30	32663	0.974	3771	0.949	363	240	43840	15.9	1.34
1959	25	32625	1.025	3498	1.035	536	262	44033	16.3	1.35
1960	21	34141	1.076	3453	1.069	342	298	46581	17.2	1.37
1961	20	36904	1.029	3615	1.036	144	306	50883	18.3	1.38
1962	17	39827	0.995	3735	1.024	187	308	54780	19.2	1.38
1963	15	42237	0.976	3735	1.038	287	287	57496	20.5	1.36
1964	15	45492	0.995	3821	1.034	197	284	61461	22.0	1.35
1965	16	48571	0.986	3863	1.032	243	285	65197	23.1	1.34
1966	15	51945	0.948	3916	1.024	240	293	69563	24.5	1.34
1967	15	55706	0.935	4023	0.991	181	288	74782	25.8	1.34
1968	16	59433	0.937	4122	0.975	214	313	80415	26.9	1.35
1969	16	62580	0.949	4172	0.979	249	299	85458	28.3	1.37
1970	16	65408	0.972	4184	0.987	320	332	90864	30.5	1.39
1971	15	67781	0.976	4137	1.001	359	312	95226	32.0	1.41
1972	15	70080	0.978	4102	0.995	309	275	99363	33.1	1.42
1973	15	73179	0.993	4132	0.987	268	297	105288	34.9	1.44
1974	15	75630	1.001	4140	0.983	290	298	111074	36.5	1.47
1975	15	75152	0.985	3950	1.019	448	258	112504	37.7	1.50
1976	14	76226	1.026	3844	1.040	337	231	114792	39.1	1.51
1977	14	79697	1.004	3888	1.027	221	265	120660	40.0	1.51
1978	14	82702	0.995	3873	1.033	281	266	125102	40.6	1.51
1979	15	88317	0.955	4011	1.004	135	274	133322	42.2	1.51
1980	15	92513	0.925	4056	0.992	201	245	139168	43.9	1.50

[1]In millions of guilders of 1963.

[2]In thousands of man years.

[3]Decrease in capacity labour demand due to technical depreciation and obsolescence in thousands of man years.

[4]Increase in capacity labour demand due to investment in thousands of man years.

[5]Capital stock in millions of guilders of 1963.

[6]Capital intensity of the youngest vintage in thousands of guilders of 1963 per man year.

[7]Aggregate capital-output ratio.

depicted—gives an even clearer idea of what was happening in the late fifties.

The clay-clay studies indicate alternating periods of capital and labour shortage. [For instance, Den Hartog and Tjan (1976) and Kuipers, Muysken and Van Sinderen (1979)]:

Figure 4.1

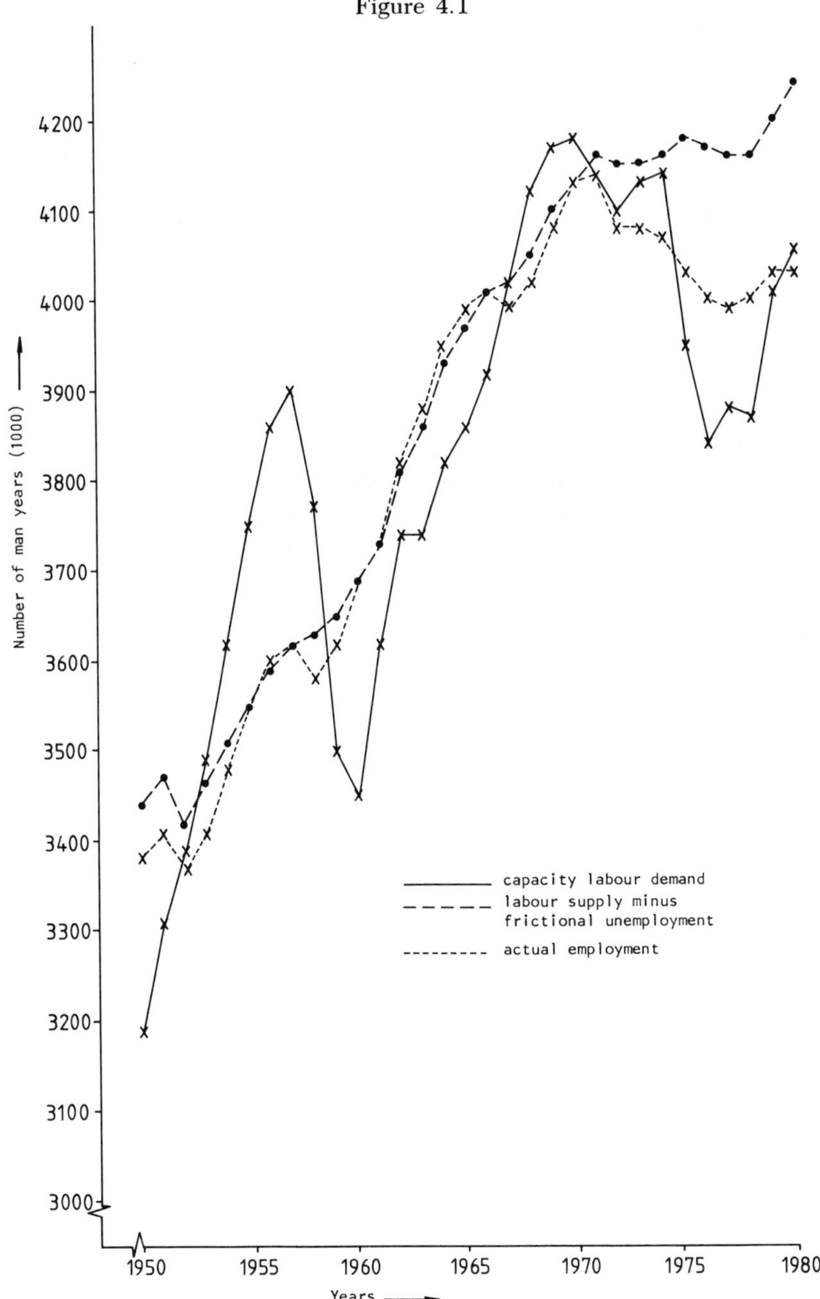

Capacity labour demand, actual employment and labour supply.

1950–1960 capital shortage
1960–1970 labour shortage
1970–1980 capital shortage

A labour shortage is defined as a situation in which the labour supply is smaller than capacity demand for labour, while in case of a capital shortage the reverse is the case. Figure 4.1 shows that the present study does not support this conclusion. Although labour shortages do indeed occur, the periods in which they do ((1952–1959) and (1967–1971)) are rather short however; they do not coincide with the periods which the clay-clay studies indicate. The overwhelming impression one gets from figure 4.1 is that of an almost continuous capital shortage with only short interruptions in those periods when the economy is short of labour.

In particular the events in the early- and mid-sixties are hard to reconcile at first sight. Although labour supply exceeds capacity demand for labour, which indicates a relatively low actual demand, employment in fact exceeds normal supply. An explanation might be that, due to high growth rates of expenditure, not only q_N was high but also q_X. Table 4.1 shows, however, that this has not been the case. On the contrary, capacity was underutilized in this period.[24]

One can only conclude that the high level of employment in the early- and mid-sixties was caused by the fact that entrepreneurs were hoarding labour. There are several arguments in support of this hypothesis.[25] First, as has already been shown in section 3, entrepreneurs adjust actual employment rather slowly to the desired level. In the current context this means that actual labour demand in the early- and mid-sixties was still influenced by the existence of labour shortage in the mid-fifites. Second, wages were still rather low and profits rather high until the mid-sixties, which may explain that entrepreneurs did not feel a strong incentive to realign their stock of manpower. Third, the tight labour market may have influenced the expectations of entrepreneurs in a destabilizing way, e.g. by making them expect a still tighter labour market in the near future, and thus induce them to demand more labour than could be efficiently used at that moment.

At the end of the sixties the phenomenon of labour hoarding came to an end. First because rapidly rising wages forced entrepreneurs to economise the use of labour. Second, the memory of the experiences in the fifties faded. Third, a strongly growing capacity demand for labour appeared in the sixties. For a short period, capital shortage changed into labour shortage. The latter situation came in turn to an end when capacity labour demand began to stagnate in the early seventies, partly caused by rising real wages (growth rates of real wages of more than 6 percent were no exception), and a decline in investment activity. Figure 4.1 shows that in particular in the deep depression of 1975, with its deterioration of the terms of trade and rise in real labour costs, has had a disastrous influence on capacity demand for labour and with that, although to a lesser extent, on actual employment. In 1976 there was a shortage of jobs of no less than 330,000 man years. Figure 4.1 also shows that the situation improved considerably after 1978. Notwithstanding a stronger growth of labour supply than was usual in the early- and mid-seventies, the job shortage decreased to 182,000 man years in 1980.

Table 4.1 shows that the capacity utilization rates were on a high level in the mid-seventies. Even in the depression year 1975 underutilization amounted to no more than 1.5 percent, while capacity was overutilized in 1976 and 1977.[26] This reveals that the bad employment situation in the mid-seventies was entirely due to too low a capacity demand for labour. Since 1978 things began to change, however. On the one hand there is an improvement in the structural situation, on the other hand one can observe a growing underutilization of productive capacity. Due to a lagged response of employment, the latter has not led to underutilization of capacity demand for labour up to 1979. Then, in 1980 the first symptoms of a declining capacity utilization rate appear. The danger of falling employment in the early-eighties because of capacity underutilization may therefore not be just a hypothetical one.

5. Consequences for Economic Policy

At the end of the preceding section we concluded that the worsening of the employment situation in the mid-seventies must be entirely attributed to the fall in capacity demand for labour. Since 1978 however, the decline in the rate of capacity utilization also makes its influence felt. Table 5.1 shows that the latter tendency will probably occur in the early eighties as well.[27] Although the growth rate of capacity labour demand as such is not sufficient to undo capital shortage, the actual employment situation will be much worse than the structural position of the economy warrants. It is the low and still deteriorating degree of capacity utilization which must be held responsible for this. Whereas employment in the private sector might grow by about 10,000 man years per annum if capacity would be fully utilized, it is actually declining by about 40,000 man years a year, a difference of about 50,000 man years. For this period 1981–1985 this

Table 5.1

Forecasts, 1981–1985	
	Average yearly percentage changes
Capacity output	3.2
Capital stock	3.4
Capacity labour demand	0.2
Employment	−1.0
	Level in 1985
Capacity utilization	0.85
Utilization rate with respect to capacity labour demand	0.93
Unemployment (1000 man years)	506
Life time of oldest equipment	17

means an additional unemployment of 250,000 man years. Stated otherwise: by restoring full capacity utilization, unemployment in 1985 might be halved.

The above makes the dilemma of present-day economic policy quite clear. On the one hand a policy of wage restraint is necessary in order to achieve a lower scrapping rate and a slower growth of the capital intensity of newest equipment, which is prerequisite to increase capacity demand for labour. Such a policy is also necesssary in order to improve profitability, and, hence, investment growth. On the other hand, economic policy has to prevent a further deterioration of capacity utilization. A wage restraint policy may seriously endanger its realization, because it will depress national expenditures and hence actual output, a tendency which may be weakened somewhat by the improvement of the competitive position. As a consequence, employment growth will be retarded or worse, not be restored. Besides, the recovery of investment growth may also be undone which will inevitably have its effects on capacity demand for labour. This implies that recovery of output and employment growth cannot be achieved by a restrictive monetary and budgetary policy as a way to achieve suitable market conditions for the desired wage restraint. On the contrary, however necessary this restraint may be, a restrictive stance of demand management will worsen the situation.

The nature of the policy dilemma clearly points in the direction of a two-track policy: an expansionary budgetary and monetary policy to improve capacity utilization and a wage policy to restrict the rise in real wages. A possible scenario of economic recovery might be the following. In order to improve the structural position of the private sector, the government reduces the tax and social security burden of enterprises. As a further deterioration of the degree of capacity utilization should be avoided, this reduction should not involve an increase in the tax burden of households or a reduction in government spending. This makes an increase in the budget deficit inevitable. To prevent a further tightening of the capital market the deficit should be money financed. As a result the money rates of interest may tend to fall. This will lead to capital outflows, which—as long as the current account of the balance of payments has not improved—may depress the exchange rate. Under a system of fixed, but adjustable exchange rates—which applies *de facto* to the case of the Netherlands—a devaluation of the currency will probably become inevitable. As a result the competitive position will improve not only in the short run but also in the intermediate and long run in so far as the price increases due to the devaluation are not compensated in wages. The wage policy has to guarantee that this does not happen.

One may expect that the improvement of the competitive position, the increase in profits and the fall in real interest rates will eventually lead to an increase in exports and investments and a decrease in imports. The consequence will be an acceleration in actual output growth and hence an improvement in capacity utilization, which will stimulate in turn investment growth and hence aggregate demand. As soon as capacity limits are reached the government has to reduce aggregate demand growth by means of an increase in the tax burden. In its turn wage policy has to prevent that the increase in the tax burden is shifted towards entreprises. Finally, the budget deficit will decrease again, not only as a result of the rise in tax rates but also as a result of the recovery of output growth.

The scenario above is not necessarily the only way to escape from the dilemma in question. The analysis has made clear, that whatever policy is chosen, on the one hand it has to restrict the rise in real wages in order to solve the structural problem of too low a level of capacity labour demand, while on the other hand it has to prevent a structural solution giving a new deflationary momentum to the economy.

6. Concluding Remarks

In this paper an attempt has been made to estimate a putty-clay vintage model for the Netherlands in order to test the assumption, usually made in the Dutch vintage model discussion, of complementarity ex ante.

The estimation led to the following conclusions: an elasticity of substitution of about 0.32, a planning period of 13 years and apart from the fifties the existence of embodied labour-augmenting technical progress only. Although the probability distribution of the parameters is unknown and as a consequence a proper test of the hypothesis of complementarity ex ante is not possible, the estimation results give rise to the surmise that substitutability ex ante is indeed a real phenomenon.

The model outcomes force a somewhat different interpretation of the postwar growth performance than was usual up to now. In contrast with the clay-clay studies, which normally point to a capital shortage in the fifties and the seventies and a labour shortage in the sixties, the present study gives rise to the surmise that, with the exception of some short periods in the fifties and the late-sixties, capital shortage is the ruling phenomenon. This makes it impossible to explain the tight labour market in the early and mid-sixties by means of capital abundance. Instead, the explanation probably has to be found in labour hoarding.

The conclusions with respect to the seventies do not deviate however from that of the clay-clay studies. These years are characterized by a shortage of jobs due to an excessive growth of real wages and a slow growth of investments until the late seventies. In the latter period the rise in real wages is more moderate which is the main cause of the decreasing shortage of jobs during these years. The greatest danger for employment growth in these years seems to be too slow a growth of actual output and as a consequence underutilization of productive capacity. Predictions for the period 1981–1985 suggest that underutilization will also be the main cause of the decline in employment in the early-eighties.

The simultaneous occurrence of capital shortage and underutilization creates a dilemma for present-day economic policy. From a structural point of view real wages should be restricted whereas from a conjunctural point of view a fall in real wages should be resisted in order to prevent a further decline in the degree of capacity utilization. A two-track policy consisting of an expansionary stance of monetary and budgetary policy and a restrictive wage policy may offer an escape from the dilemma in question. By using this policy it can be avoided that the structural measures give a further deflationary momentum to the economy which may seriously endanger its recovery.

Notes

[1]Den Hartog and Tjan (1976), Central Planning Bureau (1977). A forerunner of this medium-term model was developed in: Den Hartog, Van de Klundert and Tjan (1975).

[2]The only exceptions are Sandee (1976) and Surie (1975).

[3]This applies, for instance, to Baum et. al. (1971) and Mizon (1974). See for this kind of criticism also Malcolmson and Prior (1979).

[4]This approach has been taken in Nickell (1974); Nickell (1975); Malcolmson (1975); Malcolmson and Prior (1979).

[5]See for instance, Kuipers, Muysken and Van Sinderen (1979). According to this study labour-augmenting technical progress is embodied for 75 percent and disembodied for 25 percent. The Den Hartog-Tjan (1980) article points in the same direction.

[6]See, for instance: De Klerk, Van der Laan and Thio (1975) and Den Hartog and Tjan (1975). A way to overcome this anomaly is to assume the capital-output ratio to be variable. This way is in line with those suggested by Den Hartog and Tjan (1980) and Van Schaik (1976). See also, Van Schaik (1981), ch. 3.

[7]Examples of the application of a critical pay-off period and of minimization of the pay-off period are respectively: Kaldor and Mirrlees (1962) and Minne and Tjan (1972).

[8]In the estimation w_T is defined as a three year rectangularly distributed lag.

[9]The economic life time is not necessarily equal to the span of life of oldest equipment, as—due to cyclical variations in real wages—younger equipment may be scrapped earlier than older equipment. This will lead to discontinuities in the vintage structure of the capital stock. However, during the estimation stage it appeared that a continuous vintage structure of the capital stock could be observed in almost all cases, including the one associated with the chosen optimal parameter set.

[10]For a detailed description see Kuipers and Van Zon (1981).

[11]This function has the drawback, well-known from the Dutch vintage model discussion, that it presupposes that in the estimation period actual output and actual employment are on the average equal to capacity output and capacity labour demand. If this is not the case, the estimation procedure may lead to under- or overestimation of the capacity quantities. The reason for the use of this objective function, notwithstanding this drawback, is that other objective functions, for instance those used in Den Hartog-Tjan (1976) or Mizon (1974), did not lead to convergence in the preliminary phase of this research. This point needs further attention, however.

[12]Den Hartog and Tjan (1976). In Den Hartog and Tjan (1980) a distinction has been made between working hours per day and working days per year. The elasticity of labour and capital productivity with respect to the former has been put equal to 0.35 and that with respect to the latter has been put equal to 1. Den Hartog and Tjan (1980), p. 145.

[13]For the source of this value see appendix D of Kuipers and Van Zon (1981).

[14]Den Hartog and Tjan (1979), mimeographed version of Den Hartog and Tjan (1980). Time series of nominal wages and the output deflator before 1950 are taken from Kuipers, Muysken and Van Sinderen (1979).

[15]The data and their sources are presented in Kuipers and Van Zon (1981).

[16]Of course this is no guarantee that the solution obtained in this way is the definite final solution. It is always possible that it is a local minimum.

[17]The non-linear estimate of A, B and ρ converged in 16 steps.

[18]It must be admitted however that this is a rather speculative hypothesis. Further information is needed to test this hypothesis.

[19]This is the case under the following circumstances: labour requirements and output do not change over the life of a machine, the discount rate is between 10% and 15%, and expected life time is equal to actual life time. Under these circumstances life time varies between 11 and 14 years. This estimate is, however, very sensitive with respect to the assumptions concerning output and labour requirements over the life of a machine and with respect to the assumed discount rate. Malcolmson and Prior (1979), pp. 731–735.

[20]Sandee assumes a planning period of one year.

[21]Terms in parentheses are t-values: R^2 is the coefficient of determination; DW is the statistic of Durbin and Watson.

[22]According to Den Hartog and Tjan (1980), pp. 181 and 182, in one year 25% of

the difference between log N_t^a/N_t and log N_{t-1}^a/N_{t-1} is eliminated.

[23]The fit is comparable with that obtained by Den Hartog and Tjan (1980), p. 184.

[24]Clay-Clay studies also lead to this conclusion. However, in these studies underutilization is caused by labour shortage. See Den Hartog and Tjan (1976) and Kuipers, Muysken and Van Sinderen (1979).

[25]The same conclusion is drawn for the U.K. by Taylor (1976).

[26]The implication of this result is that the slowdown of output growth in these years is mainly caused by a structural decrease in competitiveness of Dutch industries and only to a small extent by a fall in aggregate demand at still profitable relative prices.

[27]The forecasts are based on the following assumptions: output growth by 1.5 percent a year, gross investment growth by 1 percent a year, growth of real wages by 2.5 percent a year, decline in working hours by 1 percent a year and a working population of 5.095 thousand man years in 1985. Source: Central Planning Bureau (1981).

References

Baum, D., B., Görzig and W. Kirner, "Ein Vintage-capital Produktionsmodell für die Bundesrepublik Deutschland," *Vierteljahreshefte zur Wirtschaftsforschung,* Heft 4, 1971.

Berndt, E. K., B. H. Hall, R. E. Hall and J. A. Hausman, "Estimation and Inference in Nonlinear Structural Models," *Annals of Economic and Social Measurement,* 3/4 (1974), pp. 653–665.

Central Planning Bureau, *Een macro model voor de Nederlandse economie op middellange termijn* (Vintaf II), Occasional Papers, No. 12, The Hague, 1977.

Central Planning Bureau, *De Nederlandse economie in 1985, Een verkenning,* The Hague, 1981.

Driehuis, W. and A. van der Zwan, "De voorbereiding van het economisch beleid kritisch bezien," *Economisch-Statistische Berichten,* LXII (1977), pp. 316–319, 348–359 and 376–387.

Driehuis, W., "An Anlaysis of the Impact of Demand and Cost Factors on Employment," *De Economist,* CXXVII (1979), pp. 255–286.

Hartog, H. den, Th. van de Klundert and H. S. Tjan, "De structurele ontwikkeling van de werkgelegenheid in macro-economisch perspectief," in: *Werkloosheid,* Preadvies van de Vereniging voor de Staathuishoudkunde, The Hague, 1975.

Hartog, H. den and H. S. Tjan, *Investeringen, lonen, prijzen arbeidsplaatsen,* Central Planning Bureau, Occasional Paper, Nr. 2, The Hague, 1974.

Hartog, H. den and H. S. Tjan, "Commentaar," *Economisch-Statistische Berichten,* LX (1975), pp. 484–489.

Hartog, H. den and H. S. Tjan, "Investments, Wages, Prices and Demand for Labour (A Clay-Clay Vintage Model for the Netherlands), *De Economist,* CXIV (1976), pp. 32–55.

Hartog, H. den and H. S. Tjan, "A Clay-Clay Vintage Model Approach for Sectors of Industry in the Netherlands," *De Economist,* CXXVIII (1980), pp. 129–188.

Hartog, H. den and J. Weitenberg, "Econometrische modellen en economische politiek," *Economisch-Statistische Berichten,* LXII (1977), pp. 1236–1243 and 1269–1273.

Kaldor, N. and J. A. Mirrlees, "A New Model of Economic Growth," *Review of Economic Studies,* XXIX (1962), pp. 174–192.

Klerk, R. A. de, H. B. M. van der Laan and K. B. T. Thio, "Het C.P.B. en de ontwikkeling van de werkgelegenheid," *Economisch-Statistische Berichten,* LX (1975), pp. 480–484.

Klerk, R. A. de, H. B. M. van der Laan and K. B. T. Thio, "Unemployment in the

Netherlands: A Criticism of the Den Hartog-Tjan Vintage Model," *Cambridge Journal of Economics,* I (1977), pp. 291–306.

Kuipers, S. K. and H. F. Bosch, "An Alternative Estimation Procedure of a Clay-Clay Type of Vintage Model: The Case of the Netherlands, 1959–1973," *De Economist,* CXXIV (1976), pp. 56–82.

Kuipers, S. K., J. Muysken and J. van Sinderen, "The Vintage Approach to Output and Employment Growth in the Netherlands, 1921–1976," *Weltwirtschaftliches Archiv,* Band 115 (1979), pp. 485–507.

Kuipers, S. K. and A. H. van Zon, *Output and Employment Growth in the Netherlands in the Postwar Period: A Putty-Clay Approach,* Mimeographed, Groningen, 1981.

Malcolmson, J. M., "Replacement and the Rental Value of Capital Equipment Subject to Obsolescence," *Journal of Economic Theory,* X (1975), pp. 24–53.

Malcolmson, J. M. and M. J. Prior, "The Estimation of a Vintage Model of Production for UK Manufacturing," *Review of Economic Studies,* XLVI (1979), pp. 719–736.

Minne, B. and H. S. Tjan, *Een macro putty-clay produktiefunctie,* Central Planning Bureau, Notitie nr. 14, 5-11-1972.

Mizon, G. E., "The Estimation of Non-Linear Econometric Equations: An Application to the Specification and Estimation of an Aggregate Putty-Clay Relation for the United Kingdom," *Review of Economic Studies,* XLI (1974), pp. 353–369.

Muysken, J. and C. H. van Ardenne, "Den Hartog and Tjan's Vintage Model as a Tool for the Determination of Structural Employment: Some Critical Remarks," *De Economist,* CXXIV (1976), pp. 83–102.

Nickell, S. J., "On Expectations and the Pure Theory of Investments," *Review of Economic Studies,* XLI (1974), pp. 1–20.

Nickell, S. J., "A Closer Look at Replacement Investment," *Journal of Economic Theory,* X (1975), pp. 54–88.

Sandee, J., *A Putty-Clay Model for the Netherlands,* Paper to be read at the European Meeting of the Econometric Society, Helsinki, August 1976.

Schaik, A. B. T. M. van, "Een direct verband tussen economische veroudering en bezettingsgraadverliezen?; Gevoeligheidsanalyse," *Reeks ter Discussie,* nr. 38, Katholieke Hogeschool Tilburg, December 1976.

Schaik, A. B. T. M. van, *Naar een nieuwe macro-economie,* Leiden, 1981.

Surie, G. O., *De invloed van investeringen, reële loonkosten en economische levensduur op de werkgelegenheidsontwikkeling in Nederland,* Doctoral Paper, Amsterdam, 1975.

Taylor, J., "The Unemployment Gap in Britain's Production Sector, 1953–73," in: G. D. N. Worswick (ed.), *The Concept and Measurement of Involuntary Unemployment,* Londen, 1976, pp. 146–167.

Résumé

On a essayé d'évaluer dans cet article un modèle pour la Hollande afin de vérifier l'hypothèse de complémentarité ex ante habituellement faite dans la discussion du modèle hollandais. On arrive aux conclusions suivantes: une élasticité de substitution de 0,32, une période de planification de 13 ans et, à l'exception des années 1950, l'existence d'un travail organisé augmentant seulement le progrès technique. Les résultats de l'estimation laissent penser que la subsituabilité ex ante est en fait un phénomène réel.

Les résultats du modèle permettent de conclure que la pénurie des capitaux est la règle pour la période d'après-guerre avec seulement quelques courtes périodes d'abondance des capitaux dans les années 50 et la fin des années 60. Depuis la fin des années 70, la croissance de l'emploi n'est pas seulement déprimée par une croissance trop lente de la demande globale de travail, destinée à répondre à une augmentation des capacités de production, mais aussi par suite d'une croissance de la sous-utilisation des capacités de production. Cette dernière conclusion ressort aussi des prévisions à moyen terme pour la période allant jusqu'à 1985.

L'analyse des années 1970 et la prévision pour les années 80 rend très net le dilemme de la politique actuelle. D'une part, une politique de modération des salaires est nécessaire afin d'atteindre un plus faible taux d'obsolescence et une plus faible croissance de l'intensité capitalistique des nouveaux équipements productifs, ce qui est une condition préalable à une augmentation de la demande globale de main-d'oeuvre. Une telle politique est aussi nécessaire pour améliorer la profitabilité et donc accroître la croissance de l'investissement. D'autre part, la politique économique doit empêcher une détérioration accrue de l'utilisation des capacités productives. Une politique de modération des salaires peut sérieusement menacer sa réalisation, car elle diminuera la dépense nationale et la production réelle. En conséquence, la croissance de l'emploi ne sera pas restaurée. En outre, la reprise de la croissance de l'investissement risque aussi d'en souffrir, ce qui aura inévitablement des effets défavorables sur la demande globale de travail.

Ceci implique que la reprise de la croissance de la production et de l'emploi ne peut être réalisée par une politique monétaire et budgétaire restrictive permettant de créer les conditions favorables au freinage de la hausse des salaires. Par contre, aussi nécessaire que puisse être ce freinage des salaires, une politique restrictive de la demande aggravera la conjoncture. Les caractéristiques de ce dilemme conduisent clairement à envisager une politique à deux voies: d'une part, une politique expansioniste pour accroître l'utilisation de la capacité de production et, d'autre part, une politique des salaires pour limiter la croissance des salaires réels. Une variante spécifique de cette politique pourrait être une réduction de poids des charges fiscales et sociales payées par les entreprises grâce à une augmentation du déficit budgétaire financé par la création monétaire et une politique salariale garantissant que la profitabilité accrue des investissements ne conduira pas à de nouvelles demandes d'augmentations réelles.

Human Capital Formation and Public Finance: A Dynamic Model*

Karl W. Roskamp
Manfred Neumann

A. Introduction

The historical records of developed countries show that human capital formation has been of great importance for long-run economic growth and for that matter the attainment and maintenance of high standards of living.

Intertemporal human capital formation as discussed in the literature is most often concerned with the human capital formation by one individual. The interest in this case is to trace out an optimal intertemporal investment-consumption time path. This in itself is a considerable task, given the constraints an individual faces in such a process, to wit: a finite length of life, the non-transferability of human capital at death but transferability of real capital, retirement requirements and uncertainties about health, learning capacity, obsolescence of accumulated knowledge and the possibility of earning higher incomes with greater human capital formation under changing economic conditions. Much useful work has been done in this area. Yet if society believes that a certain welfare distribution is desirable and if this distribution depends on the consumption of individuals having different earning capacities, an important social aspect of human capital formation comes to the fore. If income earning capacities—and for that matter life-time income earning capacities—are closely correlated with human capital, helping underprivileged groups to acquire this capital is one way of improving their long-run economic lot.

*The authors gratefully acknowledge constructive comments and suggestions from the discussant, Professor Hans van de Kar.

Public Finance and Economic Growth. Proceedings of the 37th Congress of the International Institute of Public Finance. Tokyo, 1981, pp. 207–216

On the other hand redistribution through human capital formation might reduce economic growth and, one stage further removed, general economic welfare. Therefore, economic policy with respect to human capital formation should heed both economic growth and distribution requirements.

If poorer sections of the population are to be helped to increase their human capital formation over and above those levels they would reach by themselves, resource transfers are required. For this the more well-to-do sections of the population will have to give up some of their consumption or forego some of their capital formation. From a technical point of view the resource transfer can occur through a tax-subsidy scheme, or a tax-subsidy scheme combined with the provision of public goods helpful for human capital formation, such as schools, libraries, etc. The cardinal problem is then the following: what are the optimal stocks of human capital and what is the optimal stock of public capital, both from the efficiency and from the equity point of view? Furthermore, what is the optimal consumption of the different individuals concerned and what optimal tax rates should be applied. These are the problems with which we are concerned with in this paper.

B. The Model

In this section we will link various elements affecting human capital formation. We shall investigate how, over time, optimal human capital formation can be influenced by taxation and government expenditures. Ours is an inter-temporal optimization model with two persons and the government as decision-makers. If one wishes, the two persons may be taken to represent two different groups or parties in an economy. The structure of the model was kept simple so that involved dynamic relationships could be handled. Nevertheless we believe it to be realistic and helpful for the understanding of inter-temporal human capital formation under a public finance constraint. We explain first the relationships which enter into our model.

We assume that the economy consists of two persons, Mr. Schwarz (s) and Mr. Weiss (w). Both persons receive, over time, utilities from consumption. The utility function for Schwarz we write as:

$$U^s = \int_0^T U(c_s)e^{-r_1 t}dt. \qquad (1)$$

In order to consume he must earn some income Y_s. How much he can earn shall be a function of the capital stocks at his disposal. Accordingly, the "production function" is written as:

$$Y_s = F^s(K_s, K_p) \tag{2}$$

where K_s is the amount of human capital at his disposal and K_p is the amount of public capital which he can use as a citizen. K_p is in the nature of a public good entering the production function. Schwarz must use part of his income for consumption c_s. The latter he shall be able to control. Further he has to pay a fraction of his income, τ^s, in the form of taxes to the government. Once taxes are paid and the amount to be consumed is determined, Schwarz shall then use the rest of his income for human capital formation. To simplify our model it is assumed that no real capital formation takes place. The net human capital formation which will occur is thus:

$$\dot{K}_s = \eta^s[(1 - \tau^s)F^s(K_s, K_p) - c_s] - \mu^s K_s \tag{3}$$

In (3) the symbols have the following meaning:

η^s	transformation parameter for s, telling us how efficiently income is transformed into human capital
τ^s	tax rate for s, flat income tax rate without exemptions
μ^s	depreciation rate for s, pertaining to existing capital
r_1	rate of time preference of s
K_s	stock of human capital of s
K_p	stock of public capital
c_s	consumption of s
$\dot{K}_s$	net human capital formation of s
t	time

The objective of s is to maximize (1) subject to (3). Similarly the second person, w, tries to maximize

$$U^w = \int_0^T U(c_w)e^{-r_2 t}\, dt \tag{4}$$

subject to:

$$\dot{K}_w = \eta^w[(1 - \tau^w)F^w(K_w, K_p) - c_w] - \mu^w K_w \tag{5}$$

In (4) and (5) the symbols have the following meaning:

η^{w} transformation parameter for w, telling us how efficiently income is transformed into human capital
τ^{w} tax rate of w
μ^{w} depreciation rate for w pertaining to existing human capital
r_2 rate of time preference of w
K_w stock of human capital of w
K_p stock of public capital
c_w consumption of w
$\dot{K}_w$ net human capital formation of w
t time

We now introduce a government which desires to form public capital subject to a budget constraint. The constraint is written as:

$$\dot{K}_p = \eta^{p}[\tau^{s}F^{s}(K_s,K_p) + \tau^{w}F^{w}(K_w,K_p)] - \mu^{p}K_p \tag{6}$$

The additional symbols in (6) have the following meaning:

η_p transformation parameter for the government, telling us how efficiently tax receipts are transformed into public capital
μ_p depreciation rate pertaining to public capital

A look at equations (1) and (2) reveals that s, given certain values for r, η^{s}, τ^{s}, and μ^{s}, can influence the rate of his human capital formation $\dot{K}_s$ through c_s. Thus c_s is his control variable. Similarly, the control variable for w is c_w.

Inspection of equation (6) shows that the government, with μ_p given, has two control variables at its disposal, namely, the tax rates τ^{s} and τ^{w}.

The equations (1) to (6) form an interdependent dynamic system. Before continuing with our analysis, we point out a few features which concern the relationship between human capital formation and public finance. If there were no government—which in our model has a voice in determining the welfare distribution and which affects this distribution through taxation and the supply of public goods enhancing human capital formation—the two individuals s and w would accumulate human capital between $t = 0$ and $t = T$ only according to individual preferences. Without taxes to pay and with no public good K_p each individual would follow a particular optimal time path for his human capital formation. The optimality conditions would, in this case, be the same as for real capital formation in the theory of economic growth. These are well known in the literature. Yet the experience is that governments do have a considerable influence on human capital formation. In many countries a large part of all education is tax financed and a variety of public goods often aid in the formation of human capital. Individuals who wish to achieve an optimal human capital formation in such a setting must, therefore, take public policy measures into consideration. Taxes and public expenditure variables will have to enter their maximization calculus.

We define optimality by the Pareto criterium. We are thus looking for a situation where the level of individual consumption and the rates of taxation—or subsidization—and the ensuing amounts of capital are such that nobody can be made better off without making somebody worse off. The initial distribution of utility is assumed to be given. In this paper we are not concerned with the process of how such a Pareto optimal situation can be brought about. We are interested in describing the properties of such an optimum.

From a mathematical point of view, a Pareto optimum can be found by maximizing a social welfare function subject to the constraints given in (3), (5), and (6).[1]

The social welfare function is given by:

$$W = \int_0^T [U(c_s) + \bar{\lambda} U(c_w)] e^{-r_3 t}\, dt \tag{7}$$

where $\bar{\lambda}$ denotes a welfare parameter chosen by the government. The rate of discount applied by the government is r_3. For the sake of simplicity we assume that the rates of time preference are the same, that is, $r_1 = r_2 = r_3 = r$. Applying the Maximum Principle we can write the Hamiltonian as:

$$\begin{aligned} H = {} & [U(c_s) + \bar{\lambda} U(c_w)]e^{-rt} \\ & + y_1\{\eta^s[(1-\tau^s)F^s(K_s,K_p) - c_s] - \mu^s K_s\} \\ & + y_2\{\eta^w[(1-\tau^w)F^w(K_w,K_p) - c_w] - \mu^w K_w\} \\ & + y_3\{\eta^p[\tau^s F^s(K_s,K_p) + \tau^w F^w(K_w,K_p)] - \mu^p K_p\} \end{aligned} \tag{8}$$

In terms of the maximum principle analysis we have in (8):

c_s, c_w, τ^s, τ^w	control variables
K_s, K_w, K_p	state variables
y_1, y_2, y_3	co-state variables.

Necessary conditions for an interior maximum are as follows:[2]

$$\partial H/\partial c_s = U'(c_s)e^{-rt} - y_1\eta^s = 0 \tag{9}$$

$$\partial H/\partial c_w = \bar{\lambda} U'(c_w)e^{-rt} - y_2\eta^w = 0 \tag{10}$$

$$\partial H/\partial \tau^s = (-y_1\eta^s + y_3\eta^p)F^s = 0 \tag{11}$$

$$\partial H/\partial \tau^w = (-y_2\eta^w + y_3\eta^p)F^w = 0 \tag{12}$$

Further, the co-state variables must fulfill the differential equations:

$$\dot{y}_1 = -\partial H/\partial K_s = -y_1(\eta^s F^s_{K_s} - \mu^s) \tag{13}$$

$$\dot{y}_2 = -\partial H/\partial K_w = -y_2(\eta^w F^w_{K_w} - \mu^w) \tag{14}$$

$$\dot{y}_3 = -\partial H/\partial K_p = -y_3[\eta^p(F^s_{K_p} + F^w_{K_p}) - \mu^p] \tag{15}$$

Observing that from (9) to (12) we have

$$-y_1\eta^s + y_3\eta^p = 0 \tag{16}$$

$$-y_2\eta^w + y_3\eta^p = 0 \tag{17}$$

$$U'(c_s) = \bar{\lambda} U'(c_w) \tag{18}$$

the co-state variables can be eliminated in (9) to (15). Doing this one obtains the optimality conditions:

$$\dot{U}'(c_s)/U'(c_s) = r + \mu^s - \eta^s F^s_{K_s} \tag{19}$$

$$\dot{U}'(c_w)/U'(c_w) = r + \mu^w - \eta^w F^w_{K_w} \tag{20}$$

$$\dot{U}'(c_s)/U'(c_s) = \dot{U}'(c_w)/U'(c_w) = r + \mu^p - \eta^p(F^s_{K_p} + F^w_{K_p}) \tag{21}$$

The conditions (19) to (21), plus (3), (5), (7), and (18) form a system of seven equations which determine the seven endogenous variables, K_s, K_w, K_p, c_s, c_w, τ^s, and τ^w. The exogenously given parameters of the system are η^s, η^w, η^p, the efficiency parameters, and the depreciation rates, μ^s, μ^w, and μ^p. The given welfare distribution parameter is $\bar{\lambda}$.

Above dynamic system describes the optimal paths of the various variables. In this paper we shall concentrate on the stationary state of the model. In it all time derivatives are zero and the system can thus be written as:

$$\eta^s[(1 - \tau^s)F^s - c_s] - \mu^s K_s = 0 \tag{22}$$

$$\eta^w[(1 - \tau^w)F^w - c_w] - \mu^w K_w = 0 \quad (23)$$

$$\eta^p[\tau^w F^w + \tau^s F^s] - \mu^p K_p = 0 \quad (24)$$

$$U'(c_s) = \bar{\lambda} U(c_w) \quad (25)$$

$$r + \mu^s = \eta^s F^s_{K_s} \quad (26)$$

$$r + \mu^w = \eta^w F^w_{K_w} \quad (27)$$

$$r + \mu^p = \eta^p(F^s_{K_p} + F^w_{K_p}) \quad (28)$$

A look at the system (22) to (28) reveals an interesting recursive relationship between the subset of equations (22) to (25) and (26) to (28), respectively. The last three equations show that the marginal productivities of K_s, K_w, and K_p are solely determined by r, the η's and the μ's. For equations (26) to (28) to hold it is necessary that the capital stocks attain particular magnitudes. We may denote them by K_s^*, K_w^*, and K_p^*. These are the optimal capital stocks. It is worth pointing out that they are totally unaffected by taxation.

The optimal capital stocks being given, tax rates, τ^s, τ^w, as well as private consumption, c_s, c_w, are determined by the first subset of equations, i.e., by (22) to (25), after the optimal values of the capital stocks have been inserted.

Thus far the mathematical analysis. We now turn to the economic interpretation of the solution.

C. Interpretation of the Results

With the aid of system (22) to (28) we can compare different stationary states implied by different sets of the given exogenous parameters.

It follows from equations (26) to (27) that the stock of human capital is the larger the greater the respective private efficiency parameters and the smaller the respective rates of depreciation.

Thus, for example, $\eta^w > \eta^s$ implies $F^s_{K_s} > F^w_{K_w}$ provided $\mu^s \leqq \mu^w$, and consequently $K_s^* < K_w^*$.

Similarly, the larger the parameter η^p, i.e., the greater the efficiency of transforming tax receipts into public capital, and the smaller μ^p, the greater the optimal stock of public capital.

Moreover, provided the cross derivatives $F^i_{K_pK_i}$ $(i = w,s)$, are positive, which can normally be assumed, a larger private human capital entails a larger optimal public capital. Therefore, if one of the individuals of our model, say w, is particularly efficient in attaining and maintaining a comparatively large human capital it will cause favourable external effects for the other, comparatively disadvantaged, individual. Conversely, as public capital exerts a favourable influence on the marginal productivity of individuals, the existence of public capital leads to a higher level of private human capital.

We should like to point out the close relationship of equations (26)–(28) to the familiar Samuelsonian rule for the optimal provision of a pure public good. Assume that $\mu^s = \mu^w = \mu^p$. Thus:

$$\eta^s F^s_{K_s} = \eta^w F^w_{K_w} = \eta^p (F^s_{K_p} + F^w_{K_p})$$

and, consequently,

$$\frac{F^s_{K_p}}{F^s_{K_s}} + \frac{F^w_{K_p}}{F^s_{K_s}} = \frac{\eta^s}{\eta^p}$$

$$\frac{F^s_{K_p}}{F^w_{K_w}} + \frac{F^w_{K_p}}{F^w_{K_w}} = \frac{\eta^w}{\eta^p}$$

As is evident from the recursive structure of the system of equations (22) to (28) the optimal stocks of capital necessitate particular optimal rates of taxation and private consumption. It can be shown that the individual optimal tax rates to be imposed will rise with larger individual efficiency parameters.

We now consider a simplified case where depreciation rates are zero, utility functions are identical and where $\bar{\lambda} = 1$. Assume $\eta^w > \eta^s$. Thus Mr. Weiss is more efficient than Mr. Schwarz in transforming savings into human capital. Then, according to (26) and (27), $K^*_w > K^*_s$. Consequently $\bar{F}^w > F^s$. Thus private income of w exceeds the income of s. Since $\bar{\lambda} = 1$ and utility functions are identical by assumption, equation (25) implies $c^*_s = c^*_w$. Therefore, according to (22) and (23), $(1 - \tau^s)F^s = (1 - \tau^w)F^w$. As $F^w > F^s$, we obtain $(1 - \tau^s) > (1 - \tau^w)$ which immediately yields $\tau^w > \tau^s$. This result can easily be generalized.

The more efficient and wealthier individual should be more heavily taxed than the comparatively disadvantaged individual. In the simplified case considered private consumption is equalized. In a more general case, where $\bar{\lambda} \neq 1$ and where individual utility functions are different the wealthier individual may still enjoy a higher private consumption in spite of being taxed at a higher rate. Although taxation of the wealthier person does not immediately lead to increases in human capital formation of the poor, it does so in a round-about way because public human capital augments the marginal productivity of individual capital, as indicated above.

It remains to investigate why it is beneficial to supply public capital goods at all. Wouldn't it be better to leave human capital formation entirely to individuals and to obtain the welfare condition (25) solely via taxation and transfers?

In order to answer this question let us assume K_p to be equal to zero. Condition (25) must be met through appropriate taxation and transfers. Hence $\tau^w > 0$ (tax rate) implies $\tau^s < 0$ (a transfer) and vice versa. Equations (3), and consequently equation (24), reduces to a static budget constraint. y_3 assumes the role of a constant Lagrangean multiplier. As a consequence, equation (28) disappears.

It will be noted that, in this case, too, human capital formation is totally unaffected by taxes and transfers once a stationary state has been attained. According to equations (26) and (27), the optimal stocks of human capital are solely determined by the rate of time preference and by the individual efficiency and depreciation parameters. To satisfy equation (25) taxes are levied on the wealthier individual and transfers are made to the poorer individual. Taxes and transfers, however, do not affect capital formation. Because no public capital is now available, incomes of *both* individuals are lower compared to the previously investigated situation where public capital, too, contributed to production. The formation of public capital entails a deferring of consumption but eventually everybody will be better off.

Our analysis thus suggests that, in the interest of both economic efficiency and distributional equity, the accumulation of human capital should not be left to individual efforts alone. To further economic efficiency and an equitable distribution of income human capital formation can only be beneficial for rapid economic growth, the main concern of this Congress. To the extent that human capital formation through a supply of public capital can be accelerated, government should favor the building-up of a stock of public capital in order to aid individual human capital formation.

Notes

[1]There is an equivalent method. We could have started with a more general framework in which the utility of one individual, say Mr. Schwarz, is maximized subject to a given level of utility of the other individual, in our case Mr. Weiss. In such a framework λ is a Langrangean multiplier denoting the marginal decrease of utility of Mr. Schwarz as a result of an increase of the initial level of utility of Mr. Weiss. There would be a movement along the contract locus of Pareto optima.

[2]In particular, since the Hamiltonian is linear in τ^s and τ^w, the Kuhn-Tucker conditions require:

$$\frac{\partial H}{\partial \tau^s} \leqq 0, \quad \tau^s \frac{\partial H}{\partial \tau^s} = 0$$

$$\frac{\partial H}{\partial \tau^w} \leqq 0, \quad \tau^w \frac{\partial H}{\partial \tau^w} = 0$$

implying (11) and (12) provided $\tau^s \neq 0$, $\tau^w \neq 0$.

References

G. S. Becker, *Human Capital. A Theoretical and Empirical Analysis, with Special Reference to Education*, 2nd ed. University of Chicago Press (1975).

Y. Ben-Porath, "The Production of Human Capital and the Life Cycle of Earnings," *Journal of Political Economy* 75, (1967), p. 352–65.

E. Denison, *Why Growth Rates Differ*. Postwar Experience in Nine Western Countries, The Brookings Institution, Washington, D.C., 1967.

Z. Griliches and W. Mason, "Education, Income and Ability," *Journal of Political Economy* 80, (1972) pt. 2, p. 74–103.

D. Levhari and Y. Weiss, "The Effect of Risk on the Investment in Human Capital," *American Economic Review*, 64 (1974), p. 950–63.

J. Mincer, "The Distribution of Labor Incomes. A Survey, With Special Reference to the Human Capital Approach." *Journal of Economic Literature*, 8 (1970), p. 1–26.

L. Olson, H. White and H. M. Shefrin, "Optimal Investment in Schooling when Incomes are Risky," *Journal of Political Economy*, 87 (1979), p. 522–39.

Y. Weiss, "Ability and the Investment in Schooling: A Theoretical Note on J. Mincer's "Distribution of Labor Incomes," *Journal of Economic Literature*, 9 (1971), p. 459–61.

Résumé

Le sujet de l'article concerne la formation du capital humain au cours du temps. Si les classes les moins aisées d'une population doivent être aidées pour former leur capital humain un transfert de ressources est nécéssaire. Ces transferts peuvent être effectués de deux façons: à l'aide d'un système impôt-subvention ou à l'aide d'un système impôt-subvention combiné avec l'approvisionnement des biens publics qui aident à la formation du capital humain. Le problème central est donc: quel est le stock optimal de capital humain détenu par chaque individu et quels sont les taux d'impôts optimaux à appliquer.

Finances Publiques et Formation du Capital Humain: Elements d'une Strategie alternative de Financement de l'Enseignement superieur

*Guy Terny**

Introduction

Ce qu'il est aujourd'hui convenu d'appeler l'Etat Providence (Welfare State)[1] a indéniablement contribué, d'une part, au développement économique et social des pays industriels fondés sur la propriété privée et l'économie de marché et, d'autre part, au nécessaire renforcement des liens de solidarité entre les diverses classes sociales. L'ensemble des dispositifs, mis en place au lendemain de la seconde guerre mondiale et au cours des quarante dernières années, connaissent cependant depuis que la plupart des pays subissent un net ralentissement de leur croissance économique, de telles difficultés dans leur financement qu'ils sont remis en cause, dans leur principe même, par certains, qu'ils font, par d'autres, l'objet de propositions de réforme radicales qui tendraient à améliorer leur efficacité, impact et équité.

L'enseignement supérieur, en tant qu'élément constitutif des institutions caractéristiques du "Welfare-State," n'échappe bien évidemment pas à ces critiques. Dans tous les pays du monde occidental, en France notamment, l'enseignement supérieur universitaire, au même titre que l'éducation nationale en général, souffre d'une perte de confiance de

*L'auteur est professeur d'économie publique et directeur du Groupe de Recherche en Economie Publique (G.R.E.P.), Université de Paris X (France). Il est également professeur-visitant à l'Institut de Management Public—CESMAP. Il a bénéficié, pour la rédaction de la 3ème partie de cette communication, de la collaboration de P. BARADUC.

Public Finance and Economic Growth. Proceedings of the 37th Congress of the International Institute of Public Finance. Tokyo, 1981, pp. 217–250

la part de la population et a perdu, depuis la fin des années 60, la place privilégiée qu'il occupait dans la hiérarchie des objectifs de la puissance publique et, corrélativement, dans la part relative des ressources qui lui sont affectées. Partout l'enseignement supérieur semble aujourd'hui être frappé par une triple crise: crise de pertinence, crise financière, crise de gestion et de management. Dysfonctionnements, inefficacités, insatisfaction des "usagers," dégradation de la valeur marchande des diplômes, etc. semblent être les traits les plus couramment retenus, parfois injustement, pour caractériser l'enseignement supérieur.

La thèse soutenue dans cette communication, thèse qui se situe dans l'exacte perspective de celle avancée par Th. W. SCHULTZ et par bien d'autres économistes britaniques et nord-américains, est la suivante: la plupart des problèmes et inefficacités qui affectent les systèmes universitaires trouvent en partie, selon nous, leur source principale dans l'insuffisance et l'inadéquation des modes de régulation et, plus particulièrement, dans l'inadaptation des procédures actuelles de financement et de production publics de l'enseignement supérieur.

Il existe, certes, de notables différences dans les divers modèles d'organisation des institutions universitaires des pays occidentaux, notamment en ce qui concerne les contrôles exercés par le pouvoir central (fédéral ou étatique) sur l'accès aux formations supérieures (éligibilité, sélection des étudiants), le contenu de celles-ci, la délivrance des diplômes, etc. . . ., mais tous se caractérisent cependant par une propriété commune: la quasi gratuité des services et le recours croissant et, progressivement généralisé aux ressources et prélèvements fiscaux pour assurer le financement des activités universitaires. C'est par et au travers d'un financement principalement public, complété par une planification et par un ensemble de réglements et contrôle directs que le centre régule ou gouverne les organisations périphériques (les établissements), oriente l'offre, accroît ou freine son développement, ne laissant aux organes de décisions périphériques (et aux étudiants) qu'une marge d'initiative et de choix souvent réduite, créant, aussi bien au niveau macro-économique qu'au niveau micro-économique, des distorsions et inefficacités allocatives et productives. Nous souhaiterions, en d'autres termes, démontrer que l'enseignement supérieur n'est pas actuellement doté des instruments de régulation économique susceptibles de promouvoir un investissement optimal en capital humain. Les inefficacités économiques du système, le caractère inéquitable de ses résultats se situent principalement, dans les modes actuels de financement, de tarification et d'offres des services éducatifs.

L'orientation générale de cette communication étant ainsi, en termes encore très généraux, précisée, l'argumentation sera maintenant développée dans une triple perspective:

—en premier lieu, nous nous interrogerons sur le point de savoir si le financement public de l'enseignement supérieur est économiquement fondé;
—en deuxième lieu, nous analyserons succinctement les "effets pervers" engendrés par un financement public, accompagné d'une production principalement publique, sur l'affectation des ressources et la production des services éducatifs;
—enfin, nous tenterons d'esquisser ce que pourraient être les principaux éléments d'une stratégie alternative de financement, donc de l'offre, susceptible d'améliorer l'efficacité et l'équité du système.

Il est évident que cette contribution, nécessairement limitée, repose sur un certain nombre d'hypothèses:

—il s'agit d'une analyse utilisant les instruments économiques néoclassiques; dans cette perspective, l'hypothèse est faite que l'investissement optimal en cette forme de capital humain qu'est l'enseignement supérieur est principalement fondé sur les micro-décisions d'individus se comportant de façon économiquement rationelle
—il est supposé que les activités de formation et d'enseignement peuvent être disjointes de l'ensemble des autres activités et productions universitaires; bien qu'il existe des liens entre enseignement, recherche, services divers à la collectivité, etc. . . ., ces divers outputs sont ici considérés comme étant séparables;
—l'enseignement supérieur, ainsi que l'éducation en général, sont indéniablement des services complexes, aux composantes multiples; la demande de ces services revêt des aspects de consommation privée et collective; elle donne lieu à des décisions individuelles d'investissement dont bénéficient directement l'individu mais aussi, soutiennent certains, la collectivité tout entière; seules les composantes investissement et consommation privés seront ici étudiés à titre principal.
—l'évaluation en termes économiques, de la régulation et du financement de l'enseignement supérieur, de même que toute proposition de réforme, ne peuvent être appréciées qu'en prenant simultanément en compte l'efficacité et l'équité globales du dispositif.

1. L'offre et le financement publics de l'enseignement supérieur sont-ils économiquement fondés?

En France, comme dans la plupart des autres pays, l'enseignement supérieur est financé par le canal de subventions publiques directement allouées aux établissements. De ce fait, toute personne éligible et sélectionnée bénéficie d'un même montant de subvention publique qui correspond à la quantité, à la qualité et au type de formation qu'elle reçoit. Le système se caractérise donc par une subvention indifférenciée attribuée au produit et non par une aide spécifique qui serait affectée à la personne en fonction des revenus dont celle-ci disposerait. Il en va ainsi, mais à des degrés variables, aussi bien pour un enseignement supérieur quasi-gratuit (France) que pour un enseignement payant mais dont le prix directement mis à la charge de l'utilisateur ne correspond qu'à une partie seulement du coût (moyen, marginal) de production du service (U.S.A., Grande-Bretagne).

Partant de ce constat, la question se pose de savoir quels sont les arguments économiques couramment avancés à l'appui d'un financement public dont les principes fondamentaux viennent d'être sommairement décrits.

D'une façon générale, il est couramment affirmé que le financement public de l'enseignement supérieur trouve sa justification économique dans une double série de considérations correspondant à deux objectifs de la puissance publique:

—un objectif *d'équité:* l'offre publique et la gratuité de l'enseignement supérieur seraient des instruments efficaces permettant de promouvoir une égalisation des chances et une redistribution des revenus des plus favorisés vers les plus défavorisés;

—un objectif *d'efficacité:* le subventionnement public de l'enseignement supérieur se justifierait par l'existence d'économies externes associées aux utilisations individuelles dudit service.

Financement public de l'enseignement supérieur et objectif d'équité

Une analyse minutieuse de l'abondante littérature traitant de cet aspect du problème, permet de décomposer l'argument en deux interrogations:

—le financement public de la production d'enseignement supérieur contribue-t-il à une égalisation des chances des individus?
—le financement public de la production d'enseignement supérieur constitue-t-il un instrument efficace de redistribution des revenus?

Financement public, égalisation des chances et démocratisation. Ce premier argument, qui est d'ailleurs de nature plus politique qu'économique, repose sur l'idée suivante: l'offre publique d'éducation et sa gratuité seraient de nature à promouvoir une égalisation des chances d'accès aux niveaux les plus élevés de la culture et des qualifications et, ce faisant, engendreraient des effets bénéfiques sur la démocratisation de l'enseignement non-obligatoire. C'est ce que traduit J.Cl. EICHER lorsqu'il écrit:

> Il semble généralement admis qu'en pays démocratique, la politique d'éducation doit s'efforcer d'égaliser les chances des individus devant l'enseignement. Mais, si l'on interprète cette expression dans son sens le plus étroit, en ne prenant en compte que les chances d'accès à l'enseignement non-obligatoire, on se trouve devant le problème suivant: l'école fournit des services dont l'acquisition requiert à la fois une capacité financière et des qualités intellectuelles minimales. Il ne suffit donc pas de rendre l'école gratuite pour en permettre un accès égal à tous.

Cet argument, valable pour l'école, est encore plus puissant appliqué à l'enseignement supérieur qui, de par sa situation dans le cycle de formation des individus, se trouve placé en aval des périodes de formation primaire et secondaire au cours desquelles en dépit de la gratuité ou quasi-gratuité, les critères de sélection intellectuels et culturels ont progressivement écarté du système tous ceux qui n'avaient pas ces qualités intellectuelles minimales dont parle J.Cl. EICHER. Le résultat de ces éliminations successives est simple: la population qui se présente aux portes d'accès à l'enseignement supérieur à une structure qui est déjà très fortement déformée par rapport à celle de la population totale des classes d'âge correspondantes ventilées par niveaux de revenu. Dans tous les pays, cette population candidate à l'enseignement supérieur est très largement composée de personnes appartenant aux catégories sociales moyennes et élevées dans des proportions bien supérieures à celles des effectifs composant les dites catégories par rapport à l'ensemble de la population.

Des évolutions favorables aux catégories sociales défavorisées ont, certes, été constatées au cours des vingt dernières années mais elles n'ont pas eu pour effet de promouvoir l'égalisation des chances d'accès et de réussite dans l'enseignement supérieur que déclarent vouloir réaliser les décideurs politiques. C'est dire que l'expansion considérable des effectifs de l'enseignement supérieur, l'offre gratuite et indifférenciée de ce type d'enseignement n'ont eu que très partiellement pour conséquence de garantir le progrès social et la mobilité sociale.

Financement public de l'enseignement supérieur et redistribution des revenus. Le deuxième argument en faveur d'un contrôle et d'un financement publics de l'éducation serait, dans l'optique de la recherche d'une plus grande équité socio-économique, que l'enseignement supérieur ouvert à tous et subventionné sur fonds publics constituerait un instrument efficace de redistribution des revenus.

L'argumentation proposée peut être présentée (et réfutée) en décomposant ici encore l'analyse en deux étapes:

—l'étude des liens entre éducation et distribution des revenus, en dehors de toute considération des modes de financement de celle-ci;
—l'étude des conséquences du financement public de l'enseignement supérieur sur la redistribution des revenus proprement dite.

Enseignement supérieur et distribution des revenus. En dehors de toute considération des modes de financement de l'enseignement supérieur, il convient de poser la question de savoir si la considérable augmentation des effectifs d'étudiants, qui est intervenue tout au long des années 1950 et 1960, a effectivement entraîné une amélioration de la distribution des revenus.

Les très nombreux travaux récents qui ont été effectués dans cette perspective ne semblent pas confirmer l'idée fort répandue suivant laquelle l'éducation améliorerait la répartition des revenus. Il s'agit-là d'une controverse encore très vive à propos de laquelle des conclusions définitives ne sauraient être avancées avec certitude. Il semble néanmoins prouvé, qu'aux U.S.A. par exemple, la répartition des revenus est demeurée pratiquement constante depuis la IIème guerre mondiale alors que pendant toute la période allant des années cinquante à nos jours, des progrès considérables ont été réalisés dans la répartition des chances face à l'enseignement supérieur et que les pourcentages des classes d'âge des personnes de 18 à 25 ans ayant accès à ce niveau d'enseignement s'accroissaient plus que partout ailleurs.

De même, une étude de R. HOLLISTER réalisée pour l'O.C.D.E. conclue que dans la plupart des pays industrialisés,il semble n'y avoir pratiquement aucun rapport entre la distribution de l'éducation et celle du revenu, mesurées toutes les deux à l'aide des indices de Gini. Si l'on s'intéresse à la situation qui semble prévaloir dans les pays en voie de développement, en Amérique Latine notamment, les constats que l'on peut faire sur ce point sont encore plus nets que dans les pays industrialisés: il suffit, pour s'en convaincre de se reporter aux travaux de J. P. JALLADE. Un pays comme le Mexique a vu s'aggraver l'inégalité des revenus entre 1960 et 1970 au moment où des progrès considérables étaient réalisés dans le domaine de l'accès à l'éducation.

Plusieurs explications de cet échec peuvent être ainsi résumées:

a) On a sans aucun doute surestimé l'étroitesse de la relation entre éducation et revenu. Or, comme le souligne J. P. JALLADE, l'existence de cette relation est indispensable pour que la distribution de l'éducation puisse avoir une influence sur la répartition du revenu. S'il est incontestable que l'éducation accroît le potentiel de revenu d'un individu, il est tout aussi probable que de nombreux autres facteurs agissent sur la détermination dudit revenu: le milieu socio-économique d'origine de l'individu, les effets exercés par l'environnement familial (éducation du père, de la mère, le métier du père et/ou de la mère), les facultés innées de l'individu, etc. . . ., ont, à côté de l'éducation proprement dite, une influence indéniable dans la détermination du revenu.

Tout cela nous conduit bien naturellement à penser que, si l'objectif d'une meilleure répartition des revenus figure parmi ceux que s'assignent les décideurs publics, l'offre gratuite d'éducation et son accès libre ne sont sans doute pas le moyen le plus efficace d'y parvenir. Son coût est élevé pour des résultats relativement médiocres.

b) Par ailleurs,pour que l'éducation considérée isolément puisse contribuer à améliorer la distribution des revenus,il conviendrait que l'analyse tienne compte de l'inégalité qui prévaut avant toute action en ce domaine. Cette inégalité initiale a pour conséquence l'inégalité de l'épargne, et, donc celle des possibilités d'investissement en capital humain. Il apparaît que pour améliorer la répartition des revenus par le canal de l'investissement en éducation en général, dans l'enseignement supérieur en particulier, il conviendrait que deux conditions soient satisfaites.

(i) Les catégories à faible revenu devraient investir davantage dans l'éducation que les catégories à revenus moyens et élevés;

(ii) Le taux de rentabilité de l'investissement en éducation des premières devrait être au moins aussi élevé que celui des catégories à revenu moyen et élevé.

De très nombreuses études faites, tant dans les pays développés que dans les pays en voie de développement, montrent que ces conditions ne sont pas remplies. Ces constatations empiriques renforcent donc l'hypothèse suivant laquelle l'éducation en tant que telle ne peut, à court ou moyen terme, réduire les inégalités. On peut même penser que la généralisation de l'éducation tend à entraîner une diminution de l'influence de celle-ci sur le revenu et que de ce fait, le rôle joué par des facteurs autres que l'éducation sur le revenu, telles que les aptitudes intellectuelles et l'origine socio-économique, devient prépondérante dans le détermination du revenu. Il semble donc évident que la démocratisation d'un niveau d'éducation, de l'enseignement supérieur en particulier, annule le rôle sélectif de ce niveau pour laisser place à l'influence grandissante d'autres facteurs dans la détermination du revenu, et notamment celle du facteur "accès à l'emploi."

Financement public de l'enseignement supérieur et redistribution des revenus. Il apparaît, au travers de l'argumentation précédente, qui ne constitue pas une véritable démonstration, laquelle demanderait de très longs développements, que la très large ouverture de l'éducation à toutes les catégories socio-économiques, et plus particulièrement, que la "massification" de l'enseignement supérieur, n'a pas eu pour effet de provoquer une amélioration de la distribution des revenus. Encore n'avons-nous pas, dans le raisonnement précédent, pris en compte le fait que les individus n'investissent que rarement seuls dans l'enseignement supérieur et que les gouvernements participent très largement à cet investissement par le canal de dotations budgétaires financées sur fonds publics issus de la fiscalité générale. Le problème se pose donc de savoir quelle est la conséquence de ce financement public sur la distribution des revenus. L'une des thèses les plus couramment avancées en faveur d'un financement public, total ou partiel, de l'enseignement non obligatoire, post-secondaire notamment, serait qu'il favoriserait une juste redistribution des revenus. Nous allons voir que loin de contribuer à la réalisation de cet objectif, les subventions publiques, indifféremment accordées à tous les étudiants entrant dans le système supérieur, peuvent être à l'origine d'"effets pervers" en matière de redistribution, c'est-à-dire avoir des conséquences contraires aux objectifs annoncés par les décideurs publics.

Partant donc de la constatation suivant laquelle il semble exister une assez forte préférence des gouvernements et des contribuables pour des subventions en nature par rapport à des transferts monétaires non affectés, il n'en reste pas moins que l'on peut se poser la question de savoir si une intervention publique de ce type en matière de financement de l'enseignement supérieur est justifié et conduit aux "bons" résultats attendus, en matière de redistribution des revenus notamment. Plusieurs arguments, que nous allons résumer ici, donnent à penser que les résultats d'une politique de subvention telle que nous l'avons sommairement décrite ne sont pas toujours conformes aux objectifs affichés par les pouvoirs publics.

Pour porter, de ce point de vue, une appréciation sur ce système de financement, il convient de procéder à la mesure de son incidence nette (bénéfice moins impôts) pour les différentes classes de revenu et se demander si les impôts payés par les classes "favorisées" sont supérieurs aux avantages qu'elles retirent des services éducatifs.

Ainsi que nous l'avons précédemment souligné, les modalités actuelles de financement public de l'enseignement supérieur font que le "produit" est subventionné sans tenir compte du niveau de revenu. Il est alors tout à fait possible que la subvention soit, dans le meilleur des cas, "neutre" en ce qui concerne l'inégalité des revenus. Il est même permis de penser qu'elle peut avoir des conséquences négatives sur la distribution des revenus dans la mesure où les groupes à revenus élevés font, en général, des études plus longues que les groupes à revenus faibles et moyens, et que les premiers sont, de ce fait, plus largement subventionnés par l'Etat que les seconds. Dans les pays où la fiscalité est assez, voire très progressive, les groupes à revenus élevés peuvent soutenir qu'ils paient l'éducation de leurs enfants par le biais des impôts directs et que les enfants de ces groupes ayant le plus longuement bénéficié des subventions de l'Etat remboursent les subventions reçues tout au long de leur vie dans la mesure où les revenus élevés sont plus lourdement frappés par l'impôt progressif. Mais, pour que cet argument soit acceptable, il conviendrait que dans les pays où l'accès à l'enseignement supérieur est très inégal, et où la répartition des subventions à l'éducation favorise des groupes à revenus moyens-supérieurs et supérieurs, la fiscalité dans son ensemble soit très progressive pour compenser les effets néfastes d'une distribution régressive des subventions publiques sur la répartition du revenu (J. P. JALLADE, p. 783).

Ce problème fondamental a donné lieu, au cours des quinze dernières années, à des études statistiques et économétriques nombreuses et ce en un grand nombre de pays.

Il est bien évidemment difficile de dresser un bilan précis des résultats de ces diverses études, et ce d'autant plus qu'elles portent sur des pays très divers, tant du point de vue des taux et de la structure de la scolarisation au niveau de l'enseignement supérieur que du point de vue de la structure fiscale qui les caractérisent. Il semble cependant possible de constater que, dans l'ensemble, le financement public de l'enseignement supérieur n'a pas, en matière de redistribution des revenus, les effets redistributifs escomptés. Ainsi, HANSEN et WEISBROD (pour la Californie), WINDHAM (pour la Floride) ont démontré que l'effet net instantané des subventions publiques à l'enseignement supérieur dans ces deux états américains, s'analyse en une redistribution des revenus s'opérant au détriment des groupes ayant les revenus les plus faibles. JUDY, pour le Canada, conclue son analyse de la façon suivante:

> L'enseignement principal des ces travaux est de montrer qu'aucune redistribution sensible entre classes de revenus n'est réalisée par le canal de programmes d'enseignement supérieur financés sur fonds publics. Les bénéficiaires de ces programmes sont, ou seront, très largement concentrés dans les tranches de revenus les plus élevés, mais sont aussi concentrées dans ces tranches les personnes qui paient les impôts dont sont issus les ressources publiques servant à financer les aides accordées aux universités.

D'autres études montrent, qu'entre autres résultats possibles, l'enseignement supérieur pourrait avoir pour effet de promouvoir une meilleure distribution du revenu lorsque sont pris en compte les revenus perçus par les individus sur la totalité de leur vie active. Quoi qu'il en soit, il apparaît difficile, comme on le fait parfois, d'affirmer que les "pauvres subventionnent l'enseignement supérieur reçu par les riches" (encore que dans certains pays en voie de développement, il semble bien qu'il en aille ainsi).[2]

Mais à l'inverse, il apparaît également, qu'au mieux, le financement public de l'enseignement supérieur est neutre en matière de redistribution des revenus et que dans de nombreux pays, dont la France semble-t-il, ce mode de financement bénéficie principalement, lorsque l'on compare les avantages reçus aux coûts financés sur fonds publics, aux catégories appartenant aux classes moyennes. En tout état de cause, il est difficile d'admettre au travers des résultats de ces diverses études, que le financement public de l'enseignement supérieur est un instrument efficace de redistribution des revenus alors même qu'il s'agit-là de l'argument qui est le plus couramment avancé par les décideurs publics et les politiques lorsqu'il s'agit pour eux d'apporter un élément de justification à l'intervention de l'Etat en ce domaine. Il semble indéniable en d'autres termes, que l'enseignement supérieur n'échappe pas de ce point de vue à "la loi de Directeur," explicitée par George J. STIGLER.

S'il apparaît donc difficile, d'un point de vue strictement

économique d'apporter une argumentation solide en faveur du financement public de l'enseignement supérieur, argumentation qui serait fondée sur les effets redistributifs positifs qu'exercerait une telle intervention, le problème se pose de savoir si des arguments tenant cette fois, non plus à l'équité, mais à l'efficacité dans l'affectation des ressources seraient de nature à justifier le financement public, total ou partiel, de l'enseignement supérieur. Nous allons voir que, de ce point de vue, les raisons les plus couramment avancées par les économistes ne revêtent pas, lá encore, un caractère totalement convainquant.

Financement public de l'enseignement supérieur et efficacité économique

La théorie économique classique nous enseigne qu'une source possible de l'intervention de l'Etat en matière d'affectation des ressources résulte de l'existence d'économies externes importantes qui seraient "sacrifiées" si les décisions de production et/ou de consommation de certains biens ou services étaient entièrement laissées à la seule et entière initiative d'agents isolés (consommateurs et producteurs).

En ce qui concerne ici notre propos, tous ceux qui cherchent à justifier une intervention publique, sous forme d'une subvention à l'enseignement supérieur, soutiennent qu'en l'absence de toute action visant à infléchir les décisions et choix individuels, il y aurait, en présence d'économies externes, sous-production d'enseignement par rapport à la quantité correspondant à l'optimum collectif.[3]

Nous voudrions ici montrer que les avantages qui sont couramment présentés comme constituant les économies externes de l'enseignement supérieur sont qualitativement incertains et quantitativement difficilement mesurables. La littérature sur un tel sujet est particulièrement abondante et trouve principalement son origine dans des travaux menés aux U.S.A., en Grande-Bretagne, et, plus récemment, en France.

Tous ces auteurs, pris collectivement, fervents avocats de l'intervention de la puissance publique, énumèrent huit catégories d'effets[4] qu'ils considèrent comme constituant autant d'avantages collectifs associés à l'enseignement supérieur: celui-ci aurait, en dehors des avantages individuels qu'il procure, pour effet de:[5]

—provoquer des changements dans les attitudes, comportements et valeurs;

—promouvoir le "leadership politique" et une meilleure participation aux affaires politiques et collectives;
—promouvoir une meilleure distribution des revenus;
—accroître la mobilité sociale;
—accroître la quantité et la qualité de la recherche;
—améliorer la structure des qualifications professionnelles;
—abaisser le niveau de chômage
—provoquer une élévation de la productivité du capital physique.

Provoquer des changements dans les attitudes, comportements et valeurs. Ces changements d'attitudes et de comportements ont, de tout temps et dans tout pays, été l'un des fondements et l'une des principales justifications du contrôle et du financement public de l'enseignement primaire et secondaire (obligatoires): il s'agit de faire "pénétrer" dans tous les esprits d'un groupe national certaines valeurs communes et certains comportements communs. Cet objectif constitue, certes, un argument en faveur d'un contrôle public sur le contenu de la formation mais peut-il à lui seul justifier un financement public?

Par ailleurs, quelle peut être la validité de cet argument lorsqu'il est appliqué à l'enseignement supérieur? Il apparaît que deux propositions peuvent, à ce sujet, être avancées:

—nul ne pourrait définir et préciser une liste, recueillant un accord unanime, des valeurs et des attitudes devant être transmises aux générations actuelles d'étudiants;
—à supposer même que l'on puisse préciser ces valeurs, comment pourrait-on s'assurer qu'elles exercent des effets positifs, neutres, voire négatifs, sur l'ensemble de la collectivité?

Au total, l'évaluation d'attitudes et de comportements nous semble relever d'un processus par trop subjectif pour pouvoir être sérieusement (et quantitativement) prise en compte dans une évaluation objective des ressources publiques devant être affectées à l'investissement éducatif non obligatoire.

Promouvoir une plus grande participation aux affaires politiques et collectives. L'enseignement supérieur contribuerait à accroître le sens des responsabilités et à promouvoir le degré de participation des diplômés aux affaires politiques et collectives; il a été ainsi démontré qu'étudiants et diplômés de l'enseignement supérieur prennent une part plus active dans les affaires que ceux ayant bénéficié d'un niveau de formation plus faible. Mais, pour qu'il s'agisse là d'une économie externe, il faudrait être sûr que cet accroissement de participation des diplômés n'est pas un obstacle à l'accession à des responsabilités politiques d'autres catégories de population, des non-diplômés notamment. Or, à ce sujet, l'expérience, semble montrer, en France comme ailleurs, qu'il y a rivalité et que des solidarités se nouent entre diplômés ayant une origine commune. L'avantage ainsi conféré par une formation supérieure échoit principalement au bénéficiaire de celle-ci et à la classe à laquelle il appartient; il ne saurait, dans ces conditions, être considéré comme une économie externe générale, indivisible et collective.

Promouvoir une meilleure distribution des revenus. Ce point a été longuement abordé et l'on se souvient que les conclusions tirées de cette étude montrent que l'enseignement supérieur n'exerce aucun effet sensible sur la distribution des revenus et peut engendrer des "effets pervers" en matière de redistribution.

Accroître la mobilité sociale des individus. De nombreuses études semblent montrer que l'enseignement supérieur peut avoir des effets significatifs sur la mobilité individuelle mais n'exerce que des effets relativement secondaires sur la mobilité d'un groupe social tout entier vers un autre groupe du statut socio-économique plus élevé. Dans la même optique, les travaux de S. BOWLES, S. BOWLES et H. GINTIS, M. CARNOY, H. M. LEVIN pour les U.S.A., de P. BOURDIEU, P. BAUDELOT et R. ESTABLET pour la France, conduisent tous à la conclusion que, dans un système d'économie concurrentielle et de propriété privée, la fonction de l'éducation est au mieux de maintenir et, probablement, d'aggraver les inégalités. La conclusion suivant laquelle les niveaux supérieurs d'éducation et de formation ne constituent pas un moyen très efficace au service d'une plus grande mobilité sociale semble devoir s'imposer à tous les analystes, quelle que soit leur orientation philosophique et/ou politique!

Accroître la quantité et améliorer la qualité de la recherche. Parmi les autres types d'économies externes associées à la production d'enseignement figure, de façon quelque peu surprenante, le fait que la société tout entière beneficierait, sous la forme d'un sous-produit de l'enseignement, d'un avantage commun résultant des travaux de recherche menés par les membres du corps professoral. Voilà un traitement bien particulier fait à la recherche qui ne correspond ni à la réalité, ni aux objectifs d'une véritable politique de la recherche.

L'enseignement bénéficie de la recherche (dans des limites d'ailleurs plus étroites qu'on ne l'affirme généralement) plus que la recherche bénéficie de l'enseignement! Par ailleurs, une grande partie de la recherche menée dans les universités est un produit direct, souvent défini par contrat, des établissements d'enseignement supérieur. Elle ne saurait être, en aucune façon, analysée comme étant une externalité fortuite!

Améliorer la structure des qualifications professionnelles. Il s'agit d'un type d'économie externe très couramment mentionné, notamment par les responsables des politiques d'éducation des pays en voie de développement. L'argument avancé est le suivant: le rôle majeur de l'enseignement supérieur serait de produire les types de formations et qualifications dont l'économie a besoin. Cette contribution de l'enseignement supérieur au développement économique constituerait alors la principale justification des subventions publiques versées au système. En fait, une grande désillusion semble aujourd'hui se faire jour à propos de cette liaison formation-qualification-développement économique et, en tout état de cause, l'intervention publique destinée à promouvoir une meilleure structure des qualifications pourrait prendre des formes beaucoup plus efficaces que celle consistant en un "subventionnement" général et indifférencié du système d'enseignement supérieur. Si un type particulier de formation qualifiée est nécessaire et si l'intervention gouvernementale semble être le seul moyen de parvenir à cette production, il serait préférable que le gouvernement subventionne cette formation particulière ou améliore le système d'information et de "signaux" émis par les demandeurs de cette formation.

Contribuer à la réduction du niveau de chômage. Il est en général bien établi que, dans la plupart des pays développés, le taux de chômage des diplômés de l'enseignement supérieur est inférieur à celui qui caractérise ceux qui ont reçu un niveau d'éducation plus faible. Mais, il faut être prudent dans l'interprétation de ce constat lorsqu'il s'agit de l'ériger en un effet externe positif de l'enseignement supérieur: en effet, bien qu'une probabilité réduite de chômage soit indéniablement un avantage pour ceux dotés d'un diplôme d'enseignement supérieur, il n'en reste pas moins vrai que l'avantage collectif n'existe que dans la mesure où celui-ci n'est pas compensé par une probabilité de chômage plus élevée pour les autres diplômés. En fait, les résultats empiriques de la plupart des études faites en ce domaine au cours des dix dernières années semblent indiquer que la croissance et la "massification" de l'enseignement supérieur n'ont pas conduit à une diminution des taux globaux de chômage et que la moindre augmentation du taux de chômage des diplômés s'est faite au détriment de celui des non-diplômés. Ce phénomène résulte probablement du fait que les diplômés de l'enseignement supérieur, ne trouvant pas d'emploi dans des postes auxquels les destinait leur formation, ont accepté des postes de moindre qualification les plaçant dans une situation de concurrence qui leur est favorable par rapport à ceux ayant un niveau moindre de formation (phénomène de déqualification ou de déclassement des diplômés).

Provoquer une Amélioration de la Productivité du Capital Physique. Si les diplômés de l'enseignement supérieur contribuent, dans l'exercice de leurs fonctions, à l'amélioration de la productivité générale du capital physique et ne reçoivent pas en contrepartie de cette amélioration les avantages correspondant sous forme de rémunérations personnelles, alors cette amélioration de la productivité peut, mais peut seulement, bénéficier à l'ensemble de la collectivité sous la forme d'un abaissement des coûts et/ou sous la forme d'un accroissement de l'emploi. Il est cependant plus probable que le "surplus" créé par ces travailleurs diplômés, qui ne récupèrent qu'une partie de leur contribution à l'amélioration de la productivité du capital physique sera accaparé non par la collectivité dans son ensemble, mais par les employeurs eux-mêmes. L'enseignement supérieur peut donc être ici à l'origine d'une économie externe, d'une nature, il est vrai, très particulière, mais son incidence ne pourra qu'exceptionnellement être qualifiée de collective et généralisée.

Au total, il ressort de ce rapide examen des divers types d'effets externes que l'on associe couramment à l'enseignement supérieur, que de tels effets ont une existence incertaine, que leur importance et leur distribution restent difficiles à préciser et que la quasi totalité d'entre eux ne peut donner lieu à une quantification et encore moins à une valorisation en termes monétaires.

Mais, même si tous les problèmes que nous venons d'évoquer pouvaient être résolus de manière à établir la liste et l'importance réelle de tels effets, l'existence d'économies externes associées à l'enseignement supérieur pourrait certes constituer une justification de l'intervention de la puissance publique dans le financement (ou l'offre) d'enseignement supérieur mais elle ne justifierait, en aucun cas, le maintien d'une subvention quasi-totale directe et indifférenciée du produit.

Envisagé dans cette perspective, les modes de financement publics les plus couramment mis en oeuvre ne semblent donc pas avoir toutes les vertus qu'on leur attribue généralement: ils ne contribuent pas efficacement, ni à l'égalisation des chances, ni à une redistribution équitable des revenus (ils peuvent même avoir en ce dernier domaine des "effets pervers"); ils ne sont que très incomplètement justifiés par des impératifs associés à la recherche d'une affectation optimale des ressources dans la mesure même où les économies externes associées à l'enseignement supérieur sont incertaines dans leur généralité, qualitativement douteuses et difficiles à mesurer. Ces modes de financement semblent, en outre, être à la source de graves inefficacités allocatives et productives, tant au plan global ou macro-économiques qu'au niveau micro-économique (ou organisationnel), inefficacités qu'il nous faut, ne serait-ce que très brièvement, analyser.

II. Inefficacités économiques engendrées par un système de financement public direct du produit "enseignement supérieur"

Nous pourrons, sur ce point, nous limiter à quelques rappels seulement car il s'agit de phénomènes bien connus et qui ont donné lieu à de nombreuses et pertinentes analyses largement admises dans leurs principes et conclusions.

Financement public du produit et inefficacités globales ou macro-économiques

En dehors d'une inefficacité en matière de redistribution des revenus sur laquelle nous ne reviendrons pas ici, un financement public du produit "enseignement supérieur" est de notre point de vue, de nature à engendrer des gaspillages de ressources rares à usages alternatifs.

Un système efficace de financement serait, en effet, celui qui permettrait de satisfaire, au moindre coût, les demandes des usagers du service et de provoquer des adaptations, rapides et souples, de l'offre aux variations de la demande.

Le financement public, tel qu'actuellement mis en oeuvre, financement qui contribue à la concentration du pouvoir de décision entre les mains des autorités centrales, entrave la réalisation de l'efficacité telle que précédemment définie et l'adaptation de l'offre à la demande. En d'autres termes, le système éducatif étant caractérisé par une forte autonomie par rapport à son environnement et par de longs délais de réaction aux changements de ce dernier, il n'est pas, dès lors, surprenant que les désajustements entre formation du capital humain et emploi soient l'une des principales manifestations de l'inefficacité dans la production des systèmes universitaires.

La démonstration de ce qui n'est ici qu'une simple affirmation demanderait de longs développements qu'il est impossible de faire figurer dans cette communication.[6] Seuls seront rappelés quelques indices, quelques signes manifestes de l'inefficacité globale du système.

a) L'accroissement constaté, bien avant que n'intervienne ce qu'il est convenu d'appeler la "crise" économique des années 1970, du chômage des jeunes diplômés de l'enseignement supérieur.

b) Parallèlement à cette aggravation continue du chômage des jeunes diplômés de l'enseignement supérieur, subsistent des pénuries persistantes de personnels qualifiés dont témoignent les offres d'emploi non satisfaites. Un système économique qui fonctionnerait correctement ne devrait pas avoir d'autres excédents (chômage) et d'autres pénuries (offres d'emploi non satisfaites) que "frictionnelles," c'est-à-dire passagères et limitées dans leur ampleur. Or, comme tel n'est pas le cas depuis plusieurs années, force est de constater que la persistance de niveaux élevés de chômage et d'offres d'emploi nombreuses tient à une durable inadéquation entre l'offre et la demande des formations.

c) La déqualification des diplômes constitue une autre manifestation des rigidités du système; en France, comme dans la plupart des autres pays, l'absence d'une régulation institutionnelle véritable a favorisé la "massification" des enseignements supérieurs sans que pour autant ne s'élargissent parallèlement ni le nombre, ni l'éventail des postes de travail auxquels ils conduisaient dans un passé encore récent. Les conséquences de ce phénomène sont nombreuses et souvent douloureuses, notamment pour les plus vulnérables de ces diplômés, c'est-à-dire ceux qui, issus de milieux modestes ou moyens, ne disposent pas du capital social et culturel nécessaire à l'obtention du plein rendement et à la valorisation marchande de leurs titres. Cette déqualification moyenne des diplômes résultant d'une "création anarchique de faux droits et de faux espoirs" (LEVY-GARBOUA), s'est, bien évidemment, traduite par la baisse du taux de rendement de l'enseignement supérieur et par une intensification de la sélection expost, menée par les universités, s'analysant en un rejet d'un nombre croissant d'étudiants sans diplôme et en l'élévation sensible des abandons, redoublements, etc. . . .

d) Un autre signe de la mauvaise adéquation entre formation du capital humain et emploi doit aussi être recherché dans la très grande mobilité (mieux vaudrait dire "instabilité") des jeunes au cours des premières années de leur vie active. Il est bien connu aujourd'hui que cette mobilité (ou instabilité) effective ou potentielle, tient principalement à l'insuffisante connaissance concrète, réelle, vécue que les jeunes peuvent obtenir, au cours de leur période de formation, du milieu de travail et de la vie active en général, du type de métier ou d'emploi qu'ils choisissent ou vers lesquels ils sont orientés. Le décloisonnement des systèmes d'enseignement supérieur et de formation serait sans aucun doute de nature à atténuer les rigueurs de cette instabilité et les inquiétudes qu'elle suscite.

Les autorités publiques et planificateurs centraux ne disposent pas, en l'absence d'un "marché" organisé de l'enseignement supérieur, des informations qui permettraient de remédier à ces inefficacités. Il leur faudrait, pour ce faire, disposer d'informations sur les préférences des usagers-consommateurs à l'égard des formations et sur celles des employeurs à l'égard des diverses qualifications. Il leur faudrait, en outre, obtenir une connaissance précise des disponibilités et combinaisons possibles des ressources éducatives avant qu'ils ne soient à même de fixer quels types de formation offrir et quelles techniques de production mettre en oeuvre. En ce qui concerne le premier point, il est inutile de faire ici l'historique des méthodes de planification de l'enseignement et des échecs successifs rencontrés en ce domaine. Il paraît clair que les centres de décision centraux ont tenté de planifier l'offre, sans être en mesure, faute de volonté politique et d'information, de connaître et de maîtriser la demande. Ils ont, ce faisant, sinon engendré, du moins laissé se développer des déséquilibres profonds dans le développement et le fonctionnement du système. Il semblerait essentiel, dans une perspective d'efficacité dynamique, que les universités proprement dites puissent bénéficier d'une véritable autonomie et soient incitées, par de nouveaux modes de régulation et de financement, à répondre aux variations de la demande exprimée à l'égard de divers types de formation. La mise en oeuvre d'un système cohérent d'incitations nouvelles devrait, selon nous, avoir pour principal objectif de réduire "l'impérialisme de l'offre," de susciter la reconnaissance et la prise en compte de la demande, en bref, de favoriser la confrontation des deux forces capables d'assurer une meilleure régulation globale d'un "quasi marché" de l'enseignement supérieur.

Financement public du produit et inefficacités micro-économiques ou organisationnelles

Les inefficacités précédemment mentionnées sont de type "allocatif" dans la mesure où elles se traduisent par une affectation des ressources qui ne correspond pas à l'optimum social de type parétien. Mais, le financement public de l'enseignement supérieur, qui confère le quasi-monopole de la production à des organisations publiques non-marchandes (OPNM) ou organisations publiques bureaucratiques, génère indéniablement des inefficiences "productives" se traduisant par des gaspillages de ressources et, par voie de conséquence, par des surcoûts de production. Ces inefficiences qui semblent être caractéristiques, non seulement des institutions universitaires mais, sinon de toutes, du moins de la plupart des OPNM, ont été particulièrement bien analysées par les économistes-théoriciens de la bureaucratie[7] et, dans une perspective plus générale, par H. LEIBENSTEIN, auteur de la théorie de "l'inefficience-X," et Ch. WOLF qui a récemment proposé une stimulante description des "déficiences du secteur non-marchand" ("non-market failures"). Pour notre part, nous nous bornerons ici à remarquer que les modalités actuelles de financement, de production, de gestion et de contrôle des établissements universitaires publics, qui, en France, détiennent un quasi-monopole de l'offre, ne suscitent guère, de leur part, la recherche de combinaisons techniquement et économiquement efficaces des facteurs de production. Les systèmes d'incitations-sanctions-récompenses qui prévalent les vouent "naturellement," en quelque sorte à "l'inéfficience-X." L'encouragement, dans un système centralisé de financement public, de pratiques minimisantes en matière de coûts supposerait la mise en place d'une bureaucratie coûteuse et "oppressive" dont le moins que l'on puisse dire est qu'elle est peu désirable lorsqu'il s'agit de la production d'enseignement (ou de recherche) et qu'elle conduirait à un renforcement du pouvoir exercé par les autorités centrales sur les organisations périphériques. C'est donc vers d'autres perspectives de financement et de régulation qu'il convient d'orienter les recherches.

III. Éléments d'une stratégie alternative de financement de l'enseignement supérieur

La logique de l'analyse et du raisonnement économiques permet d'affirmer que la meilleure façon de porter remède aux inefficacités redistributives, allocatives et productives précédemment recensées ne saurait consister à affecter un volume croissant de ressources publiques à l'enseignement supérieur, même dans l'hypothèse où ces ressources seraient issues d'un système fiscal fortement progressif. Le problème à résoudre consiste moins, d'ailleurs, selon nous, à envisager une impossible et indésirable privatisation du financement et de la production de l'enseignement qu'à déterminer quelles sont les activités éducatives devant faire l'objet de subventions financées sur fonds publics d'une part, les modalités d'utilisation des ressources publiques affectées à l'enseignement supérieur d'autre part.

Or, en ce domaine, une littérature considérable alimente depuis plus de vingt ans un débat qui reste ouvert, tant au niveau des fondements théoriques qu'au niveau des modalités d'application pratique des réformes envisagées. Nombreux sont ceux qui, parmi les animateurs de ce débat, ont par trop tendance à vouloir faire triompher, de façon dogmatique, leur philosophie et conception personnelles d'une organisation économique et sociale idéale, au détriment, parfois, de la rigueur scientifique et, presque toujours, du plus élémentaire pragmatisme. Nous ne souhaitons pas, quant à nous, nous engager dans cette voie.

S'il est pourtant nécessaire de modifier les modes de financement et de régulation de l'enseignement supérieur, comme celui, d'ailleurs, de nombreux autres services collectifs divisibles (santé, éducation, culture, transports, etc. . . .) ce changement ne peut être conçu qu'au travers d'une stratégie présidant à la mise en oeuvre de réformes coordonnées entre elles, la première ètape consistant en la recherche d'une reconnaissance par le plus grand nombre d'exigences d'efficacité et de justice d'une part, en la traduction en termes économiques de cette double nécessité d'autre part. C'est l'esprit qui préside à la formulation des réflexions qui suivent.

Les exigences d'efficacité et d'equité

Pour prétendre provoquer la réalisation simultanée d'une plus grande efficacité et d'une meilleure équité du système, tout nouveau mode de financement et de régulation de l'enseignement supérieur doit permettre et/ou encourager simultanément:

—une gestion efficace des organisations universitaires;
—la liberté des choix individuels et l'égalité des chances;
—l'efficacité des choix sociaux;
—la réduction des inégalités de revenus et de richesse.

La première exigence étant largement admise, nous limiterons ici notre propos à l'explicitation rapide du sens et de la portée des trois autres.

La liberté des choix individuels et l'égalité des chances. Il a largement été démontré que les inégalités de réussite tout au long de la scolarité sont fortement liées aux inégalités de fortune, de milieux sociaux et familiaux des individus. Il paraît, de même, acquis que l'absence de contrôle des connaissances ou son affaiblissement conduit à aggraver la sélection économique des étudiants. Dès lors, le contenu que prend la notion d'égalité des chances en matière d'enseignement supérieur ne peut-il refléter que le souci de ne pas amplifier les distorsions existantes et non (on peut le regretter) l'espoir de corriger les situations engendrées par les scolarités primaire et secondaire.

L'égalité des chances d'accès et de réussite au niveau de l'enseignement supérieur implique, en conséquence, l'absence de contraintes financières pesant sur l'individu ayant fait la preuve de ses capacités à suivre la formation de son choix, contraintes qui, si elles existaient, seraient susceptibles de l'y faire renoncer. L'égalité des chances c'est la possibilité pour les individus éligibles de ne pas être obligés d'arbitrer, dans leur fonction d'investissement et de consommation au détriment de l'acquisition d'une formation supérieure. Elle constitue donc l'une des conditions de la liberté individuelle des choix.

L'adhésion à ce principe n'est pas sans avoir de conséquences sur les modalités de financement de l'enseignement supérieur que l'on peut envisager. Mais, elle n'implique pas, comme le soutiennent certains, sur le base d'un "principe social," la gratuité pour tous. Au contraire, et si l'on admet en outre que le financement de l'enseignement supérieur peut et doit concourir à la réduction des inégalités de revenus et de richesse, cette adhésion impose que le système de financement tienne compte de la diversité des situations économiques des individus.

L'efficacité des choix sociaux. La liberté des choix individuels peut ne pas conduire nécessairement, pour toute une série de raisons, nous l'avons vu, à l'efficacité sociale. Cette "évidence" sert bien souvent d'argument pour justifier que l'Etat, en échange de la gratuité, contingente à sa guise les filières de formation, sous couvert de réguler l'offre de diplômés sur le marché du travail tout en satisfaisant la demande d'enseignement supérieur.

Il est cependant vrai que les choix des candidats aux formations et diplômes ne peuvent que difficilement et systématiquement être fondés sur un juste calcul prévisionnel des gains (monétaires ou non) que les diplômés recueilleront et auxquels concourront les mécanismes d'ajustement des marchés du travail. Mais, il est beaucoup moins sûr qu'on aide les étudiants à "gérer" leur formation et à obtenir effectivement les satisfactions qu'ils en attendent par un système de financement qui est assorti d'un numérus clausus, explicite ou implicite, ex-ante ou ex-post, qui, dans bien des cas entraîne l'éviction d'individus réalisant un investissement en capital humain au profit de "purs consommateurs." La gratuité peut ainsi avoir un coût élevé, non seulement pour la collectivité, mais aussi pour les individus qui en bénéficient. Un système de financement efficace devrait donc permettre, à tous ceux soucieux de faire un investissement, de faire le meilleur calcul possible et de ne se heurter dans la réalisation de leurs projets qu'aux seules limites de leurs capacités intellectuelles. Un tel système devrait également permettre de modifier les incitations perçues par les candidats lorsque la collectivité peut retirer des avantages associés au développement de certaines formations et qualifications.

L'efficacité sociale suppose aussi que l'offre s'adapte à la demande avec souplesse, flexibilité et rapidité. Or,il a été précédemment démontré que la gratuité ou quasi-gratuité de l'offre est un système injuste et injustifié. Il a en outre le défaut de faire dépendre le volume de services produits, non pas d'une confrontation de l'offre et de la demande, mais de choix politiques sous contrainte d'une capacité fiscale. En assurant la pérénnité et l'impérialisme de l'offre, un tel système entrave l'efficacité des choix sociaux.

La réduction des inégalités des revenus et des richesses. Certains pourraient s'étonner que l'on demande à un système de financement de l'enseignement supérieur de contribuer à la réduction des inégalités de revenus et de fortune. On peut cependant remarquer que, dès lors qu'on adhère à cet objectif social, il n'y a aucune raison de l'écarter dès lors qu'il est possible de l'intégrer à une quelconque politique, en en atténuant ainsi les conséquences coûteuses en termes réels pour certains, les conséquences psychologiquement douloureuses pour les autres. Mais, en l'espèce, cette exigence sociale est une nécessité dynamique, permettant de faire converger le système économique et social vers toujours plus de souplesse, de perméabilité entre les catégories socio-économiques, de liberté et de choix, rendant l'intervention nécessaire de la collectivité moins complexe et moins lourde financièrement, diminuant d'autant les risques d'une crise financière accrue et des arbitrages défavorables à l'enseignement supérieur.

Telles sont, selon nous, rapidement exprimées, les exigences et nécessités qu'une politique de financement de l'enseignement supérieur doit prendre en compte. Le problème est maintenant celui de développer une stratégie de réforme dudit financement qui soit acceptable par le plus grand nombre.

Fondements d'un financement plus efficace et plus équitable

Les éléments qui seront analysés sont à la fois les parties constitutives d'un tout et le reflet d'une progression logique tendant vers une amélioration continue de l'efficacité et de la justice. De ce fait, ils sont autant des étapes d'un raisonnement que d'une possible réforme par expérimentations successives à partir d'un système de gratuité ou quasi-gratuité des services résultant d'un financement public direct des organisations universitaires et de leurs facteurs de production.

Le dispositif proposé se compose de trois éléments:

—la tarification au coût marginal des services;
—la "privatisation" de la demande;
—une politique discriminatoire de financement et de régulation.

La tarification au coût marginal. La tarification des productions de l'enseignement supérieur n'a indéniablement pas le mérite de la nouveauté.[8] Nous pourrons donc ici nous limiter à l'énoncé des avantages qui semblent pouvoir être associés à une vente au coût marginal des services de l'enseignement supérieur. Il s'agit-là d'un moyen susceptible d'engendrer, au sein des organisations universitaires, une gestion plus efficace des ressources mais aussi, dans le cadre d'un financement public, de promouvoir un moindre gaspillage social et une plus grande clarté politique des choix budgétaires. Supposant nécessairement la tenue d'une comptabilité analytique fine, la tarification au coût marginal permet de déterminer le coût effectif de la formation d'un individu dans chaque filière de chaque établissement, autorise des comparaisons et surtout, le choix rationnel de "l'acheteur" des services et des productions; elle améliore, en outre, la fluidité du "marché" et rend ainsi possible la pénalisation d'une mauvaise gestion.

Un tel "marché" peut d'ailleurs fort bien ne faire intervenir qu'un "acheteur" unique, l'Etat ou la collectivité. Cette formule serait déjà supérieure à celle de la subvention publique des moyens de production. Elle obligerait en effet l'autorité publique à expliciter ses choix, et, notamment, à arbitrer, pour un budget donné, entre qualité et quantité, au lieu de s'en décharger, comme elle le fait actuellement dans de nombreux cas, sur les éstablissements.

Pourquoi préconiser, comme nous le faisons ici, la tarification au coût marginal plutôt qu'au coût moyen? Ne risque-t-on pas, en effet, de favoriser les grands établissements au détriment des petits dès lors que les rendements seraient croissants avec l'échelle de la production et, par conséquent, les coûts marginaux décroissants? Ne risque-t-on pas, de même, de favoriser les formations peu coûteuses au détriment de *formations plus onéreuses (formations scientifiques, techniques, technologiques, médicales,* etc. . . .)? Les problêmes ainsi évoqués conduisent certains théoriciens à privilégier une tarification fondée sur l'avantage, privé ou collectif, qui s'attache à la valeur du service offert à chaque étudiant. De notre point de vue, la réponse à ce probléme est claire: la tarification au coût marginal constitue le meilleur compromis entre les impératifs d'une gestion efficace, de l'élasticité de l'offre par rapport à la demande et de l'efficacité des choix individuels et collectifs. A tous les niveaux de désagrégation comptable, le coût marginal conserve le même sens économique: le prix réel d'une unité de formation supplémentaire.

La tarification à l'avantage marginal, même si elle est pour certains l'outil de l'optimalité par excellence, poserait indéniablement d'importants problèmes en matière d'enseignement supérieur dans la mesure où elle impliquerait la connaissance "fine" des dispositions marginales à payer de chaque étudiant éligible d'une part, la mise en oeuvre d'une pluralité de prix (à la limite, un prix par étudiant), peu compatible avec le principe, ancré dans les esprits, d'une égalité devant le service rendu, d'autre part.

La "privatisation" de la demande. La collectivité comme tout agent économique, est dotée d'une fonction de préférence et d'une contrainte de revenu, donc de capacité de financement. Les ressources qu'elle accepte de (ou qu'elle peut) consacrer à l'enseignement supérieur sont donc limitées ou commandées par ces deux éléments. Compte-tenu des imperfections du marché politique et des rigidités bureaucratiques, les choix ainsi formulés peuvent ne pas correspondre à la demande, privée et/ou collective, d'enseignement. Si l'on souhaite créer un marché de l'enseignement supérieur, il convient donc de permettre à la demande de s'exprimer sur ce marché, donc, pour reprendre l'expression proposée, de la "privatiser."

Il s'agit là, d'ailleurs, d'une pratique qui tend à s'établir dans de nombreux pays occidentaux, mais les conditions dans lesquelles elle intervient semblent, toutes choses étant égales par ailleurs, peu conformes aux principes d'équité et d'efficacité que nous avons précédemment évoqués. Dans ces pays, la diminution des ressources publiques, exprimés en termes réels, affectées aux établissements, conduit ces derniers ou bien à relever, de façon indifférenciée, les droits payés par les étudiants, ou bien à accepter la détérioration de la qualité de l'enseignement, ou bien encore à mettre en place (comme en France par exemple) des dispositifs de numerus clausus, explicites ou implicites.

Dans la mesure où les difficultés financières des établissements se traduisent, notamment, par un relèvement indifférencié des droits, ne tenant pas compte des capacités contributives des étudiants, il est indéniable que cette privatisation partielle du financement de l'enseignement supérieur tend à aggraver les inéquités par rapport à une offre gratuite puisqu'elle contribue à éliminer, au nom de la seule sauvegarde des apparences, les demandeurs financièrement les plus démunis. Dans le même temps, cette pratique peut provoquer l'élimination "d'investisseurs" au profit de "purs consommateurs."

La solution juste et équitable réside, certes, compte-tenu des caractéristiques des avantages associés à l'investissement en enseignement, en un partage du financement entre ressources publiques et ressources privées, mais il convient pour y parvenir, d'inverser, en quelque sorte, les termes du problème: c'est-à-dire, fixer les droits d'inscription à un montant correspondant aux coûts marginaux de production et substituer, à une aide indifférenciée au produit, une aide publique à la personne permettant à la demande individuelle de s'exprimer (c'est ce que nous appelons privatiser la demande) et tenant compte des capacités contributives (nulles pour certains) de chaque étudiant éligible. Efficacité et équité se trouveront alors réconciliées.

Une politique discriminatoire de financement et de régulation. Rappelons que l'enseignement supérieur donne lieu à une demande de nature privée susceptible d'être soumise au principe d'exclusion, que la propension à investir et à consommer dépend, entre autres éléments, de la fortune présente et des espérances d'utilité, et que les choix individuels peuvent engendrer des économies externes qualitativement et quantitativement variables, voire incertaines. Dans ce cadre, la régulation financière de la collectivité doit tendre à maximiser les avantages et gains sociaux d'utilité, c'est-à-dire:

—permettre la maximisation des gains d'utilité de tous les individus éligibles, donc jugés aptes à entrer dans l'enseignement supérieur;
—minimiser les risques de déséconomies externes résultant de choix individuels erronés (en raison de l'imperfection de l'information, de la segmentation des marchés du travail, etc. . . .);
—harmoniser le court, le moyen et le long terme.

Pour parvenir à la réalisation de ces divers objectifs, il conviendrait de mettre en oeuvre une politique de financement et de régulation discriminatoire. Dans le domaine de l'enseignement supérieur, une telle politique est la nécessaire traduction, en termes économiques, des exigences d'efficacité et de justice sociales dans la mesure où elle est la seule qui puisse réconcilier morale et économie. Elle devrait être le slogan de tous ceux qui militent en faveur d'une société plus égalitaire, car existe-t-il d'autres moyens de lutter efficacement contre une discrimination de fait que d'agir de manière discriminatoire?

Les trois axes d'une telle politique discriminatoire de régulation de l'enseignement supérieur devraient être:

—l'aide financière personnalisée;
—l'incitation financière à l'orientation des études;
—l'aide différentielle selon les niveaux d'étude.

La première (aide financière personnalisée) aurait pour double but d'égaliser les chances (condition nécessaire à la liberté réelle des choix) et de réduire les inégalités de revenus et de fortune telles que ces exigences ont été précédemment formulées.

La seconde (incitation à l'orientation des études) viserait à tenir compte des externalités résultant des choix individuels et, notamment, des déséconomies externes à long terme qui pourraient résulter des calculs d'utilité des étudiants "investisseurs." Il s'agirait là de tenir compte des différences objectives et subjectives de "valeur actualisée nette" des diplômes selon les types de formation et de réguler, non plus par une planification en termes quantitatifs, mais par un système d'incitations financières et de décentralisation des décisions, l'offre sur les marchés du travail.

La troisième, enfin, aurait pour but de favoriser, si besoin est, l'investissement par rapport à la consommation pure en enseignement supérieur.

Modalités de mise en oeuvre d'une politique discriminatoire de régulation et de financement de l'enseignement supérieur

La littérature spécialisée et l'expérimentation nous offrent de nombreuses perspectives opérationnelles quant à la mise en oeuvre de modes alternatifs de financement de l'enseignement supérieur.

Les droits d'inscription. Chaque étudiant éligible devrait être appelé à payer des droits d'inscription ("tuitions and fees") égaux aux coûts marginaux de production du service qui lui est fourni.

De tels droits, correspondant à la vérité des prix et des coûts, capables d'orienter les décisions des usagers, payables individuellement par ces derniers, constitueraient la modalité de financement correspondant à la nécessaire amélioration de l'efficacité allocative, de la gestion productive des établissements et de la flexibilité de l'ajustement de l'offre et de la demande. Mais, une telle réforme ne saurait être envisagée seule; elle devrait être accompagnée d'un volet répondant aux exigences de justice et d'efficacité des choix sociaux.

L'aide financière personnalisée. Une telle aide financière personnalisée pourrait prendre la forme d'un prêt ou d'une allocation monétaire ou d'une combinaison des deux formules.

Le prêt.[9] Le prêt permettrait de différer la charge financière associée à la préparation et à l'obtention d'un diplôme sur la période d'activité professionnelle de l'individu. Bien des formes sont envisageables et sont effectivement mises en oeuvre: prêts privés, prêts publics, prêts bonifiés, par "tranches" ou cycles de formation, à remboursements dépendant du revenu futur (Université de Yale) ou à amortissement différé simple, etc. . . .

Toutes ces propositions sont, on le voit, étroitement fondées sur les principes et les enseignements de l'investissement en capital humain d'une part, et s'associent aisément avec la thèse d'une tarification à l'avantage marginal d'autre part.

Pour notre part, l'octroi de prêts aux étudiants nous semble devoir soulever des difficultés à la fois de nature théorique, opérationnelle et psychologique. L'échec ou le quasi-échec des expériences tentées en divers pays ne fait que renforcer cette attitude. En dehors même des imperfections, voire même de l'inexistence d'un marché des capitaux destiné à faciliter l'investissement en éducation, les incertitudes du marché du travail et des prévisions individuelles posent ensemble le problème de la compensation nécessaire aux différentiels d'espérances de gains résultant de la confrontation des revenus futurs avec les coûts actuels de diverses formations. Si la rémunération est largement fonction du diplôme, elle n'en a pas moins que peu de rapport avec le coût réel de l'enseignement et de la formation. Ainsi, les formations les plus longues et les plus onéreuses ne conduisent pas nécessairement aux diplômes les plus valorisés sur les marchés du travail.

Mais, ce qui nous incite le plus à douter des vertus d'un système de prêts personnels aux étudiants, c'est le problème des inégalités sociales, celui de leurs effets sur l'attitude des plus défavorisés à l'égard du risque lié à un endettement. Qui plus est, ce système n'est guère de nature à satisfaire l'objectif de justice: il favoriserait indéniablement les étudiants appartenant aux catégories sociales les plus aisées; s'il était uniquement réservé aux plus favorisés, il ne constituerait pas l'instrument le plus rapide et le plus efficace de réduction des inégalités.

Même si certains auteurs, parmi les meilleurs en la matière, estiment que paiement individuel, prêts et allocations monétaires doivent être combinées, nous pensons, pour notre part, que le meilleur système de financement est celui du paiement individuel de la formation (tarification au coût marginal) donnant lieu à compensation de manière discriminatoire, par une allocation publique personnalisée sous la forme, administrativement peu coûteuse, d'un "bon" ou "chèque d'éducation" (voucher).

L'attribution personnalisée de "bons d'éducation." Le système proposé est, en définitive, très proche d'un dispositif dans lequel les étudiants paieraient leur formation, se verraient attribuer des bourses différentielles d'entretien et rembourser, en tout ou partie, leurs droits d'inscription. Mais les "bons d'éducation" seraient à la fois économiquement plus efficaces, bureaucratiquement moins lourds à gérer et plus équitables que le système précédent.

Les étudiants éligibles recevraient ou non des "bons" ou "chèques-éducation" de valeur nominale variable que les établissements habilités présenteraient au "réescompte" du Ministère des Universités et du Trésor.

Quant au principe de leur distribution, il est esquissé dans les fonctions que nous avons assignées à la collectivité en matière de financement de l'enseignement supérieur. De nombreuses modalités sont concevables[10] mais, pour simplifier l'analyse on peut imaginer deux formes d'allocation à l'individu:

—l'une "synthétique" ou globale qui regrouperait sous la valeur nominale d'un bon unique l'ensemble des critéres de l'aide publique auxquels un individu satisferait;
—l'autre, "analytique" ou "segmentée," consisterait en divers bons ou coupons dont la valeur de chacun traduirait les différents critères d'allocation possibles définis par la puissance publique, coupons qui se cumuleraient, pour un même individu, en fonction des divers droits qu'il réunirait en un lieu et en un temps donnés.

Cette deuxième formule, bien que plus complexe que la première, nous semble cependant plus apte à promouvoir une adaptation immédiate de l'aide personnalisée à l'évolution de l'environnement et des critères d'intervention fondant l'attribution des bons.

Parmi les critères d'attribution devant être retenus, nous avons déjà dit que trois nous paraissent essentiels: la situation socio-économique et de fortune des individus; l'orientation des choix de formations et la prééminence de l'investissement sur la consommation.

Mais la formule proposée comporte une indéniable souplesse: elle permettrait d'ajouter des "coupons" visant très directement la situation personnelle des demandeurs (femmes ayant élevé des enfants, chômeurs, retraités, etc. . . .) tant "investisseurs" que "consommateurs," ou des "coupons" visant à compenser les disparités régionales etc. . . . La formule proposée permet aussi de contribuer à la réalisation conjointe de plusieurs politiques (par exemple, inciter des chômeurs d'une région particulière à se recycler dans des formations spécifiques).

Les bons-éducation sont donc de nature à provoquer par un financement public différencié, une réduction de la charge privée du coût de la formation supportée par les individus, réduction variable selon les agents, la formation qu'ils choisissent et le niveau qu'ils atteignent. Une telle discrimination volontaire a pour but d'égaliser les chances, d'atténuer les effets néfastes résultant des inégalités d'origine et de fortune tout en assurant l'efficacité des choix individuels et collectifs.

Mais un ou des bon(s) dont la valeur ne correspondrait qu'à la couverture des coûts directs de la formation pourrait s'avérer insuffisant dans certains cas dans la mesure où les coûts indirects de l'éducation (le manque à gagner) constituent une source de renoncement à l'investissement. Il conviendrait donc de maintenir un système de bourses, elles aussi progressives, de manière à ce que, pour tout individu éligible, le cumul de sa bourse et des bons atteigne la valeur minimale nécessaire à un arbitrage réellement libre entre la poursuite et l'abandon de ses études.

Conclusion

L'incompatibilité entre "gratuité" et "rareté des ressources" est sans aucun doute au coeur de la controverse et des désaccords profonds qui portent sur les principes essentiels d'un modèle idéal d'enseignement supérieur. Entre les deux principales thèses en présence, "enseignement supérieur gratuit" et "investissement optimal en enseignement supérieur," nous avons, quant à nous, privilégié la seconde et proposé un certain nombre d'orientations susceptibles de favoriser sa mise en oeuvre effective, efficace et équitable. Il est cependant certain, comme le souligne Th. W. SCHULTZ /35, p. 519/ que:

> Les problèmes posés par l'enseignement supérieur se situent bien au delà des seules possibilités du calcul économique. L'enseignement supérieur ne constitue pas un monde clos; il est le résultat de l'activité

d'un très grand nombre d'organisations, publiques et privées qui, tant socialement que politiquement, sont solidement enracinées dans la société.

C'est dire que l'économiste doit en ce domaine, plus qu'en tout autre, prendre conscience du caractère partiel (voire, aussi, partial) de son analyse et du fait que les recommandations qu'il peut être conduit à formuler, même si elles lui apparaissent techniquement fondées, peuvent ne pas avoir tous les effets escomptés sur les changements d'orientation des politiques publiques. La politique, au sens large du terme, peut avoir des raisons que l'économiste ne connaît pas ou n'est pas encore en mesure, actuellement, d'insérer, ni correctement, ni complètement, dans ses analyses.

Notes

[1]Par Etat-Providence nous désignons ici ainsi que le propose B. CAZES (p. 7): "l'ensemble des activités civiles de fourniture de services, de réglementation et de versement de revenus de transfert qui sont exercées par la puissance publique en vue soit d'augmenter le bien-être de la collectivité nationale soit de modifier la répartition de ce bien-être au sein de la population."

[2]L'étude menée par O. Mehmet sur le système de financement de l'enseignement supérieur en Ontario conclue de façon formelle que: "Cette étude montre de façon évidente que le financement et l'offre actuels caractéristiques du système universitaire de l'Ontario sont tout à fait régressifs . . . Les principaux bénéficiaires nets du système universitaire sont les groupes à revenus moyens et supérieurs et ce aux dépends des groupes à faibles revenus. On peut donc dire que, de ce point de vue, le système universitaire constitue un programme important de dépenses publiques à l'occasion duquel les groupes relativement pauvres subventionnent les groupes relativement riches." On ne saurait être plus clair!

[3]Seules les économies externes, associées aux décisions individuelles d'investissement en capital humain sont étudiées dans cette communication. Il convient cependant de remarquer que d'autres éléments peuvent être avancés en faveur d'une intervention publique dans le financement de l'enseignement supérieur; citons, pour mémoire ici, l'existence (problématique) d'économies avec l'échelle de la production, des phénomènes de production jointe, l'inexistence ou les imperfections d'un marché des capitaux capable de faciliter l'investissement en éducation. Sur ce dernier point on pourra se reporter aux articles de R. M. Bird, J. P. Jallade.

[4]Les huit catégories d'économies externes prises en compte dans le texte sont celles à propos desquelles les discussions les plus vives sont intervenues, au cours des années 1960–1970, entre les théoriciens. D'autres avantages collectifs associés aux décisions individuelles de consommation et/ou d'investissement en enseignement supérieur méritent cependant d'être mentionnées: amélioration de la productivité des individus dans la production non-marchande et domestique, influence sur les goûts des individus, amélioration des aptitudes perceptives, influence positive sur les activités qui nécessitent une collecte d'information, sur le développement de la personnalité, sur les aptitudes au changement, etc. Tous ces effets positifs sont indéniables mais ils méritent de faire l'objet de deux remarques: d'une part ils restent, dans leur formulation actuelle, purement qualitatifs et impalpables; d'autre part, s'agissant d'effets associés à l'enseignement supérieur, ils contribuent à renforcer le caractère régressif

d'un investissement, qui, gratuit pour les bénéficiaires directs, est financé par la fiscalité générale.

[5]L'analyse proposée s'inspire très directement des travaux de D. M. Windham cidessus mentionnés.

[6]On pourra sur ce point se reporter aux articles de G. Terny et de Lévy-Garboua.

[7]La théorie économique de la bureaucratie a été principalement développée, au cours des vingt dernières années, par A. Downs, G. Tullock, W. Niskanen, etc. On trouvera dans l'ouvrage de G. Terny et alii une bibliographie complète et une analyse des divers modèles proposés.

[8]On pourra sur ce point se reporter aux travaux de J. L. Azad; M. A. Grew and A. Young; O. Eckstein; S. A. Hoenack and W. C. Weiler; C. Kaysen; M. Nerlove; R. D. Tollison and T. D. Willett (1972, 1976), etc.

[9]Divers systèmes de prêts et d'aides aux étudiants ont été analysés par T. Giller; R. W. Hartman; A. Maynard, M. Nerlove; J. P. Jallade; M. Woodhall, etc.

[10]Les quelques propositions esquissées dans ces paragraphes doivent beaucoup à la lecture des ouvrages et articles de: M. Blaug; D. K. Cohen et E. Farrar; M. Friedman; St A. Hoenack; A. Maynard; E. O. Olsen; A. T. Peacock et J. Wiseman; C.K. Rowley; C. K. Rowley et A. T. Peacock; E. G. West (1964, 1970).

Références/bibliographiques

AZAD, (J. L.): "Financing Institutions of Higher Education in India: The Need for a Realistic Fee Policy," *Higher Education,* vol. 5, n° 1, 02/76, pp. 1–8.

BAUDELOT (G.) et ESTABLET (R.): *L'école capitaliste en France,* Paris, Ed. Maspero., 1972.

BIRD (R. M.): *Charging for Public Services. A New Look at an Old Idea,* Toronto Canada, Canadian Tax Foundation, 1976 (chap. 19: The Benefit Approach in Postsecondary Education).

BLAUG (M): "Economic aspects of vouchers for education" in I.E.A. *Education a Framework for Choice,* Readings in Political Economy, 1, London, G.B., The Institute of Economic Affairs, 1970, pp. 21–47.

BOURDIEU (P.) et PASSERON (J. C.): *La Reproduction. Eléments pour une théorie du système d'enseignement,* Paris, France, Ed. de Minuit, 1970.

BOWLES (S.): "Schooling and Inequality from Generation to Generation" in T. W. Schultz (ed.): *Investment in Education,* Chicago, U.S.A., University of Chicago Press, 1972.

BOWLES (S.) and GINTIS (H.): Schooling in Capitalist America: Educational Reform and the Contradictions of Economic Life, New York, U.S.A., Basic Books 1976.

CARNOY (M.): Education as Cultural Imperialism, New York, U.S.A., David Mc and Co, Inc, 1974.

CAZES (B.): "L'Etat-Protecteur contraint à une double manoeuvre," *Futurible* Janvier 1981, pp. 5–21.

CILLER (T.): "The Economics of a Service-Loan Program in Financing Higher Education in the Middle-East," *Higher Education,* vol 4, n° 2, 05/1975, p. 47–50.

COHEN (D. K.) and FARRAR (E.): "Power to the Parents? The Story of Education Vouchers," *The Public Interest,* n° 48, Summer 1977, pp. 72–97.

CREW (M. A.) and YOUNG (A.): Paying by Degrees. A Study of the Financing of Higher Education Students by Grants, Loans and Vouchers, I.E.A., London, *U.K., (Hobart Paper 75), 1977.*

ECKSTEIN (Otto): "The Problem of Higher College Tuition," *Rev. of Econ. and Stat.* Supplt August 1960, vol XLII, pp 61–72.

EICHER (J. Cl.) et LEVY-GARBOUA (L.): *Economique de l'éducation,* Paris, France, Economica, 1979.

FRIEDMAN (M.): "The Role of Government in Education" in *Capitalism and Free-*

dom the University of Chicago Press, Chicago, U.S.A. 1962, pp. 85–107.

HANSEN (W. L.) and WEISBROD (B.): "The Distribution of Costs and Direct Benefits of Public Higher Education: the Case of California," *Journal of Human Resources,* Spring 1969.

HARTMAN (R. W.): "Equity Implications of State Tuitions Policy and Student Loans" *Journal of Political Economy,* vol. 80, n° 3, Part III, May–June 1972, pp. S-142 S-171.

HOENACK (St. A.) "The Efficient Allocation of Subsidies to College Students" *American Economic Review,* vol. LXI, n° 3, part 1, June 1971, pp. 302–310.

HOENACK (S. A.) and WEILER (W. C.): "Cost-Related Tuition Policies and University Enrollments," *Journal of Human Resources,* vol. 10, n° 3, Summer 1975, pp. 332–60.

HOLLISTER (R.): "Enseignement et distribution du revenu: quelques incursions exploratoires" in O.C.D.E.: *Conférence sur les politiques d'expansion de l'enseignement,* Rapport de base n° 11, Paris, OCDE, 1973.

KAYSEN (C.): "Some General Observations on the Pricing of Higher Education" *Rev. of Eco. and Stat.* Supplement August 1960, pp. 55–60.

JALLADE (J. P.): "Financing Higher Education: the Equity Aspects," *Comparative Education Review,* June 1978, pp. 309–325.

JALLADE (J. P.): "Education et répartition du revenu en Amérique Latine" *Revue Tiers Monde,* t. XIX, n° 76, Oct–Dec. 1978, pp. 771–799.

JUDY (R. W.): "On the Income Redistributive Effects of Public Financial Assistance to Higher Education in Canada," *Systems Analysis for Efficient Resources Allocation in Higher Education,* Series n° 20, Institute for Policy Analysis, University of Toronto, 1970.

LEVIN (H. M.): "Educational Opportunity and Social Inequality in Western Europe," *Social Problems,* vol. 24, 12/1976, pp. 148–172.

LEVY-GARBOUA (L.): "Planification et régulation de l'enseignement supérieur en France," *Cahiers de l'ISMEA,* Sciences de Gestion, série S.G. n° 1, 1980, p. 737–773.

MAYNARD (A.): Experiment with Choice in Education: an Analysis of New Methods of Consumer Financing To Bring More Resources Into Education By Vouchers and Loans, London, G. B., Institute of Economic Affairs, 1975.

MEHMET (O.) and TSANG (L.): Who Benefits from the Ontario University System A Benefit-Cost Analysis by Income Groups. Toronto, Ontario, Canada, Ontario Economic Council, Occasional paper 7, 1978, 62 pages.

NERLOVE (M.): "On Tuition and the Costs of Higher Education: Prolegomena to a Conceptual Framework" *Journal of Political Economy,* vol 80, n° 3, Part II, May–June 1972, pp S 178–S 218.

NERLOVE (M.): "Some Problems in the Use of Income Contingent Loans for the Finance of Higher Education," *Journal of Political Economy,* vol 83, n° 1, 02/1975, pp 157–183.

OLSEN (E. O.): "Some Theorems in the Theory of Efficient Transfers," *Journal of Political Economy,* vol 79, n° 1, 01–02/1971, pp 166–176 (and Rand Corporation, 1969, P. 4018-1).

PEACOCK (A. T.) and WISEMAN (J.): Education for Democrats: A Study of the Financing of Education in a Free Society, London, G. B., Institute of Economic Affairs, 1964.

ROWLEY (C. K.): "The Political Economy of British Education" *Scottish Journal of Political Economy,* vol 16, n° 2, 06/1969.

ROWLEY (C. K.) and PEACOCK (A. T.): Welfare Economics. A liberal Restatement Cambridge, U.K. Martin Robertson, 1975, pp. 112–128.

SCHULTZ (Th. W): "Optimal Investment in College Instruction: Equity and Efficiency" *Journal of Political Economy,* vol 80, n° 3, Part II, May–June 1972, pp S-2, S-30.

STIGLER (G. I.): "Director's Law of Public Income Redistribution," *Journal of Law and Economics,* vol 13, April 1970, pp 1–10.

TOLLISON (R. O.) and WILLET (T. D.): "A Proposal for Marginal Cost Financing of Higher Education," *Public Finance*, vol 27, n° 3, 1972, pp. 375–380.

TOLLISON (R. O.) and WILLET (T. D.): "The University and the Price System" in Amacher R. A., R. D. Tollison and Th. D. Willet (eds): *The Economic Approach to Public Policy*, New-York, U.S.A., Cornell University Press, 1976, pp. 153–167.

TERNY (G.): Economie des services collectifs et de la dépense publique, Paris, France, Dunod, 1971, (chap. X: les prix publics des services et nuisances collectifs).

TERNY (G.): "Quelques réflexions sur les liaisons Education-Formation-Emploi" *Revue d'Economie Politique*, vol 90, n° 4, Juillet-Août 1980, pp. 353–370.

TERNY (G.): Eléments d'une théorie économique des organisations publiques non-marchandes: bilan et perspectives, Université de Paris X Nanterre, France, G.R.E.P., 1980, 238 pages.

WEST (E. G.): "Private Versus Public Education: a Classical Economic Dispute," *Journal of Political Economy*, vol 72, Octobre 1964, pp. 465–475.

WEST (E. G.): Education and the State. A Study in Political Economy, London, G.B., The Institute of Economic Affairs, second ed., 1970.

WINDHAM (D. M.): Education, Equality and Income Redistribution, Lexington, Mass, U.S.A., Health, Lexington Books, 1970.

WINDHAM (D. M.): "The Efficiency-Equity Quardary and Higher Education Finance," *Review of Educational Research*, n° 3, 1973.

WINDHAM (D. M.): The Economics of Higher Education, in P. G. Altbach (ed) Comparative Higher Education: Bibliography and Analysis, New York, Prager Press for ICED, 1976.

WINDHAM (D. M.): "Social Benefits and the Subsidization of Higher Education: a Critique," *Higher Education*, vol 5, 1976, pp. 237–252.

WINDHAM (D. M.): Incentive Analysis and Higher Education Planning: Alternatives in Theory, Research and Policy, Research Report 29, International Institute for Educational planning, Paris, 1978.

WOLF (Ch. Jr): "A Theory of Non-Market Failure Framework for Implementation Analysis," *Journal of Law and Economics*, vol XXII, n° 2, 1979, pp. 107–139.

WOODHALL (M.): Student Loans: A Review of Experiences in Scandinavia and elsewhere, London, G. B., Harrap, 1970.

Summary

The central argument in this paper is the following one. Most of the difficulties and inefficiencies which in our time seem to afflict nearly all of the higher education systems can be traced to insufficient and inadequate regulations of the former. This is particularly true with respect to the financing of these systems.

In the first part of the paper it is shown that economic reasons which are currently advanced to justify non-differentiated public financing of higher education cannot stand up under close analysis. The present principles of financing contribute little to assure equal chances for all individuals, they entail no significant redistribution of revenues, yet they are a source of serious inefficiencies in allocation and production, on a global, microeconomic and organizational level. This is shown in the second part of this paper. Starting from here we outline a new strategy of financing. (Third part of paper.) Its main feature is a substitution of a voucher system with direct payments to the person concerned for the system. Such a system would have, in our opinion, the advantage to equilibrate supply and demand more rapidly, to reduce bureaucratic controls, to safeguard the liberty of individual choice, to increase the efficiency of social choices, to contribute to a reduction of inequalities in income and wealth, and finally to promote a more efficient management of university organizations.

Federalism versus Centralism in Regional Growth

Albert Breton

I

I am, like many other economists, generally uneasy about postulating economic growth or development as an objective of economic organization and activity. This for at least two reasons. First, as one can readily verify, economic development measured as increments to net national product does not always lead to improvements in living standards and in welfare. Second, fixing such a goal tends to simplify economic science—not in its mathematical-technical aspects, but in its theoretical-conceptual expressions—to the point of making it sometimes almost trivial.

There are, I suspect, two main reasons why economic development as a goal for economies and economics has come to be attractive to a large number of individuals. One is the fascination, especially, but by no means exclusively, of untutored minds, with the notions of economic planning and orderly progress; the other is that, to a degree, we have all come to accept the collectivist goals of modern nation-states, whether democratic or dictorial: military power, diplomatic ascendency and nationalistic sovereignty. None of these goals are obviously conducive to improved living standards, but their achievement is made much easier with rapid economic development.

The above strictures notwithstanding, I will develop the argument of this paper within the terms of reference that have been laid down for these meetings. I will, consequently, focus almost exclusively on the production efficiency and supply dimensions of the problem I have accepted to discuss, without paying much attention to its welfare aspects. Extension to the latter may be straightforward, but until such an extension has been performed, that view is pure conjecture.

Public Finance and Economic Growth. Proceedings of the 37th Congress of the International Institute of Public Finance. Tokyo, 1981, pp. 251–263

II

The proposition I wish to defend is that, from the point of view of production efficiency, a federal governmental structure will lead to an allocation of local public goods that is superior to the "best" allocation achievable by a centralized governmental structure and, consequently, that, *ceteris paribus*, the rate of economic development will be greater in a federation than in a central state. Federalism is still a poorly understood phenomenon and, for that reason, real world federations are not optimally designed. But my argument does not require an optimal design; it states that, even in the very imperfect world in which we live, one should expect that, *ceteris paribus*, economic growth of federations will exceed that of centralized states.

If the proposition appears obvious, let me reassure you immediately that it is not. All the literature that I know which relates to the question rejects the proposition in one way or the other. Consider the issue of the competitive bidding that junior governments sometimes engage in to attract capital, usually manufacturing enterprises, to their jurisdictional domains. The consensus in the profession surely is that such bidding is a wasteful undertaking and that the "best" jurisdictional (i.e., spatial) location of capital assets is achieved by a central government doing the "appropriate" calculations and making a locational decision based on these calculations. Or consider the question of differential factor taxes between jurisdictions. Again, the consensus surely is that such tax differences lead to wasteful interjurisdictional movement of labour and/or of capital, and that the optimal tax structure is one for which all these differences are eliminated.

A final example should convince even the most skeptic that I will not be dealing with a problem whose solution is obvious. The literature on customs unions and the practices of common markets are replete with discussions of policy harmonization, an expression which is used as a shorthand for the kind of outcome that would be generated by a central government which had control over all policy instruments.

In its most simplified form, the proposition that, in terms of economic development, federalism is superior to centralism rests on the notion that a competitive outcome is superior to a monopolistic one. It will, therefore, be necessary to define the nature of the competitive process and the characteristics of the underlying structure of property rights without which the concept of competition is formal and empty. To do this in a meaningful way, I will, however, have to circumscribe with care the domain over which competition takes place. That will require a few words on the nature of local public goods.

III

It is never clear how one should define a federation or, for that matter, a centralized state. Since much of the theoretical work of economists on federalism and federal finance has been rooted in one way or another in a Tiebout-type paradigm, even before the letter of Tiebout's paper [1956], there has been a tradition in the profession to consider governments at the local or municipal jurisdictional level as *bona fide* members of federal structures. That practice has meant that even such quintessentially non-federal states as France and the United Kingdom have been treated by economists as federations on the same footing as Australia and Canada. Political scientists, who know better, have in their more generous moments treated economists as poor souls with a model in need of an application.

Political scientists are not always wrong nor are the practices of economists, even if these lead to the mildly funny aberration of calling France and other unitary states federations. In many instances, the approximation of reality through fictitious prototypes can be productive. In the remainder of this paper, I shall suppose that federations are constituted of two tiers only: a senior and a junior tier. The junior tier is assumed to be made up of all governments below the national government which in turn defines the senior tier. A more general model would postulate a three-tier federation and analyse the nature of the competitive adjustment in such a structure. At the level I am casting the argument of this paper, very little would be gained with this added degree of generality.

I shall begin by assuming "full autonomy" of the two jurisdictional levels and then relax this assumption. By "full autonomy," I mean that the governments and governmental bureaus at each level or tier compete among themselves, but do not compete with governments and public bureaus at the other level. In the language of constitutional law, this assumption implies that all functions or powers are assigned in a nonoverlapping way; there is no concurrent authority. This definition will do for the purposes I have in mind. The reader should, however, remember that there is no real world counterpart of any significance to the concept of "full autonomy." The more general case of partial autonomy is, therefore, the only one that has real empirical significance.

Initially, any arbitrary assignment of powers between the two jurisdictional tiers will do. Therefore, I assume that the junior tier—on which I shall focus attention to begin with—has been assigned responsibility for policies pertaining to housing and therefore zoning, including street lighting, police protection, etc.; transportation and therefore roads (possibly not all the country's roads, but those within the frontiers of jurisdictions), railways, trucking, bridges, etc.; education; social services in which one can include, in addition to day-care centers, hospitals and welfare, other social overheads such as theaters, museums, and concert halls. In addition, it must be assumed that the governments at that jurisdictional level have been assigned responsibility over certain tax bases, that is, these governments must be able to vary tax rates, to extend tax credits, to give tax holidays, etc., as pertains to certain bases such as income, sales, property, land or others.

The question we face is the following: how will the various governments at that junior jurisdictional level decide on the level of supply with respect to the policies for which they have responsibility and at what level will they set tax rates, tax holidays, tax credits, etc., pertaining to the bases over which they have been assigned responsibility? If we postulate a competitive environment, the answer must be that whatever objective function is being maximized by whosoever inhabits these governmental units, that behaviour and those decisions must be determined by whatever is being done by other governments. To put it differently, if factors of production—whatever they are and to whatever use they are put—are mobile, the decisions of a government are going to be determined by the actions of the other governments within the domain in which the effects of factor mobility manifest themselves.

Below I shall briefly return to this proposition if for no other reason than the presence of at least one factor—what economists identify by the very abstract label of land and natural resources—which is not mobile. But, I would be remiss in my duty if I did not pause to ask: what is a competitive environment? What is competition in the public sector? It is the implicit, or sometimes the explicit, answers given to these questions which constitute the major stumbling block to the central proposition of this paper on the superiority of federalism over centralism.

IV

In mainstream neo-classical economics, the concept of competition does not refer to a process nor to decisions which economic agents make; it refers only to the outcome of this unmodelled process. It is a solution to a problem that was never posed, an answer to a question that was never asked! Such a declaration is slightly exaggerated and a trifle caricatural since it neglects to take account of the important work of Knight [1921], Chamberlin [1933], and of those who have worked on the meaning and place of product differentiation for market adjustment, and it slights the work of Arrow [1959] and the work of those who have sought to incorporate a notion of "transitory monopoly" in the yet-to-be formulated theory of price formation.[1]

But more importantly the above assertion does not take account of the meaning given to competition by those economists of the "Austrian school," although in defence of my earlier statement, it is fair to recognize that not much of that work has ever been part of the mainstream. However, I would like to argue here that an understanding of competition in the public sector should be based on this Austrian model—incorporating some insights from the Chamberlinian approach—and not on the purified and strictly formal view of competition that undergirds mainstream neo-classical economic theory. This for at least two reasons.

The first has to do with the fact that public sector competition on the whole is not, and cannot be, price competition. The fiction of "tax-prices" or "pseudo-prices" which now occupies center stage in much of the literature of Public Choice is not very useful, mostly because it is virtually impossible to identify anything that resembles a price for the very great bulk of policies supplied by governments. What, indeed, is the price of international diplomacy to any tax-paying citizen? What is the price of regulating the hertzian spectrum for broadcasting? What is the price of a unit more of national defence? Even for local goods such as street cleaning, noise abatement, dog catching, tree pruning, snow removal, garbage disposal, it is not easy to point to any index that would measure their individual unit prices to each consumer.

But even if tax-prices could be identified, the fiction of a *crieur* or auctioneer who oversees (regulates?) a *tâtonnement*, re-contracting or other similar process does not appear to mimick any of the competitive behaviour one can observe in the public sector, whatever views one may hold about the descriptive value of these processes for the market adjustments of the private sector.

The Austrian notion of competition—although it is still quite undeveloped and certainly not formally modelled—is first, and above all, a process which corresponds to effective decisions by individuals who have to respond or react to actions taken by other individuals. One of the best outlines of this competitive process is still that given by Schumpeter [1961, 1975]. One could summarize it in stylized fashion in the following way. Assume that an entrepreneur detects a need for a new product which he proceeds to produce and to sell; assume also that the new product did in fact satisfy a need which was hitherto unsatisfied. What is the likely response of competing entrepreneurs who feel the effect of this new product through a reduction in the demand for their own output? Will they simply reduce the price of their own output in an effort to forestall the movement away from them, as one would have to assume if one formulated one's answer within the framework of canonical theory?

Schumpeter and the Austrians would argue that what are supposed to be imperfections in mainstream economics constitutes the very essence of the competitive response: reacting entrepreneurs would differentiate their own products, would introduce new commodities of their own, new methods of production, would seek out new sources of supply, would search for new forms of industrial or commercial organization, and would intensify marketing via advertising, packaging and other similar efforts? So, I suggest, would behave public entrepreneurs when they are required to respond to the behaviours and actions of other public entrepreneurs.

Consider, for the sake of illustration, the case of industrial location alluded to above. Suppose that the government of a particular jurisdiction decides for whatever reason that it wishes to attract a particular manufacturing enterprise. To that effect, it develops an industrial park in which property taxes are lower; in which access roads, parking facilities, storage, etc., are supplied at subsidized rates or even free of charge; it permits accelerated depreciation for tax purposes, etc. Whether the manufacturing enterprise will move to that jurisdiction depends on the response and reaction of the governments of other surrounding jurisdictions. These may decide to match every concession offered by the first jurisdiction but, in addition—or as a substitute—they may decide to offer alternative policies. They may seek to attract that manufacturing enterprise by developing a "complete" industrial strategy that will be attractive to a large number of related enterprises by encouraging the development of research facilities, by setting up developmental loan facilities, by promoting a philharmonic orchestra, a theatre company or a local art museum, by placing a large volume of resources in educational facilities, by offering better "law and order" through a better police force or through specially designed zoning ordinances and/or by a host of other local public policies.

One could go on describing the possible responses which competition between jurisdictions could in principle, elicit, or has historically elicited. The point is, that interjurisdictional competition can, and does, exist and that such competition will have an influence on the movement and, hence, on the location of capital and labour. At the same time it will help to determine the configuration of public policies supplied by all governments at the junior tier, something which we are now going to analyse.

V

The question that we must now address is whether that competition is optimal in the sense that it leads to the best possible allocation of productive resources, one that will produce the highest rate of growth for all regions together, i.e., for the whole country. This is, of course, the central question of this paper. It is the question on which hinges the proposition about the superiority of federalism over centralism. As noted earlier, the general view among economists about intergovernmental competition is that it is not optimal. For that reason economists either favour a centralized form of government or, when they are forced by political necessity to accept the existence of federalism, they favour the maximum degree of policy harmonization.

Neither time nor space allow me to dwell on the notion of policy harmonization. Let me only note that the meaning that can be given to that concept is clear only for a world in which governing politicians are not motivated by self-interest, but pursue some agreed-upon objective measure of the common good. In such a world, the tasks of governments are simply to correct for market failures (which, of course, includes the failure to achieve full-employment)—in socialist economies, for organizational failures—and to redistribute income according to some socially accepted norm. The methods of implementing these tasks constitute the substance of welfare economics, whether of the first or second best variety.

But very little of welfare economics can be salvaged once governing and non-governing politicians are assumed to be motivated by their own interest. One thing that can surely not be saved is the notion of policy harmonization. In addition, it is fruitless to ask whether the allocation of resources derived in welfare economics is superior to that achieved in an economics that assumes self-seeking politicians. This is like asking whether we would be better governed by angels than by men or women! Consequently, things that are called "distortion" in the literature of welfare economics may or may not be distortions—non-harmonized policies—in an economics that acknowledges real governments.

Not much help can be expected from standard neoclassical theory because in that theory all competition is either price competition and the prices are all attached to homogenous products. The fact that, under certain conditions, competition in that framework is efficient, cannot take us very far. If we knew that Schumpeterian or Austrian competition was efficient, that would be helpful. But the fact that, even for the simplest cases of industrial and commercial adjustment, that question has not been resolved, implies that one cannot hope to obtain general support for the proposition that under certain conditions intergovernmental Austrian competition is optimal in the sense defined above. What are these conditions?

There are many approaches to formulate an answer to that question. The one I have chosen to explore in this paper rests on the proposition that, if the structure of property rights is appropriate, competition between jurisdictions will be optimal. What meaning should be given to the term appropriate? First, that the benefits and the costs of decisions made within a jurisdiction are borne within that jurisdiction.[2] To explore that assertion, let us consider two different cases. The first, and least interesting, one obtains when every firm in a jurisdiction has the same production function, and there are no fixed factors such as land entering production because, let us say, land is so abundant that it is free. Under such circumstances, the full appropriation of all costs and benefits of public policies simply means the absence of uncompensated interjurisdictional spillovers. There are many ways of achieving that result. They have been examined in the theoretical literature on federalism.[3] It would serve no purpose to review these conclusions here.

In the second case, the production function of private firms differ, and land and other fixed factors may be present. Full appropriation of benefits and costs now, imply that these are equalized over the long run for everyone inside the jurisdiction. This equalization can be achieved by the departure of losers and the arrival of potential gainers but also by the implementation of a set of compensatory taxes and subsidies (inter-jurisdictional grants) that would take account of direct benefits and costs resulting from the implementation of the various policies and of the spillover flows associated with them.

The absence of internal and external "beggar-thy-neighbour" policies and actions or full appropriation does not, of course, imply that all jurisdictions will have the same pattern of production or will grow at the same rate. Some jurisdictions are better endowed than others. It would imply that capital and labour would be located in areas where their net yield was the highest. In other words, if full appropriation existed, no government at the junior level would offer, by way of a competitive bid, more than it would expect to receive. In the presence of fixed factors, such as land and natural resources, the competitive bidding would generally stop short of the exhaustion of all rents by all jurisdictions.[4]

This first condition, which I have called full appropriation, is not sufficient to guarantee the optimality of competition or, what is equivalent, the appropriateness of property rights. A second condition must be fulfilled. That condition pertains to the relationship between citizens and governments.[5] In a way, this second condition is more basic than the first because, under certain—admittedly "ideal"—conditions, it will insure that the first is satisfied.

If one assumes that governments are fully responsive to the preferences of citizens—following the approach adopted in my theory of representative government [Breton, 1974] this is equivalent to assuming that elected governing politicians have zero degrees of freedom—competition will lead to full appropriation and be optimal. Why? Because, whenever a government makes a tax concession (say), the size and other properties of that concession would be matched by benefits which, at the margin, would be of equal size and characteristics. To put it differently, a government which had to face up to the full consequences of all its actions would not compete by granting concessions of one type or another to attract capital, labour, or other factors of production, unless the benefits accruing from these "purchases" were at least as large as the costs.

Therefore, if such a government chose to compete by whatever means—supplying local public goods, offering tax advantages, or buying the output of the sought-after enterprises—to attract businesses and firms, it would do so up to a point determined by its command over resources and by the extent to which the other jurisdictions are competing. In general, its command over resources would be determined by the rate at which it is losing popular support in relation to what it is doing. The less responsive the popular support to the actions of governments—the larger the number of degrees of freedom governments dispose of—the less efficient competition as a result of a greater ability of any jurisdiction to export net costs to other jurisdictions and, therefore, to evade appropriation of the benefits and costs of their actions.

This last proposition must be qualified in an important way. If the governments of all the jurisdictions possess (approximately) the same number of degrees of freedom, they will be able to compete against each other with (approximately) the same vigour. Consequently the differences between benefits and costs—due to the presence of degrees of freedom which representative governments enjoy—will be minimized.

Since this last proposition constitutes the heart of the matter under consideration, let me dwell on it a bit longer. A typical representative government can engage in actions which will lead to costs in excess of benefits or product and still be re-elected because of the existence of such institutional factors as non-unanimity decision rules, election periods extending over years, the existence of full-line supply [Breton, 1974, Chapter 3], and the presence in the electorate of a longterm fiscal illusion (a term that should be given its widest possible meaning). The ability to engage in such actions is more or less proportional to the strength of these institutional factors. To put it differently, the ability of a representative government to impose excess costs on its citizens without costs to itself is more or less proportional to the number of degrees of freedom conferred by these institutional factors. What the proposition of the last paragraph states is that the ability of any representative government to exploit its available degrees of freedom to its own advantage is minimized in a federal structure by the competition originating from the other constituent governments. This will be the case as long as no government has an infinite number of degrees of freedom.

In short this is simply another way of stating that competition will force all governments of a federation to forego the advantages conferred to them by a positive number of degrees of freedom, at least as long as a sub-set of junior governments does not possess sufficient degrees of freedom liberating it from the necessity to compete with the other governments.

VI

We are now in a position to enquire into the role of a federal government in this scheme of things and, therefore, into the assignment of functions or powers in a two-tier federation. There is a classical, but naive view, that one of the characteristics of an optimal assignment of powers is that powers should not overlap, that is, no concurrent authority should exist.[6] Such an assignment is not easy to define, as anyone who seeks to analyse efforts along that line can verify. But assuming that it could be done, it would imply that for all the powers that had been assigned to the senior level, there would be, by definition, no competition since, at that level, only one government is to be found in all real world federations. Consequently, there would be a tendency for all policies designed and implemented by the central government—under the powers assigned to it in exclusivity—to be marked by a large excess of costs over benefits, indicating that that government possesses many degrees of freedom.

However, if the assignment of powers displayed a large degree of concurrency—the functions being assigned simultaneously to the governments at both tiers or levels—the senior and the junior governments would always be competing with each other and the extent to which excess-costs would be inflicted on citizens would be minimized. In the present context of regional economic development a minimization of excess-costs must be interpreted as a minimization of the excess-costs produced by a non-optimal localization of factors of production. It implies maximum aggregate regional growth.

I should emphasize that the demonstration, that generalized concurrent authority is superior to the non-overlapping of powers, constitutes at the same time a demonstration that federalism dominates centralism as a mode of organizing for the provision of public policy. This is so because, in a non-overlapping situation, a central government is, with respect to the powers assigned to it, similar to the government of a centralized country.

VII

By way of conclusion, I would like to point out that I have not relied, for the demonstration of the superiority of federalism over centralism, on the fact that the former requires a smaller amount of information than the latter, a line of argument which, I believe would be valid but which, to my knowledge, has not yet been developed. Nor have I relied on the argument that a federal structure will usually set in motion a mechanism which will tend to eliminate "trade distortions" in a way a centralized structure cannot achieve. This is also a valid but unexploited line of argument.

I have solely relied on the very simple, but very powerful, line of reasoning that competition tends to reduce the wedge between price and value when property rights are defined in an appropriate fashion.

Notes

[1]For a recent survey of this work, see M. Rothschild [1973].

[2]It is generally believed that this condition is not satisfied. Without going into the validity of that view, I would like to note here that establishing or denying it is not as easy as is sometimes assumed. The key to an understanding of the difficulty lies in appreciating the meaning of interjurisdictional competition. For a statement of the accepted view, see C. E. McLure, Jr. [1967].

[3]A virtually complete overview of these can be found in A. Breton and A. Scott [1978].

[4]See D. Epple and Z. Zelenitz [1981]. Their model is different from mine, but the effect of fixed factors is recognized there.

[5]One cannot focus here on the relationship between producers and governments alone, unless one also assumes that producers are the sole consumers or citizens of the jurisdictions. In a way, the need to consider all citizens forces a departure from the narrow confines of production economics to which I am restricting myself in the bulk of this paper.

[6]A standard formulation of that view can be found in K. C. Wheare [1953]. In Canada, it has been incorporated in the proposed constitution of the Quebec Liberal Party [1980] without critical appraisal.

References

Arrow, K. J., "Toward a Theory of Price Adjustment" in M. Abramovitz, ed., *The Allocation of Economic Resources* (Stanford, Ca.: Stanford University Press, 1959).

Breton, A., *The Economic Theory of Representative Government* (Chicago, Ill.: Aldine, 1974).

Breton, A. and A. Scott, *The Economic Constitution of Federal States* (Toronto: University of Toronto Press, 1978).

Chamberlin, E. H., *The Theory of Monopolistic Competition* (Cambridge, Mass.: Harvard University Press, 1933, 1950).

Commission constitutionnelle du Parti Libéral du Québec, *Une nouvelle fédération canadienne*, 1980.

Epple, D. and Z. Zelenitz, "The Roles of Jurisdictional Competition and the Collective Choice Institutions in the Market for Local Public Goods," *American Economic Review* (May 1981).

Knight, F. H., *Risk, Uncertainty and Profit* (Boston, Mass.: Houghton Mifflin, 1921).

McLure, Jr., C. E., "The Interstate Exporting of State and Local Taxes: Estimates for 1962," *National Tax Journal* (March, 1967).

Rothschild, M., "Models of Market Organization with Imperfect Information: A Survey," *Journal of Political Economy* (Nov./Dec., 1973).

Schumpeter, J. A., *The Theory of Economic Development* (New York, N.Y.: Oxford University Press, 1961).

———, *Capitalism, Socialism and Democracy* (New York, N.Y.: Harper and Row, 1975).

Tiebout, C. M., "A Pure Theory of Local Expenditures," *Journal of Political Economy* (October, 1956).

Wheare, K. C., *Federal Government*, 3rd. ed., (London: Oxford University Press, 1953).

Résumé

Dans les pays fédéraux, les gouvernements de chacun des états de la Fédération rivalisent souvent entre eux pour attirer l'industrie, le commerce et les autres activités économiques. Ils font cela à l'aide de moyens variés: réductions fiscales, subventions salariales, garanties d'emprunt, facilités culturelles, pour n'en nommer que quelques uns.

En général, les économistes condamnent de telles pratiques concurrentielles parce qu'il n'est pas facile de les rationaliser car elles ne relèvent pas de ce que l'économie du bien-être considère comme le rôle de l'état. La concurrence est "bonne" pour les institutions privées, mais "néfastes" pour les institutions publiques.

Cet article soutient que les conditions relatives aux droits de la propriété et de là à l'appropriation des charges fiscales et des bénéfices peuvent être spécifiées afin de rendre la compétition inter-étatique optimale, car elle conduira à une meilleure localisation globale des industries et du commerce.

Bref, la compétition améliore les décisions locales en mettant à la disposition des entrepreneurs publics des moyens dont ils ne disposeraient pas autrement. On démontre que les systèmes centralisés ne peuvent disposer de cette amélioration des ressources qu'amène la concurrence inter-étatique et que par conséquent l'allocation ceteris paribus des ressources et le taux de croissance économique de ces systèmes seront inférieurs à ceux qu'il est possible d'obtenir dans les systèmes fédéraux.

Intergovernmental Fiscal Relations and Regional Growth in a Federal Context

Russell Mathews

This paper is concerned with the interaction of intergovernmental fiscal arrangements and regional growth in a federal country, with special reference to the development of different kinds of grants arrangements. The focus is on responsibility sharing and revenue sharing between governments and on the role of federal and regional governments in reducing economic and fiscal disparities between regions (states or provinces in a federation). To this end, the paper consists of two parts. The first examines the role of and relationships between governments when they take the initiative in promoting regional growth, either through development planning or through the provision of financial assistance for specific developmental purposes. The emphasis here is on responsibility and cost sharing. The second part of the paper examines the response of governments to regional disparities associated with the development of mineral resources, with particular reference to different kinds of fiscal equalization arrangments. The emphasis in this part is on revenue sharing.

I. Responsibility Sharing and Regional Growth

Assumed Conditions for Regional Development Assistance

For the purpose of promoting regional development, the most appropriate fiscal instruments are specific purpose (or conditional) development grants and loans from the federal government to regional governments. In the following discussion, it will be assumed that development assistance is provided to regional governments in these forms,

Public Finance and Economic Growth. Proceedings of the 37th Congress of the International Institute of Public Finance. Tokyo, 1981, pp. 265–296

for the purpose either of encouraging the growth of rural, manufacturing and service industries or of establishing the social and economic infrastructure needed to support private sector growth. The discussion will apply to both less developed and economically advanced federal countries, it being assumed that they share a common problem in the form of significant disparities in incomes and economic activity between and within regions. In the case of less developed countries, federal and regional governments are likely to join in general planning arrangements designed to increase incomes all round as well as to reduce regional disparities. In advanced countries, more emphasis is likely to be placed on stimulating regional growth through specific purpose programs designed to deal with particular problems in particular areas. But the grants model which will be developed will be applicable to both cases.

The discussion will be restricted to financial relationships between federal and regional governments, although most of the analysis is applicable to regional-local or even federal-local financial relations. In the case of less developed countries, the federal government will be assumed to have a major role in determining planning strategies, mobilizing and allocating financial resources, and co-ordinating federal and regional development policies. In economically advanced countries, the federal government may have a less dominant role. However, in both cases it will be assumed that federal and regional governments, their economies and their development activities are so interdependent as to require effective intergovernmental consultation, co-operation and policy co-ordination if regional development is to proceed efficiently, equitably, responsibly and responsively.

Although it may be expected that taxation and other revenue collections will be concentrated to a significant extent in the hands of the federal government, it will be assumed that, through revenue-sharing arrangements or independent taxing powers, regional governments have the power to determine the size of their revenue collections at least at the margin. As part of the revenue-sharing arrangements, some form of horizontal fiscal equalization may operate to compensate for differences in the capacity of regional governments to provide comparable services if they impose comparable levels of taxation. In less developed countries the fiscal equalization arrangements may be subsumed under the provisions for determining and financing plan expenditures, but in any case it is possible to design a development grants model which incorporates provision for fiscal equalization; such a model is developed below. The fiscal equalization arrangements may include provision for the assessment of fiscal needs by an independent finance or grants commission, but in the case of less developed countries it will be assumed that an intergovernmental planning commission has been established to advise on the level, pattern, financing and interregional distribution of the planning or development assistance which is intended to promote regional growth.

Specific Purpose Grants for Regional Development

Specific purpose grants and loans for development purposes may take many forms. In this paper, attention will be directed mainly to grants (which may take the form of regional governments' entitlements under revenue-sharing arrangements). However, much of the discussion will be applicable to specific purpose loans or advances, while an important aspect of development policy will be concerned with deciding on the extent to which planning or development assistance should take the form of loans rather than grants.

Although by definition specific purpose grants are conditional grants, the conditions which may be attached to them include both expenditure and revenue conditions. The expenditure conditions may require the grants to be spent on narrowly defined purposes (such grants are usually described as categorical grants) or broad purposes (described as block grants). A somewhat similar distinction is that between project or program grants, which are allocated on the basis of specific proposals, and formula grants, which are available to all governments for broad functional purposes, for example for economic development generally, without restrictions or detailed specifications as to how they are to be spent.

Revenue conditions may take the form of general conditions which require recipient governments to maintain existing or prescribed revenue efforts as their contribution to the financing of the assisted programs. Alternatively, they may take the form of conditions which require recipient governments to match the grants with contributions in prescribed ratios from their own revenue sources. Matching ratios may be fixed (e.g., $1 for $1) or variable, the size of the matching ratio depending on the revenue effort required of the recipient governments, which may in turn depend on their relative fiscal capacities. In Canada, the federal share of regional develoment grants administered by the Canadian Department of Regional Economic Expansion may range from 90 per cent in Newfoundland to 50 per cent in Ontario, Alberta and British Columbia.

Specific purpose grants may also be open-ended or closed-ended, the latter being fixed in amount or subject to an upper limit and the former being dependent on the level of expenditure which the recipient government undertakes.

Many grants for regional development are inefficient, in the sense that they fail to achieve the purposes for which they are given, or inequitable, in the sense that they fail to take account of the relative revenue-raising capacity and expenditure needs of the governments being assisted. A general problem with grants for development purposes is that they involve federal government intervention in activities which are constitutional responsibilities of regional governments.

This raises the question as to which level of government is to determine the purposes, priorities and policies of the assisted programs, with the possibility of conflicts between competing national and regional interests, proliferation of programs, duplication of bureaucracies and a tendency to encourage unnecessary public sector growth, failure to distinguish between policy formulation and policy execution, inadequate accountability and an inability to establish clear responsibility for the performance of programs. Fixed grants for narrowly defined purposes presuppose a much greater knowledge of detailed regional problems and needs than federal governments are likely to possess. Block or formula grants are likely to be too generous to some regions and inadequate for others, while failing to meet the national interests which provide the justification for federal intervention.

Open-ended cost-sharing grants will tend to increase expenditures beyond the limit that either level of government acting by itself would consider economically or politically justified, even if externalities are fully taken into account, because each unit of government will tend to relate the total benefits of programs to its share of costs instead of to total costs. Closed-ended or fixed grants may fail to achieve the federal government's purpose of stimulating or influencing the pattern of expenditures in the assisted field, if the recipient governments are able to substitute the grants for their own revenues. On the one hand, revenue or expenditure substitution of this kind enables regional governments to retain their spending priorities at the expense of the federal government. On the other hand, matching conditions imposed to prevent such substitution have the effect of distorting the pattern of regional government expenditures by inducing the regional governments to depart from their preferred choice.

These problems and conflicts of interest suggest that, in the case of regional development as for other specific purpose programs, governments need to pay particular attention to grant design, the machinery for formulating, co-ordinating and implementing policies, and the development of an efficient and equitable grants distribution model.

Grant Design

In designing regional development grant programs, governments will thus need to consider spending conditions, revenue conditions, possible limitations on the level of grants and other specifications in relation to the purposes they seek to achieve. It has thus been suggested that, if the objective of specific purpose grants is to internalize the spillover effects which result from the spending decisions of regional governments,[1] an open-ended matching grant is the appropriate instrument.[2] More generally, it may be argued that matching conditions should be imposed when the granting government seeks to achieve expenditure stimulation or reallocation effects, and that fixed grants should be limited to programs where the recipient governments act as administrative agents of the federal government.[3]

If the purpose of the grants is to provide general revenue support, formula or block grants will be preferred to project or categorical grants, but under these circumstances the question must be asked whether there is a case for specific purpose grants at all or whether they should be replaced by general purpose grants or a reallocation of taxing powers.[4]

The application of the foregoing criteria will still tend to result in specific purpose grants being evaluated by reference to the interests of one or other level of government. However, the essential need in relation to regional development is to establish co-ordinating machinery which will adequately represent the interests of all governments and assign responsibilities in accordance with the relative competence and mandate of different governments to perform particular tasks.

Machinery for Co-ordinating Regional Development Policies

The machinery problem is partly one of relating development plans or grant programs to the budget priorities and processes of each of the governments concerned, and partly one of co-ordinating the strategies and policies of granting and recipient governments. Depending on the generality of the planning arrangements, several approaches to this problem have been developed in federal countries.

In India, where economic and social planning is listed as a concurrent function of federal and state governments in the Constitution, a Planning Commission has been established as a federal government agency under the chairmanship of the prime minister.[5] Its role is to assess resources and consider developmental options, formulate five-year and annual plans and the detailed disaggregation of those plans, advise on financing and other policies necessary to implement the plans, determine planning machinery, and appraise progress and evaluate performance. As well as acting as a ministry of planning for the federal government, the Planning Commission consults with the states in determining their own five-year and annual plans and in assessing the level and forms of federal government assistance.

The Planning Commission also serves as the secretariat of the National Development Council, which includes among its members the prime minister and all state chief ministers as well as members of the Planning Commission and the federal cabinet. The National Development Council plays a major role in reviewing the five-year plans as they evolve through preliminary discussions of planning objectives and options, the formulation of draft plans and the endorsement of final plans. Despite its broad base and great power, the National Development Council's role is essentially an advisory one. It makes recommendations to federal and state governments, but the final responsibility for planning decisions rests with those governments.

The general purpose of these arrangements is to co-ordinate all planning and policy decisions of federal and state governments, their broad policy goals, sectoral plans and projects, and financing arrangements. In addition to federal government assistance through grants and loans for state plans, which is determined by the Planning Commission on the basis of agreed annual plan expenditures, the states receive federal assistance for their nonplan expenditure needs based on recommendations of a separate Finance Commission.

As in many other respects, the Federal Republic of Germany has developed, through its so-called joint tasks and grants-in-aid programs, a highly integrated system of responsibility sharing between the federal and Länder (state) governments, which incorporates joint planning, decision making and financing arrangements. Under West Germany's Basic Law or Constitution, the federal government and Länder governments must exercise joint responsibility for three joint tasks, concerned respectively with the expansion and construction of universities, the improvement of regional economic structures and the improvement of the agrarian structure and coast preservation.[6]

For each joint task, a framework plan is adopted, which establishes the planning goals, the expenditure programs to achieve the goals and the financial contributions of federal and Länder governments by budget periods. Policy co-ordination is effected by a planning board on which federal and all Länder governments are represented. Initiatives for joint tasks come from the Länder and they are responsible for implementing the programs. The federal government cannot be out-voted by the Länder in the planning board but requires the support of half the Länder to carry its own proposals.

Similar joint decision-making machinery operates in the case of federal grants-in-aid for such purposes as educational planning and research, urban renewal, transport and stabilization policy. Both the joint tasks and grants-in-aid programs followed constitutional amendments in 1969, which were intended to overcome earlier criticisms of specific purpose grants programs to the effect that they breached constitutional law and infringed the autonomy of the Länder. In 1975, the federal Constitutional Court ruled that the federal government and all Länder must agree on the allocation of federal-Länder grants; that funds must be allocated on a uniform basis; and that the selection of projects must conform to Länder priorities.

There have been two Australian responses to the problem of establishing appropriate machinery for the purpose of co-ordinating regional development or other public policies. The first has taken the form of federal-state ministerial councils supported by committees of the permanent heads of the relevant federal and state departments. The most important ministerial councils are the Premiers' Conference and the Australian Loan Council, which have the same membership in the form of the federal prime minister and all state premiers. The Premiers' Conference usually meets only two or three times a year to discuss intergovernmental financial arrangements and such other matters as may be raised by members. It is a consultative body which makes few collective decisions. Although some intergovernmental bargaining takes place about taxation and grants arrangements, in the face of federal financial domination the Conference has tended to become merely a forum in which the federal government announces its decisions.

The Australian Loan Council formally has a major role in intergovernmental policy co-ordination, having been established following constitutional amendment in 1928 to determine the amounts, conditions and intergovernmental allocation of all public sector borrowing—federal, state and local. But although the federal government may be out-voted in the Council if it fails to obtain the support of two states, its monopoly over the major tax sources and the discriminating use of its central banking powers have enabled it effectively to control the level of state and local borrowing.

A ministerial council was also established by the federal and two state governments in 1973 for the purpose of co-ordinating the development of the Albury-Wodonga region on the border of New South Wales and Victoria. The three governments also jointly established a development corporation to act as a statutory planning and development authority for the region. Most of the funds for the development were to be provided by the federal government through specific purpose grants and loans, but the federal government's support for the project has since largely been withdrawn.

The second Australian institutional development, which is concerned especially with intergovernmental grants arrangements, has involved the establishment of independent statutory commissions by the federal government to assess the fiscal needs of the states and advise on the level and interstate distribution of grants and the design of grant programs. The prototype of these bodies was the Commonwealth Grants Commission, which was established in 1933 to advise on the fiscal needs of states which, because of their low fiscal capacity, needed special equalization assistance. The Commission still exercises this role, while in 1981 it completed a major review of the revenue-raising capacities and expenditure needs of all states for the purpose of assessing, on the basis of fiscal equalization principles, the distribution of state tax sharing entitlements. This inquiry, which was carried out over a period of two and a half years and involved voluminous submissions by federal and state treasury departments and most state government spending departments, is probably the most ambitious fiscal equalization exercise which has ever been attempted in any country.[7]

Advisory commissions have also been established in Australia to advise on the financial needs of the states, as a basis for specific purpose grants from the federal government, in functional fields of state constitutional responsibility. Such bodies have operated at various times in respect of universities and other tertiary education institutions, schools, roads, hospitals and health services, cities and social welfare, although now only the tertiary education and schools commissions remain in existence. They have never operated as intergovernmental agencies and the extent of their consultation with the states has tended to vary from one commission to another. But their recommendations have had significant implications for state budgets and policies even when matching grants were not being proposed.

The Australian use of advisory commissions may be contrasted with the American and Canadian approach to the development of specific purpose grants machinery, which typically involves the use of legislation administered by federal government departments or agencies, project grants based on applications by regional governments as well as formula grants, and intergovernmental agreements. In Canada, for example, the federal Department of Regional Economic Expansion was established in 1969 to administer all federal regional development programs and agencies. One of the main roles of the Department has been to negotiate so-called general development agreements with provincial governments as a basis for federal financial assistance. The general development agreements establish joint federal-provincial strategies for regional development on the basis of co-operative arrangements in which other federal departments, local governments and the private sector may also participate. The general development agreements are followed by subsidiary agreements, which provide the basis for the formulation of specific program proposals and determine administrative and financing arrangements. Implementation of the subsidiary agreements is the responsibility of the provinces, which have established their own development departments or agencies. As noted above, federal financial support for programs varies from province to province in accordance with their relative fiscal capacities.[8]

A Regional Development Grants Distribution Model

Irrespective of whether financial assistance for regional development takes the form of general planning assistance along Indian lines, shared contributions as in West Germany or specific purpose grants as in Australia and Canada, a general distribution model may be developed on the basis of the following steps. It is assumed that there is appropriate intergovernmental machinery for deciding on total expenditures, systematically assessing the relative expenditure needs of regions and determining the relative capacity of governments to contribute towards the cost of the development expenditures.

First, decide on the level of the total expenditure program and its distribution among regions. This is a political decision which must be taken in the context of the determination of budget priorities by both federal and regional governments, but it may be supported by cost-benefit studies or other quantitative analysis directed towards the problem of assessing total and relative expenditure needs.

Second, allocate the responsibility for financing the program between the federal government and regional governments in general. This also is a political decision, the outcome of which will depend on the respective interests of federal and regional governments in the program as well as on the vertical distribution of taxing and other revenue powers. This decision will determine the aggregate level of specific purpose grants or assistance.

Third, assess the relative capacities of the regional governments to contribute to the regions' share of the total expenditure program. The following distribution model will then determine the level of specific purpose grants or assistance received by each regional government:

$$G_i = E_i - \left[\Sigma R_i \cdot \frac{Y_i}{\Sigma Y_i} \right] \tag{1}$$

where G_i = the grant to government i
E_i = the assessed expenditure program for government i where ΣE_i equals the aggregate expenditure program for all regions
ΣR_i = the total financing contribution required from regional governments' own revenue sources
$Y_i/\Sigma Y_i$ = the fiscal capacity of government i relative to the total capacities of all regional governments

This model will result in each regional government receiving a grant equal to the difference between its assessed expenditure program and its assessed financing contribution based on its relative fiscal capacity.

It may be noted that the application of a fixed matching ratio implies that the relative contributions of regional governments should be proportional to their assessed expenditure programs, that is that $Y_i/\Sigma Y_i = E_i/\Sigma E_i$, so that no account is taken of relative fiscal capacity. The Canadian regional development grants referred to above effectively determine $Y_i/\Sigma Y_i$ for each province in accordance with the assessment that has been made of the province's relative fiscal capacity.

If the specific purpose grants are being made in a country which already has a general system of fiscal capacity equalization in operation and the equalization is complete, all regions may be assumed to have equal per capita fiscal capacity and the contributions of regional governments will be proportional to regional populations, that is $Y_i/\Sigma Y_i$ will be determined by $P_i/\Sigma P_i$.

If, as has been the case with most Australian programs, the distribution of specific purpose grants among regions has not taken account of differences in fiscal capacity (for example, if only expenditure needs have been assessed or if the grants take the form of cost-sharing or fixed matching grants), the specific purpose grants may be treated as a revenue item for the purpose of the general fiscal equalization arrangements. Differences in per capita specific purpose grants will thus be treated as differences in revenue-raising capacity and brought into the assessment of revenue needs.[9]

II. Revenue Sharing and Regional Growth

Sharing Resource Revenues

So far we have been concerned with the manner in which governments share the responsibility for, and the costs of, those forms of economic development which, at least in their initial stages, impose a net burden on their budgets. It has been assumed that the purpose of the governments has been to promote regional growth and reduce regional economic disparities through rural and industrial development.

In this part, a different question is examined. This concerns the manner in which different levels and units of government share the revenues from highly profitable development, in particular the development of mineral and energy resources.

The first problem is to determine the basis on which the resource revenues are shared between the federal government and the governments of the regions in which the resource development takes place. This will depend partly on the distribution of taxing powers among the two levels of government and the manner in which those powers are exercised, and partly on the ownership of the mineral rights and the basis on which rents and royalties are levied.

The level and pattern of resource development and the distribution of the resulting revenues will also be influenced by the level of the resource rents and the profitability of projects; by the manner in which the federal government exercises its powers with respect to foreign investment and exchange, resource and environmental management, monetary and exchange rate policies; and by the manner in which the regional governments exercise their powers with respect to the provision of social, community and economic services (for example, by requiring mining companies to contribute to the cost of infrastructure development), the pricing of rail and electricity services, and resource and environmental management.

The two levels of government will be so interdependent in relation to these matters as to necessitate a substantial degree of coordination of their taxation and other policies if the resource development is to be carried out efficiently and equitably. Two major issues will concern the extent to which the federal government should control resource development either to protect national interests or to prevent wasteful competition among regional governments; and the extent to which resource revenues should be subject to equalization arrangements among the regions themselves. The resolution of these issues will depend on the nature of the federal compact and the extent to which the interests of regions are seen by the citizens of those regions as overriding national interests.[10]

In the rest of this paper, it will be assumed that there is a system of horizontal fiscal equalization in force. The principal purpose will be to show that the nature of the equalization arrangements will have a crucial result on the sharing of resource revenues, not only among the regions themselves but also between the federal and regional governments.

Fiscal Equalization and the Sharing of Resource Revenues

A general equalization grants model to achieve horizontal fiscal capacity equalization may take the following form:

$$G_i = P_i \cdot \frac{R_s}{Y_s}\left[\frac{Y_s}{P_s} - \frac{Y_i}{P_i}\right] + P_i \cdot \frac{E_s}{P_s} \cdot \gamma_i \qquad (2)$$

where
G = equalization grant
P = population
R = revenue collections
Y = revenue base
R/Y = revenue effort
E = government expenditure
γ = additional cost of providing services relative to standard per capita cost
i = government being equalized
s = equalization standard

Separate calculations are made for each revenue source R_j and each expenditure category E_j.

Three federal countries have adopted variants of this model as the basis for their equalization arrangements, and the analysis which follows is designed to show how the differences in the arrangements affect the sharing of resource revenues.

In the Federal Republic of Germany, G_i represents the horizontal fiscal transfer which Land government i must make or receive, depending on whether its fiscal capacity exceeds or falls short of the equalization standard. The equalization standard in West Germany is the average fiscal capacity for all Länder. The fiscal equalization process is confined mainly to revenue equalization, that is to the first term on the right-hand side of equation (2), but there is some allowance for differences in expenditure needs arising from special burdens, population density and the degree of urbanization. The aggregate horizontal transfers for all Länder will sum to zero.[11]

The Canadian fiscal equalization arrangements are restricted to revenue equalization, that is to the first term on the right-hand side of equation (2). The equalization standard is again a national average standard, based on the tax effort and revenue bases of all provinces. Separate calculations are made for 29 revenue sources and the results (both positive and negative) are added. Any province which has below-standard capacity as measured by the net amount of its entitlements receives an equalization grant from the federal government. Provinces with above-standard capacity are not directly affected by the equalization process.[12]

The traditional Australian fiscal equalization arrangements have involved the payment of equalization grants by the federal government to the states on the recommendation of the Commonwealth Grants Commission, which assesses expenditure needs of states seeking special financial assistance as well as revenue needs. Thus the equalization grant is calculated by reference to all recurrent revenues and expenditures and covers both terms in equation (2). Further, the equalization standard is the average of the two states with the highest fiscal capacity.[13]

Fiscal Equalization and the Sharing of Resource Revenues

In comparing the effects of these three kinds of fiscal equalization systems on sharing of resource revenues, we shall assume that there are three governments, namely the federal government, the government of an underdeveloped region with a small population and rich resources waiting for development, and the government of a rich industrialized region with a large population. Although the government of the industrialized region (which we shall designate government A) originally has a higher revenue-raising capacity than the resource-rich regional government (which we shall designate government B), as a result of mineral discoveries and exploitation the latter's revenue base is about to be substantially increased.

The analysis will be restricted to revenue equalization and will ignore the question of the vertical sharing of resource revenues between the federal and regional governments, by assuming that federal resource revenues are the same under each system. It will also be assumed that there are no differences in revenue-raising effort as between the regions and that, prior to the resource development, only one revenue source is available to the two regions.

The three systems of fiscal equalization which will be compared are then:

(a) horizontal fiscal equalization transfers between the two regions, based on a national average equalization standard (the West German system);

(b) vertical fiscal equalization transfers from the federal government to the region with below-standard revenue-raising capacity, based on a national average equalization standard (the Canadian system); and

(c) vertical fiscal equalization transfers from the federal government to the region with below-standard revenue-raising capacity, based on an equalization standard derived from the region with the highest fiscal capacity (the Australian system).

The analysis loses something through the simplifying assumptions which are made, because in the real world the equalization arrangements are likely to depend on such matters as the extent of regional fiscal disparities, the number of regions with relatively small revenue bases, the year-to-year variations in revenue bases, whether poor regions have large or small populations, the relative political and financial strength of federal and regional governments, the treatment of differences in revenue-raising effort and the extent to which fiscal equalization is accepted as a major policy objective.

It will be demonstrated that, if a system of fiscal equalization is operating in a federation and substantial resource development takes place in a region which has been receiving equalization grants, the distribution of the resource revenues resulting from the development depends on the nature of the equalization arrangements. In particular, it will depend on which level of government has been financing the equalization transfers, whether the system is closed-ended or open-ended, what equalization standard is adopted and whether the equalization is complete or partial.

Fiscal Equalization Before Resource Development

The comparisons will be based on the following data, which relate to the period before the development results in increased resource revenues:

Region	*Population* P	*Revenue Base* Y	*Revenue Collections* R
		$	$
A	10	1,000	200
B	5	250	50
Total	15	1,250	250

Equalization transfers will be calculated as follows under the three systems:

West German System.

$$G_A = P_A \cdot \frac{R_s}{Y_s}\left(\frac{Y_s}{P_s} - \frac{Y_A}{P_A}\right)$$

$$= 10 \cdot \frac{250}{1250}\left(\frac{1250}{15} - \frac{1000}{10}\right)$$

$$= -\$33.3$$

$$G_B = P_B \cdot \frac{R_s}{Y_s}\left(\frac{Y_s}{P_s} - \frac{Y_B}{P_B}\right)$$

$$= 5 \cdot \frac{250}{1250}\left(\frac{1250}{15} - \frac{250}{5}\right)$$

$$= \$33.3$$

Region B will thus receive a grant of $33.3 which will be financed by the negative grant of $33.3 calculated for region A. The budgets after equalization will permit equal expenditure per head of population (E/P) in each region, so that equalization is complete:

Budgets After Equalization

Government	*R*	*G*	*E*	*E/P*
	$	$	$	$
A	200	−33.3	166.7	16.7
B	50	+33.3	83.3	16.7

The federal government is not affected, while the equalization is internal to the revenue-raising arrangements and is therefore closed-ended.

Canadian System. In this case, only the government with below-standard revenue-raising capacity (government B) receives a grant, which is financed by the federal government. Government A retains the whole of its revenue collections:

$$G_A = 0$$

$$G_B = P_B \cdot \frac{R_s}{Y_s}\left(\frac{Y_s}{P_s} - \frac{Y_B}{P_B}\right)$$

$$= \$33.3$$

The budgets after equalization will not permit equal expenditure per head because, although region B has been equalized up to the standard, region A has not been equalized down; the equalization is therefore partial:

Budgets After Equalization

Government	*R*	*G*	*E*	*E/P*
	$	$	$	$
A	200	–	200	20
B	50	+33.3	83.3	16.7
Federal		−33.3		

The federal government finances the grant to region B by means of a supplementary payment, which is external to the regional revenue-raising arrangements. The system is open-ended except to the extent that it is constrained by the equalization standard.

Australian System. Again government B receives a grant from the federal government while government A is not affected by the equalization process:

$$G_A = 0$$

$$G_B = P_B \cdot \frac{R_A}{Y_A}\left(\frac{Y_A}{P_A} - \frac{Y_B}{P_B}\right)$$

$$= 5 \cdot \frac{200}{1000}\left(\frac{1000}{10} - \frac{250}{5}\right)$$

$$= 50$$

The budgets after equalization permit equal expenditure per head at a higher level than in the West German case, because the revenue collections of the regions have been supplemented by a federal grant which equalizes to the highest fiscal capacity and not the average:

Budgets After Equalization

Government	*R*	*G*	*E*	*E/P*
	$	$	$	$
A	200	–	200	20
B	50	50	100	20
Federal		−50		

With the federal government financing the grant, the system is open-ended in the same sense as the Canadian system.

Fiscal Equalization After Resource Development

It will now be assumed that resource development in region B results in an increase in government B's revenue base to the extent necessary to eliminate B's shortfall in revenue-raising capacity, and that both regions continue to collect other revenues as before:

Region	*P*	*Y*	*R*
		$	$
A	10	1,000	200
B	5	500	100
Total	15	1,500	300

The increase of $50 in government B's revenue will have the effect of eliminating all equalization grants, while regional budgets after equalization will be the same in each of the three systems:

Government	*R*	*G*	*E*	*E/P*
	$	$	$	$
A	200	–	200	20
B	100	–	100	20

However, a comparison with the equalized budgets before resource development shows that the resource revenues of $50 have been shared among the three governments in different ways, depending on the form of the equalization arrangements:

West German System. Under this system, government A benefits to the extent of $33.3 from B's resource revenues while government B gains $16.7. That is, both A and B gain equally in per capita terms, by $3.3 per head. If they maintain expenditure at previous levels but reduce tax rates, they will likewise share equally in the gains in per capita terms. The federal government is not affected.

Canadian System. Under this system, government A is not affected by the resource development but the budgetary positions of government B and the federal government both improve, government B by $16.7 or $3.3 per head and the federal government by $33.3.

Australian System. Under this system, government B's grant is wholly replaced by the increase in its resource revenues. Governments A and B neither gain nor lose by the increase in resource revenues, but the federal government benefits to the full extent of the revenues ($50).

Effect of Varying Assumptions

The main interest in the foregoing analysis centres on the light it throws on the equalizing effects, development incentives, political acceptability and financial stability of the different equalization systems. In this context, it is useful to consider the effect of varying the assumptions, for example by assuming that government B's total revenue base increases as a result of the resource development to such an extent that its revenue-raising capacity exceeds the standard capacity, so that in effect the equalization is reversed; or by assuming that the resource development takes place in region A, the government of which already has the higher revenue-raising capacity, so that the equalization need of region B is increased.

It can be shown that, under the West German system, the resource revenues will continue to be shared between the two regional governments under each of the changed assumptions, and that the federal government will remain unaffected.

Under the Canadian system, government A will benefit from reverse equalization because it will now receive an equalization grant, while government B will benefit to the extent that its resource revenues exceed the grant it was formerly receiving. Whether the federal government gains or loses under the equalization arrangements will depend not only on the amount of resource revenues and their effect on the equalization standard, but also on the fact that the per capita equalization grant now has to be paid to a region with a larger population. Under the assumption that government A receives the resource revenues, the Canadian system will have the effect of leaving government A with the full benefit of those revenues but, because of the higher equalization standard, government B will receive a larger grant at the expense of the federal government.

Under the Australian system, government A will benefit under reverse equalization by the amount of the equalization grant, while government B will benefit by the amount by which its resource revenues exceed the equalization grant it was previously receiving. For an equal (but opposite) per capita difference in revenue-raising capacity before and after the resource development, the federal government will be worse off because the equalization grant will now have to be paid to a region with a larger population. When government A receives the resource revenues, it will retain the whole of the benefit while B will improve its position to a comparable extent at the expense of the federal government.

Evaluation of Equalization Systems

The effects of the three equalization systems may now be summarized and contrasted. Insofar as the equalizing effects are concerned, the West German and the Australian systems are fully equalizing in their treatment of resource revenues. The Canadian equalization system is only partly equalizing; although it equalizes all regions up to the national average revenue-raising capacity, it does not equalize regions with above-standard capacity down to the national average. Another feature of both the Australian and the Canadian arrangements is that standard states or above-standard provinces derive no benefit from resource development in states or provinces receiving equalization assistance, unless the resource revenues received by the latter are so large as to reverse the eligibility for equalization grants.

Because it is fully equalizing at all times, the West German system will offer less incentive to a regional government to encourage resource development than there will be in a federal country with no regional fiscal capacity equalization, such as the United States. There, for example, Alaska may retain the whole of its mineral revenues for itself, whereas under the West German system a regional government must share its gains with other regions. The West German system will also tend to discourage resource development relative to a unitary state such as the United Kingdom, the central government of which has control over the whole of its North Sea oil and gas revenues. Whether the Canadian and Australian systems have disincentive effects similar to those of the West German system will depend on whether the regional governments have previously been receiving equalization grants which will be lost as a result of the resource development.

It is possible to exaggerate the significance of these revenue substitution effects, because regional governments will no doubt have other reasons for wishing to promote resource development, including its effects on regional employment and incomes. Nevertheless, as far as possible such disincentives should be minimized. In principle, it would be preferable to measure revenue bases by reference to revenue potential when comparisons are being made between regions for the purpose of assessing their revenue-raising capacities. Differences in policy or efficiency in exploiting mineral resources should not be reflected in equalization grants.

However, it will usually be difficult to identify revenue potential as a basis for assessing equalization grants, except in a negative way. Thus if one state government declares that, as a matter of policy, it will not develop its proved uranium resources while another state proceeds to develop its resources, it is clearly inappropriate for the former to receive an equalization grant to match the latter's resource revenues from the uranium development.

Because the Canadian system does not fully equalize regional budgets, it provides a greater incentive than the Australian system for a government receiving equalization assistance to develop its revenue bases so as to reach or exceed the equalization standard. There is not a complete substitution of resource revenues for equalization grants under the Canadian arrangements, because the equalization standard itself rises when the resource revenues are brought into account. By contrast, the Australian system involves a \$1 for \$1 substitution of resource revenues for equalization grants up to the point where the revenue-raising capacities of the assisted and standard governments become equal. In effect, the federal government withdraws its equalization grants by imposing a 100 per cent levy on all resource revenues received by the government which has previously been assisted, up to the point where it ceases to be eligible for grants.

The conclusions of the previous paragraph must be modified when the assumption of a uniform revenue effort for all regional governments is relaxed. This is because, under the Australian system, a government which is in a below-standard region but which is receiving resource revenues can vary its revenue effort without affecting the size of its equalization grant, which is calculated by reference to an external standard revenue effort. If regional governments are free to determine their own tax rates, neither the West German nor the Canadian system is policy neutral in this sense. In both cases, a greater revenue effort by the government in the region with below-standard revenue-raising capacity will raise the national average tax rate and thus increase its equalization grant, while a reduction in the revenue effort of the region with above-standard capacity will have the opposite effect and reduce its negative grant (in the West German case) or the grant payable by the federal government (in the Canadian case).[14]

The political stability of the three equalization systems depends to an important extent on whether the federation itself is robust or fragile. This will depend on the degree of national as opposed to regional consciousness, which will determine the extent to which the citizens of a financially strong region accept the case for equalization grants to fiscally disadvantaged regions and the extent to which citizens of a region undergoing resource development are prepared to share the resulting revenues with the citizens of other regions.

The problem will be eased if a uniform system of collecting and sharing revenues is operating under constitutional provision (as in West Germany) or under the aegis of the federal government (as in Australia). A system involving grants from regions with high fiscal capacity to regions with low fiscal capacity is only likely to be politically acceptable to the former if it is subsumed in general tax-sharing arrangements of the kind which exist in West Germany or Australia, so that vertical fiscal transfers from the federal to the regional governments are distributed among the latter in accordance with fiscal equalization principles.

It is unlikely that, if regional governments have themselves collected the resource or other revenues from a high-capacity revenue base, they will voluntarily share those revenues with other less affluent regions.[15] This means that, in practice, if it is to work effectively, the West German no less than the Canadian and the Australian equalization systems requires federal government involvement.

The West German system nevertheless has an advantage over the other two systems in that, being a closed system, it is financially stable, whereas the dependence of the Canadian and Australian systems on supplementary grants from the federal government makes them potentially unstable.

Factors Contributing to the Financial Instability of Equalization Arrangements

In practice, the conditions giving rise to financial instability operate to a much greater extent in Canada than in Australia. This is because a number of special circumstances have combined in Australia to minimize the political and financial problems of horizontal fiscal equalization arrangements financed by the federal government. These include: the absence of marked disparities in personal incomes, social composition and economic conditions among the states; a relatively even distribution of mineral and energy resources among all states, relative to state populations, combined with a relatively low ratio of resource revenues to other state revenues; a concentration of population in the two states with the highest fiscal capacity, so that the absolute amounts of equalization grants to other states based on their per capita fiscal disabilities impose a relatively small burden on the federal government's budget; and, as noted above, the operation of what is essentially a two-stage equalization process which has the effect of reducing the need for supplementary equalization grants from the federal government to financially weak states, because some equalization is carried out in the vertical distribution of tax-sharing payments.

By contrast, none of these conditions holds in the Canadian case. There are substantial financial, social and economic disparities among the provinces; resource revenues are very unevenly distributed and in some provinces are very high indeed relative to other revenues; the resource-rich provinces have relatively small populations while the revenue-raising capacity of the province with the second-largest population (Quebec) is well below the national average, necessitating very large equalization grants to that province; and there is no general federal-provincial tax-sharing arrangement containing explicit or implicit provision for horizontal fiscal equalization, so that the whole burden of horizontal fiscal equalization falls on the federal budget.

The form of the Australian equalization arrangements also has the advantage, from the viewpoint of states with relatively low revenue-raising capacity or relatively high costs of providing services, that the equalization is complete and includes expenditure as well as revenue equalization. Expenditure equalization tends to favour the resource-rich states and thus to offset their negative equalization in respect of resource revenues.

By contrast with the Australian system, the Canadian equalization arrangements do not make it possible for all regional governments to provide standard levels of services provided they impose standard levels of taxes and charges. The Canadian provinces are equalized only for differences in revenue-raising capacity and then only to the national average, so that substantial inequalities in the capacity of provinces to provide services remain.

The financial instability of the Canadian equalization system does not only result from the fact that the federal government has to carry the burden of financing very large equalization payments. It also follows from the inbuilt tendency of the equalization process, through what is essentially a multiplier effect, to generate increases in the expenditures of all below-standard provinces whenever any one of the ten provinces has its revenue capacity improved as a result of increasing resource revenues (or, indeed, from any other cause). Although similar problems exist to a marginal degree under the Australian system, they have reached chronic proportions in Canada. There is no such effect under the West German arrangements.

Both problems have their origin in the design of the Canadian arrangements, whereby the federal government has to finance equalization payments from sources other than the provincial revenues which are subject to equalization. This may be illustrated by changing the form of the Canadian equalization model so as to emphasize differences between relative populations and relative resource revenue bases instead of differences between per capita revenue bases:[16]

$$G_i = \Sigma R_i\left(\frac{P_i}{\Sigma P_i} - \frac{Y_i}{\Sigma Y_i}\right)$$

where R_i = the resource revenues of province i and ΣR_i the resource revenues of all provinces

Y_i = the resource revenue base of province i and ΣY_i the resource revenue base of all provinces

The problem for the federal government is that any increase in provincial revenues ΣR_i results in a higher grant for every province whose share of population exceeds its share of the resource revenue base. If a province with a relatively small population has most of the revenue base for a particular revenue source and collects substantial revenue therefrom, the level of equalization entitlements theoretically required for other provinces in respect of that revenue source will approach the level of the province's revenue collections.

Suppose, for example, that a province has 10 per cent of the country's population and collects 100 per cent of all provincial oil and natural gas revenues, a situation which is not very far removed from the actual position of Alberta. In the absence of offsetting equalization entitlements for other revenue sources and other modifications to the equalization arrangements discussed below, the federal government will need to make equalization payments of 90 cents for every $1 of oil and gas revenues collected by the resource-rich province.

Furthermore, except to the extent that it can exploit the oil and gas revenue base itself, the federal government will need to finance the equalization payments by means of taxes and charges which are likely to bear mainly on the citizens of the provinces receiving equalization. If the revenue bases of federal taxes are proportional to population, 90 per cent of the equalization payments in the above example will be collected from taxpayers in the provinces receiving equalization and only 10 per cent from taxpayers in the province with the resource revenues. The distributional problem will be accentuated if, as has happened in Canada, taxpayers in other provinces are faced with increased oil and gas prices as well as higher taxes.

The foregoing discussion must be qualified, because it has overstated the intergovernmental fiscal effects of increases in resource revenues under the Canadian equalization arrangements. This is partly because the equalization entitlements of some provinces for resource revenues may be offset by negative entitlements for other revenue sources, and partly because the federal government has modified the equalization formula and taxation arrangements in various ways in order to limit its liability. It has thus eliminated the open-endedness of the equalization formula by limiting equalization on non-renewable resource revenues (that is, revenues from oil, natural gas and other minerals) to one-half of those revenues and by restricting the amount of equalization entitlements in respect of resource revenues (both renewable such as forestry and non-renewable) to one-third of total equalization payments.[17]

Although the Canadian federal government was unable to obtain direct access to provincial resource revenues as a means of financing equalization payments to other provinces, it increased its own revenues from minerals and energy sources by imposing oil export, excise and other energy taxes and making oil and gas royalties non-deductible for income tax purposes. But the essential problem with the Canadian arrangements is that the resource revenues which give rise to the need for equalization cannot themselves be used to finance the equalization payments. This is due to an inherent defect in the Canadian equalization system, to which the federal government's major response has been to limit equalization on resource revenues.

Conditions for a Stable Equalization System

It has been suggested that the Canadian problem could be dealt with by permitting the federal government to tax provincial resource revenues as though they originated in the private sector.[18] Alternatively, it has been suggested that a system of interprovincial equalization transfers should be established under which the resource-rich provinces would themselves finance the payments to the other provinces.[19]

Whether or not these proposals are politically practicable is a question which only Canadians can answer in the context of their continuing debate on the structure of the Canadian federal system. But it may be noted that the West German and Australian tax-sharing arrangements avoid the Canadian financing problem (altogether in the West German case and substantially under the existing Australian arrangements) by incorporating the equalization transfers in the general arrangements for the collection and distribution of revenues among federal and regional governments. Provided the amount of the shared tax revenues is sufficiently large to permit a distribution among regional governments which will fully equalize their fiscal capacities, there is no need for supplementary federal equalization payments.

In its report on the distribution of state tax-sharing entitlements,[20] the Commonwealth Grants Commission concluded that what has been described above as the Australian equalization system, whereby individual states can apply for supplementary grants of special financial assistance from the federal government, is incompatible with provision for horizontal fiscal equalization through the personal income tax-sharing arrangements.

The Commission suggested that Australia should adopt a more general and unified approach to fiscal equalization, based on a system of annual reviews of state tax-sharing relativities with no provision for supplementary grants. The annual reviews would be intended to provide a systematic basis for distributing the states' total share of tax collections wholly in accordance with fiscal equalization principles.

The following distribution model will achieve that purpose. If the states' total share of tax collections G is equal to the sum of their equalized (or standardized) deficits $\Sigma\beta_i$, where a state's equalized deficit β_i is the difference between its equalized expenditure and its equalized revenue,[21] each state's tax sharing entitlement G_i may be calculated as follows under the Commission's procedures:

$$G_i = \frac{\beta_i}{\Sigma\beta_i} \cdot G$$

where

$$\beta_i = P_i\left[\frac{E_s}{P_s}(1 + \gamma_i) - \frac{R_s}{P_s}(1 - \rho_i)\right]$$

P_i = state i's population

E_s/P_s = standard expenditure per capita (separate calculations being made for each expenditure category E_j)

R_s/P_s = standard own-source revenue collections per capita (separate calculations being made for each revenue source R_j)

ρ_i = state i's differential revenue-raising capacity relative to standard revenue-raising capacity = $(1 - r_i)$ where $r_i = (Y_i/P_i)/(Y_s/P_s)$ and Y_i is the revenue base of state i and Y_s is the standard revenue base

γ_i = state i's differential cost of providing standard services relative to standard per capita cost = $(u_i \cdot s_i \cdot d_i \cdot e_i - 1)$ and u_i, s_i, d_i and e_i are units of service, scale, dispersion and environmental factors representing costs of providing services in state i relative to standard costs

s is subscript indicating a national average standard.[22]

Such an equalization model will provide complete equalization in respect of the state expenditures and own-source revenues which are brought into the calculations. In the Australian case, these are restricted to recurrent expenditures and revenues, including the results of certain business undertakings (such as transport authorities) which have an impact on state budgets. All resource revenues are subject to equalization.

Personal Income and Regional Economic Disparities

The fiscal equalization systems which have been described in the preceding sections are designed in varying degrees to equalize the fiscal capacity of regional governments to provide standard levels of government services if they also impose standard levels of taxes and charges. The resulting fiscal transfers are directed explicitly to budget equalization and not to the equalization of personal incomes or economic disparities across regions. Ironically, the failure of fiscal equalization to deal with these other kinds of regional disparities has been more of an issue in the U.S.A., which alone among the major federations makes no systematic provision for horizontal fiscal equalization at the state level, than in the federations which do have fiscal equalization arrangements.

The rationale for restricting equalization to regional budgets in a federal system is that it is only the existence of differences in the fiscal capacities of regional governments which prevents citizens in different regions from being treated comparably across the nation, at least so long as the federal government has the primary responsibility for income distribution and macro-economic policies.

In the case of redistributive taxation and other fiscal policies, social security arrangements, monetary and balance of payments policies, tariff and industry assistance arrangements, prices and incomes policies, and policies relating to internal trade, migration and capital movements, the assumption is that the federal government will act in the same way as a central government in a unitary state.

Again the U.S.A. is an exception, because of the extent to which state and local governments in that country have to assume responsibility for social welfare and other equalizing income transfers which in other federal countries are financed by the federal government.

However, even if there is general acceptance of the need for uniform interpersonal income distribution and economic policies throughout the nation, without regard to regional disparities, the emergence of large and unevenly distributed resource revenues is likely to have interregional political implications. These will be accentuated if there is a strong regional consciousness which transcends national loyalties.

The political acceptability of intergovernmental fiscal equalization arrangements, if they operate to the exclusion of measures for interpersonal income and interregional economic equalization, is likely to be influenced by the level of income and economic disparities and by whether the resource revenues subject to equalization have been generated in low-income regions. A region with relatively low levels of personal incomes and industrial development is not likely to accept readily the view that its resource revenues should be equalized without regard to any action for equalizing personal incomes and regional economies. If federal tariff and industry assistance policies which have had the effect of favouring highly industrialized regions have been major factors contributing to relatively low incomes, relatively high prices and other disabilities in less developed but resource-rich regions, the latter are even less likely to accept the need to share resource revenues through fiscal equalization arrangements without insisting on some form of income redistribution and regional economic equalization. The problem thus reverts to the one discussed in the first part of this paper.

A related issue is whether revenues from non-renewable resources, which are in the nature of temporary additions to the budgets of regional governments and which will cease when the energy and mineral deposits have been fully exploited, should be treated in the same way for equalization purposes as other recurrent revenues. In a continuing system of full fiscal equalization, this will not involve potential budgetary problems as such for the resource-rich provinces. Nevertheless, they may be expected to insist on political and economic action to ensure that the depletion of their natural resources is accompanied by other programs designed to develop and diversify their economies.

The exclusion of 50 per cent of non-renewable resource revenues from equalization in Canada, when supplemented by federal regional development programs, represents one approach to this problem. Another possible response, which is essentially the one that has been adopted by Alberta in Canada and Alaska in the U.S.A., is for portion of the regional government's resource revenues to be earmarked for development purposes. The Alberta Heritage Savings Trust Fund thus receives 30 per cent of the province's annual non-renewable resource revenues and invests part of the proceeds in projects designed to strengthen and diversify the Alberta economy and thus provide long-term social and economic benefits to Albertans. The Fund also makes loans to the federal or other provincial governments and invests in marketable securities.

The problem turns around when, again as has happened in Alberta and Alaska, the resource revenues accruing to a region are so vast as to place it in a position of fiscal and economic superiority relative to other regions. The response to this situation will depend on the extent to which the resource-rich regions are able to establish regional as opposed to national ownership over the resources and to earmark the revenues for development within their regions or use them exclusively to benefit their own citizens, through tax reductions, increased government expenditures or even direct cash payments to citizens.[23] Each of these options is likely to pose problems for the governments of resource-rich regions, some internal and some in their relations with the federal government and other regions, as they attempt to find profitable or efficient avenues of investment and equitable methods of distributing the revenues.

In any case, the development of natural resources is likely to result in significant interregional migration and capital flows and shifts in incomes, prices, employment and economic activity. Quite apart from the fiscal and development response of governments to the growth of revenues, the resource development itself is likely to induce major structural changes in the national and regional economies.

The inflow of overseas capital to finance the resource development and the ensuing growth in export earnings will generate upward pressures on exchange rates and the money supply, with implications for the country's traditional rural and manufacturing industries. Wage costs are also likely to rise in these industries as a spillover from the resource development.

Irrespective of the manner in which the federal government responds to these pressures—whether through reductions in tariffs and other forms of protection, appreciation of the exchange rate, increases in interest rates, other restrictions on the money supply or fiscal measures—the resulting structural adjustments are likely to have painful consequences for many existing industries and those employed in them. And just as there may be a case for using resource revenues to stimulate other forms of economic development in resource-rich regions, so may it be necessary to use them to facilitate structural adjustments in other parts of the national economy.

The regional impact of fiscal, monetary, balance of payments and industry policies will depend on the location of industries and the pattern of economic activity, but all regions will be affected in varying degrees by such policies. As was the case with development planning designed to stimulate economic growth in poor regions, the development of resource-rich regions in a federal country will therefore need to be planned and monitored by federal and regional governments acting together. This means that revenue-sharing and fiscal equalization arrangements will need to be accompanied by responsibility sharing arrangements, designed to co-ordinate both the resource development policies themselves and the structural changes which will be necessary in other parts of the national and regional economies.

Conclusion

This paper has been concerned with intergovernmental fiscal arrangements during two separate phases of economic growth, one involving responsibility or cost sharing and the other revenue sharing between governments. In both cases the purpose has been to demonstrate the inter-dependence of governments and the importance of establishing suitable kinds of intergovernmental fiscal relationships if regional disparities are to be reduced and the other objectives of public policies achieved.

The paper has been specifically directed to the task of developing grants or revenue-sharing distribution models which will enable fiscal equalization and regional growth policies to be pursued in harmony. It has been shown that the different kinds of grants arrangements which operate in federal countries play a vital role in determining the manner in which the costs and benefits associated with resource development are shared between governments. Special attention therefore needs to be paid to the design of grant systems to ensure that they achieve their intended purposes.

Notes

[1]See Break, George, E. *Intergovernmental Fiscal Relations in the United States.* Washington, D.C.: Brookings, 1967: 77–79.

[2]See Oates, Wallace, E. *Fiscal Federalism.* New York: Harcourt Brace Jovanovich: Chapter 3.

[3]The Swiss federal government thus makes payments to the cantons to reimburse them for expenditures in respect of certain tasks, such as building national roads and meeting certain costs of universities, which they perform for the federal government. See Bieri, S. *Fiscal Federalism in Switzerland.* Canberra: Centre for Research on Federal Financial Relations, ANU Press, 1979: 62.

[4]The Canadian shift to a system of so-called established programs financing in 1977, whereby the federal government transferred personal income tax room and equal per capita cash transfers to the provinces in substitution for cost-sharing grants for post-secondary education, medicare and hospital insurance, seems to have been partly based on arguments of this kind, although it also reflected federal government concern over the open-endedness of its commitments under the cost-sharing arrangements and provincial concern about restraints on spending autonomy.

[5]The Indian planning system is described in detail by Dar, R. K. *Recent Developments in Federal Financial Relations in India.* Canberra: Centre for Research on Federal Financial Relations, ANU Press, 1981: Chapter 2; and Dar, R. K. 'The Role of the States in the Indian Planning System'. In *Regional Disparities and Economic Development*, edited by Mathews, R. L. Canberra: Centre for Research on Federal Financial Relations, ANU Press, 1981: Chapter 4. See also Grewal, B. S. *Fiscal Federalism in India.* Canberra: Centre for Research on Federal Financial Relations, ANU Press, 1974.

[6]The joint task arrangements are critically examined by Reissert, B. 'Responsibility Sharing and Joint Tasks in West German Federalism'. In *Principles of Federal Policy Co-ordination in the Federal Republic of Germany: Basic Issues and Annotated Legislation*, edited by Spahn, P. B. Canberra: Centre for Research on Federal Financial Relations, ANU Press, 1978; and by Marheineke, H. D. 'The Impact of Federalism on Economic and Fiscal Policy with Special Reference to the Implementation of Projects and Tasks'. In *Federalism in Australia and the Federal Republic of Germany*, edited by Mathews, R. L. Canberra: ANU Press, 1980.

[7]The Commission's report was published in three volumes: Commonwealth Grants Commission. *Report on State Tax Sharing Entitlements 1981*, Volume I—Main Report, Volume II—Appendixes, Volume III—Reports of Consultants. Canberra: Australian Government Publishing Service, 1981.

[8]The work of the Department of Regional Economic Expansion in relation to general development agreements and other programs is described by the Canadian Tax Foundation in *The National Finances 1980–81.* Toronto: 1981: Chapter 11.

[9]Commonwealth Grants Commission. *Report on State Tax Sharing Entitlements 1981*, Volume I: 43–50.

[10]These and other issues relating to efficiency and equity in the sharing of resource revenues are examined by Anthony Scott in *Central Government Claims to Mineral Resources.* Canberra: Centre for Research on Federal Financial Relations, The Australian National University, 1978.

[11]The description of the West German arrangements is somewhat over-simplified, because in practice there is a Bund-Länder revenue-sharing arrangement which involves a two-stage equalization process, the first of which is incorporated in the distribution of shared value-added taxes and the second of which involves horizontal transfers between Länder in accordance with differences in fiscal capacity generally. Equalization also falls somewhat short of full equalization. For details of the arrangements see Spahn, P. Bernd. 'The German Model of Horizontal Federal Decentralisation.' In Spahn (ed.), P. Bernd, *op. cit.*; Traber, Theo. 'Receipts and Burden Sharing, the Taxation System and Fiscal Equalisation in the Federal Republic of Germany'. In

Federalism in Australia and the Federal Republic of Germany, edited by Mathews, R. L., *op. cit.*; and Hunter, J. S. H. *Federalism and Fiscal Balance*. Canberra: ANU Press, 1977.

[12]This description is also over-simplified, and as noted below there are restrictions on the extent to which resource revenues are equalized. For a detailed description see Clark, Douglas H. *Fiscal Need and Revenue Equalization Grants*. Toronto: Canadian Tax Foundation, 1969; and Boadway, Robin W. *Intergovernmental Transfers in Canada*. Toronto: Canadian Tax Foundation, 1980.

[13]The equalization arrangements which have been described will be called the Australian system for purposes of the following analysis. The actual arrangements in Australia are more complex, because under the federal-state tax-sharing arrangements there is some implicit equalization in the distribution of state shares and this may affect a state's ability to claim a special (equalization) grant. The Commonwealth Grants Commission has recently completed a review of the distribution of state tax-sharing entitlements based on fiscal equalization principles, the general approach of which is closer in concept to the West German than to the traditional Australian arrangements. See Commonwealth Grants Commission. *Report on State Tax Sharing Entitlements 1981*. The method of averaging under the Australian system also differs from the Canadian method, in that each standard state's tax rate schedule is applied to the revenue bases of that state and the state being equalized and a simple average is taken of the two sets of calculations (one for each standard state). In Australia, R_s/Y_s represents a tax rate structure whereas in Canada it is the ratio of actual collections to the total revenue base; the difference in the two methods is especially significant when there is a progressive rate structure or exemption limit.

[14]In practice, Länder governments are not free to adopt different tax rates in West Germany, because (with minor exceptions at the local level) taxes are collected on a uniform basis throughout the federation and shared between the different levels and units of government in accordance with constitutional provisions.

[15]However, the authors of a recent paper have proposed a system of interprovincial transfers designed to equalize Canadian resource revenues as one element of a two-tier equalization system, the other part of which would involve federal government grants to equalize other provincial revenues along the lines of the existing system. See Courchene, Thomas J. and Copplestone, Glen H. 'Alternative Equalization Programs: Two-Tier Systems'. In *Fiscal Dimensions of Canadian Federalism*, edited by Bird, Richard M. Toronto: Canadian Tax Foundation, 1980.

[16]Cf. Clark, Douglas H. *Fiscal Need and Revenue Equalization Grants*, *op. cit.*: 28–29; and Courchene, Thomas J. and Copplestone, Glen H. 'Alternative Equalization Programs: Two-Tier Systems', *op. cit.*: 11. It can be shown that this formulation is equivalent to the one used earlier in this paper:

$$G_i = P_i \frac{\Sigma R_i}{\Sigma Y_i}\left(\frac{\Sigma Y_i}{\Sigma P_i} - \frac{Y_i}{P_i}\right)$$

$$= P_i \Sigma R_i \left(\frac{1}{\Sigma P_i} - \frac{Y_i}{\Sigma Y_i P_i}\right)$$

$$= \Sigma R_i \left(\frac{P_i}{\Sigma P_i} - \frac{Y_i}{\Sigma Y_i}\right)$$

See also Mathews, Russell, 'Fiscal Equalisation Models', in Mathews (ed.), R.L. *Fiscal Equalisation in a Federal System*. Canberra: Centre for Research on Federal Financial Relations, ANU Press, 1974: 27–30; and McMillan, M. L. *Natural Resource Prosperity: Boon or Burden for Canadian Federalism*? Canberra: Centre for Research on Federal Financial Relations (1981).

[17]Special provisions relating to Ontario are described by Courchene and Copplestone, *op cit.*: 14–16.

[18]Gainer, W. D. and Powrie, T. L. 'Public Revenue from Canadian Crude Petroleum Production'. *Canadian Public Policy* (Winter 1975): 1. See also McMillan, M. L. *Natural Resource Prosperity: Boon or Burden for Canadian Federalism?*, *op cit.*

[19]Courchene, Thomas J. and Copplestone, Glen H.: 37–45. See footnote 15 above.

[20]Commonwealth Grants Commission. *Report on State Tax Sharing Entitlements 1981.* Volume I, Main Report: 296.

[21]It will be seen from the formula that equalized expenditure equals standard expenditure plus expenditure needs while equalized revenue equals standard revenue minus revenue needs. Equalization thus involves standardization.

[22]The formulation is considerably over-simplified because it ignores such problems as timing differences, the possibility of differences between G and $\Sigma\beta_i$, the possibility of standard budget surpluses or deficits, problems of averaging, the detailed treatment of revenue and cost differences among the states, and the treatment of federal specific purpose grants. An alternative but equivalent formulation on the basis of the simplifying assumptions may be used to calculate each state's per capita share as the sum of an equal per capita share of total states' tax-sharing entitlements plus or minus fiscal equalization adjustments:

$$\beta_i = P_i \left[\frac{G}{\Sigma P_i} + \frac{R_s}{P_s} \cdot \rho_i + \frac{E_s}{P_s} \cdot \gamma_i \right]$$

See also Commonwealth Grants Commission. *Report on State Tax Sharing Entitlements 1981*, Volume I—Main Report: Chapter 2; and Mathews, Russell, *The Distribution of Tax Sharing Entitlements Among the States*, The Fourth Newcastle Lecture in Political Economy. Canberra: Centre for Research on Federal Financial Relations, The Australian National University, Reprint Series 31.

[23]See McMillan, M. L. and Norrie, K. H. 'Province-Building vs. a Rentier Society'. *Canadian Public Policy*, Supplement on The Alberta Heritage Trust Fund (February 1980): 213, for a proposal to treat resource revenues as though they are private rents by distributing them as dividends to residents.

Résumé

Cet article considère 2 aspects de l'interaction qui se produit entre des aménagements fiscaux intergouvernementaux et la croissance régionale, on se réfère en particulier à différentes sortes d'aménagements possibles pour les subventions.

On met l'accent sur le partage des responsabilités et des recettes entre les pouvoirs publics et sur le rôle des différents niveaux du pouvoir dans la réduction des disparités économiques et fiscales entre régions (états, provinces ou départements).

Cet article contient 2 parties. La première partie étudie le rôle des pouvoirs publics et les relations qui existent entre eux quand ils prennent l'initiative de promouvoir le développement régional, on insiste sur le partage des responsabilités et du coût. La deuxième partie étudie quelle est la réponse apportée par les pouvoirs publics à des disparités régionales lorsqu'elles se trouvent associées au développement de ressources minières, on se réfère en particulier à l'interaction entre développement des ressources et égalité de traitement fiscal. On insiste dans cette deuxième partie sur le partage des revenus.

Grants to Communities in their Relation to National Growth

Horst Zimmermann

I. The Grants System and National Growth

Objectives of the Grants System and of National Growth

The numerous fiscal flows from state and federal governments to communities bear at first sight no direct relationship to the objective and instruments of promoting national growth. National growth policy is seen here mainly as an attempt to increase, or at least maintain, the volume or the medium- and long-term rate of growth of gross domestic product (GDP). In either form the objective is expressed in national terms. The instruments used by growth policies also pertain most often to the national level. Examples are general tax incentives for private investment and (or) for research and development activities.

Fiscal flows to communities, on the other hand, are—in the Federal Republic of Germany at least—aimed at different objectives. The formalized system of state grants to communities follows three objectives:

(1) to raise an insufficient level of local budgets,
(2) to equalize fiscal burdens and expenditures among communities and
(3) to strengthen central place functions.

Many categorical grants outside this system have the objective

(4) to increase spending in specific fields like housing or transportation according to the preferences of state and federal

Public Finance and Economic Growth. Proceedings of the 37th Congress of the International Institute of Public Finance. Tokyo, 1981, pp. 297–313

governments. They are thus an indication of state merit goods vis-à-vis communities.

National growth does not appear in this list and is hardly found to underly any specific grant program (see Part III). On the contrary, the objective of fiscal equalization between communities may be in direct conflict with growth objectives.[1]

One reason for dealing with the relationship between the two fields of policy is a renewed interest in policies to promote national growth. For a number of years economic policy has focused on redistributing income from rich to poor people and on allocating GNP from private to public use, the tacit assumption being that growth, or at least preservation of real GDP, was assured. Today the question is raised again, how GDP (even in its conventional form) may be maintained at a high level, as it is now surmised that a substantial degree of redistribution reduces the national growth potential. The search for the reasons of lagging national growth also leads to a study of sectors and regions of the economy, whereas in times of satisfactory growth rates the sectoral and regional origin of national growth was frequently neglected.[2]

As national growth becomes again a major political issue, it is justified to ask, how grants to communities relate to it. The magnitude of these grants (see Table 1) as well as their share in all budgets and in gross national product (GDP) are considerable. Since they explicitly aim at regional units they are of interest for the analysis of the re-

Table 1

Grants to Communities

	1971		*1981*[1]		
	Bill DM	*Share of Local Expenditures*	*Bill. DM*	*Share of Local Expenditures*	*Increase*
Grants to Communities, Total	17,11	23,4%	40,50	26,0%	137%
—for current expenditures	11,80	16,1%	28,30	18,2%	140%
—for capital expenditures	5,31	7,3%	12,20	7,8%	130%
Local expenditures	73,22	100,0%	155,80	100,0%	113%
GNP	756,00		1 580,50		109%

[1]Estimated

Sources: Grants and Local Expenditures: Karrenberg, H. and E. Münstermann (1981), p. 23 and 29; GNP: Sachverständigenrat zur Begutachtung der gesamtwirtschaftlichen Entwicklung (1980), pp. 138 and 248.

gional origin of GDP. Moreover, the fact that many grants serve the equalization objective suggests that they have a negative effect on national growth. The funds to finance these grants were raised nation- or statewide so that the total regional distribution process may induce flows from more promising to less promising regions under the national growth objective. We must, therefore, look at the total fiscal flows between regions and upper level governments (Part II).

Even if one or the other research work should demonstrate effects of the grants system, which are clearly favorable or detrimental to growth, it does not imply that the grants system should be changed. To reach such a conclusion, the conflicting objectives—essentially equalization and growth—would have to be weighted first. Therefore research on the relation between grants to communities and national growth is in essence research on the side-effects of a policy on some other political objective, in this case national growth.

Ways of Relating Grants to National Growth

There seem to be two types of connections between these policy areas (with communities being regarded as parts of regions; see Part II):

(i) First, it may be asked whether the receiving regions are the most promising ones under the growth objective (Part II). In the investigation of the choice among regions it suffices to think of just one unspecified type of grant, for instance, an unconditional grant. Types of grants with specific effects are of no significance in this context. The question whether the right regions receive the resources would have to be answered in the context of a comprehensive, empirically applicable, theory of regional growth. No such theory appears to exist at the moment. Hence we must be satisfied with partial empirical foundations and plausible hypotheses. Complicating matters is the fact that regional development policy, e.g. in the Federal Republic of Germany, directs some grants to communities in problem areas with emphasis on regional development and growth, without judging the contribution to national growth.

(ii) Next it may be asked whether those types of fiscal flows which are distributed regionally are the most promising under the growth objective (Part III). To concentrate on this aspect all regions can be thought of as being equally promising under the aspect of national growth. This eliminates consideration of the growth contribution of regions, and allows focussing on the type of flows they receive. Here again knowledge about the growth effects of different types of grants seems to be lacking, something which makes it difficult to answer the question even partially.

(iii) Considering the absence of empirically applicable theories, the two approaches—types of regions and types of grants—will be highly unsatisfactory for an evaluation of actual grants programs. Therefore the question, whether the right regions receive the right flows, cannot be answered satisfactorily. If the question is nevertheless asked, it is done in order to show how far we are still away from a state of the discussion, in which it would be possible to scrutinize how close a given grants system comes to an ideal situation (ideal under the national growth objective alone), that is, a situation in which the most growth-promising regions receive the most growth-promising types of grants.

II. Growth Aspects of Grants by Types of Receiving Regions

The Difficulty of Determining Growth Regions

Communities and Regions. To tackle the question which regions are most promising under the growth objective, communities have to be considered as types of regions. Arguments relevant to regions cannot, however, be applied identically to all communities. As regional units, many communities are too small to observe growth effects. Under growth aspects small communities should therefore be thought of and discussed as parts of regions only. It depends on the purpose of a study, what size of region is chosen,[3] but usually they will surpass that of most communities. The regions as sums of communities can then be grouped into different categories, for instance by density, by the share of primary, secondary, or tertiary activities, by per capita GDP, etc., whichever seems adequate under the growth hypothesis.

Contributions from Regional Economics. The problem of the most promising regions is not a specific one for national growth. It is a prerequisite for any policy dealing with regions, among other regional development policy (see Part II). Because a review of these problems would need a specialist in regional economics, the question is dealt with only briefly. To indicate its importance one may think of a national program to increase the grants program by a major amount with the instruction that the resources be distributed regionally so as to increase national growth. Following Richardson's review of regional growth theory, the relation of regions to national growth under this heading should be viewed as "generative," meaning that the national rate of growth is the result of the different regional activities.[4] The contribution of a particular region to national growth may be the result of a greater than average factor input in this region. This aspect is disregarded for the moment, because many of these factors are, at least over a medium-term period, mobile among regions and thus available wherever they are needed. Policies to increase their mobility usually are not aimed at a particular region, but are applied nationally and thus have effects wherever insufficient mobility occurs. Emphasis lies instead on the "positive feed-back on the growth rate of the aggregate economy" which may result from "intra-regional spatial efficiency of an area" [Richardson (1979) p. 218 ff.]. Regional output would thus depend not so much on how factors are allocated among regions, but on how a particular region is spatially and socially organized. One would then have to focus on

(1) the degree of agglomeration,
(2) the position of a community in the overall settlement pattern, for instance its central-place functions,
(3) the equipment with human and social capital investments,
(4) the position in the transportation network [ibid.], etc., but also on the organization of the private sector (predominance of big enterprises versus a mixture of different-sized enterprises, predominance of one branch of business, etc.).

As to private activities the potential of influencing private investment through public activities is of primary interest here. One kind of influence results from direct subsidies to business, i.e. from fiscal flows other than grants. The remaining and probably most important effect stems from infrastructure. Unfortunately "the generative impact of public capital stocks and infrastructure on private investment and location decisions . . . is a virgin research question" [ibid. p. 135]. The operationally defined theory, which tells the planner what type of infrastructure in a given region will induce a noticeable increase in private investment, thus does not yet seem to exist, especially since obvious bottleneck situations usually have been remedied in many of the highly developed countries.

From this field of factor-oriented analysis (as opposed to demand-oriented approaches) [Hoover (1975) p. 218 ff.] some recent studies can be drawn upon. In 1964 Giersch asked for an approach based on regional development potential [Giersch (1964) p. 393 ff.], and in 1975 Biehl put this in an operational form which since then has been further expanded. In a cross-section analysis of the 178 regions (of the Federal Republic) potential p.c. GDP is explained by factors like infrastructure, agglomeration, or sector mix, and the difference between potential and actual GDP of each region is interpreted as under- or over-use of existing resources [Biehl (1980)]. For most regions the development potential is explained rather satisfactorily, and, what is important here, all regions are grouped under the national perspective of how much growth they can produce. The results are tentative in so far as on the input side certainly not all relevant factors of regional production have been included. Concerning the output side the question has been asked by the author himself, to what degree an unused growth potential in a big city, based on above average infrastructure, agglomeration, optimal position in a settlement structure, etc., can by itself be accepted as an inducement to further such growth. Environmental damages of many kinds suggest that there is rather an overuse of regional potential [Biehl and Münzer, (1980)] (or an overestimation of GDP as conventionally measured).

Presumably there exist not one, but several agglomeration optima, depending on what problem is looked at.[5] Some of them are related to central-place functions, which indicates that well equipped central places are a prerequisite for an adequate functioning of the economy. Taking central-place functions together with localization and urbanization economies, it seems that big cities are especially advantageous for national growth, particularly if they are not dominated by old industries.[6] Moreover, an open question is, whether one cannot organize major agglomerations internally in a way which retains high p.c. GDP and reduces negative effects like congestion and environmental damages. After all, the major part of national GDP (if not of its short-term growth) and of state and local taxes originates in more or less agglomerated regions. If high p.c. GDP and its growth is again regarded as a major policy objective, it could be hazardous to change this growth pattern by an adverse distribution of fiscal flows, as long as there is no substantial evidence of overused resources (including all benefits and losses of operating such agglomeration).

Other results of regional economics suggest that there are no reliable tools to forecast the growth prospects of specific regions. In general, backward rural areas without any growth center are regarded as probably lacking almost all prerequisites for a not too costly start into growth, unless tourism offers a chance. Taking this and the previous observations together, the only conclusion for an analysis of fiscal flows to communities thus is the dichotomy of

(1) rural regions with actual low growth performance, which can be—tentatively—regarded as less promising, and of
(2) big cities with major central-place functions and a modern sector mix that may be particularly advantageous under the objective of national growth.

The Special Role of Regional Development Policy. The system of communities and regions in its entirety is rarely the object of growth-promoting policies on the national level. Instead, in many countries regional policies are pursued which sometimes try to "contain" large agglomerations (London, Paris) by means of non-fiscal instruments; and mostly such regional policies consist of fiscal flows to businesses and local governments in less developed areas to promote regional growth there. Under the national growth perspective such policies and the concomitant grants to communities may, from what was said, very well be suboptimal as far as the "containment" of major agglomerations is concerned, or even detrimental as far as rural areas are concerned.

The German federal/state "Joint Task" of "Improvement of Regional Economic Structure" concentrates in rural areas on development centers, where investment grants are extended to local governments and where subsidies to newly located or expanding firms are highest. The effect on national growth is possibly still rather high, partly because of this regional pattern, but partly also because by now more than 60% of the area of the Federal Republic is included in the program. This reduces the relative advantage, which the backward rural areas draw from the program, and it tends to include medium-sized cities like Saarbrücken, Wilhelmshaven, etc., and even segments of the Ruhr agglomeration, where funds may produce a rather high GDP per unit of the grants, if agglomerated regions are *per se* regarded as regions with above average growth potential.

Grants to Communities by Types of Regions

The grants to local governments in the Federal Republic of Germany are taken as an empirical example to check which types of communities receive how much of the grants. In Germany most grants are extended by state governments, and only few selected programs provide federal money. The greater part of the state grants is given within a formalized system and without ties [Zimmermann (1981a) for details]. They make up the major part of the grants "for current expenditures" in Table 1 (Part I). The grants "for capital expenditures" are mostly investment grants, part of them out of Federal programs.

If it is assumed that bigger cities are on the average more growth-promising—because they may be the central places for agglomerated regions with high per capita GDP—Table 2 shows that total p.c. grants increase with community size up to 500,000 inhabitants. Beyond this the amount decreases slightly, because p.c. grants for current expenditures drop considerably. P.c. grants for capital expenditures increase continuously with community size.

Within the formalized grants system this effect is partly brought about by the technique of assessing fiscal capacity, because above average local tax revenue is not taken away, but leads at most to the point, where no grant is received. Thus very rich communities, which are found quite often in larger size groups, are not "taxed" in this process. A second influence stems from fiscal needs assessment. Fiscal need can be calculated more or less from original local figures as in England. [Smith (1981)]. It can also be approximated, for instance through allowing for higher per capita spending with increasing community size[7] as is the case in Germany. This approach is defended on the grounds of past expenditure experience (which however has been shaped, among other things, by the same equalization scheme over decades). It covers (implicitly) various expenditure determinants at the same time [Zimmermann (1981c)]:

(1) number of cases causing expenditure,
(2) intensity of dealing with each case,

Table 2

Grants to Communities by Community Size

	Grants to Communities 1979		
Inhabitants	*For current expenditures DM p.c.*	*For capital expenditures DM p.c.*	*Total DM p.c.*
500 000 and more	339	185	524
200 000 – 500 000	391	168	559
100 000 – 200 000	345	138	483
50 000 – 100 000	281	145	426
20 000 – 50 000	250	119	369
less than 20 000	n.a.	n.a.	n.a.

Source: *Statistisches Jahrbuch Deutscher Gemeinden*, 67. Year, 1980, p. 442 f.

(3) higher input costs (for instance due to a higher price level in agglomeration regions),
(4) (dis-)economies of scale, and finally
(5) public inefficiency in producing a service.

Such an acknowledgement of higher per capita expenditure in big cities works in favor of agglomeration regions.

Table 3 gives some examples of which types of cities within a size class receive most of the grants. For this purpose the cities are listed within each size class in declining order of their tax potential (which correlates highly with p.c. GDP). In the first size class (500,000 and more) the first three are modern cities, the last are rather "old industrial" cities of the Ruhr region. The formalized grants system (most of the grants "for current expenditures") favors the latter, the

Table 3

Grants to Selected Communities

Inhabitants	*Grants to Communities 1975* For current expenditures DM p.c.	For capital expenditures DM p.c.	Total DM p.c.
500 000 and more			
Frankfurt	172	297	469
Stuttgart	204	147	351
Düsseldorf	125	106	231
Duisburg	296	230	526
Essen	320	160	480
Dortmund	319	179	498
100 000–200 000			
Leverkusen	115	91	206
Ludwigshafen	16	330	346
Pforzheim	265	149	414
Trier	139	223	362
Wilhelmshaven	275	283	558
Bottrop	432	115	547
20 000–50 000			
Bietigheim	142	137	279
Schwäbisch-Hall	114	272	386
Neu-Isenburg	32	27	59
St. Wendel	254	66	320
Bergkamen	343	339	682
Osterholz-Sch.	189	30	219
Federal Republic[1]	227	152	379

[1]Average of communities of 20 000 and more inhabitants
Source: *Statistisches Jahrbuch Deutscher Gemeinden*, 63. Year, 1976, p. 450 ff.

other grants, mainly investment grants, also the first, especially Frankfurt. The picture is similar for the other size classes. On the average, the economically less strong communities receive more total grants p.c., mainly out of the formalized grants system. This is due to the technique of fiscal capacity assessment, because with fiscal need being regarded as almost equal within the same size class, the higher fiscal capacity of the richer cities reduces their grants (but not equally their budgets, because very rich cities retain their high tax revenue and simply receive no, or fewer, grants, as mentioned before).

Three of the eight area states (which together with the three city states, Hamburg, Bremen, and Berlin, constitute the Federal Republic) have in recent years substituted a *central-place functions* bonus for the *larger population* premium. The two approaches are similar insofar as with increasing community size more central-place functions are on the average fulfilled. Within the same size class however the distribution changes considerably. If, therefore, it is assumed that cities with many central-place functions are more growth-promising than equally big cities without such functions, this change could be growth-promoting.

Taking the total effects of the grants system, they favor bigger communities, among communities of the same size those with less fiscal strength and, in some states, those with central place functions. So far, however, communities have not been grouped by regions. This is done, for one example, in the following section, where grants are also pictured as part of total fiscal flows between regions and upper levels of government.

Grants to Communities in the System of Fiscal Flows

A Wider Conceptual Framework. Assuming the spatial and social organization within a region to be a growth factor (see Part II), it may, for the evaluation of the effects of grants, be helpful to interpret a region as a productive unit. To take a growth region as an example, it possibly produces high GDP from factor inputs, because these inputs are combined in a highly productive manner, due to the fact that this region is favored by a medium to high degree of agglomeration, an advantageous position in the settlement structure, a high level and good mixture of infrastructure, etc. In order to retain its productive capacity, i.e. to produce private income and public revenue, such a regional unit must be given or allowed to keep enough private and/or public funds and legal power to provide and retain its specific mix of productive inputs, which allows it to realize its comparative advantage within the efforts of all regions to further their growth and thus, taken together, national growth.[8]

The first question to be asked in this context is, how much of "earned" income in a region has to be retained within the region in order to keep it workable. If too much income is withdrawn, for instance through state and federal taxes, there may not be enough money for local public reinvestment,[9] especially if the equalization mechanism on the grants' side does not lead to grants for this region. Of course, a national tax system has to draw its revenue—part of it in a progressive manner—to a considerable degree from the growth centers. This process of public revenue-raising and -spending, which favors less developed regions, can certainly be explained by the objectives underlying each flow. However, a point may be reached in this development, where an uncoordinated drain on growth regions, accumulated over many separate decisions, may prevent these regions from remaining the nation's growth centers in the future. In times past such monitoring was not as necessary, because regions were able to finance themselves from their own resources, partly from fees for schools, hospitals, even roads, etc., partly from their own taxes. A growth region was thus able to recover its private and public input cost directly from the benefiting private households and enterprises. Today the responsibility for keeping a region economically viable lies more than before with the upper level governments.

In order to judge whether the position of a region is advantageous or disadvantageous, it is necessary to determine its situation in the total of all fiscal flows to and from a region, of which grants to communities are only part. Though these fiscal flows influence growth through their effects on regional income, employment, etc., the regional distribution of fiscal flows can be taken as a first approximation of the regional distribution of these effects.[10]

An Empirical Example. Table 4 presents the overall results of a German study on fiscal flows to and from selected regions each made up of many communities. Total public inflows and outflows show that the underdeveloped region (Trier) receives considerably more than the state average, and the agglomerated region (Ludwigshafen) receives considerably less than the state average. This is partly due to inflows other than grants. For instance, the underdeveloped region receives a great deal of personnel expenditure and public investment because it houses a sub-unit of the state government (Bezirksregierung). As far as grants are concerned, most of the advantage of the underdeveloped region in the total of public inflows is due to "state general equalization" (most of the mentioned "grants for current expendi-

Table 4

Total Fiscal Interregional Flows
Two Regions, Federal Republic of Germany
(1975, DM per capita)

	Underdeveloped Region (Trier)	*Agglomerated Region (Ludwigshafen)*	*State Average (Rheinland-Pfalz)*
I. Inflowing public payments			
Intergovernmental			
State general equalization	282	71	177
Other	302	215	162
Purchases, investments	461	233	399[1]
State and federal personnel	782	459	777
Transfer payments	975	740	799
Total of listed public inflows	2802	1718	2314
II. Outflowing state and federal taxes			
Income tax	576	1812	1177
Property and inheritance taxes	19	70	48
Automobile tax	87	84	88
Share of business tax	65	162	98
Outflowing taxes, regional figures	747	2128	1411
(Other taxes, breakdown of national figures)	(1085)	(2252)	—

[1]Figure actually higher; state figure for defense purchases not available.
Source: Condensed version of two tables in: Zimmermann and Stegmann (1981).

tures"). The grants thus increase the effect in favor of the underdeveloped region, which already occurs through the other fiscal flows.

Outflowing taxes show the reverse picture and to an even higher degree. The agglomerated region delivers about three times as much in taxes p.c. to state and federal budgets as the underdeveloped region. Taking fiscal inflows and outflows together, the agglomerated region under review contributes substantially to state and federal governments and at the same time receives far less than the average. This is due to the correlation of taxes and regional p.c. GDP, but also to the grants equalization effect. As both taxes and the formalized grants system serve mainly the distribution objective, the conflict in objectives becomes clearly visible (Part I).

III. Growth Aspects of Grants by Types of Flows

Thus far the grants to communities have not been differentiated by types of flows. In most countries there exist side by side many types of flows, with different objectives and different effects. If we now assume that regions are homogeneous, we may analyze which types of flows would best further national growth.

No hypotheses concerning the growth effect can—at least initially—be derived from regional economics, or the theory of grants, unless its contributions happen to be specific about national growth. Instead, we would need initially hypotheses about the strategic factors in the national economy in general which tend to further growth. The theories of economic growth seem to be too general to translate into direct policy recommendations [Dürr (1980)]. Private and public investments are considered to be at the heart of the growth process, but already the desirable mix between the two cannot be determined except in specific situations. Public infrastructure is regarded as a major growth factor in general [Frey (1972) Ch. 5], but whether an existing stock of infrastructure is "sufficient" and just has to be kept up, or which degree of expansion of public investment (and its segments) is desirable, is apparently a decision which has to be made case by case.

What follows from this discussion, is the notion that it may be advantageous under the national growth objective to improve on all types of investments, but not on transfers to private households (unless they raise the quality of labor). Because many transfers to private households have the objective of redistributing (real and/or money) income, the same conflict of objectives between equalization and growth shows up again. Table 1 shows that investment-oriented grants ("for capital expenditures") amount to less than half of all grants to communities, without much change between 1971 and 1981. They already include special programs like the Federal program for "future-oriented" local investments, which however was not limited to particularly growth-promising investments, if growth is defined narrowly. Moreover, unconditional grants could also be used in equally growth-promising ways by the receiving community itself, if there are other incentives to induce the community to use them for investments or for other growth-oriented activities. To judge this structure of grants, one would have to know whether the unrestricted use of funds by the local level leads to more growth than categorical grants by the state and federal level.

Table 4 shows that p.c. grants to local governments amount to only about 15% of the state average of inflowing public p.c. expenditures. The position of a region is determined much more by the other flows, which mainly reach the private sector directly and are thus only indirectly related to the subject of this paper. Transfer payments amount to 35% and the rest is made up by expenditures for personnel and goods. They should all be considered in addition to grants, if the question is to be answered, whether the right regions receive the right flows.

IV. Concluding Remarks: The Right Flows to the Right Regions?

In the beginning we said that the question whether the right flows go to the right regions cannot be answered satisfactorily. This is not so much due to lack of empirical data, but to the lack of precision and workability in the underlying theories.[11] This is particularly true for the contribution to growth by types of grants, and reflects the unsolved problem as to which determinants constitute growth in general and how local public activities are to be judged among these determinants in particular. Even the importance of investment grants, though they are apparently tied to a growth-relevant factor, seems doubtful in the light of the recent debate on fiscal federalism with its emphasis on decentralized decision-making and financing.

As to the question of whether the right regions receive most of the grants, the reliability of the—still very tentative—results above depends on whether the assumptions concerning growth regions seem acceptable. If so, then the empirical evidence is mixed for the Federal Republic. Big cities receive more p.c. than small cities. Among cities of the same size, the economically weak receive most, but in some states those with central place functions are favored.

Moreover, if communities are seen as parts of regions and for these regions all fiscal flows are considered, then the economically strong regions—in the example given—are at a considerable disadvantage. If a region is viewed as a productive unit, the conclusion can be drawn that the agglomeration region must have a remarkable economic and fiscal power, if it would be able, at the same time,

(1) to stand a heavy withdrawal through taxes,

(2) a less than proportionate share in the regionally not targeted fiscal flows, while receiving
(3) a very small amount of grants, and still be able
(4) to reinvest publicly and privately enough to ensure its high p.c. GDP in the future.

The reverse is true for the underdeveloped region. It would have to have a tremendous growth performance, if the sum of all public inputs were to be justified under the national growth objective. This is not to be expected, because many of the flows under consideration pursue distributional objectives. In this conflict of objectives the present paper was merely meant to point out the—in most cases unintended—effects on one objective of national economic policy, namely national growth of GDP.

Notes

[1]On the equalization objective compared to other objectives of influencing regions see Zimmermann (1981b).

[2]The analysis here is not only concerned with regional growth rates, but also with the level of GDP involved. Under the perspective of keeping national GDP high it may be more important to at least maintain GDP at present levels in regions with high per capita GDP and a considerable share in national GDP than to increase the growth rate in regions with low per capita GDP and a small contribution to national GDP.

[3]For instance labor market areas can be used (Klemmer (1981), Berry (1973), Vol. I), but they will often be much bigger than even some of the largest cities of a country.

[4]Richardson, H. W. (1973) and Richardson, H. W. (1979), p. 145 ff.—Another view would be "competitive," meaning that the national rate of growth is regarded as exogenously fixed, with regions competing in a zero-sum-game for the shares of this given volume; the notion of national GDP being ex post always the sum of all regional GDPs, can imply this view.

[5]Richardson, H. W. (1973), p. 120 ff.; for the different types of costs associated with urban size see Stone (1973), p. 239 ff.

[6]A recent example is the resurgence of the business district of some of those previously more or less distressed U.S. cities which could be termed "regional cities" (Peter Hall) due to their wide-ranging central-place functions: Chicago, Los Angeles and San Francisco.

[7]For Germany see Zimmermann, H. (1981c); for Holland see Hoff, J. (1981).

[8]As A. Breton pointed out in the discussion of this paper, regions in this sense are usually not acting units, unless they are coterminous with a city, a metropolitan government, or some other jurisdiction. For the promotion of regional economic growth it would certainly be better, if they were acting units so that the function of growth promotion could be given, and the principle of fiscal equivalence be applied to, them.

[9]The unfavorable outlook for many old industrial cities in the U.S.A. is probably due to a degree to the local fiscal inability to reinvest in public infrastructure.

[10]For the methodological details, see Zimmermann, H. (1981d).

[11]H. Giersch (1977) notes that so far there exists no "region-related growth theory with empirically valid evidence," p. 285.

References

Berry, B. J. L. (1973), *Growth Centers in the American Urban System,* 2 Vols., Cambridge, Mass. (Ballinger).

Biehl, D. (1980), "Determinants of Regional Disparities and the Role of Public Finance," in: *Public Finance,* Vol. XXXV, p. 44–717.

Biehl, D. and U. Münzer (1980), "Agglomerationsoptima und Agglomerationsbesteuerung. Finanzpolitische Konsequenzen aus der Existenz agglomerationsbedingter sozialer Kosten," in: *Ballung und öffentliche Finanzen,* Forschungs- und Sitzungsberichte der Akademie für Raumforschung und Landesplanung, Vol. 134, Hannover (H. Schroedel), p. 113–150.

Frey, R. L. (1972), *Infrastruktur,* 2. ed., Tübingen-Zürich, (J. C. B. Mohr/Paul Siebeck).

Giersch, H. (1964), "Das ökonomische Grundproblem der Regionalpolitik," in: Jürgensen, H., Ed., *Gestaltungsprobleme der Weltwirtschaft,* Göttingen (Vandenhoeck & Ruprecht), p. 386–400.

Giersch, H. (1977), *Konjunktur- und Wachstumspolitik,* Wiesbaden (Gabler).

Hoff, J. (1981), "The Financial Relationship Between Central and Local Government in the Netherlands," in: OECD (1981), p. 283–301.

Hoover, E. M. (1975), *An Introduction to Regional Economics,* 2. ed., New York (Alfred A. Knopf).

Karrenberg, H. and E. Münstermann (1981), "Gemeindefinanzbericht 1981," in: *Städtetag,* 34. Year, p. 3–33.

Klemmer, P., B. Bremicker and A. Ortmeyer (1981), "Analyse der regionalen Produktionsgesetzmäßigkeiten in der Bundesrepublik Deutschland," unpublished manuscript.

OECD (1981) (Organisation for Economic Co-operation and Development), Cameron, J. and J. Lotz, Eds., *Measuring Local Government Expenditure Need,* Paris 1981 (OECD).

Richardson, H. W. (1973), *The Economics of Urban Size,* Westmead (Saxon House).

Richardson, H. W. (1977), Regional Growth Theory, 3. printing, London and Basingstoke (Macmillan).

Richardson, H. W. (1979), *Regional Economics,* 2. printing, Urbana, Chicago, London (University of Illinois Press).

Sachverständigenrat zur Begutachtung der gesamtwirtschaftlichen Entwicklung (1980), *Jahresgutachten 1980/81,* Bundestagsdrucksache 9/17.

Smith, J. (1981), "Principles of a Grant Distribution System," in: *OECD* (1981), p. 251–290.

Stone, P. A. (1973), *The Structure, Size and Costs of Urban Settlements,* Cambridge (University Press).

Wienen, H.-J. (1980), "Räumliche Verteilung der Zuweisungen und Baumaßnahmen des Landes Nordrhein-Westfalen 1969/1975," in: *Ballung und öffentliche Finanzen,* loc. cit., Biehl, D. and U. Münzer, (1980), p. 97–111.

Zimmermann, H. and H. Stegmann (1981), *Öffentliche Finanzströme und regionalpolitische Fördergebiete. Anwendung einer Methodik der Regionalisierung öffentlicher Finanzströme am Beispiel der Region Trier und einiger Vergleichsräume,* Bonn (Gesellschaft für Regionale Strukturentwicklung).

Zimmermann, H. (1981a), *Studies in Comparative Federalism: West-Germany.* Washington, D.C. (Advisory Commission on Intergovernmental Relations).

Zimmermann, H. (1981b), "Fiscal Impact on Regional Disparities, Basic Issues and European Examples," in: *Fiscal Policy in Regional Economics,* special issue of: Regional Science and Urban Economics, forthcoming.

Zimmermann, H. (1981c), "Local Expenditure Needs Under Alternative Policy Objectives," in: OECD (1981), p. 231–242.

Zimmermann, H. (1981d), *Regionale Inzidenz öffentlicher Finanzströme. Methodische*

Probleme einer zusammenfassenden Analyse für einzelne Regionen, Baden-Baden (Nomos).

Résumé

Le volume des subventions aux communautés dans des pays comme les Etats-Unis et la République Fédérale d'Allemagne est si important qu'il est probable que des effets sur la croissance nationale en découlent. L'accroissement des contraintes budgétaires et le renouveau d'intérêt porté à la croissance nous poussent à évaluer la direction et l'intensité de ces effets. Ces effets seraient positifs, si les flux destinés à promouvoir la croissance étaient dirigés vers des régions susceptibles de croître. C'est pourquoi nous envisageons deux cas d'étude dans cet article:

1) Sans tenir compte du type de flux, on se demande si les régions adéquates reçoivent les subventions? L'ensemble de la théorie sur la croissance régionale n'est pas assez opérationnelle pour déterminer quelles sont les régions qui apportent une contribution maximale à la croissance nationale dans le monde réel. Il semble exister un consensus sur le fait que les régions purement rurales et régions à industrie ancienne n'offrent pas de perspective d'avenir. Des systèmes de subventions avec une prime à la taille de la population comme en Allemagne de l'Ouest et en Hollande pourraient ainsi avoir des effets positifs, tandis qu'une égalisation fiscale en faveur des régions rurales n'en auraient pas.

2) Sans tenir compte du type des régions bénéficiaires, on se demande si les flux choisis sont adéquats? Les théories de la croissance économique nationale citent l'investissement et l'innovation comme des facteurs majeurs de croissance; des flux fiscaux liés à l'investissement seraient donc ainsi particulièrement favorables.

De nombreux systèmes de subventions aux communautés, dont celui de l'Allemagne de l'Ouest cité comme modèle, visent à une égalisation fiscale et en théorie devraient pour des raisons de distribution éviter d'être liés à l'investissement ainsi qu'à tout autre lien. Dans ce cas, ils ont tendance à entrer en conflit directement avec la croissance nationale. Cette tendance jointe à leur volume nous permet d'affirmer combien le conflit est grand dans un pays donné.

Contributions of Regional Public Enterprises to Regional Economic Development

Aldo Chiancone

1. Introduction

In the process of preparing a general survey paper on regional public enterprises and regional development, one thing comes clearly to one's attention: just as in the case of interventions through national public enterprises, it is difficult to find a general theory that "explains" intervention by regional public enterprises,[1] a theory, that is, that goes beyond justifying such interventions on the basis of some public need to "correct" market imperfections, or, more generally, as a means of achieving given aims of economic policy. In fact, an analysis of the existing literature reveals that what these aims are, and consequently, what are the motives underlying interventions by public enterprises, is generally determined on the basis of *ad hoc* reasoning.[2]

In order to find a coherent theory of the intervention by means of local public enterprises one has to go back to the work of Montemartini (1900 and 1917). After discussing Montemartini's theory, we will analyze the theoretical principles that could serve as a basis for justifying an intervention in the development process by means of regional public enterprises and to relate them to concrete experiences in various countries. A final paragraph will be devoted to a comparison between regional public enterprises and systems of incentives in a growth process.

2. Montemartini's Theory of Public Enterprises

Montemartini's theory of local public enterprises, or of municipalization as he calls it, is based on his general theory of public fi-

Public Finance and Economic Growth. Proceedings of the 37th Congress of the International Institute of Public Finance. Tokyo, 1981, pp. 315–328

nance, which in turn, is based on a political theory. It is therefore useful to begin with the following quotations:

> The fundamental starting principle is . . . the following: every political organization is an industrial enterprise. The important question is to determine the nature of this special organization which is called a political enterprise (Montemartini, 1900, p. 138).

> The entire theory of public enterprise consists in an appropriate formulation of the fundamental theorem by which pure economics explains the activity of the private entrepreneur. *Theorem:* "The (individual or collective) public or political enterprise supplies services or goods up to the point at which its supply equals the demand for the said goods; it is supplied with factors of production up to the point at which its demand for them is met" . . . The agent of the political enterprise, or the political entrepreneur, is that economic unit, or that group, or that class which, at its own risk and peril, co-ordinates factors of production in a manner such as to compel an entire community to participate in the production of particular goods or in the performance of particular services. (Montemartini 1900, p. 139)

> The public enterprise can be defined as "a productive organization designed to obtain the participation of an entire community in the purchase of given goods or services." (Montemartini 1900, p. 138)

For Montemartini, the public enterprise does not aim at producing goods and services in the usual sense, but rather a "special service": the "compulsory distribution of certain costs over the community." This is the consequence of the activity of

> those who find it to their advantage to distribute the costs they have to bear for certain productions, on other economies, when these costs are compared with those that they have to bear to reach their goal. (Montemartini 1900, p. 138)

So if three individuals, *A*, *B*, and *C*, have to satisfy the same need and, having conquered the necessary political power, decide to act, by

> causing the cost of the enterprise to be shared also by other economic units *D*, *E*, *F*, *G*, etc., which do not form part of the enterprise, that is to say, by distributing the cost of the enterprise over a community, (Montemartini 1900, p. 138)

they will give rise to a public enterprise. The choice between private and public enterprise depends solely on the relative costs of the two forms of organization. If the individuals opt for the public enterprise, it will be because "this enables them to achieve their purpose in the most economical way." (Montemartini 1900, p. 138)

Municipal enterprises in no way differ from other public enterprises:

> Municipal enterprises have the aim of distributing, by means of coercion, over all members of the community, the costs of some productions of goods and services . . . The productions to which the municipality devotes itself are contingent upon the times, the countries and the economies which, in a given moment, give rise to the enterprise. (Montemartini 1917, p. 47)

Municipal enterprises can be created either in order to produce goods and services to be used directly by the local public administration itself in the process of carrying out its activities, or to produce goods and services to be sold on the market. It is to this second group of municipal enterprises that Montemartini devotes the greatest attention, and it is also this group of enterprises which is the more interesting for our purposes.

> A group of consumers powerful enough to influence the decisions of the municipal government causes an industrial enterprise to be founded. The municipal government compels the local community to bear in advance the administrative and industrial costs along with the risk of the enterprise. (Montemartini 1917, p. 91)

But the products that are produced by the municipal enterprise are

> almost never of a general use; nor in this general use . . . is to be found the main cause of the enterprise. (Montemartini 1917, p. 91)

In conclusion, Montemartini states two general theorems that explain the recourse to public enterprises:

> Theorem 1—Every class aims at constituting as public needs, that is, needs that have to be satisfied at the cost of the community, its own class needs. (Montemartini 1917, p. 347)
> Theorem 2—Every class will try to pass off the greatest share of the weight of public expenditures on other classes, . . . thereby reducing to a minimum its own burden of taxation. (Montemartini 1917, p. 349)

This brief and necessarily sketchy summary of Montemartini's theory must suffice for our own purposes. Those who have studied modern theories of property rights will have recognized, in Montemartini's theory, many of the most important characteristics of these theories: above all the need to "look through," as it were, the organic structure of the organization and to consider not the abstract, or publicly proclaimed aims of the organization itself, but the concrete aims of the individuals that take part in it and actually determine its economic behavior. Indeed, it is only by considering the aims of those taking part in the organization that it is possible to "explain" the variety of economic policy aims which public enterprises take it upon themselves to carry out in those countries where they are considered an instrument of economic policy.[3]

Montemartini's theory contains some points that can be used as a basis for our discussion. Intervention by means of public enterprises, or any kind of intervention at that, is essentially a political act relating to the type of society that the dominant elements in the community wish to create and to the speed at which they hope to advance towards it. Consequently, there are no fields or sectors of economic activity in which public intervention by means of public enterprises can be considered "natural" or "normal."

More specifically, in the case of regional economic growth, regional public enterprises will distribute over the community the same type of costs as national public enterprises with the same aims, namely, the costs connected with the accumulation of capital to start enterprises of optimum size (especially where that size requires relevant minimum investments), with the taking of risks, and with the spreading of knowledge.[4]

Once it is recognized that intervention in the economy by means of public enterprises is a political decision, we as economists cannot attempt to analyze the forces and the social groups that push for economic growth through public enterprises rather than through other instruments: such an analysis lies outside the field of public finance. What we can do, instead, is to discuss within the framework of normative analysis, at least two important questions as regards economic growth:

(i) the technical principles which an intervention by means of public enterprises should follow in order to minimize the costs of the intervention (as required also by Montemartini's theory);

(ii) the effects of public enterprises on economic growth when compared to its main alternative: a policy of subsidies to private enterprises.

Since our main purpose is to concentrate on policies carried out by public enterprises, we will deal only briefly with such a comparison.

Principles of Intervention

Before we begin, a constraint must be noted that is particularly relevant at the regional level. This constraint is the amount of finance which can be raised and employed to pursue given ends. In general, in the case of decentralized interventions, the smaller the size of the regional government, *ceteris paribus,* the smaller the amount of capital it can raise and devote to the creation of public enterprises. Also, for any given size of regional government, the higher the level of income per head the greater the amount of finance the local government can raise. This condition is especially important for regional governments aiming at growth in countries in which there is a wide variation of incomes among local areas: unless there be some central system for reallocating funds, regional governments in the relatively poorer areas will have less capital to stimulate economic growth through regional public enterprises.

In order to analyze the specific aspects of the intervention through regional public enterprises in a growth process we must turn to the general models of regional economic development policy. There are no specific theoretical contributions to the subject. The limited amount of specific experiences will be dealt with in the notes.

Models of regional economic development are based, in essence, on two fundamental principles.

In the first place, as input-output analysis shows, each productive activity is, at the same time, a market for the products of other enterprises and a source of intermediate and final goods. Consequently, it can be supposed that each new productive activity will promote the growth of other new activities which either satisfy its needs for intermediate goods and services, or use its products for final consumption or further production.

Following a distinction introduced by Hirschman (1958) technical interdependencies within a productive system give rise to *linkage* effects, which are of two kinds:

(a) *backward* linkages, in consequence of which each non-primary activity stimulates the creation of a local supply aimed at satisfying its needs with respect to inputs;
(b) *forward* linkages in consequence of which each non-final activity stimulates the creation of local activities aimed at utilizing its supply of inputs.

In the second place, it is maintained that a series of costs, connected more or less directly with physical distance, induce these further activities to locate themselves in the neighborhood of that plant, which therefore exerts a kind of territorial attraction, whose force with respect to other activities depends on the relevance which those costs have for these activities.

As Klaasen (1967) points out, these costs are not necessarily transportation costs (which may even be irrelevant for most products in a modern economy), but more generally costs of communication. These costs can be briefly defined as all those costs that are connected with the physical distance from other economic agents with whom the entrepreneur has to entertain a continuous flow of contacts. The lower these costs in a given region, and they are not necessarily connected linearly with physical distance, the more probable it is that industrial plants will be located in that region.

Methods have been devised (e.g., by Klaasen and Van Wickeren 1969 and Cella 1978), by means of which it is possible to specify and measure the network of relationships among industries and to determine how the growth of one industry in a given region directly influences growth of other industries in the same region. For any given region, the location of a particular industry is more attractive the higher its growth-rate and the higher the effects produced through backward and forward linkages.

On the basis of such studies, the type and dimension of regional public enterprises to be used in the process of regional economic development could be adequately determined.[5] Moreover, intervention by means of public enterprises allows the establishment of exactly the right productive units, of the required dimension needed for economic growth, and to locate them in the proper areas. (To anticipate, these results can hardly be achieved by means of incentives/subsidies.) If this is certainly the general picture, the role of public regional enterprises has to be examined in greater detail.

First, notwithstanding what some authors would seem to believe (e.g., Klaasen and Van Wickeren, 1969, p. 266), it is not necessary that an enterprise which is important for regional economic development be a regional public enterprise: in a State in which one of the aims of the ruling classes is equal economic development in different regions, those key industries for regional development may well be nationally-owned enterprises. In fact, aside from the problem posed by the amount of capital that may be needed, intervention through national public enterprises will guarantee such a choice and distribution of the various activities among the regions that not too different growth levels will be achieved.

What is then the place of regional public enterprises in the process of regional growth? Regional public enterprises have at least three very important functions: they will have to be concentrated

(i) in those sectors in which relatively medium-sized or small enterprises are needed, which may or may not be complementary to the key sectors in which there is State intervention;

(ii) in those sectors which involve aspects or problems which are specific of the given region;

(iii) finally, in the key sectors, if nationally-owned enterprises fail to intervene.

Let us discuss these three points in greater detail.

Intervention in Sectors Requiring Small Enterprises

A process of regional development may, and usually does, require intervention not only in the key sectors, but also in other sectors. This may be necessary for at least two reasons. In the first place, there may be a need of diversifying the industrial structure:

> the stronger an industry is represented in a given region, the more its economy will depend on this activity and the more urgent is the need for additional employment in other industries. . . . For these reasons, additional employment in other industries, although maybe not as attractive from a general point of view, does seem appropriate in all cases where one-sidedness is a characteristic of the economy. (L. H. Klaasen and A. C. Van Wickeren, 1969, p. 267)

Secondly the development process may require the intervention not only of large enterprises, but also of medium-sized or small enterprises to complement or support the effects of the large ones. At this "lower" level, regional public enterprises will generally be quite useful also because typically, national public enterprises are, in fact, though not by logical necessity, better able to operate on a larger rather than a medium or small scale.

The relatively smaller size of regional public enterprises can thus, very adequately, help in solving the problem raised by the need of diversifying the industrial structure and of contributing to the creation of a network of viable enterprises for regional economic development.

Intervention in Connection With Specific Regional Problems

Aside from, or in addition to the purposes mentioned, regional public enterprises may be active in sectors which, although relevant from the point of view of the region, may not be dealt with at the central level because of their specifically regional character.

Again some examples will have to suffice.

In the primary sector, regional public enterprises may be needed for interventions in agriculture, fishing, forestry and the like. It is true that some of the older economic growth theories, and especially those based on such models as the ones we have seen before, do not lay great stress on growth in the primary sector (because here backward linkages are presumably scarce). Nonetheless, the contribution of the primary sector to the growth process has been stressed by many authors (e.g., Johnston and Mellor, 1961).

In general, political and social pressure in favor of direct private ownership of agricultural land is so strong that, even in cases of land reform and of land reclamation carried out by public bodies, land is in most cases eventually apportioned to private owners. At this level, public intervention is generally limited to the creation of more or less compulsory cooperatives of various kinds among producers. But such organizations do not come under our definition of public enterprises.

And, in fact, it is not the cost of the ownership and of the management of agricultural land in these circumstances that is usually apportioned among the members of the community by means of public enterprises. The costs that usually are thus distributed over the community are those which are connected with:

(a) institutional facilities for servicing agricultural production;
(b) research and the application of its results to develop improved production possibilities.[6]

Hence, the creation of public enterprises, e.g., for constructing storage facilities or marketing agricultural products, in order to increase and stabilize, over time, the incomes of the agricultural sector. Hence, on the other hand, the creation of regional public enterprises to study and introduce at the local level, new methods of cultivation and new crops especially suited to specific local conditions. In all these instances, the intervention by regional public enterprises is justified by their special and specific knowledge of local problems and needs. What has been said about intervention in agriculture can be extended, with proper modifications, to interventions in other primary sectors.

The same points could be raised in favor of intervention in the industrial sector, but a discussion of them would entail, basically, a repetition of the main arguments of the previous paragraphs.

Industrialization, however, may also have to rely on the provision of adequate capital to the "right" kind of individuals, to those, that is, that are ready and willing to start new industrial enterprises.[7] A process of regional development may therefore also require public regional financial organisms ready to provide long term finance to local entrepreneurs.

Regional financial bodies have been created as a technical instrument for fostering economic development through the concession of financial support to small and medium-sized private enterprises.[8] They are set up with public capital, sometimes with a minority shareholding of private parties. Their financial support can take various forms ranging from long-term loans at better-than-market conditions, to minority shareholding in the enterprises. From many points of view, financial bodies seem to be a rather flexible instrument, especially since it can be used not only as an aid to growth, both of existing but feeble enterprises and of new ones, but also as an instrument of localization policies.

With all financial instruments, however, and of all discretionary ones, the use of this one may run into well-known difficulties. It may be conditioned by political pressures, and it may be directed not towards enterprises that offer good prospects for growth, but to already existing and declining ones, which can also exist in a developing region. Pressure in this latter sense may be very great, especially in an area where these enterprises are one of the few sources of employment, and it may come not only from the owners, but also from trade unions.[9]

Finally the service sector. At the regional level, the importance of communication costs has already been stressed. The reduction of these costs may require specific action through regional public enterprises, and is generally connected with the stock of social overhead capital in the region.

This is, obviously, one of the traditional fields of public intervention also at the regional level. Here the motives that justify intervention through a public enterprise rather than through the general administration are based on the greater managerial flexibility of the enterprise compared to administrative action. This is the reason why, both in developing and in developed countries, there is a large number of instances in which regional public enterprises are used to carry out tasks that traditionally belong to the field of intervention of public administration.

Regional Public Enterprises in Lieu of National Public Enterprises

The final case which we have to consider is the one in which national public enterprises fail to intervene in the process of regional growth. Regional enterprises would then have to base their intervention in the process of economic growth also on the criteria that we have considered before as applicable to national public enterprises.

Here, however, the constraint posed by the probably limited amount of finance available to regional bodies could exert all its strength: the type and the size of the intervention required may well be beyond the financial possibilities of the local body. Regional authorities would then have to choose, if at all possible, a different, possibly non-optimal, path towards growth, concentrating on one or more of the sectors and types of intervention that we have considered in the previous paragraphs.

Public Enterprises vs. Incentives

As we pointed out before, a detailed comparison with a policy of incentives is beyond the scope of this paper because it would entail analyzing the large variety of incentives which are usually applied. Policies entailing incentives (of various kinds) which can be justified more easily from a *laisser faire* point of view and, consequently, can be more easily employed by "liberal" governments, have been widely used in most Western countries.[10] Much more limited has been the recourse, for purposes of economic development, to public enterprises and even more to regional public enterprises.

Public enterprises distribute over the community the full costs of getting the enterprise started. Incentive/subsidy systems may or may not, depending on how they are designed, have the same characteristics: usually, however, not all the initial costs are distributed over the community.

Whereas the efficacy of regional public enterprises in a growth process has not been questioned, the efficacy of incentive systems has often been called into doubt:[11]

> incentives to manufacturing investment do, in all probability, increase the amount of investment in manufacturing, but they do so not by raising the total level of investment but in effect by crowding out investment somewhere else. (R. M. Bird, 1980, p. 47–8)

Furthermore, we should remember the problems connected with the undesirable distortions that any incentive system usually introduces in the relative prices (and hence the use) of capital and labor as witnessed by all actual experiences.[12]

Aside from their dubious effects on economic growth, systems of incentives have different characteristics and uses when compared with public enterprises. To summarize, incentives are of a general nature and cannot be used where specific interventions are needed for the purposes of economic growth. The specificity of the intervention, as we have seen in the previous paragraphs, can refer both the the type of enterprise needed and to its size. For these ends, only public enterprises can be used.

Moreover, incentives can hardly be used for purposes of localization when there are many regions in a State that pursue autonomous or semi-autonomous policies of economic growth: in such cases, incentives policies may well compete with one another and, consequently, neutralize each other.

From the point of view of the efficiency of public intervention, A. Peacock (1981) has pointed out some of the welfare problems connected with subsidies. We do not intend to discuss here the superiority of the one or the other means of intervention from a welfare point of view: we must remember, however, that public enterprises, too, may give rise to inefficiencies in the allocation of resources, caused, for instance, by the difficulty of controlling these enterprises.

A final point of comparison has to do with the flexibility of the instruments. In general terms it would seem that, on this score, incentives have clear advantages, because they can be discontinued easily once the aims of economic growth have been achieved. Public enterprises, on the other hand, can be turned over to private entrepreneurs with greater difficulty. In practice, however, the difference between the two instruments may not be so great. In the case of incentives, important authors (see e.g., J. Wiseman, 1981) have stressed the difficulty of suppressing them once they are introduced, whereas there are some instances in which public enterprises have been transferred to the private sector once their public policy aims had been achieved.[13]

Notes

[1]In this essay we will be using the term "public enterprise" in the familiar sense, to mean public ownership, organization and control of industrial, agricultural, financial and commercial undertakings. The existence of regional public enterprises will be taken to mean that, up to a certain extent, the process of decision-making in economic policy is effectively decentralized. We will not concern ourselves with the legal form of ownership and/or control of regional public enterprises. We will not consider regional public enterprises as a means of raising revenues and thereby mobilizing resources for growth, because this possibility, especially at the local level, seems either unrealistic or irrelevant. It is unrealistic in the case in which public enterprises face competition in open markets. It is irrelevant because the cases of monopoly public enterprises seem to be few at the local level and, consequently, the amount of revenues that it would be possible to raise is relatively small.

[2]In fact, even a recent work like that of R. Minns and J. Thornley (1978) which would appear at the outset to be based on Marxian theory, does not, in the end, go beyond *ad hoc* theorizing. It could also be added that the theory of the second best

goes a long way to limit large scale interventions by means of public enterprises based on Paretian welfare economics.

[3]It may not be without interest to note that a contemporary of Montemartini, A. Puviani, had in the same years come to similar conclusions as regards the nature of the State: "at the very heart of its structure, the state appears as an aggregation of forces which aims at the defense and the growth of one part of society against the rest." (1896, p. 9) Consequently, against marginalist theories, Puviani maintained that public finance can only be defined as "a form of political activity, whose aim is to extract from a community the means that are needed for the victory of the interest of one of its parts." (1896, p. 303)

[4]For concrete evidence on all these points, see now e.g., R. Minns and J. Thornley, 1978.

[5]So, for instance in Great Britain, the primary objectives of local agencies are:

> helping to establish an improved industrial structure upon which a sounder economy can be developed, improving the profitability and efficiency of industry and increasing employment [Northern Ireland Financial Corporation]; economic and social development in the area through the creation and maintenance of viable enterprises [Highlands and Islands Development Board]; the promotion of industrial development and employment by the encouragement and establishment of new enterprises; acting as an investment bank to industry in the area and undertaking joint commercial ventures [Scottish Development Agency and Welsh Development Agency].

Quoted in R. Minns and J. Thornley, 1978, p. 8.

[6]See e.g., the experience in Scotland and Northern Ireland as reported in R. Minns and J. Thornley, 1978, p. 63–65 and 86; the experience in Senegal as reported in G. Mizzau, 1979; and in Turkey, as reported in A. H. Hanson, 1959, p. 122.

[7]A number of important authors stress this need: see e.g., A. Gerschenkron 1957 and A. H. Hanson 1959, p. 59.

[8]Such regional financial bodies could also, for instance, counter-balance the tendency of private financial institutions towards syphoning off capital from backward regions in order to support the growth of other regions. For an example of this kind of behavior in the United States, see N. H. Hansen, 1971.

[9]Examples in this sense are not uncommon in the Italian experience: see D. Cuzzi, 1977, p. 97. For a general picture of the British experience, see R. Minns and J. Thornley, 1978, various places.

[10]On this, see e.g., N. H. Hansen, 1974.

[11]For a recent assessment of investment incentives, see R. M. Bird, 1980.

[12]Cf. for instance such distant cases as the Northeast of Brazil and Southern Italy. On the Brazilian case, see D. Goodman, 1972; on the Italian case, F. Momigliano, 1965.

[13]Cf. for instance the case of South Korea as reported in F. Buffoni, 1979.

References

Bird, R. M., *Tax Incentives for Investment: The State of the Art,* Toronto, Canadian Tax Foundation, 1981.

Buffoni, F., "*Corea del Sud: intervento pubblico e sviluppo economico*" [South Korea: Public Intervention and Economic Development], in Sciolli, G., (ed.), *Meccanismi dell'intervento pubblico nei paesi in via di sviluppo,* [Mechanisms of Public Intervention in Developing Countries], Milan, Ciriec-F. Angeli, 1979, pp. 451–463.

Cella, G. "Interdipendenze produttive e effetti di polarizzazione: un tentativo di applicazione all'economia italiana," [Production Interdependencies and Polarization Effects: An Attempted Application to the Italian Experience], in Costa, P., (ed.), *Interdipendenze industriali e programmazione regionale* [Industrial Input-Output

Relationships and Regional Programming], Milan, F. Angeli, 1978, pp. 334–53.
Cuzzi, D., "Le attività delle finanziarie regionali," [The Activities of Regional Financial Institutions], *Economia Pubblica,* No. 3, 1977, pp. 97–101.
Gerschenkron, A., "Riflessioni sul concetto di 'prerequisiti' dell'industrializzazione moderna," [Some Reflections on the Concept of 'Prerequisites' of Modern Industrialization], *L'Industria,* n.2/1957 reprinted in: *Economic Backwardness in Historical Perspective, A Book of Essays,* Cambridge, Mass., Harvard University Press, 1962, ch. 2, pp. 31–51.
Goodman, D., "Industrial Development in the Brazilian Northeast. An Interim Assessment of the Tax Credit Scheme of Article 34-18," in R. Roett (ed.), *Brazil in the Sixties,* Nashville, Vanderbilt University Press, 1972.
Hansen, N. H., *Financing Rural Development,* Lexington, Ky., National Area Development Institute, 1971.
———, *Public Policy and Regional Economic Development. The Experience of Nine Western Countries,* Cambridge, Mass., Ballinger, 1974.
Hanson, A. H., *Public Enterprise and Economic Development,* London, Routledge and Kegan Paul, 1959.
Hirschman, A. O., *The Strategy of Economic Development,* New Haven, Yale University Press, 1958.
Johnston, B. F., Mellor, J. W., "The Role of Agriculture in Economic Development," *American Economic Review,* Sep; 1961, 566–91.
Klaasen, L. H., *Méthodes de Sélection d'Industries pour les Régions en Stagnation* [Methods for Selecting Industries for Stagnating Regions], Paris, OCDE, 1967.
Klaasen, L. H., Van Wickeren, A. C., "Interindustry Relations: An Attraction Model. A Progress Report," in Bos, H. C., (ed.), *Towards Balanced International Growth,* Amsterdam, Elsevier, 1969.
Minns, R., Thornley, J., *State Shareholding. The Role of Local and Regional Authorities,* London, Macmillan, 1978.
Mizzau, G., "Senegal. L'intervento dello Stato e delle cooperative nella commercializzazione dell'arachide," [Senegal. The Intervention of the State and of the Cooperatives in the Marketing of Peanuts], in Sciolli, G., (ed.), *Meccanismi,* cit., p. 65–140.
Momigliano, F., *Ricerca sul grado di convenienza all'insediamento delle industrie in relazione ai vigenti incentivi diretti* [An Analysis of the Relative Advantages of Industrial Localization in Relation to Present Direct Incentives], Milan, ILSES, 1965.
Montemartini, G., "Le basi fondamentali di una scienza finanziaria pura" [The Fundamental Principles of a Pure Theory of Public Finance], Giornale degli economisti, 1900, II; English translation in: Musgrave, R. A., Peacock, A. T., (eds.), *Classics in the Theory of Public Finance,* London, Macmillan, 1958, p. 137–51. The quotations are from the English translation.
———, *Municipalizzazione dei pubblici servigi,* [Municipalization of Public Services], Milan, Società Editrice Libraria, 1917.
Peacock, A. T., "On the Anatomy of Collective Failure," *Public Finance,* n.1/1980, p. 33–43.
Puviani, A., "Il problema edonistico della scienza delle finanze" [The Hedonistic Problem in Public Finance], *La riforma sociale,* n.5/1896.
Wiseman, J., "Is There a Logic of Industrial Subsidization?," in Häuser, K., (ed.), *Subsidies, Tax Reliefs and Prices,* Paris, Cujas, 1981, p. 59–68.

Résumé

Sur la base d'un important article par MONTEMARTINI, les entreprises publiques régionales peuvent être considérées comme l'instrument le plus économique, adopté par les classes au pouvoir, pour distribuer les coûts du développement sur la collectivité tout entière.

Du côté normatif, l'emploi d'entreprises publiques régionales comme instrument de développement économique régional peut être justifié sur la base de modèles input-output (dans lesquels les entreprises publiques peuvent fournir le réseau productif nécessaire), aussi bien que du niveau des coûts de communication.

En général, les autorités régionales auront des bornes financières. Par conséquent, le gouvernement central devra prendre à sa charge les projets de plus grande dimension. Pourtant, les entreprises publiques régionales auront au moins trois fonctions importantes: elles seront concentrées dans les secteurs où, pour des raisons différentes, sont nécessaires des entreprises de dimensions relativement réduites; dans les secteurs caractérisés par des problèmes spécifiques de la région; dans les secteurs-clef si le gouvernement central n'intervient pas. Ces différentes possibilités sont examinées à l'aide d'exemples tirés de l'expérience concrète.

Le rapport termine avec une brève comparaison entre l'emploi d'entreprises publiques régionales et celui de primes/subventions.

Urban Fiscal Stress in U.K. Cities

*Peter M. Jackson**

> Urban fiscal stress in Britain has been avoided at the cost of national fiscal stress. A rapid expansion of local services has been achieved only by dint of an equally rapid and massive transfer of resources from the centre to the local level.
>
> Kirwan, 1980, page 73

Urban growth and development have been accompanied, in most countries, by fiscal problems. In some cases the large cities of the world are seen to be breaking down under sheer excess of size and growth. They are disintegrating administratively, institutionally and logistically in their inability to cope with the complexities which accompany size and rapid growth. [Bookchim, 1974] The older cities of the world, laid down centuries ago and which saw rapid growth in the nineteenth and early twentieth centuries, are now suffering from the problems of decline. Falling population size, a loss of manufacturing jobs, and a crumbling obsolete public infrastructure all combine to place pressures upon local and national fiscal systems.

Different countries have reacted to these universal urban problems in different ways. The most celebrated example is that of New York.[1] While the New York example has been analyzed in depth and reported extensively, the experiences of other cities outside the USA seem to have received little attention. It is both important and interesting to ask how the fiscal systems of different countries are re-

*Director, Public Sector Economics Research Centre, University of Leicester, Leicester LE1 7RH, England. The paper borrows from earlier work that I have carried out with my colleagues, Justin Meadows, Steve Bailey and Andy Taylor. I would like to thank them, for their stimulating collaboration and for allowing me to borrow from the work for this paper. I am also indebted to the Department of Environment and to the Social Science Research Council for their research grants and to the British Academy for a travel grant to Japan. I am also grateful to Ian Byatt, and Richard Bird, who provided valuable comments on an earlier draft; the usual disclaimer applies.

Public Finance and Economic Growth. Proceedings of the 37th Congress of the International Institute of Public Finance. Tokyo, 1981, pp. 329–347

flected in their treatment of the fiscal stresses created by urban growth and decline.

This paper examines the nature of urban fiscal stress in the United Kingdom. In comparison to the United States and other federalised countries U.K. city governments are less autonomous in their powers of budgetary decision-making. It is, therefore, interesting to examine how urban fiscal stress manifests itself in urban governments which operate within a highly centralised set of local-central-government fiscal relationships. This paper will demonstrate that while urban governments in the U.K. have faced similar pressures from urban growth and decline the means used to finance local public expenditures have been different. These differences have prevented an "urban fiscal crisis" on the scale of New York. Nevertheless, U.K. urban governments have been confronted with growing fiscal stress. The source of this stress is to be found not only in the pressures which cause public expenditures to rise but also in the grant-in-aid relationships between central and local governments which have become increasingly complex and uncertain.

The British Urban Fiscal Context

In this section we consider the problems of urban decline and fiscal stress in U.K. cities. One initial set of questions of interest is whether or not the underlying models of local public expenditure determination and fiscal flight from the cities, which have become so characteristic of the U.S. literature, apply with equal weight to the U.K. Do the location decisions of firms and the migration patterns of households respond to changes in local expenditures and taxation? While partial answers to these questions can be provided the analysis is far from complete. A systematic analysis of the fiscal impact of urban decline in the U.K. has, until recently been severely hampered by a lack of suitable historical data on city finances.[2] We present an outline of the results which are currently available.

Socio-Economic Decline

The older cities in the U.K. such as Newcastle, Birmingham, Manchester, Glasgow, Liverpool and Leeds have suffered both a decline in their populations and a contraction in the manufacturing base of their local economies. Tables 1 and 2 show the changes in their

Table 1

Population Changes in U.K. Major Cities 1951–75

	1951/61	*1961/71*	*1971/76*
Birmingham	−0.3%	−8.6%	−3.6%
Leeds	+0.9%	−2.9%	+0.8%
Liverpool	−5.7%	−18.2%	−11.4%
Manchester	−5.9%	−17.9%	−9.9%
Newcastle	−7.6%	−17.6%	−4.1%

Source: (a) 1971 *Census-County Reports for England and Wales*, HMSO, 1971. (b) Office of Population Censuses and Surveys, *Population Estimates Series*, PP1, No. 2, 1977.

populations from 1951 to 1976. There has been a decline both in the absolute size of their populations and in the size of the school age population. This last group is of importance to the dynamics of local public spending since education spending is the largest item in a local government's budget accounting for 34% of current expenditure, and 12% of capital spending. The older age groups in the populations place demands on public services such as personal social services and public sector housing. In addition their low incomes make them eligible for transfer payments such as rent and property tax subsidies. Table 3 gives an indication of one element of this demand by showing the increase in the numbers of pensioners.

From these population data the characteristic changes in the composition of city population can be seen. The proportions of young and old in the cities' populations are increasing. This implies a large out-migration of middle aged groups. The fall in school pupil numbers

Table 2

Changes in School Population of U.K. Major Cities 1951/71

			Proportion of Total Population		
	1951/61	*1961/71*	*1951*	*1961*	*1971*
Birmingham	+4.6%	−3.1%	16.0%	16.8%	17.8%
Leeds	+15.5%	+1.7%	14.4%	16.5%	17.3%
Liverpool	−0.5%	−17.2%	17.4%	18.3%	18.6%
Manchester	+8.3%	−15.6%	14.9%	17.2%	17.6%
Newcastle	+3.0%	−18.5%	15.0%	16.0%	16.6%
Glasgow	+1.7%	−9.3%	17.3%	18.1%	19.3%

Author's calculations made on information contained in the annual reports of the various city governments.

Table 3

Number of Pensioners Living Alone 1961/71

	1961	*1971*	*Percentage Change 1961/71*	*Proportion of Total Population*	
				1961	*1971*
Birmingham	24,811	38,495	+55.2	2.2	3.8
Leeds	16,711	23,965	+43.4	3.3	4.8
Liverpool	16,557	23,525	+42.1	2.2	3.9
Manchester	18,794	24,825	+32.1	2.8	4.6
Newcastle	8,213	11,580	+41.0	3.1	5.2
Glasgow	25,633	37,970	+48.1	2.4	4.2

Source: Author's calculations made on information contained in the annual reports of the various city governments.

reflects this movement in addition to changes in fertility rates and rates of family formation.

The economic decline of the manufacturing base of central cities in the U.K. has been documented in Cameron (1973) and Hall et al. (1973). In general the economies of these cities relied heavily upon old staple industries such as heavy engineering for which there was a long run decline in export and domestic demand. These industries were not replaced as bankruptcies accelerated with the downturns of the business cycle. The economic base of the cities changed more towards the services sector, which, while being labor intensive neither demanded the skills that had been made redundant over the cycle nor employed the same number of workers. Moreover, the new growing industries located on the greenfield sites in the New Towns. These new towns were designed as an element of regional policy in the 1960s and 1970s to attract population out of the cities. At that time it was generally thought that the congestion costs of high density living in the central cities could be alleviated through a population dispersal policy in which industries were attracted to the new towns by the offer of jobs and high quality public amenities such as housing and schools. In addition other local authorities which were in a growing economic environment were paid subsidies to accept the cities' population overspill. At the time of the introduction of the policy the costs to the old cities of population decline were not counted.[3]

While the population was moving out of the city there was, surprisingly, no dramatic change in the socio-economic composition, as is seen in Table 4. The decline in the number of economically active males is, however, interesting. It has important implications for the

Table 4

Socio-Economic Composition of Economically Active Males

	Employers, Managers and Professionals			*Other Non Manual and Skilled*			*Semi Skilled*			*Unskilled*			*Totals*	
	1961	*1971*	*1978*	*1961*	*1971*	*1978*	*1961*	*1971*	*1978*	*1961*	*1971*	*1978*	*1961*	*1971*
Newcastle	11.8%	12.6%	12.9%	61.3%	59.8%	58.3%	14.6%	14.5%	16.5%	12.3%	13.2%	12.2%	81,560	66,540
Manchester	9.8	12.6	9.8	61.4	61.0	55.0	17.6	18.4	23.2	11.2	8.0	12.0	204,590	144,760
Liverpool	10.1	11.0	8.7	54.8	55.5	53.8	19.4	19.5	21.7	15.7	140	15.8	219,670	168,420
Birmingham	10.1	14.5	11.1	61.8	57.2	56.6	19.8	19.9	21.9	8.4	8.4	10.3	352,880	314,230

Source: *Census of Population*, HMSO 1971; and information obtained from the Department of the Environment.

burden of the local property tax since fewer persons remain in the city to finance the tax bill.

Finally, the cities have experienced in recent years unemployment rates which have in some cases been well above the national average. (Table 5) Some cities such as Liverpool, Newcastle and Glasgow (the Northern Cities) have consistently had unemployment rates well above the GB average. Within Scotland, which has had above average unemployment rates, unemployment was concentrated in Glasgow. Other cities such as Birmingham, Leeds and Manchester have had worsening employment rates. The general picture which emerges is that the major cities of the U.K. have poor and deteriorating local economies. While they have shed large numbers of their populations those who have remained in the city are the least mobile, their skills either being redundant or non-existent. Moreover, recent research (Eversley and Bonnerjea, 1980) has demonstrated that these high levels of city unemployment are concentrated in particular areas within the cities. These inner city zones typically tend to be concentrations of multiple social, economic, and physical deprivation and are the flash points for city riots.[4]

There are many possible indices which can be used to obtain some measure of the scale of multiple deprivation. Social indicators have been heavily criticized. They nevertheless provide some insights to the nature of the problems which the inhabitants of the inner cities face. A number of studies has demonstrated conclusively that on almost any dimension chosen, the central cities score high in terms of social, economic and physical deprivation. In welfare terms the inhabitants of these areas are worse off than their counterparts in the growing and developing towns although there is much debate and controversy about whether or not they are worse off than those who

Table 5

Unemployment Rate in Cities as a Percentage of the Rate for Great Britain as a Whole: Males and Females, 1960–75

	1960	*1965*	*1970*	*1975*
Birmingham	60	50	100	133
Leeds	53	64	96	94
Manchester	66	71	85	100
Liverpool	240	193	177	204
Newcastle	167	179	196	149
Glasgow	233	207	212	135
(Scotland)	220	193	173	118

Source: *Regional Statistics,* Central Statistical Office, HMSO, 1976.

live in rural areas where access to amenities and public services is low and where unemployment levels are also high.

In what sense do the inhabitants of central city areas face deprivation? The indices typically used include: homelessness; the degree of overcrowding; the number of households without exclusive use of amenities; age and quality of the housing stock and public infrastructure; number of single parent families; number of ethnic minorities; number of educationally subnormal children; number of children receiving free school meals; and unemployment rates. Those who have studied the relative position of U.K. cities in terms of their rank order in these indices have shown that in all cases the declining cities come out on top (Holterman, 1975; Evans, 1980, and Eversley and Bonnerjea, 1980).

Multiple urban deprivation gives rise to a demand for public expenditure. Traditional urban public policy argues that the disequilibrium in the urban economy can be stabilized through urban and regional aid programs while the social and physical environments can be improved by public investments in housing and other areas of social infrastructure. Thus, in the U.K., as in the USA, there are strong pressures to increase public expenditures in the central cities.

The Fiscal Context

Local government spending in the U.K. has grown from 9.3% of GDP (at current market prices) in 1960 to 12.9% in 1979. About 12% of the working population is employed by local governments and about 30% of all capital spending carried out in the U.K. economy is done by local government mainly on housing, road building and school building.

A closer examination of local public spending reveals that per capita expenditures have increased more rapidly in the major metropolitan areas than elsewhere. Despite their decline in population the cities of Birmingham, Manchester and Liverpool had large increases in their real per capita spending over the period 1965/77 (see Table 6) compared with small increases and decreases in other areas.

These large increases in per capita spending have to be compared to the very modest increases in the real value of the property tax receipts. The property tax in the U.K. is assessed on rental values, not capital values as in the U.S.A. This gives the U.K. property tax a number of undesirable features. First, it is difficult to assess since the private market for rental housing in 1980 is only about 15% of the total rented sector (compared to 53% in 1951). Second, the tax is

Table 6

Fiscal Indicators of U.K. Cities

	Rateable Values (£m)		*Change in Tax Base Per Capita at Constant Prices of 1965 1965/77 (%)*	*Total Expenditure Per Capita (£)*			*Change in Per Capita Spending at Constant Prices of 1965 1965/77 (%)*	*Central Government Grants as a Proportion of Total Expenditure 1965/66*	
	1965	*1977*		*1965*	*1974*	*1977/78*			
Declining Cities									
Birmingham	49.9	157.9	+6.2	46.6	130.3	252.9	+74.1	44.2	61.3
Manchester	27.7	71.2	+8.8	51.7	156.8	345.2	+114.3	49.0	58.2
Liverpool	26.6	71.3	+16.5	50.4	154.1	283.1	+80.3	59.3	68.5
Areas of Expansion									
Blaby (Leics)	2.1	8.2	+1.5	42.6	n.a.	111.8	−15.8	57.9	53.9
Fareham	2.5	10.2	+3.0	42.8	105.6	136.9	+2.8	53.1	45.0
Medium Sized Manufacturing Cities									
Derby	6.7	27.9	−18.3	44.6	113.1	143.6	+3.4	43.3	35.5
Ipswich	5.1	18.0	+13.0	41.3	109.0	130.3	+1.3	49.1	26.3

Source: Kirwan (1980) and Chartered Institute Public Finance and Accountants: *Statistical Series*, (various years)

very inelastic. Revaluations of the tax base should be made every five years, but there have only been five revaluations in the last fifty years with the last in 1976. This means that during periods of rapid inflation as they occurred during the 1970s the tax base does not expand in line with the unit costs of public services. The consequence is that property tax rates will (*ceteris paribus*) rise rapidly.

Another important feature of the U.K. property tax is its incidence on domestic and non-domestic (i.e., industrial and commercial) tax payers. On the average non-domestic property tax payers contribute more than 50% of the value of the tax receipts although they account for only 10% of the assessments. Moreover, only a small proportion of the local taxpayers pay the property tax.[5] Payers of the industrial and commercial rate do not have the vote (they lost their vote in 1969) and it is only the owner of domestic property who pays the property tax. Domestic voters paid through their local taxes, 30% of total expenditure in 1938. This figure has fallen to 8% in 1980. Thus, those local voters who do pay the property tax contribute only 8% to local public spending.[6] The principal sources of finance to local governments in the U.K. are non-domestic rate tax revenue, central government grants-in-aid, and borrowing.

Because the property tax accounts for a decreasing share of local government revenues (31% in 1966 and 28% in 1979) and because local voters finance such a small proportion of local public spending through the property tax, it becomes difficult to adopt wholesale the neo-classical models of public expenditure determination which have been developed in the American public finance literature. These models are typically set up in a form which chooses a vector of public service outputs and taxes such that the utility of the median voter is maximized.

There are a number of reasons why the explanatory power of this model is weakened in the context of U.K. local government budgeting. First, local fiscal affairs seem to have little effect on local voting outcomes. They are more sensitive to the performance of central government. Thus, in order to register their displeasure with a Conservative central government's mid-term performance the local electorate will return a Labour majority at the level of local government. Second, the local "tax price" information faced by the local electorate is highly distorted. The average local tax payer suffers from a good deal of fiscal illusion since not only does he not know how much his local public services cost in terms of local taxes, he doesn't know how his central government tax payments finance the grants-in-aid to local government. Third, the median voter model applies to a single voting issue space. Real life politics are however a set of multi-dimensional issue spaces. This implies that vote trading takes place and that politicians attempt to trade off the interests of a large number of pressure groups in their attempts to win votes. The politics of the budgetary processes simulated in a series of complex games provides a more realistic picture of local public expenditure determination than the standard neo-classical median voter model. Moreover, the relevant budget constraint facing decision makers in local government depends heavily upon non-domestic property tax income and grants-in-aid. Even if the median voter did play a dominant role in determining the *mix* of local public services, the *level* of public expenditures will depend upon the behavior of the grants-in-aid program.

Fourth, central government does not only influence local government spending through grants-in-aid; it uses other instruments as well. Broad base spending decisions are made at the level of central government but they are *implemented* by local governments. For example, an educational policy question whether or not to introduce nursery schools is decided by central government. Local government does not have the statutory powers to introduce new programs but they do have discretionary power when it comes to interpreting the policy or the timing of its implementation. From a public expenditure viewpoint, however, much of the expenditure is determined by central government. Local government can, of course, make additions to the levels of existing programs which are then financed through the property tax. However, it should be realized that because of the high "gearing"[7] of the local tax and the inelasticity of this base any large increase in local spending not covered by grants will cause local tax *rates* to increase rapidly. Although the local property tax is relatively unimportant to taxpayers, it is nevertheless a politically extremely unpopular tax, which means that dramatic increases in the rate could have important repercussions for local policies. In other words, local fiscal affairs have not had a significant impact upon local politics because the local "tax price" information has always been incomplete. Central government also influences local capital spending through a system of loan sanctions. Before a local government can proceed to incur capital spending it must secure permission to borrow from central government. As part of its demand management policy central government regulates loan sanctions closely.

Local fiscal behavior in the U.K. depends heavily upon a complex set of central-local government relationships. It is within this context that the urban fiscal crisis must be viewed. Central government provides grant-in-aid to local government through the Rate Support Grant (RSG). The total amount of grant is decided by the Treasury when it makes its annual expenditure plans and is calculated as a percentage of total relevant spending.[8] This total grant is then distributed to each of the local authorities according to three elements, (a) the needs element, (b) the domestic element, and (c) the resources element.

The needs element is designed to equalize the spending needs of different local governments. Thus, according to the principles of territorial justice, those authorities with a high concentration of population, young children, and poverty should receive bigger grants. To determine the needs allocation a formula is used based upon those variables which are supposed to reflect needs. An indication of the variables used is shown in Table 7.[9]

From the point of view of urban decline and urban fiscal stress it is interesting to note that the formula has changed over time insofar as population plays a less dominant role whereas urban stress factors are more significant. This change occurred in 1974 when it was decided to shift grants to those areas in greatest need. The effect of this is seen in Table 6 where grants as a proportion of total expenditure increased significantly for the declining cities but fell elsewhere. One

Table 7

Rate Support Grant and its Elements

(a) R.S.G. Components 1978–79

Component	*£M*	*%*
Domestic Element	674	10.3
Resources Element	1901	29.2
Needs Element	3946	60.5
TOTAL RSG	6521	100.0

(b) Needs Element Proportions 1964–65 to 1978–79

1964–65 General Grant		*1978–79 Multiple Regression Formula*	
Factors	%	Factors	%
Population	62.5	One Parent families	32.9
School Children	28.4	Pupils	30.3
Low Density	4.6	Population	16.4
Under 15s	1.3	Persons per acre	7.0
Metropolitan Weighting	0.8	Lack of Amenities	6.8
High Density	0.7	Labour Cost	4.0
Declining Population	0.6	Acreage	2.6
Over 65's	0.6		
Under 5's	0.5		
TOTAL	100.0	TOTAL	100.0

Source: T. Rhodes and S. Bailey (1974), *Equity Statistics and the Distribution of the Rate Support Grant, Policy and Politics*, Vol. 7, 1979.

of the features of the highly centralized fiscal system in the U.K. is that through its grants-in-aid programs central government is able to redistribute resources among local authorities. To be more precise: because it cannot take away locally raised resources from a local authority it can nevertheless level up those in greatest need.

The domestic element of RSG, which accounts for about 10% of the grant, is allocated on a flat rate basis. Those areas with a high rateable value (i.e., property tax base) but a low rate poundage (i.e., tax rate) will receive less grant money. Those local authorities which have a high proportion of non-domestic rate income fall into this category. They tend to be the central cities. Thus, while the needs element operates in favor of the central cities, the domestic element will act against them. Domestic rate relief has increased from 3.6% of average rate bills in 1967/68 to 27.5% in 1975/76. This represents quite a shift in the burden of local public expenditure and further distorts the tax price information.

The resources element of RSG is designed to partially equalize the tax resources of the local authorities. It is about one third of total grants. Since the operational variable used for the allocation of this component of grants is rateable value per capita, declining cities can be badly hit. In order to regenerate the economic base of the city, local governments attempt to attract new industry. However, as new industry moves in and adds to the property tax base the city will lose grant money pound for pound through the resources element. Thus the inner city cannot attract additional fiscal resources *per se*. However, the worst feature of the system is that as population leaves the city (*ceteris paribus*) the rateable value per capita rises and grant money is lost. Declining areas with greatest spending needs are, therefore, losing income because of the arithmetic quirk of a ratio. It is not known whether or not increases in the needs element for declining cities more than offset the loss in the resources element.

Finally, there are a number of specific (open ended categorical) grants paid to local governments mainly for police and housing. In 1979, 9% of the total Exchequer Grant was distributed through specific grants. One set of specific grants are those on the urban aid program. Some commentators have mistakenly thought that the increase in the urban aid program implied that central government was allocating additional resources. Not so. Since the Treasury decides on the total amount of grant, RSG and all specific grants, any increases in specific grants such as urban aid are offset by reductions in RSG. So far it has been difficult to figure out whether or not the increases in urban aid to the inner city have been compensated by reductions in grants elsewhere.

A significant difference between the problems of urban fiscal stress in the U.K. and the USA is, therefore, the amount of federal grants-in-aid that have been allocated to the central declining cities in the U.K. This has undoubtedly kept down property tax increases and reduced the pressures which U.S. cities have experienced. Another important difference is the behavior of local authority debt. Gramlich (1976) has shown that the fiscal crisis in New York resulted in a rapid build-up of debt. In the U.K., however, the local governments of declining cities have not increased their debt ratios. Kirwan (1980) has shown that between 1965 and 1977 the ratio of outstanding debt to rateable values has fallen in most declining cities. Cities in the U.K. have, therefore, continued to be good risks and have not faced loss of creditworthiness as cities have done in the U.S.

While the role of central government has in recent years undoubtedly had a major influence upon the financial stability of local governments in the U.K., especially those with declining populations and a shrinking economic base, this situation has been changing since 1975. After 1979, local government in the U.K. moved into a new era of central-local fiscal relationships which has threatened the stability of the system. This followed the election of the Thatcher government and the introduction of a new system of central government grants-in-aid which contained penalty clauses for overspending local authorities.

Since 1974/75 both central and local governments were confronted with very rapid rates of inflation. Between 1974 and 1979 local government current expenditures (at current prices) rose by 98%, i.e., on average 20% p.a. This was partially offset by a fall of 5% p.a. on capital account. The rate of inflation for local government costs was about 18% p.a. which was mainly accounted for by money wage increases. This rapid increase in local authority costs was financed by an acceleration in the money value of grants-in-aid which, in turn, increased public sector borrowing by a central government reluctant to increase taxes. The outcome was that as central governments in the U.K. became increasingly monetarist in their underlying macro-economic strategy they placed tighter controls on local government spending.

The first set of controls was introduced in 1976 when RSG became for the first time subject to a cash limit. Until then inflationary cost increases had been fully indexed through supplementary increases to RSG made during the fiscal year. Because grants were subject to a cash limit any inflationary increases over and above those budgeted for when the limit was set had to be met from large property tax revenues generated by increases in the property tax rate. Such increases in the rate were likely to be large, given the size of the "gearing effect." The full force of such controls was not felt until 1979. Until then a statutory incomes policy was in force which made it comparatively easy to forecast the rate of inflation in local government costs when setting RSG. This incomes policy was abandoned in 1979 with the incoming Conservative Government. The result was that pressures built up for increases in the property tax rate.

The second set of controls which was introduced and which placed pressures on the property tax rate related to the size of grants allocated to the local authorities by central government. In calculating the grants central government has reduced the percentage of total relevant expenditure it is willing to finance. Changes in these proportions are shown in Table 8. While this change in central government policy towards the size of grants-in-aid has placed pressures on property tax rates the full impact has been moderated by local governments' own reactions. Because grants are such an important source of finance, local governments have responded to this degree of uncertainty by reducing their expenditures [Hepworth (1981)]. The grant settlement is announced late in the local government's budget cycle. Rather than underestimate the extent of the cut in grants, local governments have over-estimated it with the result that since 1975 expenditure increases have been moderated. Cutbacks have been made along the lines of the strategies outlined above. Vacated posts have not been renewed, early retirement has been introduced, maintenance, etc. has been cut back. The impacts of these policies are shown in Table 9.

Finally, central government has, from 1981, introduced a more stringent set of controls. Central government now calculates how much it expects each local authority to spend. This is based upon some assessment of its needs. It then calculates what it *hopes* local authority cost inflation will be based upon, how much it is willing to pay in wage increases, etc. On the basis of these calculations total grants are determined and then allocated in the normal way. If local government employees settle for wage increases above the figure calculated by central government, these increases can only be paid by the local au-

Table 8

Percentage of Relevant Expenditure Met from Grants

1973–74	*1974–75*	*1975–76*	*1976–77*	*1977–78*	*1978–79*
60.6	65.5	67.0	63.8	61.0	60.7

Source: The Government's Expenditure Plans for 1982 to 1985, Cmnd 8494, HMSO, 1982.

Table 9

Property Tax Rates 1977/78–1979/80				
	1977–78 (pence)	*1978–79 (pence)*	*1979–80 (pence)*	*Percentage Increase 1977–1980 (%)*
Liverpool	82.1	86.2	101.0	23.0
Newcastle	99.0	114.0	133.0	34.3
Birmingham	77.7	80.0	90.0	15.8
Leeds	66.2	72.7	86.4	30.5
Manchester	109.0	115.3	125.7	15.3

Source: Extracted from several tables in *Rate Collection Statistics: 1979/80*, Chartered Institute of Public Finance and Accountancy.

thorities if they cut back on non-wage cost items elsewhere in their budgets or if they increase the property tax rate. Moreover, local authorities are now penalized if they spend above the figure which central government considers to be appropriate for them. This penalty is implemented by withholding grants from the overspenders. The amount of grants withheld depends upon the degree of overspending. Overspenders are then forced to finance the deficit through supplementary increases in the property tax rate, which it is hoped will make them unpopular with the local electorate and thereby force them to reduce spending. The situation is, however, significantly different in Scotland. There local authorities who overspend and now lose grant money are *not* allowed to finance the difference through increases in the property tax rate. Expenditures have to be reduced immediately. This can, however, only be done by making local government employees redundant on a large scale. Given the nature of the contracts which most U.K. public employees have, the implementation of this policy is likely to take time and to be expensive since the employer (in this case the local government) will have to pay redundancy compensation in order to buy out the term labor contracts.

Because these measures are so recent it is not possible to discuss their implications. However, from the perspective of the declining cities they do raise a number of interesting issues. It is generally assumed that because population is declining, service levels can be reduced in order to maintain financial balance. However, a basic assumption of the analysis of fiscal stress is that different parts of the budget adjust at different speeds and not necessarily in the way which is required.

Growing expenditure needs, inflation and improvements in the quality of services have all caused expenditures to rise. The decline of the tax paying population would have caused problems of fiscal stress for U.K. cities had it not been for the grants-in-aid programs of central government. Still even that policy and especially the new policy of constraining local government spending does not take into account that there are costs associated with population decline. Returning to Table 7 it can be seen that while the needs formula does recognize and does take into account some of the particular problems of expenditure needs in the declining central cities, it does not recognize that because of the indivisibilities in service provision and the fixity of many expenditure items (e.g., debt charges), per capita spending will rise and total *real* costs will decline only slowly, despite the fall in the client group population. For example, if the school age population in a city is falling it does not follow that total education costs will decrease rapidly. Schools remain open until some critical point is reached when a decision must be made to close them. In the meantime, total costs are maintained and per capita costs rise.

Unless the costs of decline and the speed of adjustment to population decline are recognized, grants-in-aid policies towards the central cities in the U.K. are likely to spill over into increased multiple deprivation. Moreover, while declining central cities in the U.K. have so far been sheltered from the fiscal stresses experienced by their U.S. counterparts, this situation is rapidly changing. Current policies are placing greater burdens upon local governments already faced with mounting demands for expenditure increases. How this burden will be accommodated remains to be seen.

Notes

[1]So much has been written about New York's fiscal crisis that it is best to give an indication of the most succinct treatments. See, Gramlich (1976); Bahl, Campbell and Greytak (1974). For a comparison of U.S. cities, see Howell and Stamm (1979). See also, Bahl, Jump and Puryear (1976); Ginzberg (1974); Hirsch, Vincent, Terrell, Shoup and Roset (1971) and Nathan and Adams (1976).

[2]Work currently being carried out at Leicester University has amassed a suitable data set. Earlier studies include, Eversley (1972, a and b) and Kirwan (1973, 1980). These were not detailed studies.

[3]Eversley (1972, a and b) was one of the first in the U.K. to recognize this problem.

[4]City rioting in the U.K. broke out on a large scale for the first time during the summer of 1981. It started in Brixton, London, and spread to other areas such as Toxteth in Liverpool, Manchester, Leicester, and Hull.

[5]Nothing is being assumed about the shifting of the property tax.

[6]The net property tax accounted for 2.2% of personal disposable incomes in 1980 compared to 2.6% in 1966.

[7]The gearing effect refers to the impact upon the local tax system, in particular the local tax rate, arising from a reduction of the proportion of local public spending which is financed from central government grants-in-aid. Thus, for example, if the

proportion was reduced from 60% to 50% then local tax rates would rise by more than 10%, that is they will be geared in an upward direction.

[8]"Relevant spending" is all local government spending minus mandatory elements such as student awards and rent rebates.

[9]The needs formula has been criticized on a number of grounds. It is conceptually very weak and it is not clear if it reflects spending needs accurately. Moreover, it preserves the status quo by favoring those who were heavy spenders in earlier years.

References

Bahl, R. W., Campbell, A. K. and Greytak, D. (1974), *Taxes, Expenditures and Economic Base: Case Study of New York City,* Praeger.

Bahl, R. W., Jump, Bernard and Puryear, D. (1976), *The Outlook for State and Local Government Fiscal Performance,* Testimony prepared for the Joint Economic Committee, January 22, 1976, (mimeo, Syracuse University, New York).

Baumol, W. J. (1963), "Urban Services, Interactions of Public and Private Decisions," in H. G. Schaller (ed.), *Public Expenditure Decisions in the Urban Community,* Resources for the Future, Inc., The Johns Hopkins Press, pp. 1–18.

Baumol, W. J. (1967), "The Macroeconomics of Unbalanced Growth," *American Economic Review,* Vol. 57, pp. 415–426.

Baumol, W. J. (1972), "The Dynamics of Urban Problems and its Policy Implications," in B. Corru and M. Preston, (eds.), *Essays in Honour of Lord Robbins,* Weidenfeld and Nicolson, London.

Boochkim, M. (1974), *The Limits of the City,* Harper Row.

Borcherding, T. E. (ed.) (1976), *Budgets and Bureaucrats,* Duke University Press, Durham, North Carolina.

Borcherding, T. E. and Deacon, R. T. (1972), "The Demand for the Services of Non-Federal Governments," *American Economic Review,* December, Vol. 62, No. 5, pp. 891–901.

Bradford, D. and Kelejian, H. (1973), "An Econometric Model of Flight to the Suburbs," *Journal of Political Economy,* Vol. 81, No. 31.

Bradford, D. F., Malt, S. and Oates, W. E. (1969), "The Rising Cost of Local Public Services," *National Tax Journal,* Vol. 22 (2).

Cameron, G. C. (1973), "Intra Urban Location and New Plant," *Proceedings of the Twelfth European Congress of the Regional Science Association.*

C.I.P.F.A. (Chartered Institute of Public Finance and Accountancy), *Local Government Trends,* various years (London).

Evans, A. W. (1980), "Poverty and the Conurbations," in G. Cameron (ed.), *The Future of the British Conurbations,* Longmans.

Eversley, D. E. C. (1972,a) "Old Cities, Falling Populations and Rising Costs," *G.L.C. Intelligence Unit Bulletin,* No. 18.

Eversley, D. E. C. (1972,b), "Rising Costs and Static Incomes: Some Economic Consequences of Regional Planning in London," *Urban Studies,* Vol. 9, No. 2.

Eversley, D. and Bonnerjea, L. (1980), *Changes in the Resident Populations of Inner Areas,* Inner City in Context, No. 2, Social Science Research Council, London.

Ginzberg, E. (ed.), (1974), *The Future of the Metropolis: People Jobs and Incomes,* (Salt Lake City), Olympus Publishing Co.

Gramlich, E. M. (1976), "The New York City Fiscal Crisis: What Happened and What is to be Done?", *American Economic Review,* May, 1966 (2).

Gramlich, E. M. (1980), "Models of Excessive Government Spending: Do the Facts Support the Theories?" mimeo, paper presented to IIPF Conference, Jerusalem, Wayne State University Press, 1981.

Hall, P., Thomas, R., Gracy, H., and Drewett, R., (1973), *The Containment of Urban England,* Vols. 1 and 2, George Allen and Unwin, London.

Hepworth, N. (1981), "Control of Local Authority Expenditures—The Use of Cash Limits," mimeo, *Chartered Institute of Public Finance and Accountancy*, London.

Hirsch, W. Z., Vincent, P. E., Terrell, H. S., Shoup, D. C., and Roset, A., (1971), *Fiscal Pressures on the Central City,* (New York), Praeger.

Holterman, S. E. (1975), "Areas of Urban Deprivation in Britain," *Social Trends,* No. 6, HMSO, London.

Howell, J. M. and Stamm, C. F. (1979), *Urban Fiscal Stress,* Lexington Books, Lexington, Mass.

Inman, R. P. (1979), "Central City Crisis," *National Tax Journal.*

Inman, R. P. (1979), "The Fiscal Problems of Local Governments and Interpretative Review," in P. Mieszkowski and M. Straszheim (eds.), *Current Issues in Urban Economics,* Johns Hopkins University Press, Baltimore.

Jackson, P. M., (1973), "The Rising Costs of Local Government Services," in *Proceedings of a Conference on Local Government Finance,* Institute for Fiscal Studies, London.

Jackson, P. M. (1980), "The Growth of the Relative Size of the Public Sector," in D. A. Currie and W. Peters, (eds.), *Contemporary Economic Analysis,* Croom Helm, London.

Jackson, P. M. and Ulph, D. T. (1973), "The Relative Prices of Public and Private Goods," mimeo.

Kirwan, R. M. (1973), "The Contribution of Public Expenditure and Finance to the Problems of Inner London," in D. Donnison and D. Eversley (eds.), *Urban Patterns, Problems and Policies,* Heinemann, London.

Kirwan, R. M., (1980), *The Future of the British Conurbations,* Longmans, London.

Litvack, J. M. and Oates, W. E. (1970), "Group Size and the Output of Public Goods," *Public Finance,* Vol. 23, No. 1.

Nathan, R. P. and Adams, C. (1976), "Understanding Central City Hardship," *Political Science Quarterly,* Spring, Vol. 91, No. 1.

Oates, W. E., Howrey, E. P. and Baumol, W. J. (1971), "The Analysis of Public Policy in Dynamic Urban Models," *Journal of Political Economy,* Vol. 79.

Office of Population, Census, and Surveys (1971), *Population Estimates Series PP1 N°2,* HMSO, London.

Rhodes, T. and Bailey, S. (1979), "Equity Statistics and the Distribution of the Rate Support Grant," *Policy and Politics,* Vol. 7.

Résumé

Dans la plupart des pays, la croissance et le développement urbains s'accompagnent de problèmes de pression fiscale. Ces problèmes sont caractérisés par des augmentations rapides des dépenses publiques locales sans augmentation correspondante des revenus locaux. Il en résulte une accumulation des déficits et/ou une détérioration de la qualité des services. La croissance des dépenses publiques locales dans les villes en déclin est provoquée par l'augmentation des groupes de clientèle qui bénéficient des services publics locaux, par des changements de technologie ou par l'inflation. La disparition d'offre d'emplois cause l'émigration de la base fiscale de la ville, en particulier chez les groupes à revenus moyens et supérieurs qui sont les plus mobiles. La conséquence du déséquilibre entre dépenses et revenus se traduit par des taux d'imposition qui augmentent sans cesse pour une base fiscale qui se réduit avec un déficit consécutif qui s'accumule.

Nous examinons le processus de la détérioration fiscale urbaine dans le contexte propre aux villes britanniques. Les traits caractéristiques du contexte fiscal local britannique qui diffère de façon notoire du contexte américain, tiennent à ce que (1) les collectivités locales ne fournissent pas de services sociaux ou de services de santé sur la même échelle que leurs homologues américains, (II) les subventions d'aide gouvernementales jouent un rôle bien plus important en Angleterre, ce qui protège les pouvoirs locaux des effets d'une diminution des impôts et (II) les collectivités locales n'ont pas le droit d'emprunter pour financer des dépenses courantes

Nous étudions de façon empirique la pression fiscale des villes du centre du Royaume-Uni au cours de la période d'après-guerre.

Tax Effects, Relative Prices, and Economic Growth

*Kul B. Bhatia**

I. Introduction

In a world of scarcity, if the public sector is to provide an appropriate framework for making private and public decisions, prices must reflect the relative scarcity of various goods and services after all effects of public sector activities themselves on prices are incorporated. This is important for efficient allocation of resources at a point in time as well as for economic growth because if a commodity, say a capital good, is underpriced, its output would be less than optimal. Other things being equal, future output and the economy's growth rate would be hampered. Further complications will arise if the commodity in question happens to be used as an intermediate product in the production of other goods and services. In this context, this paper offers a general equilibrium framework in which effects of factor taxes and commodity taxes on relative prices can be examined. The focus is on relative commodity prices, but obviously all prices—factor rewards as well as output prices—are inter-dependent.

In earlier work with various taxes, people have often assumed fixed input-output coefficients[1] and left out demand considerations. Besides, at least for corporation income tax (CIT) (Melvin, 1979) and value-added tax (VAT) (Aaron, 1968), it has been postulated that such taxes do not affect factor prices.[2] These assumptions can sometimes be jus-

*Department of Economics, University of Western Ontario. This research was supported by a grant from the Social Sciences and Humanities Research Council. A longer, more technical version of the paper, complete with mathematical derivations and proofs, is available from the author. I have benefitted from comments by Dr. Otto Gadó, Chairman of the session in Tokyo, Professor P. B. Boorsma, the discussant of the paper, and other participants in the session. Thanks are also due to Professor Dr. Dieter Biehl for many helpful suggestions.

Public Finance and Economic Growth. Proceedings of the 37th Congress of the International Institute of Public Finance. Tokyo, 1981, pp. 349–365

tified in the short run, but no economy can stay on a short run for too long. Also, there is plenty of evidence from econometric studies (e.g., Berndt and Wood, 1975) that production coefficients are in fact flexible (non-zero elasticities of substitution). In this paper two separate effects are identified: first, a direct "tax-effect" which can be determined by inverting a fixed-coefficient input-output matrix assuming unchanged factor prices, and second, a "factor-price-effect" emanating from changes in factor rewards for which the full general equilibrium model has to be solved. These two effects can fortify or offset each other. Their relative strength is an empirical matter. Price changes estimated in earlier studies from the "tax effect" only are, therefore, liable to be inaccurate.

The model is set out in the next section. Several analytical results are derived in Section III. A numerical illustration of CIT based on U.S. data is presented in Section IV. The last section contains implications for economic growth and the principal conclusions.

II. The Model

Two commodities, X_1 and X_2 are produced with the help of labor (L) and capital (K). Both goods are used as final products (x_1 and x_2) as well as intermediate inputs (X_{12} and X_{21}, X_{ij} is X_i used in producing X_j). Total endowment of primary factors is fixed. Constant returns to scale are assumed to exist in each industry, and technology is indicated by a set of input-output coefficients, a_{ij}, which are freely variable. Full employment of factors of production and perfect competition in all markets are assumed too. The full employment conditions are given by

$$a_{L1}(x_1 + X_{12}) + a_{L2}(x_2 + X_{21}) = L \tag{1}$$

$$a_{K1}(x_1 + X_{12}) + a_{K2}(x_2 + X_{21}) = K \tag{2}$$

Or, equivalently, by

$$R_{L1}x_1 + R_{L2}x_2 = L \tag{3}$$

$$R_{K1}x_1 + R_{K2}x_2 = K \tag{4}$$

where R_{ij} is the amount of the ith primary factor used directly or indirectly in producing one unit of the jth final good. For example, R_{K1}

$= (a_{K1} + a_{K2} \cdot a_{21})/(1 - a_{12} \cdot a_{21})$. The direct or *net* factor intensity is determined by a_{ij}'s—for instance, $K_1'/L_1' = a_{K1}/a_{L1}$—while the total or *gross* capital-labor ratio $K_1/L_1 = R_{K1}/R_{L1}$. It is further assumed that $a_{12} \cdot a_{21} < 1$, which makes all R_{ij}'s positive and ensures positive outputs for the two final goods. Production coefficients are determined by the wage rate (w), the rental of capital (r), and the price of intermediate good (p_i):

$$a_{ij} = a_{ij}(w,r,p_k)\ (i = L,K,1,2; j,k = 1,2, j \neq k) \tag{5}$$

The a_{ij} functions are homogeneous of degree zero, i.e., an equi-proportional change in all input prices will not alter input ratios.

Under competitive conditions, inputs must be priced in such a manner that excess profits are zero in both industries. Assuming that firms minimize unit costs, following Jones (1965), proportional changes (denoted by asterisks) in output prices can be expressed as weighted averages (with input shares as weights) of corresponding changes in inputs prices as in equations (6)–(9):

$$\rho_{L1}w^* + \rho_{K1}r^* + \rho_{21}p_2^* = p_1^* \tag{6}$$

$$\rho_{L2}w^* + \rho_{K2}r^* + \rho_{12}p_1^* = p_2^* \tag{7}$$

which leads to:

$$\theta_{L1}w^* + \theta_{K1}r^* = p_1^* \tag{8}$$

$$\theta_{L2}w^* + \theta_{K2}r^* = p_2^* \tag{9}$$

Here θ_{ij} denotes the *total* distributive share of the ith primary factor in industry j (for instance, $\theta_{K2} = R_{K2}\ r|p_2$), and ρ_{ij} represent direct factor shares (e.g., $\rho_{K2} = a_{K2}r/p_2$). For each industry, ρ's as well as θ's will add up to unity (e.g., $\rho_{L1} + \rho_{K1} + \rho_{21} = 1$, $\theta_{L2} + \theta_{K2} = 1$, and so on). If t_{L1} and t_{K1} respectively denote a tax per unit of labor and capital and t_1 is an excise tax in X_1, the zero-profit conditions require that:

$$\theta_{L1}w^* + \gamma\rho_{L1}T_{L1}^* + \theta_{K1}r^* + \gamma\rho_{K1}T_{K1}^* + \gamma T_1^* = p_1^* \tag{10}$$

$$\theta_{L2}w^* + \gamma\rho_{12}\rho_{L1}T_{L1}^* + \theta_{K2}r^* + \gamma\rho_{12}\rho_{K1}T_{K1}^* + \gamma\rho_{12}T_1^* = p_2^* \tag{11}$$

where $\gamma = 1/(1 - \rho_{12}\rho_{21})$, ρ's and θ's now denote factor shares gross of tax, $T^* = (1 + t)^*$, and w and r are defined net of tax. Notice that p_2 is affected by all taxes in X_1 because of interdependence in production.

The main argument of this paper is well illustrated by equations (10) and (11). The γ-terms indicate what has been described above as the direct "tax-effect," and terms involving w^* and r^* represent the "factor-price effect." Only the former is captured by inverting an input-output matrix when it is assumed that factor prices do not respond to a given tax. Under these assumptions, Melvin (1979) computed that CIT raised output prices in several U.S. and Canadian industries by 2 to 13 percent, with a mean of 4.7 percent for U.S.A. and 3.6 percent for Canada. Total price increases, allowing for changes in factor prices as well, obviously, can be much different because one cannot predict before hand the signs and magnitudes of w^* and r^* as these will be affected by capital-labor ratios in the two sectors, the various elasticities of substitution and demand, and other variables. The principal purpose of this model, therefore, is (1) to determine how various taxes affect w and r and (2) use w and r to compute movements in commodity prices. Before that is done, however, a demand function is needed to complete the specification of the model.

For the sake of simplicity, it is assumed that distribution of income among consumers does not affect aggregate demand. This, combined with the full employment assumption, ensures that there is only one independent demand function in which quantity demanded depends on relative prices alone. By differentiating this function we get:

$$x_1^* = \epsilon(p_1^* - p_2^*) \tag{12}$$

When taxes are levied, it will be assumed that the government will spend its revenue exactly as private individuals would have, so (12) continues to hold.[3]

In this model, the response of factor prices to a particular tax also holds the key to the incidence of that tax. The ultimate burden of a tax depends on how factor shares respond, and that in turn depends mainly on the behavior of factor prices because of the assumptions of full employment and fixed factor endowments. If the wage-rental ratio remains constant, relative shares of labor and capital in national income do not change, thus the two factors bear the tax burden in proportion to their initial contribution to national income. The factor whose relative price declines will suffer more than the benchmark provided by initial factor shares. Effects of various taxes on output prices thus are intimately tied to questions of tax-incidence. We turn to this matter next.

III. Taxes and Input Prices

The model is solved by equating the proportionate change in supply of x_1 to the corresponding change in its demand, after incorporating the full employment and price equations. Differentiation of equations (3) and (4) yields the following structural relations:

$$\lambda_{L1}x_1^* + \lambda_{L2}x_2^* = L^* - (\lambda_{L1}R_{L1}^* + \lambda_{L2}R_{L2}^*) \tag{13}$$

$$\lambda_{K1}x_1^* + \lambda_{K2}x_2^* = K^* - (\lambda_{K1}R_{K1}^* + \lambda_{K2}R_{K2}^*) \tag{14}$$

where λ_{ij} is the proportion of total endowment of the ith primary factor used directly and indirectly in industry j (e.g., $\lambda_{K1} = R_{K1}x_1/K$, etc.). For simplicity, all initial prices are assumed to be unity by defining appropriate units, and L^* and K^* are set to zero due to fixed factor endowments. Since only relative prices matter, the wage rate, w, is chosen as the *numéraire* in which all other prices are stated. Thus w^* is also equal to zero everywhere. It follows that proportional changes in the wage-rental ratio will be indicated by r^*. To limit the length of the paper, we discuss in detail only the case of a small tax levied on capital used directly in producing X_1. For analytical purposes, it is very similar to CIT in the United States. An analogous procedure can be applied to other taxes for which the final results will be presented and briefly analyzed.

First of all, equations (10) and (11) can be substituted into (12) after setting w^* and all tax terms except T_{K1}^* equal to zero.

$$x_1^* = \epsilon[(\theta_{K1} - \theta_{K2})r^* + \gamma\rho_{K1}(1 - \rho_{12})T_{K1}^*] \tag{15}$$

On the supply side, applying Cramer's rule to (13) and (14) yields

$$x_1^* = [R_{L2}^* - R_{K2}^* + (L_1/L_2)R_{L1}^* - (K_1/K_2)R_{K1}^*]/A \tag{16}$$

where $A = (K_1/K_2) - (L_1/L_2)$. By equating (15) to (16) and substituting the solutions for R^*'s derived in the Appendix, we get after simplification:

$$r^* = [A\epsilon\gamma\rho_{K1}(1 - \rho_{12}) - S_1N_1 - S_2N_2]T_{K1}^*/D$$

where

$$S_1 = \rho_{L1}\rho_{K1}\sigma^1_{LK} + \rho_{21}\rho_{K1}\theta_{L2}\sigma^1_{K2}(1 - \gamma\rho_{12}\rho_{K1})$$
$$+ \gamma\rho_{L1}\rho_{12}\rho_{K1}\rho_{21}\theta_{K2}\sigma^1_{L2} + \gamma\rho_{21}\rho_{12}\rho_{K1}(\rho_{L2}\theta_{K1}\sigma^2_{L1} - \rho_{K2}\theta_{L1}\sigma^2_{K1})$$
$$S_2 = \rho_{12}\rho_{L1}\rho_{K1}\sigma^1_{LK} + \rho_{21}\rho_{12}\rho_{K1}\theta_{L2}\sigma^1_{K2}(1 - \gamma\rho_{K1}\rho_{12})$$
$$+ \gamma\rho_{K1}\rho_{12}(\rho_{L2}\theta_{K1}\sigma^2_{L1} - \rho_{K2}\theta_{L1}\sigma^2_{K1}) + \gamma\rho^2_{12}\rho_{L1}\rho_{K1}\rho_{21}\theta_{K2}\sigma^1_{L2}$$
$$N_1 = \left(\frac{1}{\Omega_1}\frac{L_1}{L_2} + \frac{1}{\Omega_K}\frac{K_1}{K_2}\right) \quad N_2 = (\eta_L + \eta_k)/\eta_L\eta_K$$

and

$$D = A\epsilon(\theta_{K2} - \theta_{K1}) + (\beta + \rho_{12}\alpha)N_1 + (\alpha + \rho_{21}\beta)N_2$$

Now $\Omega_L = \rho_{L1} + \rho_{L2} \cdot \rho_{21}$ is the sum of direct and indirect shares of labor in the taxed industry, Ω_K is a similar expression for shares of capital in that industry, and η_L and η_K are the corresponding sums in the second industry, all positive by definition. α is a weighted sum of the three elasticities of substitution in $X_1(\sigma^1_{LK}, \sigma^1_{L2}, \text{and } \sigma^1_{K2})$, with various factor shares as weights, and β is the parallel expression involving the three σ's in the second industry. Here σ^j_{ik} is the partial elasticity of substitution between factors i and k in the jth industry, as defined by Allen (1969). It can be shown that α and β are positive.[4] Note further that the first term in D will also be positive because A and $(\theta_{K2} - \theta_{K1})$ will have opposite signs[5] and ϵ is negative. The sign of r^* thus depends only on the numerator of the expression.[6]

The solution for r^* in (17) summarizes everything that goes on in an economy to reach a new equilibrium when a tax such as CIT is levied. Firms in the taxed sector will attempt to increase the use of untaxed substitutes for capital and reduce complementary inputs. All elasticities of substitution in the taxed industry will play a part in such attempts. Output of X_1 will fall (depending on elasticity of demand) thereby releasing capital and labor which have to be absorbed in the second industry to restore full employment. Here capital-labor ratios in both industries and elasticities of substitution in the untaxed industry will be important. A series of complex interactions involving forces of demand and supply, will generate excess demand or supply for labor or capital which would cause factor prices to alter unless the untaxed industry somehow ends up demanding capital and labor in exactly the quantities released by the taxed industry. This will be the case, for instance, when gross capital-labor ratios are identical in the two industries and *all* production coefficients are fixed.

In general, r^*, determined by factor shares and various elasticities in a given case, can have any sign or magnitude. How does the assumption of unchanged factor prices, made in some studies, fare then? Obviously it can hold only fortuitously. Consider a case in which elasticity of demand plays no role, thus input prices are determined by supply factors only. Set ϵ, σ^1_{K2}, σ^1_{L2}, σ^2_{L1}, and σ^2_{K1} equal to naught. Now

$$r^* = \frac{\rho_{L1}\rho_{K1}\sigma^1_{LK}(N_1 + \rho_{12}N_2)}{\rho_{L1}\rho_{K1}\sigma^1_{LK}(N_1 + \rho_{12}N_2) + \rho_{L2}\rho_{K2}\sigma^2_{LK}(N_2 + \rho_{21}N_1)}$$

It should be clear that to make r^* zero even in this restrictive setting, either σ^1_{LK} will have to be zero or σ^2_{LK} must be very large. In fact, since σ^2_{LK} appears only in the denominator of r^*, irrespective of other parameters, in the limit as $\sigma^2_{LK} \rightarrow \infty$, $r^* \rightarrow 0$.

Not much else can be said in this regard on analytical grounds because the issue becomes empirical hereafter. There is no *a priori* reason to believe that A or ϵ should be zero, or that σ^1_{KL} and σ^2_{KL} should take any particular values. Let us therefore look at some empirical evidence in this connection.

In the United States, many econometric studies of production functions in different industries have been conducted, although not along the lines of the corporate-noncorporate dichotomy used in the theoretical model here. There are many estimates of partial elasticities of substitution. Berndt and Wood (1975, Table 4) report $\sigma_{LK} = 1.01$, σ_{KM} ranging from .41 to .58, and σ_{LM} from .57 to .61 for U.S. manufacturing industries. These are based on parameters of a translog cost function with capital, labor, energy, and materials (M) as inputs. The estimate used U.S. data for the period 1947 to 71. Hudson and Jorgenson (1974) do not report any σ's, but comparable estimates can be derived from their results: for 1965, $\sigma_{LK} = 1.09$, $\sigma_{KM} = .24$ and $\sigma_{LM} = .44$.[7] To conform closely to our specified model, the σ's should really be estimated separately in the two industries using cost or production functions with only K, L, and intermediate goods. These estimates nonetheless do question the assumption of fixed input-output ratios typically made in the literature, and the elasticities found are definitely a far cry from what is needed to keep factor prices unchanged ($r^* = 0$ in (17)).

As far as factor intensities are concerned, the corporate sector in the United States is probably more labor-intensive than the non-corporate sector. Harberger's computations for 1952–55 suggested that L_1/L_2 was greater than K_1/K_2 by a factor of at least 5. Ratti and Shome (1977) estimated that in 1970, the share of labor in the corporate sector was 0.8 whereas in the noncorporate sector it was about 0.3.

Turning to the elasticity of demand, there is once again no direct evidence for the corporate sector; but from some estimates of price elasticity of demand for agriculture and nonfarm housing, Harberger (1962) concludes that ϵ is probably around -0.14.

All in all, based on whatever empirical evidence on elasticities of demand, elasticities of substitution, and factor intensities we have, it does not seem reasonable to assume that a tax of the type analyzed here will leave the wage-rental ratio unchanged. The capital-labor ratio is not the same in the two sectors, σ_{LK} appears to be neither zero nor very high, and even demand for x_1 is not inelastic. The seemingly innocuous assumption that CIT leaves factor prices unchanged turns out to be a strong one indeed. This assumption will be considered further in Section IV where its quantitative effects on output prices will also be analyzed.

Other Taxes

Along the lines of CIT discussed above, the following solutions can be derived for other partial factor and commodity taxes:

A tax on labor in X_1 (t_{L1})

$$r^* = [A\epsilon\gamma\rho_{L1}(1 - \rho_{12}) + W_1N_1 + W_2N_2]T^*_{L1}/D \tag{18}$$

An excise tax on X_1 (t_1)

$$\begin{aligned} r^* = [A\epsilon(1 - \rho_{12}) &+ \rho_{12}\rho_{21}(N_1 + \rho_{12}N_2)(\rho_{K1}\theta_{L2}\sigma^1_{K2} - \rho_{L1}\,\theta_{K2}\sigma^1_{L2}) \\ &+ \rho_{12}(\rho_{21}N_1 + N_2)(\rho_{K2}\theta_{L1}\sigma^2_{K1} - \rho_{L2}\theta_{K1}\sigma^2_{L1})]\gamma T^*_1/D \end{aligned} \tag{19}$$

A tax on capital in X_2 (t_{K2})

$$r^* = -[A\epsilon\gamma\rho_{K2}\,(1 - \rho_{21}) + U_1N_1 + U_2N_2]T^*_{K2}/D \tag{20}$$

A tax on labor in X_2 (t_{L2})

$$r^* = [A\epsilon\gamma\rho_{L2}\,(1 - \rho_{21}) + V_1N_1 + V_2N_2]\,T^*_{L2}/D \tag{21}$$

An excise tax on X_2 (t_2)

$$\begin{aligned} r^* = [-A\epsilon(1 - \rho_{21}) &+ \rho_{21}(N_1 + \rho_{12}N_2)(\rho_{K1}\theta_{L2}\sigma^1_{K2} - \rho_{L1}\theta_{K2}\sigma^1_{L2}) \\ &+ \rho_{12}\rho_{21}(\rho_{21}N_1 + N_2)(\rho_{K2}\theta_{L1}\sigma^2{}_{K1} - \rho_{L2}\theta_{K1}\sigma^2_{L1})]\,\gamma T^*_2/D \end{aligned} \tag{22}$$

In all cases terms such as A, γ, D, N, etc., retain the specifications given above. The only new terms are W_1, W_2, U_1, U_2, V_1, and V_2. These are very similar to S_1 and S_2 and represent sums of various σ's premultiplied by factor shares. All of these will be unambiguously positive if intermediate goods have to be used in fixed proportions in both industries. Since D is positive, once again the sign of r^* will depend on the numerator of the different expressions. In general, for reasons discussed in connection with CIT, the sign of r^* is uncertain, and the wage-rental ratio will not be invariant ($r^* = 0$) except under rather stringent restrictions.

Effect on Output Prices

From equations (10) and (11) we get (for CIT):

$$(\theta_{K1} - \theta_{K2})r^* + \gamma\rho_{K1}(1 - \rho_{12})T^*_{K1} = p^*_1 - p^*_2 \qquad (23)$$

Here the tax effect will always tend to increase the relative output price in the taxed sector, but factor prices can reinforce or ameliorate this tendency because r^* can be zero, positive, or negative. In principle, the first term in (23) can be sufficiently negative to more than offset the tax effect. However, such a result is not very likely in practice, at least for the United States, as the numbers in the next section will show. The more likely result is that studies which consider only the tax factor will underestimate the consequent increase in the relative price of the taxed good because there is evidence in the Harberger literature cited above that $\theta_{K1} < \theta_{K2}$ and r^* has been less than zero in the United States. It is also worth noting that if factor intensities are the same in the two industries, which is neither necessary nor sufficient for making r^* zero, p_1 will rise regardless of what happens to the wage-rental ratio because θ_{K1} will equal θ_{K2}.

Price equations for other taxes will also involve two terms similar to those in (23). For example, when a excise tax is levied in the first industry,

$$(\theta_{K1} - \theta_{K2})r^* + \gamma(1 - \rho_{12})T^*_1 = p^*_1 - p^*_2 \qquad (24)$$

The crucial issue, therefore, is the comparative strength of these two effects. It is an empirical matter by and large, depending on direct and total factor shares and the particular taxes at work. The numerical results in the next section will shed more light on this matter for the CIT case.

IV. CIT in the United States: A Numerical Illustration

The analytical results presented in the preceding section suggest that before computing how output prices respond to a tax one must determine what happens to factor prices. An illustrative computation is being attempted in this section from data for 1952–55 which were used by Harberger, and later by Ballentine and Eris (1975). These data, although quite old, are sufficient to demonstrate the magnitudes involved in making different assumptions about the parameters of the model. By rearranging the Harberger data to allow for inter-industry flows, and applying the definitions given above, we get:

$$\rho_{L1} = 0.80,\ \rho_{K1} = 0.16,\ \rho_{21} = 0.4,\ \theta_{L1} = 0.82,\ \theta_{K1} = 0.18$$

$$\rho_{L2} = 0.405,\ \rho_{K2} = 0.405,\ \rho_{12} = .19,\ \theta_{L2} = 0.56,\ \theta_{K2} = 0.44$$

$$K_1/K_2 = 1.11 \text{ and } L_1/L_2 = 7.46$$

The main difference between these figures and the ones compiled by Harberger (under the assumption of final goods only) is in capital-labor ratios. There K_1/K_2 was 1 and L_1/L_2 equalled 10. Because of inter-industry flows, the "gross" factor ratios have been brought closer together. The corporate sector is still relatively labor-intensive, but the difference is by a factor of about 7 rather than 10. Other differences pertain to ρ's and θ's which will be identical in the absence of intermediate goods.[8]

These numbers can be substituted into equation (17), to derive a series of results for r^* for different elasticities of demand and substitution. In Table 1, r^* ranges from .04 to $-.97$. Most of the figures are negative and greater than 0.5 in absolute value. All these are plausible because, as discussed earlier in the paper, values of various parameters are in accordance with existing empirical literature. What are the implications of these results for the assumptions widely used in the literature, namely, unchanged factor prices, invariable input-output coefficients, and inelastic demand?

Of the 36 cases presented in Table 1, in no more than one or two is there any suggestion that the wage-rental ratio might have remained unaltered, and these involve the extreme, and probably unrealistic, assumptions of nearly inelastic demand and zero elasticities of substitution in the taxed industry. Note also that in rows 1, 2, and 3, where elasticities of substitution involving intermediate goods are zero throughout the economy, r^* is nowhere near zero. The analytical arguments in the preceding section, combined with these results, make a strong case against assuming constant factor prices, especially when fixed production coefficients are simultaneously specified.

Other implications of invariant input-output ratios can be readily seen by comparing rows 1 and 9: there is an overestimate of about 10 per cent for r^*. In other words, if possibilities of substituting capital and labor for an intermediate good in fact exist, yet the opposite assumption is made, the relative price of capital would decline by less than what the model indicates. In the present case, the error is about 10 per cent although it could be bigger (row 2) or smaller (row 3), depending on other parameters.

If demand is elastic, but ϵ is assumed to be zero, as is implicit in studies which deal only with the supply side of the model, the errors involved can be computed along any row in Table 1. For instance, if all σ's are unity but ϵ is constrained to be zero, r^* will be $-.65$ instead of $-.57$, an error of 14 per cent. The combined effect of unjustifiably postulating fixed coefficients and inelastic demand can be devastating indeed—an overestimate amounting to 35 per cent of the correct figure ($-.73$ instead of $-.54$) when all elasticities of substitution in production are unity and the elasticity of demand is about -0.2 ($\sigma_D = -1.5$).

Tax-Induced Changes in p_1

After substituting the values of ρ_{K1}, θ_{K1}, ρ_{12} and ρ_{21} reported above, equation (10) becomes (w^* and all tax terms except $T^*_{K1} = 0$) we obtain:

$$.18\, r^* + .16\, T^* = p^*_1$$

Here the factor-price effect is larger than the tax effect. If it is assumed that the wage-rental ratio does not change, r^* is zero, and $p^*_1/T^* = .16$, i.e., a one per cent increase in the tax rate will cause a

Table 1

Elasticity of Net-of-Tax Return to Capital with Respect to Tax Rate (r^*/T^*)

	$\sigma_D = -0.5$	$\sigma_D = -1.0$	$\sigma_D = -1.5$	$\epsilon = 0$
1. $\sigma^1_{KL} = \sigma^2_{KL} = 1$, Other σ's $= 0$	$-.68$	$-.63$	$-.59$	$-.73$
2. $\sigma^1_{KL} = 1$, $\sigma^2_{KL} = 0.66$, other σ's $= 0$	$-.75$	$-.69$	$-.65$	$-.80$
3. $\sigma^1_{KL} = 0.8$, $\sigma^2_{KL} = 1$, other σ's $= 0$	$-.63$	$-.58$	$-.53$	$-.68$
4. $\sigma^1_{KL} = \sigma^1_{K2} = \sigma^1_{L2} = 0$, other σ's $= 1$	.08	.12	.16	.04
5. $\sigma^2_{KL} = \sigma^2_{K1} = \sigma^2_{L1} = 0$, other σ's $= 1$	$-.89$	$-.83$	$-.76$	$-.97$
6. $\sigma^1_{K2} = \sigma^2_{K1} = 0$, other σ's $= 1$	$-.66$	$-.62$	$-.58$	$-.71$
7. $\sigma^1_{KL} = 0.66$, other σ's $= 1$	$-.50$	$-.46$	$-.42$	$-.55$
8. All σ's $= 0.66$	$-.59$	$-.53$	$-.48$	$-.65$
9. All σ's $= 1$	$-.61$	$-.57$	$-.54$	$-.65$

0.16 per cent increase in p_1, but this will be completely offset if r^* is around −0.9. If the demand elasticity is zero and input-output coefficients are invariant (rows 1 and 2), p_1^* will be either .03 or .02 instead of .16. The actual increase in the price of the taxed good thus will be $1/5^{th}$ or $1/8^{th}$ of what is computed by holding factor prices constant. It is, therefore, not unreasonable to suspect that studies which used such assumptions probably overestimated the effect of a tax like the CIT on output prices in the taxed sector.

When factor rewards are allowed to respond to tax changes, the role of various elasticities of substitution can also be isolated from the numbers in Table 1. Consider, for example, the inelastic demand case in which $\sigma_{KL}^1 = \sigma_{KL}^2 = 1$. Now, in response to a one per cent tax increase, p_1^* will be .03 if intermediate goods have to be used in fixed proportions, but .04 if these proportions are flexible (row 9). Similar conclusions are reached even if the elasticity of demand is not zero and σ_{LK}^1 and σ_{LK}^2 are neither identical nor equal to unity.[9] With these data, therefore, the assumption of fixed input-output coefficients, without any restrictions on the wage-rental ratio, leads to an *underestimate* of increase in output price.

Effect on $p_1^* - p_2^*$

Since w has been the numéraire all along, the above analysis has dealt with a change in p_1 relative to the wage rate. Although this numéraire does not affect the generality of the conclusions, for some purposes, it is more useful to look at changes in p_1/p_2, or at $p_1^* - p_2^*$. By appropriate substitutions once again, (24) can be written as:

$$-.26\, r^* + .13\, T^* = p_1^* - p_2^*$$

As long as $r^* \leq 0$, the relative price of the taxed good must increase. A negative value for r^* will indeed reinforce this result. If a tax increase of 1 per cent leads to a value of r^* equal to .5, there will be no change in relative output prices. Nothing in Table 1 comes even close to this conclusion although another set of numbers could produce such a result. The more likely outcome with the data at hand is that changes in factor prices fortify the tax effect. A few examples of the two effects are presented in Table 2.

Once again we can determine the impact of different assumptions. If factor prices are held constant, except in the rare case in which r^* is positive, increase in relative price of the taxed commodity will be understated. This is vividly brought out in Table 2 where in

Table 2

Elasticity of Relative Output Price (p_1/p_2) with Respect to Tax Rate $[(p_1^* - p_2^*)/T^*]^a$

	Factor-Price Effect[b] *(1)*	*Tax Effect*[c] *(2)*	$p_1^* - p_2^{*d}$ *(3)*
1. $\sigma_{KL}^1 = \sigma_{KL}^2 = 1$, $\sigma_D = -1$, other σ's $= 0$	.17	.13	.30
2. $\sigma_{KL}^1 = \sigma_{KL}^2 = 1$, $\epsilon = 0$, other σ's $= 0$	.19	.13	.32
3. All σ's $= 1$, $\epsilon = 0$	.17	.13	.30
4. $\sigma_{KL}^2 = \sigma_{K1}^2 = \sigma_{L1}^2 = 0$, $\epsilon = 0$, other σ's $= 1$	.25	.13	.38
5. $\sigma_{KL}^1 = \sigma_{K2}^1 = \sigma_{L2}^1 = 0$, $\sigma_D = -1$, other σ's $= 1$	−.03	.13	.10
6. $\sigma_{KL}^1 = 0.66$, $\sigma_D = -1.5$, other σ's $= 1$	.11	.13	.24
7. $\sigma_D = -1$, all other σ's $= 0.66$	.14	.13	.27

[a]Based on equation (24). All estimates of r^*/T^* are from Table 1.
[b]$(\theta_{K1} - \theta_{K2})r^*/T^* = .26\ r^*/T^*$
[c]$\gamma\rho_{K1}\ (1 - \rho_{12})$
[d]Sum of columns (1) and (2).

many instances the direct effect of the tax is smaller than what movements in the wage-rental ratio do to commodity prices. The assumption that intermediate goods are used in fixed proportions will now lead to an overestimate of $p_1^* - p_2^*$, r^* will be more negative (compare, for instance, rows 1 and 9) but that contributes a positive term in (24). If the elasticity of demand is constrained to be zero, once again the rise in the comparative output price in the taxed sector will be exaggerated.

V. Conclusions and Summary

The purpose of this paper has been to analyze the effects of various indirect taxes on commodity prices in a general equilibrium model with primary factors and inter-industry flows. By assuming flexible production coefficients and elastic demand, the model provides a sharp contrast with existing literature where fixed coefficients and inelastic demand have been generally assumed. It is shown that the assumption of constant factor prices made in some earlier studies is untenable on both theoretical and empirical grounds. Movements in commodity prices in this model depend on two distinct factors—one pertaining directly to the tax, and the other based on factor prices which inevitably change as a result of the tax. The relative strength of these two effects is an empirical matter and is affected by factor shares, elasticities of substitution and demand, and the particular taxes involved. There is no a priori reason to believe that the two effects will always reinforce each other. A numerical illustration based on U.S. data, dealing with the corporation income tax, shows that the factor-price effect is substantial and sometimes at least as large as the direct tax effect. Therefore, predictions of price changes made in earlier studies which have captured only the tax-effect, are liable to be inaccurate.

These results have a direct bearing on questions of economic policy. If a government is planning to levy a tax such as the CIT, accepting the results in the literature, it might conclude that relative price of the output of the taxed sector will rise by about .13 for a tax rate of 1 percent. The actual increase might be twice that much. Since that commodity will be used as an intermediate input by other industries, their costs will also rise and the entire structure of production would be affected. Looking at existing studies, the government might believe that the wage-rental ratio will remain unchanged. That, however, is very unlikely, as Table 1 shows. If the net-of-tax return to capital falls, the level of saving and investment in the economy would fall and adversely affect the rate of economic growth.

For more precise results along these lines, that analytical framework in the paper will have to be converted into a growth model. In keeping with much of growth theory, it could be assumed that one of the two goods is a capital good, the other becoming a wage good. Or, these two goods could be treated as final goods while an investment good is introduced as a *pure* intermediate product in lieu of inter-industry flows. It would also be necessary to replace assumptions about fixed supplies of factors by a growth function for labor and a specification of saving behavior.

Notes

[1]Friedlaender assures us, without proof, that if the assumption of fixed coefficients is supplanted by the usual neo-classical ones, the conclusions will not change. It might be so in her case, but in the present model conclusions do change on account of such assumptions as the analysis in the third and fourth sections will show.

[2]One exception is Fullerton, Shoven, and Whalley (1978), but they assumed that primary factors could not be substituted for intermediate goods (the separability assumption), nor did they derive any analytical results on tax incidence. In the present model, unrestricted substitutability among all inputs is allowed, and the approach, by and large, is analytical.

[3]Simplicity is the strongest argument in favor of (12) although the assumptions made in deriving it, and the restrictions implicitly imposed on underlying utility functions might appear to be unusually strong. We retain this equation because it has been

conventionally used in the tax-incidence literature; therefore, it is easy to compare our results with those derived in earlier work.

[4]For a proof, see Batra, pp. 178–9.

[5]If X_1 is relatively capital intensive ($A > 0$) the share of capital in that industry must be greater than in X_2 ($\theta_{K1} > \theta_{K2}$). Moreover, ϵ is negative, so the first term is also positive. It follows that D is positive in all cases. The sign of r^*, therefore, will depend on the numerator of (17).

[6]Equation (17) can be directly compared with the solution for r^* reported by Harberger (1962). If there are no intermediate goods, or such goods have to be used in fixed proportions in both industries, (17) reduces to the Harberger expression. However, when intermediate goods are present, there will be a distinction between direct and total distributive shares (ρ's and θ's), so the sign of r^* will be the same in the two cases although its magnitude could be different.

[7]The number for σ_{LK} is in Griffin and Gregory (1976), Table 2. They also report own and cross price elasticities (E_{ij}) in Table 3 from which σ's can be computed by using cost shares presented in Berndt and Wood (1975, Table 2):

$$\sigma_{ij} = E_{ij}/S_j,\ i,j = K,L,M$$

where S_j is the cost share of jth input.

Humphrey and Moroney (1975) also have several estimates of σ_{LK} (natural resources form the third variable), all positive, with a majority well above unity. However, there are no intermediate goods in their analysis.

[8]These data were also used in Bhatia (1981) where more information on these calculations is available. We have tried to match definitions in the two classifications as closely as possible. It is assumed that "Miscellaneous Agricultural Products" in Leontief's classification corresponds to "Farms" in Harberger's set up, and "Agricultural, Forestry, and Fishery Services" in the former matches with "Agricultural Services, Forestry, Fisheries" in the latter, and so on.

[9]The corresponding numbers for rows 2 and 3 with other σ's equal to unity are as follows:

$\sigma_D \rightarrow$	-0.5	-1.0	-1.5	$\epsilon = 0$
r^*/T^*_{K1}				
Row 2	−.66	−.62	−.58	−.71
Row 3	−.55	−.51	−.47	−.60

Appendix

Some of the steps required for arriving at a^*_{ij} and R^*_{ij} are given below to illustrate the general approach.

For a tax on capital in X_1

$$a_{ij} = a_{ij}(w, r_1, p_k)(i = L,K,1,2; j,k, = 1,2, j \neq k), \text{ and } r_1 = r(1 + t_{K1}) \quad (1)$$

By totally differentiating it we get ($w^* = 0$):

$$a^*_{K1} = -\rho_{L1}\sigma^1_{LK}r^* + \rho_{21}\sigma^1_{K2}p^*_2 - \rho_{L1}\sigma^1_{LK}T^*_{K1} \quad (2)$$

$$a^*_{21} = -\rho_{K1}\sigma^1_{K2}r^* + \rho_{21}\sigma^1_{22}p^*_2 \quad (3)$$

where the partial elasticity of substitution between labor and capital in the first industry can be defined as

$$\rho_{L1}\sigma^1_{KL} = \frac{\partial a_{K1}}{\partial w}\frac{w}{a_{K1}}$$

Definitions of other σ's are analogous. We know (Allen, p. 505) that

$$\rho_{L1}\sigma^1_{LL} + \rho_{K1}\sigma^1_{LK} + \rho_{21}\sigma^1_{L2} = 0 \tag{4}$$

Equations (2) and (3) can be simplified by using (4) and the zero-profit conditions (10) and (11) in the paper.

Recall that by definition $R_{K1} = (a_{K1} + a_{K2}a_{21})/(1 - a_{12}a_{21})$. Therefore,

$$R^*_{K1} = \frac{dR_{K1}}{R_{K1}} = \frac{a_{K1}a^*_{K1} + a_{21}a_{K2}a^*_{21} + a_{21}(a_{K2}a^*_{K2} + a_{12}R_{K1}a^*_{12})}{a_{K1} + a_{K2}a_{21}}$$

Simple substitutions and rearranging of terms complete the derivation.

References

Aaron, H., "The Differential Price Effects of a Value-Added Tax," *National Tax Journal*, June 1968, 162–75.

Allen, R. G. D., *Mathematical Analysis for Economists*, Macmillan, 1969.

Ballentine, J. G., and Eris, I., "On the General Equilibrium Analysis of Tax Incidence," *Journal of Political Economy*, June 1975, 83, 633–44.

Batra, R. N., *Studies in the Pure Theory of International Trade*, Macmillan, 1974.

Berndt, E. R., and Wood, D. O., "Technology, Prices, and the Derived Demand for Energy," *Review of Economic Statistics*, 47 (1965): 259–68.

Bhatia, K. B., "Intermediate Goods and the Incidence of the Corporation Income Tax," *Journal of Public Economics*, 16 (1981), 93–112.

Bishop, R. L., "The Effects of Specific and Ad Valorem Taxes," *Quarterly Journal of Economics*, May 68, 82, 198–218.

Friedlaender, A. F., "Indirect Taxes and Relative Prices," *Quarterly Journal of Economics*, February 1967, 81, 125–39.

Fullerton, D., Shoven, J., and Whalley, J., "General Equilibrium Analysis of U.S. Taxation Policy in 1978," Compendium of Tax Research Washington: U.S. Treasury Department, 1978, 23–63.

Harberger, A. C., "The Incidence of the Corporation Income Tax," *Journal of Political Economy*, June 1962, 70, 215–40.

Hudson, E. A., and Jorgenson, D. W., "U.S. Energy Policy and Economic Growth, 1975–2000," *Bell Journal of Economics*, 5 (1974): 461–514.

Humphrey, D. B., and Moroney, J. R., "Substitution Among Capital, Labor, and Natural Resource Products in American Manufacturing," *Journal of Political Economy*, 83 (1975): 57–82.

Jones, R. W., "The Structure of Simple General Equilibrium Models," *Journal of Political Economy*, 72 (1965): 557–72.

Jones, R. W., "Distortions in Factor Markets and the General Equilibrium Model of Production," *Journal of Political Economy*, May/June 1971, 79. 437–59.

Leontief, W. W., "The Structure of the U.S. Economy," *Scientific American*, April 1965, 212, 25–35.

Melvin, J. R., "Short-Run Price Effects of the Corporate Income Tax and Implications for International Trade," *American Economic Review*, December 1979, 69, 250–62.

Musgrave, R. A., *The Theory of Public Finance*, McGraw-Hill, 1959.

Ratti, R. A., and Shome, P., "The Incidence of the Corporation Income Tax: A Long-Run Specific Factor Model," *Southern Journal of Economics*, July 1977, 44, 85–98.

Taubman, P., "The Effects of Ad Valorem and Specific Taxes on Prices," *Quarterly Journal of Economics*, November 1965, 79, 649–56.

Résumé

Pour une allocation efficace des ressources à un moment donné dans le temps aussi bien que pour la croissance économique, les prix doivent refléter la rareté relative des différents biens et facteurs de production. Les prix sont influencés aussi par différents types de taxes et il est très difficile de prévoir de tels effets fiscaux quand on prend en compte la structure de production de l'économie globale car la production du secteur taxé est souvent une étape intermédiaire dans la production d'autres biens et services. Cet article, dans un cadre d'équilibre général, examine les effets des taxes frappant les facteurs de production et les produits sur les prix relatifs. L'accent est mis sur les prix à la production mais, en fait, tous les prix—à la fois pour les biens et les facteurs productifs—sont interdépendants.

Dans cette perspective, tous les coefficients d'intrant-extrant sont variables et l'on examine à la fois les facteurs de l'offre et de la demande. On isole un "effet fiscal" direct et un effet "facteur-prix" indirect. Ces deux effets peuvent s'ajouter ou s'équilibrer et leur force relative est une question d'empirisme. Des résultats numériques, basés sur des données américaines à propos de l'impôt sur le revenu des sociétés, montrent que ces deux effets, parfois de force égale, se sont renforcés l'un l'autre. Dans des études antérieures, on a admis des coefficients d'intrant-extrant fixes et laissé de côté les considérations de demande. Les changements de prix ainsi calculés ne peuvent donc être exacts. On étudie aussi les implications de ces résultats sur la croissance économique.

Taxation and the Distribution of Income and Wealth

*Yannis M. Ioannides**
Ryuzo Sato

1. Introduction

Taxation for redistribution has long been suspected of having significant effects on the labor supply, investment, and risk-taking decisions of individuals. As Joseph Stiglitz has emphasized [Stiglitz (1978)], when the endogeneity of the wealth and income distributions is recognized, taxation critically affects such distributions and not always in the ways expected. Nevertheless, surprisingly little work has been done to identify the magnitude of the alleged lasting impact of taxation on capital formation, total output, and welfare in general equilibrium models of the economy. Moreover, there has been hardly any work on the impact of taxation on factor quantities and prices in the context of a theory of the personal distribution of income.

In the present paper we explore the impact of taxation in a general equilibrium model of the distribution of income and wealth. We use a model in which parents' plans to transfer wealth to their children, on one hand, and individuals' decisions about investing in human capital and saving for retirement, on the other, interact to produce an economy-wide distribution of wealth.

The role of inheritance and of intergenerational transfers as causes of inequality in consumption and well-being has been better understood since the seminal paper by Joseph Stiglitz [Stiglitz (1969)]. Income inequality and its relationship to ability and education was elu-

*We thank David Bevan, Fischer Black, and Joseph Stiglitz for their helpful comments. Yannis Ioannides is Professor of Economics, School of Management, Boston University, U.S.A., and Athens School of Economics and Business, Greece; Ryuzo Sato is Professor of Economics, Department of Economics, Brown University, U.S.A.

Public Finance and Economic Growth. Proceedings of the 37th Congress of the International Institute of Public Finance. Tokyo, 1981, pp. 367–386

cidated by Gary Becker in his Woytinsky Lecture [Becker (1967); see also Becker and Tomes (1979), Atkinson and Stiglitz (1980), and Tomes (1981), for more recent contributions]. The basic dynamic model (in the tradition of neoclassical growth models), relating the distribution of wealth to the distribution of wages in Stiglitz, *op. cit.*, has been developed further by incorporating random return to capital, random regression of abilities to the mean across generations, and human capital investment [Stiglitz (1978)]. Stiglitz emphasizes the distinction between planned and unplanned bequests. The need for empirical research on the contribution of intergenerational transfer to aggregate capital accumulation has been forcefully emphasized by L. J. Kotlikoff and L. H. Summers [Kotlikoff and Summers (1981)] who argue that only a small fraction—in the order of .20, according to their calculation—of actual capital accumulation in the U.S. can be traced to life-cycle savings.

In this paper, we consider the total effect of several separate sources of change in the wealth distribution. Differences among individuals with respect to ability and inherited wealth combine to produce differences in life-cycle savings and transfers to descendants.[1] Its chief features are: first, that it is built on a behavioral model of individual life-cycle optimization. Thus, saving for retirement and for transfers to descendants are endogenously determined and all relevant coefficients can be computed in closed form as functions of prices and taste parameters. Second, all associated distributions of interest, such as the distribution of intergenerational transfers, of total lifetime wealth, and of income and its components are of the Pareto-Levy type with the same characteristic exponent and symmetry parameter. As a result, the Pareto distributions which approximate their upper tails have all the same exponents and skewness characteristics.

Although a relatively small number of parameters must be specified *a priori*, the general equilibrium can only be solved numerically. It is nevertheless possible to analyze the impact of taxation on the determinants of the model and the statistics of all endogenous distributions with factor prices held constant. The full impact of taxation, both through its effects on structural parameters and on equilibrium factor prices can be dealt with only computationally[2] and is the subject of another paper [Ioannides (1981)].

The remainder of this paper is organized as follows. Section 2 presents the basic elements of the model by summarizing the results of Ioannides and Sato (1981). Section 3 deals with the taxation of total individual wealth by means of a linear tax. Section 4 deals with the taxation of wealth transfers. Section 5 deals with the taxation of total income, of wage and of interest income, and discusses the subsidization of education as a policy for income redistribution.

2. The Basic Model

We shall consider first the behavior of individuals. We assume an overlapping-generations model [Samuelson (1958)] with individuals living for two periods. Each individual is endowed at birth with a certain ability—a characteristic chosen by nature—whose distribution across each and every generation is given by $\Phi(m)$. There is no population growth. In the beginning of every period each old individual gives birth to one offspring. Immediately after an individual is born he receives training (education). Training requires resources but takes place instantaneously. An individual of the tth generation with ability m_t who receives e_t units of education acquires an earning capacity $h(m_t,e_t)$. We assume that

$$h = me^{\epsilon}, \quad 0 < \epsilon < 1. \tag{1}$$

Every individual of the tth generation receives from his parent an "endowment" which is, technically, a gift *inter vivos* and which will be referred to as a transfer, as well, in the sequel. Each individual then chooses his education and lifetime consumption, saving and wealth transfer plan at the beginning of the first period of his lifetime, with knowledge of his own ability. Consumption takes place in the beginning of each period. Earnings from labor supplied during the first period and returns from savings made in the beginning of the first period are received at the end of the first period. Individuals are assumed to work only during the first period of their lives and retire in the second. Labor supply (in efficiency units) is inelastic, after education has been received.

A member of the tth generation with ability m_t and endowment x_{t-1} chooses e_t so as to maximize $(W/(1 + r))\, h(m_t,e_t) - e_t$, where r and W denote the capital rental and wage rates, respectively. No time subscripts are used for W and r because we are concerned with steady state equilibrium only. Under assumption (1), the optimal level of education, $e^*(m_t,\rho)$, is given by:

$$e^*(m_t,\rho) = \epsilon'\rho^{-1/1-\epsilon}\, m_t^{1/1-\epsilon}, \tag{2}$$

where $\epsilon' \equiv \epsilon^{1/1-\epsilon}$, $\rho = (1 + r)/W$. The dependence of education on the factor price ratio partially alleviates the effect of an inelastic labor supply.

Let us use μ_t to denote the optimum present value of the return to the individual's human capital investment net of the cost of acquiring it:

$$\mu_t = \frac{1}{\rho} h(m_t, e^*) - e^*.$$

Under the assumptions made above μ_t is given by:

$$\mu_t = \epsilon'' \rho^{-1/1-\epsilon} m_t^{1/1-\epsilon},$$

$$\text{where} \quad \epsilon'' \equiv (1 - \epsilon)\epsilon^{\epsilon/1-\epsilon} \tag{3}$$

Lifecycle Optimization and Intergenerational Transfers

If we use $p' = (p_y, p_0, p_x)$ to denote the prices of first period consumption c_t^y, second period consumption c_t^0, and endowment to his offspring x_t, an individual's lifetime budget constraint is given by:

$$p_y c_t^y + p_0 c_t^0 + p_x x_t = \mu_t + x_{t-1}. \tag{4}$$

When the produced good is used as the numeraire and there is no taxation $p' = (1, 1/(1 + r), 1/(1 + r))$. We shall use $B^*(x_{t-1}, m_t, \rho)$ to denote the right hand side of (4), an individual's total lifetime wealth, discounted to the beginning of his life: $B_t^* = x_{t-1} + \mu_t$.
Under assumption (1), this is given by:

$$B^*(x_{t-1}, m_t, \rho) = x_{t-1} + \epsilon'' m_t^{1/1-\epsilon} \rho^{-1/1-\epsilon}. \tag{5}$$

For the utility function as a function of $(c_t^y, c_t^0; B^*(x_t, M_{t+1}, \rho))$ we assume

$$U(c^y, c^0; b) = -n_1 \exp[-\nu_1 c^y] - n_2 \exp[-\nu_2 c^0] - -n_3 \exp[-\nu_3 b]; \tag{6}$$

$$n_i, \nu_i > 0, i = 1, 2, 3; \tag{6.1}$$

where b denotes the child's wealth, $B^*(x_t, M_{t+1}, \rho)$, and the n_i's and the ν_i's are constants. Maximizing $E_{M_{t+1}}[U(c_t^y, c_t^0; B^*(x_t, M_{t+1}, \rho))]$ subject to the budget constraint (4) gives a solution $(C^y, C^0; X)$ whose components are linear in $B^*(x_{t-1}, m_t, \rho)$. Specifically, the optimal lifetime consumption bundle is given by:

$$c_t^y = a_1 B^*(x_{t-1}, m_t, \rho) + b_1; \tag{6.2}$$

$$c_t^0 = a_2 B^*(x_{t-1}, m_t, \rho) + b_2; \tag{6.3}$$

$$x_t = a_3 B^*(x_{t-1}, m_t, \rho) + b_3; \tag{6.4}$$

where the coefficients a_i and b_i are defined as follows:

$$a_1 = \frac{\nu_2\nu_3}{D}, \; a_2 = \frac{\nu_1\nu_3}{D}, \; a_3 = \frac{\nu_1\nu_2}{D}; \tag{6.5}$$

$$D = \nu_1\nu_2 p_x + \nu_1\nu_3 p_0 + \nu_2\nu_3 p_y; \tag{6.6}$$

$$b_1 = [(\nu_3 p_0 + \nu_2 p_x)Z_1 + \nu_2 p_x Z_2]\frac{1}{D}; \tag{6.7}$$

$$b_2 = [\nu_1 p_x Z_2 - \nu_3 p_y Z_1]\frac{1}{D}; \tag{6.8}$$

$$b_3 = -[\nu_2 p_y Z_1 + (\nu_1 p_0 + \nu_2 p_y)Z_2]\frac{1}{D}; \tag{6.9}$$

$$Z_1 = \log\frac{n_1\nu_1 p_0}{n_2\nu_2 p_x}; \quad Z_3 = E_{M_{t+1}}[\exp[-\nu_3\mu_{t+1}]]; \tag{7.1}$$

$$Z_2 = \log\frac{n_2\nu_2 p_x}{n_3\nu_3 Z_3 p_0}. \tag{7.2}$$

Note that we do not constrain the consumption bundle—and, in particular, the transfer x_t—to be positive. We rely, instead, on parameter values to ensure such positivity. This is clearly a weakness of the model. [See Bevan (1979) and Bevan and Stiglitz (1979).] Also, for the remainder of this paper we shall assume that a child's ability is independent of that of his parents'. The resulting absence of "regression to the mean" clearly limits the generality of the model.

The Distribution of Wealth

The distribution function of total wealth can be obtained once the distribution function $\Gamma(\cdot)$ of initial endowments (transfers), x_t, is known. The latter can be obtained from solving the functional equation:

$$\Gamma(q) = \text{Prob}\,[a_3(x_{t-1} + \mu_t) + b_3 \leq q]. \tag{8}$$

This equation expresses the condition that the proportion of young members of two consecutive generations who receive initial endowments less or equal to q be the same. It can be shown that under our assumptions the equilibrium distribution Γ is a Pareto-Levy variable [Ioannides and Sato, *op. cit.*].

The proof is based on showing that a current realization of the initial wealth endowment can be expressed as a linearly weighted sum of independent and identically distributed random variables. Since individuals' net return from human capital investment, the μ's, are (positively) skewed under our assumptions, the *limit* distribution of wealth endowments $\Gamma(\cdot)$ must obey a stable law. The statistics of this limit distribution could be obtained in terms of prices, of the statistics of μ and of the various parameters. Rather than pursue this here, we seek specific results about the relationship between the statistics of the distributions of income, wealth and their components by assuming that μ *itself* obeys a stable law.

It suffices in our case, in fact, to assume that the auxiliary variable $\tilde{m}$, $\tilde{m} = m^{1/(1-\epsilon)}$ is distributed according to a stable law with parameters $(\tilde{\alpha}, \tilde{\beta}, \tilde{\delta}, \tilde{\sigma})$. These parameters are labeled, respectively, characteristic exponent and symmetry, location and scale parameters. To ensure existence of finite values for the mean and for Z_3 we must assume $\tilde{\alpha} > 1$ and $\tilde{\beta} = 2 - \tilde{\alpha}$.[3] In this case, Z_3 can be expressed in terms of the moment generating function of the distribution function of the μ's, Ψ, at $-\nu_3$. That is $Z_3 = \exp\,[-\nu_3\delta + \nu_3^{\tilde{\alpha}}\sigma\bar{\beta}]$, where $\bar{\beta} = \int[e^{-q} - 1 + q]dq/q^{\tilde{\alpha}+1}$ [Lucaks (1970), p. 125].

The location parameter $\tilde{\delta}$ is equal to the mean and the scale parameter $\tilde{\sigma}$ is a measure of dispersion (which becomes equal to one-half of the variance when $\alpha = 2$). Its characteristic function, as function of s is:

$$\exp\left[i\tilde{\delta}s - \tilde{\sigma}|s|^{\alpha}\left(1 - i\tilde{\beta}\frac{s}{|s|}\tan\left(\frac{\pi\tilde{\alpha}}{2}\right)\right)\right], \quad \text{where } i = \sqrt{-1}.$$

The parameters $(\alpha, \beta, \delta, \sigma)$ of the distribution function $\Psi(\cdot)$ of total returns from human capital investment are obtained in terms of $(\tilde{\alpha}, \tilde{\beta}, \tilde{\delta}, \tilde{\sigma})$ as follows:

$$\alpha = \tilde{\alpha},\ \beta = \tilde{\beta},\ \delta = \epsilon''\rho^{-1/1-\epsilon}\,\tilde{\delta},\ \sigma = [\epsilon''\rho^{-1/1-\epsilon}]^{\tilde{\alpha}}\tilde{\sigma}. \tag{9}$$

Some properties of the distribution function of total returns from human capital investments derive immediately from (9). Both distributions have the same characteristic exponent and symmetry parameter. The location and scale parameters of $\Psi(\cdot)$ depend upon the factor price ratio ρ.

The parameters $(\alpha_x, \beta_x, \delta_x, \sigma_x)$ of the equilibrium distribution of endowments, $\Gamma(\cdot)$, can be obtained in terms of the parameters of $\Psi(\cdot)$ by using characteristic functions and the functional equation (8). They are as follows:

$$\alpha_x = \alpha,\ \beta_x = \beta,\ \delta_x = \frac{a_3}{1 - a_3}\delta + \frac{b_3}{1 - a_3},\ \sigma_x = \frac{a_3^\alpha}{1 - a_3^\alpha}\sigma. \tag{10}$$

Some properties of the equilibrium distribution of endowments can now be discussed. The equilibrium distribution of endowments has the same symmetry parameter as the distribution of total returns from human capital investments and is skewed. Whether or not the scale parameter σ_x exceeds σ depends upon the value of a_3 and α.

The equilibrium distribution of endowments and the distribution of total returns from human capital investments are sufficient to determine all other distributions of interest for given factor prices. For example, for the equilibrium distribution of wage income and of interest income we can work as follows. The distribution H(·) of the present value of labor income, $w = (W/(1 + r))\ h(m, e^*)$, is given by the distribution function of $(1 + (\epsilon'/\epsilon''))\mu$. Thus:

$$\alpha_w = \alpha,\ \beta_w = \beta,\ \delta_w = \epsilon^{\epsilon/1-\epsilon}\ \rho^{-1/1-\epsilon}\tilde{\delta},\ \sigma_w = [\epsilon^{\epsilon/1-\epsilon}\ \rho^{-1/1-\epsilon}]^\alpha\tilde{\sigma}. \tag{11}$$

The distribution function $K(\cdot)$ of capital income $r\kappa$,

$$r\kappa = r\left[(1 - a_1)x - \left(\frac{\epsilon}{1 - \epsilon} + a_1\right)\mu - b_1\right],$$

is obtained by convolution and scaling operations on Γ and Ψ and its parameters are:

$$\alpha_r = \alpha,\ \beta_r = \beta,\ \delta_r = r(1 - a_1)\delta_x - r\left(\frac{\epsilon}{1 - \epsilon} + a_1\right)\delta - rb_1,$$

$$\sigma_r = r^\alpha\left[(1 - a_1)^\alpha\sigma_x + \left(\frac{\epsilon}{1 - \epsilon} + a_1\right)^\alpha\sigma\right]. \tag{12}$$

Both $H(\cdot)$ and $K(\cdot)$ have the characteristic exponent and symmetry parameter of the distribution of total returns from human capital investments, α and β respectively.

The distribution function of total lifetime wealth across the population, the distribution function of $B^* = x + \mu$, is given by the convolution of $\Gamma(\cdot)$ and $\Psi(\cdot)$. The parameters of the characteristic function of $\Gamma^*\Psi$, $(\alpha_b, \beta_b, \delta_b, \sigma_b)$ are given by:

$$\alpha_b = \alpha, \quad \beta_b = \beta; \tag{13.1}$$

$$\delta_b = \frac{\delta + b_3}{1 - a_3}, \quad \sigma_b = \frac{1}{1 - a_3^\alpha}\sigma. \tag{13.2}$$

The characteristic exponent and the symmetry parameter are the same, again. The dispersion parameter of the distribution of total wealth is always greater than that of the distribution of total returns from human capital investment. Under our assumptions, average total wealth, δ_b, is equal to the aggregate total wealth in the economy.

The Behavior of Firms

To complete the description of the general equilibrium model we must analyze the behavior of firms. We assume, for simplicity, a single firm, which used capital and effective labor with a constant returns to scale technology to produce the single output which is used for both consumption and investment. The output per capita available in the beginning of the tth period (when the t generation is born) has been produced with the physical capital carried forward and the labor (human capital) possessed by the $(t - 1)$ generation. Physical capital does not depreciate. Thus, output available per person of the $(t - 1)$ generation in the beginning of the tth period is given by

$$Y(k_{t-1}, \ell_{t-1});$$

where k_{t-1} and ℓ_{t-1} denote, respectively, total physical capital and total effective labor (in efficiency units) per person of the $(t - 1)$ generation.

General Equilibrium

The general equilibrium model can be fully determined by requiring that the wage rate and the interest rate are equal to the marginal products of capital and labor respectively:

$$Y_k(k, \ell) = r; \tag{14.1}$$

$$Y_\ell(k, \ell) = W. \tag{14.2}$$

Under the assumption that the characteristic exponent α is greater than unity, the means of all relevant distributions are finite and the aggregate quantities of labor and capital are given by

$$\ell = \epsilon^{\epsilon/1-\epsilon}\rho^{-\epsilon/1-\epsilon}\tilde{\delta}; \tag{15.1}$$

$$k = \delta_x - \epsilon'\rho^{-1/1-\epsilon}\tilde{\delta} - a_1\delta_b - b_1. \tag{15.2}$$

The general equilibrium model is fully determined once the tax prices $p' = (p_y, p_0, p_x)$ are given. By substituting in (14.1) and (14.2) for ℓ and k from (15.1–2) we obtain a system of equations in W and r.

The analysis of optimal taxation is substantially simplified because under the assumptions made above, the simple expression for an individual's indirect utility function $Ne^{-\nu B*}$, with $\nu = \nu_1\nu_2\nu_3/D$, and

$$N = -(n_1 e^{-\nu_1 b_1} + n_2 e^{-\nu_2 b_2} + n_3 e^{-\nu_3 b_3} Z_3),$$

leads to a closed-form expression for average social utility. That is, average individual indirect utility across the population, $V = N\,E\,[\exp[-\nu(x + \mu)]]$, can be written explicitly as follows:

$$V = N \exp\left[-\frac{\delta + b_3}{1 - a_3}\nu + \frac{\nu^\alpha \sigma}{1 - a_3^\alpha}\bar{\beta}\right], \tag{16}$$

where $\bar{\beta}$ is as defined above. The significance of this result will be appreciated in the discussion of taxation which follows. Note that $\bar{\beta}$ effectively "corrects" for dispersion even though the variance is not finite.

3. The Impact of Taxation

Redistributive taxation may affect wealth, income, and social welfare in a number of distinct ways. First, it may directly affect the parameters of the endogenous wealth transfers distribution $\Gamma(\cdot)$, which is the "state variable" in our model. Second, total savings and their allocation to physical and human capital may be affected because taxation alters behavioral coefficients. And third, relative factor prices may be affected both directly and indirectly (through the general equilibrium repercussions of taxation on factor quantities).

Our framework is general enough to allow us to examine taxes imposed on *stocks*, such as wealth and wealth transfers, and on *flows*, such as income (and its various components) and consumption. In this paper we shall seek specific results by exploring linear taxes only. All the taxes we consider are fully defined by a constant marginal tax rate τ and a redistributive lump-sum transfer T. These two parameters are not independent; they are related through the government budget constraint. All after-tax distribution functions of interest can be fully described, because we have restricted our attention to linear taxes.

As expected, the characteristic exponent and the symmetry parameter remain invariant, α and β, but the other two parameters change.

Since individuals in our model care about the welfare of their descendants, rationality suggests that they fully anticipate the effect of taxes on their descendants, as well. This assumption, along with the assumption that individuals make their endowment decisions under uncertainty about their offsprings' abilities, is responsible for introducing an additional effect of taxation. Taxation affects the riskiness of offsprings' total lifetime wealth as perceived by parents. Therefore, taxation in this model generates an efficiency effect [c.f., Eaton and Rosen, (1980)] because it provides for the sharing of a privately non-diversifiable risk.

We shall use the terms "efficient" and "optimal" to denote tax systems which maximize aggregate wealth and social welfare, respectively. Here, the former is measured by the mean total wealth, δ_b, net of education costs, and the latter by average lifetime utility across the population V—the simple utilitarian welfare criterion that we have adopted. While the values of the tax parameters of efficient and optimal tax systems can be characterized by well-defined, in each case, optimization problems, we will not discuss such formulations. Note that by restricting our attention to redistributive taxation we do not deal with the possibility that optimality may require saving (or dissaving) by the government.

Below we examine the impact on our general equilibrium system of imposing linear taxes on total wealth. In Section 4 we discuss the effects of taxing transfers of wealth, by examining wealth transfer taxes levied on donors and on recipients. Section 5 deals with the taxation of wage income and of interest income. The effects of a tax (or subsidy) on education are also discussed there. Since it is too complicated to illuminate the effect of taxation on equilibrium factor prices, we restrict our attention to the structural impact of taxation, while factor prices are held constant. The effects of taxation on factor prices and the effects of changes in factor prices on the distribution of income and wealth are discussed by Joseph Stiglitz (1978).

Taxation of Total Wealth

With a linear tax on total discounted lifetime wealth, individuals pay tax equal to $\tau(x_{-1} + \mu)$, where τ is a constant marginal rate, and receive a redistributive transfer T. We shall refrain from using subscripts as long as no confusion arises. If individuals *ignore* the impact of the tax on their descendants, when deciding on their endowments to them, optimal lifecycle decisions are given by equations (6.2–4), with $p_y = 1$, $p_0 = p_x = 1/(1 + r)$, and $(1 - \tau)(x_{-1} + \mu) + T$ in the place of B^* in the budget constraint (but not where the descendant's wealth enters the parent's utility function). If it is assumed, on the other hand, that individuals fully *anticipate* the impact of wealth taxation on their descendants' welfare, then it is the descendants' net after-tax wealth which enters the parents' utility functions. In this case, the last term of an individual's expected utility function becomes $-n_3 e^{-\nu_3(1-\tau)x} e^{-\nu_3 T} E_M[e^{-\nu_3(1-\tau)\mu}]$. By using Z_3' and ν_3' in the places of Z_3 and ν_3 respectively,

$$\nu_3' = (1 - \tau)\nu_3, \; Z_3' = \exp\left[-\nu_3 T - \delta\nu_3' + (\nu_3')^{\alpha}\, \sigma\bar{\beta}\right].$$

the expressions for the optimal lifecycle decisions (6.2–9, 7.1–2) hold. The equilibrium distribution function $\Gamma(\cdot)$ of wealth endowments is given by the functional equation (8), *mutatis mutandis*, i.e.:

$$\Gamma(q) = \text{Prob}\left[(1 - \tau)\, a_3(x_{-1} + \mu) + a_3 T + b_3 \le q\right]. \tag{17}$$

The behavioral coefficients, given by (6.5–9, 7.1–2), do not contain the tax parameters. For the parameters of the distribution of (pretax) endowments $\Gamma(\cdot)$ we have:

$$\delta_x = \frac{a_3\delta + b_3}{1 - a_3}; \quad \sigma_x = \frac{(1 - \tau)^{\alpha} a_3^{\alpha}}{1 - (1 - \tau)^{\alpha} a_3^{\alpha}}\, \sigma. \tag{18}$$

The government budget constraint $\tau(\delta_x + \delta) = T$ is simplified to become $T = \tau(\delta + b_3)/(1 - a_3)$. For the distribution of total wealth we have:

$$\delta_b = \frac{\delta + b_3}{1 - a_3}, \quad \sigma_b = \frac{(1 - \tau)^{\alpha}}{1 - (1 - \tau)^{\alpha} a_3^{\alpha}}\, \sigma. \tag{19}$$

With factor prices held fixed, an increase in the marginal tax rate has the following effects on the distribution of total wealth. As the term a_3 increases and $(1 - \tau)a_3$ decreases, dispersion, as measured by the scale parameter, decreases but the effect on average total wealth is indeterminate, because the effect on b_3 is indeterminate.

The expressions (15.1–2) for aggregate effective labor and for capital are not affected by taxation, although the tax parameters explicitly enter their coefficients a_1, a_3, b_1, and b_3. The effects of a small increase in the marginal rate on dispersion characteristics, with equilibrium factor prices being held fixed, are as follows. The dispersion of wealth endowments and of total wealth decreases, of wage income is unaffected and of interest income may increase or decrease. The characteristic exponent and the symmetry parameter remain unaffected.

The optimal linear total wealth tax is defined by the values of the tax parameters $\langle \tau, T \rangle$ which maximize V,

$$V = -(n_1 e^{-\nu_1 b_1} + n_2 e^{-\nu_2 b_2} + n_3 e^{-\nu_3' b_3} Z_3') \cdot \exp\left[-\frac{\delta + b_3}{1 - a_3}\nu' + \frac{(\nu')^\alpha (1-\tau)^\alpha}{1 - (1-\tau)^\alpha a_3^\alpha} \sigma\bar{\beta} \right], \tag{20}$$

subject to equilibrium in factor markets and the government budget constraint.

The efficient total wealth tax, on the other hand, maximizes average after tax wealth, $(\delta + b_3)/(1 - a_3)$, subject to the same constraints.

4. Taxation of Wealth Transfers

Rather than taxing total wealth, we may tax wealth transfers. There are, of course, two ways of doing so. One is to tax the recipients of wealth transfers, and the other is to tax the donors.

Taxing *donors* changes the tax price to $p' = (1, 1/(1 + r), \tau_x + 1/(1 + r))$. The accompanying lump sum grant is added to both the wealth side of a donor's budget constraint and his child's wealth where it enters the donor's utility function. Therefore, individuals' budget constraints become:

$$c^y + \frac{1}{1+r} c^0 + \left(\tau_x + \frac{1}{1+r}\right) x = x_{-1} + \mu + T; \tag{21}$$

where τ_x and T denote respectively the proportional tax rate and the redistributive transfer. The behavioral coefficients are given by (6.2–9, 7.1–2) with $p_y = 1$, $p_0 = 1/(1 + r)$, $p_x = \tau_x + 1/(1 + r)$, $B^* = x_{-1} + \mu + T$, and $Z_3' = e^{-\nu_3 T} Z_3$ in the place of Z_3. That is:

$$Z_3' = \exp\left[-\nu_3 T - \delta\nu_3 + \nu_3^\alpha \sigma \bar{\beta}\right] \tag{22}$$

The government budget constraint $T = \tau_x[a_3(\delta + \delta_x + T) + b_3]$ by using $\delta_x = [a_3(\delta + T) + b_3]/(1 - a_3)$ becomes:

$$T = \frac{\tau_x}{1 - (1 + \tau_x)a_3}(a_3\delta + b_3) \tag{23}$$

The parameters of the distribution of endowments $\Gamma(\cdot)$ are:

$$\delta_x = \frac{a_3\delta + b_3}{1 - (1 + \tau_x)a_3}, \quad \sigma_x = \frac{a_3^\alpha}{1 - a_3^\alpha}\sigma. \tag{24}$$

As expected, the characteristic exponent and the symmetry parameter remain the same. The expression for the scale parameter also remain unaltered. For the distribution function of total wealth we have:

$$\delta_b = \frac{\delta + (1 + \tau_x)b_3}{1 - (1 + \tau_x)a_3}, \quad \sigma_b = \frac{1}{1 - a_3^\alpha}\sigma. \tag{25}$$

With factor prices held fixed, an increase in the marginal tax rate has the following effects: Since a_3 decreases, dispersion of total wealth decreases, but the effect on average total wealth is indeterminate, again.

The optimal linear wealth transfer tax levied on donors is defined by the values of parameters $\langle \tau_x, T \rangle$ which maximize

$$V = -(n_1 e^{-\nu_1 b_1} + n_2 e^{-\nu_2 b_2} + n_3 e^{-\nu_3 b_3} Z_3') \cdot \exp\left[-\frac{\delta + b_3(1 + \tau_x)}{1 - (1 + \tau_x)a_3}\nu + \nu^\alpha \sigma \frac{1}{1 - a_3^\alpha}\bar{\beta} \right], \tag{26}$$

subject to equilibrium in the factor markets and the government budget constraint.

The corresponding efficient tax system maximizes average (after tax) wealth $(\delta + b_3(1 + \tau_x))/(1 - (1 + \tau_x)a_3)$ subject to the same set of constraints.

We now turn to the impact of a linear tax on wealth endowments when it is levied on *recipients*. Such a tax affects the wealth side of the budget constraint and, under the assumption that its impact on descendants *is fully anticipated* by parents, the utility function as well. Total after-tax wealth becomes $(1 - \tau_x)x_{-1} + T + \mu$, where x_{-1} is pretax endowment. The behavioral coefficients are given by (6.2–9, 7.1–2) with $p_y = 1$, $p_0 = p_x = 1/(1 + r)$, and $B^* = (1 - \tau_x)x_{-1} + \mu + T$, $\nu_3' = (1 - \tau_x)\nu_3$, and Z_3' is given by:

$$Z_3' = \exp\left[-\nu_3\tau_x \frac{a_3\delta + b_3}{1 - a_3} - \delta\nu_3 + \sigma\nu_3\bar{\beta} \right]$$

The functional equation (8), *mutatis mutandis*,

$$\Gamma(q) = \text{Prob}\,[a_3[(1 - \tau_x)x_{-1} + \mu + T] + b_3 \leq q],$$

determines the distribution of (pretax) endowments. With respect to its parameters, the characteristic exponent and the symmetry parameter remain unchanged. The expression from (10) for the average (after tax) endowment is unaltered but that of the scale parameter becomes:

$$\sigma_x = \frac{(1 - \tau_x)^\alpha a_3^\alpha}{1 - (1 - \tau_x)^\alpha a_3^\alpha}\,\sigma. \tag{27}$$

This is less, *cet. par.*, than the scale parameter for the distribution of wealth endowments when the wealth transfer tax is imposed on donors. For the distribution of total wealth we have:

$$\sigma_b = \frac{\delta + b_3}{1 - a_3}, \quad \sigma_b = \frac{1}{1 - (1 - \tau_x)^\alpha a_3^\alpha}\,\sigma. \tag{28}$$

With factor prices held fixed, an increase in the marginal tax rate reduces the dispersion of total wealth, as measured by the scale parameter of its distribution function, but its effect on average total wealth cannot be determined.

The optimal linear wealth tax levied on recipients is defined by the values of parameters $\langle \tau_x, T \rangle$ which maximize

$$V = -(n_1 e^{-\nu_1 b_1} + n_2 e^{-\nu_2 b_2} + n_3 e^{-\nu_3' b_3} Z_3')$$
$$\cdot \exp\left[-\frac{\delta + b_3}{1 - a_3}\nu + \nu^\alpha \frac{\sigma}{1 - (1 - \tau_x)^\alpha a_3^\alpha}\bar{\beta}\right] \tag{29}$$

subject to equilibrium in the factor markets and the government budget constraint. Similarly, the corresponding efficient tax maximizes $(\delta + b_3)/(1 - a_3)$ subject to the same constraints.

In our general equilibrium model, it is difficult to make comparisons among these three alternative systems of taxing wealth. Yet some general observations are possible and are summarized here. The expressions for average total wealth are the same in the cases of taxing total wealth and wealth transfers to recipients, as in the case without any taxation. For the dispersion parameter, things are different. For a constant a_3, the dispersion parameter of the distribution of total after tax wealth is equal to that of the model without taxation, when the wealth transfer tax is imposed on donors. It falls below that, where the marginal tax rate is the same, if the tax is levied on recipients and still further below, if total wealth is taxed. A definite comparison cannot, however, be made as a_3 depends on the equilibrium values of the wage and of the capital rental rates.

It is nevertheless of particular interest that the two ways of taxing wealth transfers would have, a priori, different welfare implications. When the wealth transfer tax is levied on the recipients it is a component of total wealth that is taxed; when levied on donors, it is the consumption of a particular element of individuals' consumption basket that it is taxed. It is an open question whether this asymmetry will persist, if individuals are assumed to value the (maximum) utility level attained by their descendants' rather than their descendants' (after tax) wealth.

5. Income Taxation

Taxing income or its components rather than wealth can also be easily studied by the model. If we exclude the cost of education from the tax base, neither of these taxes would distort the human capital investment decision. A tax on wage income would simply be a tax on a component of total wealth, the net total return from human capital investment, μ. A tax on savings income, on the other hand, would not only tax a component of total wealth but it would also distort the savings decision. Finally a linear tax on total income can be analyzed by combining the above two taxes.

Taxation of Wage Income

With a linear tax on wage income $\langle \tau, T \rangle$ total after tax wealth becomes $B^* = x_{-1} + (1 - \tau)\mu + T$. The expenditure side of the budget constraint is not affected and thus the tax price vector is $p' = (1, 1/(1 + r), 1/(1 + r))$. The redistributive demogrant is given by the government budget constraint, $T = \tau\epsilon''\rho^{-1/1-\epsilon}\,\tilde{\delta}$. By using Z_3' in the place of Z_3, $Z_3' = \exp\,[-\nu_3\,\tau\epsilon''\rho^{-1/1-\epsilon}\,\tilde{\delta} - (1 - \tau)\nu_3\delta + \nu_3^{\alpha}(1 - \tau)^{\alpha}\sigma\bar{\beta}]$, the expressions for the optimal lifecycle decisions (6.2–9, 7.1–2) hold. The location and dispersion parameters of the distribution function $\Psi(\cdot)$ of total after tax returns from human capital investments are given by:

$$\delta = (1 - \tau)\epsilon''\rho^{-1/1-\epsilon}\tilde{\delta}, \quad \sigma = [\epsilon''\rho^{-1/1-\epsilon}]^{\alpha}\tilde{\sigma}\,(1 - \tau)^{\alpha}. \tag{30}$$

Therefore, taxation reduces, *cet. par.*, both the mean and the scale of parameter of $\Psi(\cdot)$. All other expressions hold, with (δ and σ) as given by (31). Similarly, the expressions for average utility and average net wealth also hold. The chief effect of wage taxation is to reduce both the average and the "dispersion" of net wage income. It is through this effect that the impact on the distribution of total wealth is transmitted.

Taxation of Interest Income

With a linear tax on savings income the budget constraint becomes $c^y + 1/(1 + r))\ c^0 + (1/(1 + r)\ x + \tau_k\ (r/(1 + r))(x_{-1} + \mu - c^y) = x_{-1} + \mu + T$. Wealth, after tax, is $B^* = (1 - \tau_k\ r/(1 + r)(x_{-1} + \mu) + T$ and thus all expressions are the same as in the case of total wealth taxation above, with the following changes: $\tau_k\ r/(1 + r)$ in the place of τ and tax price vector $p' = (1 - \tau_k\ r/(1 + r), 1/(1 + r), 1/(1 + r))$.

The government budget constraint $T = \tau_k\ (r/(1 + r)) \int_{-\infty}^{\infty}\int_{-\infty}^{\infty} (x_{-1} + \mu - c^y)\ d\ \Gamma(x) d\Psi(\mu)$ yields:

$$T = \frac{\tau'}{1 + \tau' a_1} [(1 - (1 - \tau')a_1)(\delta_x + \delta) - b_1] \tag{31}$$

where $\tau' = \tau_k r/(1 + r)$. The functional equation which determines the distribution function of pre-tax endowments $\Gamma(\cdot)$ is: (17), with τ' in the place of τ. For the parameters of $\Gamma(\cdot)$ we have:

$$\delta_x = \frac{1}{1 - (1 - \tau')a_3} [(1 - \tau')a_3\delta + a_3 T + b_3]$$

which by substituting for T yields:

$$\delta_x = \frac{\delta + b_3 + \tau'(b_3 a_1 - b_1 a_3)}{(1 + \tau'(a_1 - a_3))(1 - (1 - \tau')a_3)}.$$

The scale parameter is given by:

$$\sigma_x = \frac{(1 - \tau')^\alpha a_3^\alpha}{1 - (1 - \tau')^\alpha a_3^\alpha}\, \sigma.$$

For the distribution of after tax wealth, we have:

$$\delta_b = \frac{\delta_x + \delta - \tau' b_1}{1 + \tau' b_1}, \quad \sigma_b = \frac{(1-\tau')^\alpha}{1 - (1-\tau')^\alpha a_3^\alpha}\,\sigma. \tag{32}$$

With factor prices held fixed, the dispersion of total wealth decreases, but the effect on its average value cannot be determined.

The efficient interest income tax maximizes δ_b and the optimal interest income tax maximizes average, across the population, indirect utility, V:

$$V = -(n_1 e^{-\nu_1 b_1} + n_2 e^{-\nu_2 b_2} + n_3 e^{-\nu_3' b_3} Z_3') \cdot \exp\left[-\delta_b \nu' + (\nu')^\alpha \frac{(1-\tau')^\alpha}{1-(1-\tau')^\alpha a_3^\alpha}\,\sigma\,\bar{\beta}\right] \tag{33}$$

subject to equilibrium in factor markets and the government budget constraint.

Redistribution through Education

If it is possible to use public policy to affect the cost of acquiring education, such a tool may be used as a means of redistribution. Such a policy may, in fact, be of particular interest, since dispersion in innate ability causes dispersion in net total returns from human capital investment, with the latter being a critical determinant of unequal distribution of wealth and income.

We shall now analyze the impact of subsidizing education at a constant rate θ, per unit of e. The subsidy is assumed to be paid for by a lump sum tax T. An individual chooses e so as to maximize $(1/\rho)\ me^\epsilon - (1 - \theta)e$. With a perfect capital market the human capital investment decision is not affected by the tax T. The optimal amount of education becomes $e^* = \epsilon' \rho^{-1/1-\epsilon} (1-\theta)^{-1/1-\epsilon} m^{1/1-\epsilon}$ and it increases with θ, *cet. par.*

The parameters of the (after tax) distribution function of total returns from human capital investments are given by:

$$\delta = \epsilon'' \rho^{-1/1-\epsilon}(1-\theta)^{-\epsilon/1-\epsilon}\tilde{\delta}, \quad \sigma = [\epsilon'' \rho^{-1/1-\epsilon}(1-\theta)^{-\epsilon/1-\epsilon}]^\alpha \tilde{\sigma}. \tag{34}$$

Both δ and σ increase with θ, with factor prices held fixed. The government budget constraint is:

$$T = \epsilon' \rho^{-1/1-\epsilon} \theta (1 - \theta)^{-1/1-\epsilon} \tilde{\delta}. \tag{35}$$

The average endowment is given by: $\delta_x = (\alpha_3(\delta - T) + b_3)/(1 - a_3)$ and the expression for the scale parameter remains the same. The average net wealth is $\delta_b = \delta - T/1 - a_3$, or from (35) and (36):

$$\delta_b = \frac{1}{1 - a_3} \rho^{-1/1-\epsilon} (1 - \theta)^{-\epsilon/1-\epsilon} \left[\epsilon'' - \frac{\theta}{1 - \theta} \right] \tilde{\delta}, \tag{36}$$

and the expression for the scale parameter of the distribution of wealth remains the same. All expressions for the optimal life cycle decisions hold, with Z_3' in the place of Z_3, $Z_3' = e^{\nu_3 T} Z_3$. With factor prices held constant, an increase in the marginal tax rate increases the dispersion of wealth, but average wealth may decrease or increase depending upon parameter values and the magnitude of θ.

The optimal education subsidy $\langle \theta, T \rangle$ maximizes:

$$V = -(n_1 e^{-\nu_1 b_1} + n_2 e^{-\nu_2 b_2} + n_3 e^{-\nu_3 b_3} Z_3') \cdot \exp \left[-\frac{\delta - T + b_3}{1 - a_3} \nu' + \bar{\beta} \frac{(\nu')^\alpha}{1 - a_3^\alpha} \sigma \right],$$

and the efficient one maximizes $\delta_b = \delta + b_3 - T/1 - a_3$, both subject to the same constraints.

It is clear from above that the effect of the unit subsidy is to increase both the average and the scale parameter of the total net return from human capital investment. The opposite would, of course, be accomplished if education were to be taxed rather than subsidized. Whether either policy is desirable depends upon parameter values.

In sum, taxation of wage income and of interest income can be easily analyzed by our model. Taxing wage income reduces, *cet. par.*, the average net return from human capital investments as well as its dispersion. Similarly, both total wealth and its dispersion are reduced. Interest income taxation reduces the dispersion of transfers, but its effect on the total transfer wealth depends upon the relative magnitudes of a_1, a_3, b_1 and b_3. Similar is the impact on the distribution of total wealth. Its dispersion is reduced but total wealth would decrease, if total transfer wealth does not increase, but the result is otherwise ambiguous. Finally, the effect of subsidizing education was shown to work itself through the distribution function of net returns from human capital investment.

Notes

[1]The specific model without taxation is discussed elsewhere [Ioannides and Sato (1981)] and is thus only summarized here.

[2]There is a rapidly growing body of literature on computational general equilibrium models of taxation. See D. Fullerton *et al.* (1981), for a recent review.

[3]This defines the subfamily of stable laws which exhibit maximal positive skewness. The term Pareto-Levy variable is in fact used by Mandelbrot (1960) to refer specifically to this subfamily. See also Samuelson (1965).

References

Atkinson, Anthony B., 1971, "Capital Taxes, the Redistribution of Wealth and Individual Savings," *Review of Economic Studies*, 209–227.

——— and Ragnar Sandmo, 1980, "The Welfare Implications of the Taxation of Savings," *Economic Journal, 80*, 529–549.

——— and Joseph Stiglitz, 1980, *Lectures on Public Economics*, McGraw-Hill, New York.

Becker, Gary S., 1975, "Human Capital and the Personal Distribution of Income: An Analytical Approach," Woytinsky Lecture, University of Michigan, 1967; reprinted in Becker, *Human Capital*, Second Edition, University of Chicago Press, 94–144.

——— and Nigel Tomes, 1979, "An Equilibrium Theory of the Distribution of Income and Intergenerational Mobility," *Journal of Political Economy*, *87*, 1153–1188.

Bevan, David L., 1979, "Inheritance and the Distribution of Wealth," *Economica*, *46*, 381–402.

Bevan, David L. and Joseph E. Stiglitz, 1979, "Intergenerational Transfers and Inequality," *Greek Economic Review*, *1*, 8–26.

Eaton, John and Harvey, S. Rosen, 1980, "Taxation, Human Capital, and Uncertainty," *American Economic Review*, *70*, 705–715.

Fullerton, Don, Yolanda K. Henderson and John B. Shoven, 1981, "A Comparison of Methodologies in Empirical General Equilibrium Models of Taxation," presented at the NBER Conference on Applied General Equilibrium Models.

Ioannides, Yannis M., 1981, "Taxation of Income and Wealth: Some Numerical Results," (in progress).

——— and Ryuzo Sato, 1981, "A General Equilibrium Theory of the Distribution of Wealth and Intergenerational Transfers," Working Paper No. 80–14 (revised). Boston University, Boston, MA.

Kanbur, Ravi, 1979, "Of Risk Taking and the Personal Distribution of Income," *Journal of Political Economy*, *87*, 769–797.

Kotlikoff, Laurence, J., and Laurence H., Summers, 1981, "The Role of Intergenerational Transfers in Aggregate Capital Accumulation," *Journal of Political Economy*, *89*, 706–732.

Lucaks, Eugene, 1970, *Characteristic Functions*. Griffin: London.

Mandelbrot, Benoit, 1960, "The Pareto-Levy Law and the Distribution of Income," *International Economic Review*, *1*, 79–106.

Samuelson, Paul A., 1958, "An Exact Consumption Loan Model of Interest with or without the Social Contrivance of Money," *Journal of Political Economy*, *66*, 467–482.

Samuelson, Paul A., 1965, "A Fallacy in the Interpretation of Pareto's Law of Alleged Constancy of Income Distribution," *Rivista Internazionale di Scienze Economiche e Commercialli*, April 1965, reprinted in R. C. Merton (ed), *The Collected Sci-*

entific Papers of Paul A. Samuelson, Vol. 3, 404–408, MIT Press, Cambridge, MA.

Stiglitz, Joseph E., 1969, "Distribution of Income and Wealth among Individuals," *Econometrica*, 37, 382–397.

Stiglitz, Joseph E., 1978, "Equality, Taxation and Inheritance," in W. Krelle and Shorrocks (eds.) *The Distribution of Income and Wealth*, North-Holland Publishing Co., Amsterdam.

Tomes, Nigel, 1981, "The Family, Inheritance and the Intergenerational Transmission of Inequality," *Journal of Political Economy*, 89, 928–958.

Résumé

On a longtemps pensé que taxer pour redistribuer avait des effets significatifs sur les décisions des individus en ce qui concerne l'offre de travail, l'investissement des capitaux et la prise de risque. Il est curieux cependant de constater que très peu d'études ont cherché à identifier l'amplitude de cet effet supposé durable de la fiscalité dans les modèles d'équilibre général où les répartitions des revenus et des richesses sont endogènes. Quand l'endogénéité des répartitions des richesses et revenus est reconnue, la fiscalité affecte de façon critique de telles répartitions mais pas toujours dans les sens auxquels on pourrait s'attendre *a priori*.

Dans cet article, nous abordons quelques unes de ces questions en développant un modèle dans lequel les projets de transfert de leurs biens des parents aux enfants, d'une part, et d'autre part, les décisions des particuliers d'investir en capital humain et d'épargner pour la retraite, s'interpénètrent pour déterminer la répartition économique des richesses qui dépend aussi de deux facteurs de dispersion: les différences des capacités des individus et les héritages. Un trait important de ce modèle tient à ce que toutes les répartitions endogènes, telles que les répartitions, entre individus, des transferts entre ascendants et descendants, de la fortune, des revenus salariaux et des revenus personnels globaux appartiennent à la famille des fonctions de distribution Pareto-Levy.

On peut obtenir un ensemble significatif de résultats analytiques concernant l'effet produit par la taxation de la fortune et des transferts de biens entre bénéficiaires et donateurs en se basant sur les statistiques et les propriétés générales de toute distribution endogène, aussi longtemps que les prix du capital et du travail sont supposés constants. Ce n'est que par une étude informatique que l'on peut traiter du plein effet de la fiscalité, à la fois à travers ses répercussions sur des paramètres structuraux et sur l'équilibre entre les taux de salaire et de profit.

Le Rôle de la Fiscalité dans la Lutte contre les Encombrements et les Pollutions

*Par Rémy Prud'homme**

I. Introduction

La fiscalité est généralement perçue comme un mal nécessaire. Comme un mal, parce que les impôts passent pour avoir des effets non souhaitables, et non souhaités, sur les comportements des agents économiques, et notamment sur leurs comportements de travail et d'épargne. Nécessaire, parce qu'il faut bien financer la production des biens publics. Et une partie de la littérature sur les finances publiques est précisément consacrée à comparer ce mal et cette nécessité. Elle vise à définir le taux optimal de l'impôt, qui est celui où l'utilité marginale de la dépense publique est égale à la désutilité marginale du prélèvement public qui la finance.

Cette analyse repose sur une prémice discutable. Il est vrai que tout impôt modifie le comportement des agents économiques qu'il touche. Mais il n'est pas vrai que cette modification des comportements soit nécessairement une mauvaise chose. Elle peut même être une bonne chose, si la modification a des effets socialement souhaitables ou souhaités. A côté des impôts qui se justifient, en quelque sorte, par la dépense qu'ils permettent, on peut—et on doit—imaginer des impôts qui se justifient par les changements de comportement qu'ils engendrent.

Les droits de douane sont un exemple classique, et ancien, de ce type d'impôt. Leur raison d'être n'est pas dans les fonds qu'ils procurent à l'Etat. Elle est dans la barrière qu'ils élèvent aux importations des biens et services imposés. Les droits de douane visent à modifier un comportement importateur jugé facheux pour la collec-

*Professeur à l'Institut d'Urbanisme de Paris, Université de Paris Val de Marne.

Public Finance and Economic Growth. Proceedings of the 37th Congress of the International Institute of Public Finance. Tokyo, 1981, pp. 387–398

tivité, en un mot à dissuader. L'impôt ici est une fin et non un moyen. A la limite, c'est lorsqu'il ne rapporte rien qu'il remplit le mieux sa fonction.

Le domaine de la politique urbaine et régionale est un domaine de choix pour l'instauration d'impôts de ce type. La croissance urbaine et régionale est presque toujours accompagnée, en l'absence d'interventions politiques, de phénomènes d'encombrement et de pollution, qui peuvent en effet,—ainsi que le suggère le titre de la communication que l'on m'a demandé de faire—être combattus par des mesures fiscales.

Il n'y a rien d'étonnant à ce que la croissance des villes soit accompagnée d'encombrements.

La raison d'être des villes, et le moteur de leur développement, résident dans ce qu'on appelle parfois les "effets d'agglomération" et qui sont des externalités positives engendrées ou rendues possibles par le rassemblement en un même lieu de personnes et d'activités. L'élargissement du marché du travail est un exemple classique de ces effets d'agglomération: plus l'agglomération est grande, plus le nombre d'emplois offerts et demandés est grand, ce qui profite à la fois aux travailleurs et aux enterprises. La diminution du coût d'accès aux biens, aux services, aux informations est une autre forme d'externalité poitive urbaine, menacée, du reste, notamment en ce qui concerne les informations, par le progrès des techniques de transport et de communication. L'existence de biens publics purs "localisés," c'est-à-dire produits et consommés en un lieu donné, est une autre forme d'externalité urbaine: la protection contre la guerre et le pillage est un exemple de ce type d'externalité, qui a joué un rôle essentiel dans la naissance même des villes. D'une façon générale, plus la ville est grande, et plus sont grandes les externalités positives qu'elle engendre. C'est la raison pour laquelle la productivité des facteurs est généralement fonction de la taille des villes. On en trouve une preuve, ou un début de preuve, dans le fait que les salaires et les revenus des entrepreneurs individuels sont fonction de la taille des villes.

Malheureusement, des externalités négatives sont également attachées à la naissance et à la croissance des villes. Les pollutions de l'air et de l'eau peuvent être citées en exemple. La pollution est un cas classique d'externalité. Mais les rejets polluants se diluent dans l'atmosphère, et s'épurent naturellement dans les rivières. Si les activités polluantes étaient également réparties sur tour le territoire, et le long de toutes les rivières, les niveaux de pollution seraient dans la plupart des cas faibles, et les dommages de pollution négligeables. C'est le rassemblement de ces activités dans des agglomérations qui rend les concentrations de polluants élevées, et les dommages de pollution plus élevés encore. De nombreuses données empiriques peuvent être citées à l'appui de cette affirmation. On se contentera de renvoyer aux travaux déjà anciens compilés par Hoch, qui font état de corrélations statistiquement significatives entre taille des villes et niveau de pollution (Hoch, 1974, pp. 74–76). Les encombrements et les congestions sont un autre exemple d'externalités, et sont également—Hoch le montre également en citant les données relatives à la longueur et la vitesse moyennes des déplacements urbains—liés à la taille des villes.

La notion d'encombrement et de congestion mérite sans doute d'être précisée. On dira qu'il y a encombrement lorsque la qualité d'un bien public est réduite par le nombre de consommateurs de ce bien. On a longtemps distingué entre les biens privés, dont la consommation est exclusive (si je bois ce verre de vin, vous ne pouvez pas le boire), et les biens publics, dont la consommation n'est pas exclusive (si j'écoute cette émission de radio, cela ne vous empêche pas de l'écouter). Mais il y a aussi des biens semi-publics, que S. C. Kolm appelle "biens à qualité variable," qui sont tels que la satisfaction que l'on en retire est une fonction inverse du nombre de gens qui les consomment simultanément. La route, l'exposition de peinture, le parc naturel, sont des exemples de tels biens. Ils sont publics, en ce qu'ils peuvent être consommés en même temps par plusieurs personnes; mais si le nombre de personnes qui les consomment augmente, elles se gêneront les unes les autres et un effet d'encombrement se produira, qui réduira la satisfaction que chacun retirera de cette consommation jointe. Le schéma ci-après (Fig. 1) représente ce phénomène.

Les encombrements sont, comme les pollutions, étroitement liés à la taille des agglomérations. Mais les deux phénomènes ont aussi en commun d'être des externalités ainsi que l'avait noté Rothenberg (1970). Le schéma ci-après (Fig. 2) permet d'analyser l'un aussi bien que l'autre.

Les quantités s'entendent comme le nombre de pollueurs (ou la quantité de polluant rejetée par un pollueur) ou le nombre d'usagers d'un service à qualité variable—disons une route. Le bénéfice marginal est, dans le cas de la route, le gain (brut) de temps ou de commodité associé à l'usage de la route. C'est, dans le cas du rejet de polluant, le coût de dépollution évitée; on notera que, dans le cas où Q figure les quantités de polluant rejetées, la courbe droite B devient la courbe B'; mais ce changement n'altère pas le raisonnement. Le coût privé est la gêne de pollution ou d'encombrement supportée par son auteur; elle est très faible, au moins jusqu'à un niveau de Q très élevé. Celui qui emprunte une route encombrée supporte la gêne de l'encombrement, qui vient en déduction de son gain brut; le gain se

Figure 1.

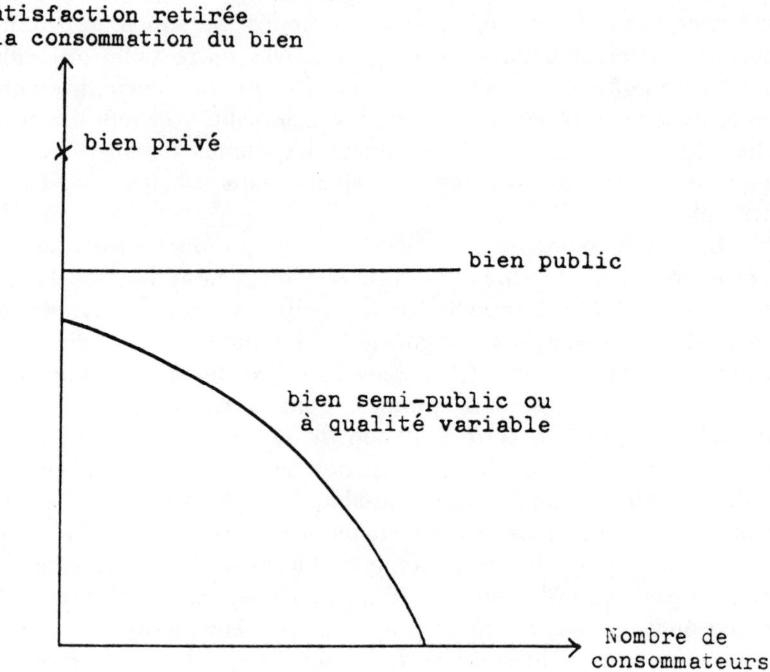

Typologie des biens

réduit, et pour le $Q_n$iéme automobiliste, il s'annule; à ce moment-là, aucun automobiliste supplémentaire n'est tenté d'utiliser la route. De la même façon, le pollueur souffre pas ou peu de la pollution supplémentaire qu'il cause, sauf s'il en rejette vraiment beaucoup ou s'il y a déjà beaucoup de pollueurs; cette gêne est très faible relativement au bénéfice qu'il en retire, et le nombre de pollueurs ou la quantité rejetée augmente jusqu'en Qn. Dans le cas de la pollution comme dans celui de l'encombrement, les coûts sociaux sont bien différents des coûts privés; le coût marginal social est la somme des coûts marginaux privés:

$$S(Q) = P(Q) \times Q$$

alors que le bénéfice marginal social est égal au bénéfice marginal privé. L'optimun social s'établit donc en Qo, où le coût marginal social est égal au bénéfice marginal social. La pollution et l'encombrement

Figure 2.

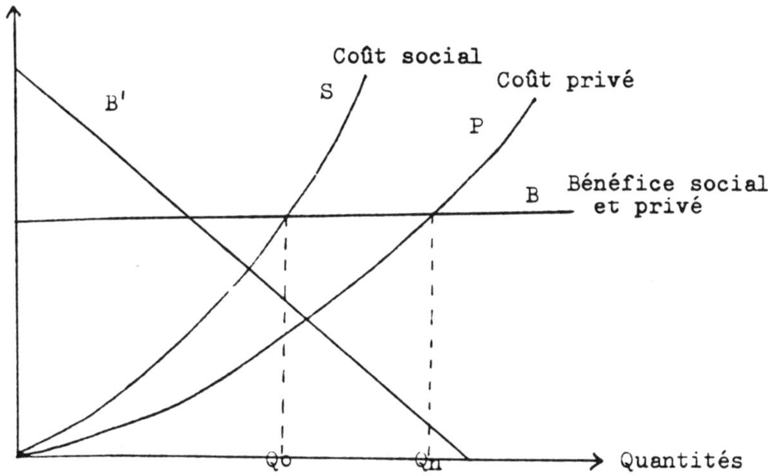

Pollution et encombrements

s'analysent donc de la même manière. Cela vient de ce que l'environnement peut être considéré comme un bien public à qualité variable. Du point de vue politique, on tire de cette analyse la conclusion évidente, et classique, qu'en l'absence d'action correctrice, il y aura trop de pollution et trop d'encombrement dans les villes. La politique urbaine et régionale doit donc mettre en oeuvre des actions correctrices.

Elles peuvent être fiscales. Le mécanisme d'action des taxes internalisantes et les raisons de préférer la fiscalité à d'autres formes d'action sont bien connues (Prud'homme, 1980). On examinera les taxes effectivement mises en oeuvre (sect. II), avant de s'interroger sur les causes du relatif insuccès de cet instrument (sect. III), et de conclure (sect. IV).

On se limitera ici aux taxes internalisantes, qui sont des "taxes positives," si l'on peut dire, par opposition à ces "taxes négatives" que sont les dégrèvements fiscaux de toutes sortes. Bien entendu, les amortissements accélérés, les crédits d'impôts, les réductions d'assiette, etc . . . peuvent être—et sont—utilisés pour encourager certains comportements de lutte contre les pollutions et les encombrements. Mais ces instruments ne sont pas particuliers à cet objet, et leur utilisation ne soulève pas de problème spécifique. Le cas des taxes internalisantes semble plus intéressant.

II. La Pratique des Taxes Internalisantes

On peut trouver un certain nombre d'exemples de taxes qui internalisent des externalités de pollution ou d'encombrement.

La France, la République Fédérale d'Allemagne, les Pays-Bas, le Canada, le Royaume-Uni, notamment, ont des redevances assises sur la pollution des eaux. En France, il est intéressant de le noter, le taux de la redevance varie selon l'Agence de Bassin (il y a six Agences de Bassin dans le pays) et selon l'objectif de qualité des eaux recherché. La Norvège, les Pays-Bas et dans une certaine mesure, le Japon, ont des taxes assises sur les rejets de SO_2.

Des redevances sur le bruit des avions existent en France, au Japon, en Suisse, et sont à l'étude aux Pays-Bas. La loi en préparation aux Pays-Bas vise également le bruit des véhicules à moteur et celui des sources fixes. Des redevances relatives aux déchets existent également, en particulier sur les emballages de liquides alimentaires (Norvège, Suède) et sur les huiles neuves (Allemagne). La taxe sur les véhicules automobiles perçue en Suède et en Norvège, et remboursée lorsque le véhicule usagé est remis à un ferrailleur agréé, peut s'analyser comme la taxation préventive d'une externalité potentielle: le coût pour la société de l'abandon n'importe où d'un véhicule.

Dans le domaine des transports, les taxes sur les encombrements, proposées par Smeed (1964), n'ont jamais été mises en oeuvre. Elles consistaient à munir chaque véhicule d'émetteurs ou de récepteurs qui auraient permis de savoir combien d'heures chaque automobile avait passé dans des embouteillages, et de le faire payer en conséquence. Cependant, le système mis en place à Singapour peut être considéré comme une version simplifiée de taxe sur les encombrements. A Singapour, dans la zone centrale et à l'heure de pointe, seuls sont admis les véhicules automobiles qui ont payé une redevance, matérialisée par une vignette apposée sur la vitre du véhicule et qui s'achète à la journée, au mois ou à l'année. Le stationnement payant s'inspire évidemment de la même philosophie.

Une façon de lutter contre la congestion associée à la concentration des hommes et des activités dans certaines métropoles consiste à lever un impôt spécial sur les créations ou les extensions d'entreprises dans ces métropoles. C'est ainsi qu'il existe en France, depuis 1960, dans la région parisienne, une redevance pour les extensions de locaux à usage de bureaux ou à usage industriel. Dans le même ordre d'idée, on peut noter, en France, l'existence d'un "versement transport," assis sur les salaires versés par les entreprises des agglomérations urbaines, et dont le taux est en pratique d'autant plus élevé que l'agglomération est plus grande: il est de 2% dans l'agglomération parisienne, de 1,5% dans les trois agglomérations d'un million d'habitants (Marseille, Lyon, Lille), égal ou inférieur à 1% dans la plupart des autres agglomérations; cette taxe est appelée "versement transport" parce qu'elle est affectée aux transports en commun de ces agglomérations, mais on peut y voir la contre-partie des externalités positives dont elles bénéficient; ces externalités proviennent de l'existence d'un vaste marché du travail, que les transports en commun contribuent du reste à créer.

On peut enfin voir dans la taxe sur le deuxième enfant récemment instituée en Chine un exemple—peut-être extrême, mais significatif—de taxe internalisante. Le fait d'avoir un enfant, qui est généralement considéré comme une affaire purement privée est aussi une affaire publique, en ce qu'il inflige des coûts à la société, c'est-à-dire des externalités. Il n'est donc pas absurde que la société cherche à internaliser ces coûts au moyen d'une taxe.

La mise en oeuvre des taxes internalisantes soulève des problèmes délicats. Mentionons pour mémoire les problèmes relatifs au taux de la taxe. On se contentera d'aborder brièvement ceux de l'assiette de la taxe, et de l'utilisation du produit de la taxe.

L'assiette de la redevance doit être étroitement liée au comportement générateur d'externalités, c'est-à-dire au rejet polluant ou au fait créateur d'encombrement. Dans le cas de pollution, qui est un phénomène complexe et multidimensionnel, cela n'est pas toujours aisé. Il faut trouver un équilibre entre une définition "juste" mais inapplicable car trop complexe, et une définition applicable mais injuste et inefficace.

C'est ainsi qu'en France, l'assiette de la redevance de pollution prélevée par les six Agences de Bassin sur les entreprises et les collectivités locales est fonction de trois variables:

—le poids de pollution déversée, mesurée en demande biologique en oxygène (DBO-5), en demande chimique en oxygène (DCO) et en matières en suspension (MES), pondérées de la façon suivante:

$$P = \frac{\text{DCO} + 2\ \text{DBO-5}}{3} + \text{MES}$$

—la salinité;
—la toxicité.

L'assiette de la redevance allemande contient à peu près les mêmes variables qui sont pondérées de façon différente. Il faut que les variables retenues soient celles dont on veut réduire la valeur. Il faut encore qu'elles soient assez faciles à mesurer, ou à estimer. En pratique, dans le domaine de l'eau, on utilise des tableaux forfaitaires qui donnent pour chaque type d'activité, la quantité de polluant rejetée. Bien entendu, les entreprises ou les collectivités locales qui justifient d'un effort de dépollution ont droit à une réduction de l'assiette, et donc de la taxe. La détermination de l'assiette doit également tenir compte des variations dans le temps des flux de pollution. En France, la redevance est assise sur la pollution du jour moyen du mois de plus grande pollution. L'expérience déjà considérable acquise dans le domaine de la pollution de l'eau montre bien qu'il est possible techniquement, administrativement et politiquement de définir l'assiette d'une redevance.

La redevance française sur le bruit des avions, en revanche, offre un bon exemple d'une mauvaise assiette. L'assiette n'est pas définie par le bruit effectif, ni même par un indicateur relié au bruit, mais par le fait du décollage. Elle n'incite pas les compagnies à faire moins de bruit. On ne peut même pas dire qu'elle décourage certains voyageurs de prendre l'avion, réduisant ainsi le nombre de vols, et le bruit des avions: le taux de la redevance exclut tout effet de ce type. On pourrait pourtant, ainsi que le montrent Alexandre et Barde (1974), définir une assiette représentative du bruit, qui inciterait les compagnies aériennes à préférer les avions les moins bruyants.

Le problème de l'assiette est lié au problème de l'utilisation du produit de la taxe. En principe, le produit d'une taxe internalisante pourrait, et même devrait, être versé au budget général de l'Etat. L'effet incitatif de la taxe en fait en quelque sorte l'impôt idéal: non seulement cet impôt n'a pas d'effet fâcheux sur les comportements, mais il a des effets favorables. On comprend mal pourquoi les ministres des Finances ne sont pas plus friands de ce type d'impôts.

Dans la pratique, cependant, le produit des redevances n'est presque jamais versé au budget de l'Etat. Il est presque toujours affecté à des dépenses de lutte contre la pollution, généralement dans le même secteur, ou à l'indemnisation des victimes, ou encore à des dépenses visant à réduire les encombrements. C'est ainsi qu'en France, le produit des redevances perçues par les Agences de Bassin sert à financer (au moyen de prêts et de subventions) les investissements de dépollution des pollueurs. La raison en est que le taux est trop faible pour être réellement incitatif. La redevance est alors davantage un moyen de financer des investissements qu'un moyen de les susciter. Dans ces cas-là, le taux est souvent fixé de manière à ce que la somme collectée soit égale au coût des programmes de dépollution envisagés. A vrai dire, la redevance ainsi envisagée mérite à peine le nom de redevance. Elle perd la spécificité de la redevance, qui est précisément son caractère incitatif. L'essentiel devient un programme de dépenses publiques qui aurait aussi bien pu être financé par l'impôt.

Il faut bien constater qu'en pratique, les taxes véritablement incitatrices, chères aux économistes, sont peu répandues. La fiscalité n'est pas l'instrument privilégié de la lutte contre les externalités de pollution et d'encombrement.

III. La Résistance aux Taxes

Il faut évidemment se demander pourquoi les redevances assises sur les comportements générateurs d'externalités sont aussi peu utilisées dans les politiques effectivement mises en oeuvre. Ces politiques font essentiellement appel à la contrainte et non à l'incitation par les prix. Mercadal (1972) réfléchissant sur la politique urbaine, arrivait à la même conclusion. Le marché fonctionne mal. On ne cherche pas à le faire fonctionner correctement, en corrigeant les signaux erronés transmis par les prix, comme le voudraient les économistes. On lui substitue le plan. Les praticiens ne suivent pas les prescriptions des théoriciens; la question se pose de savoir pourquoi. Plusieurs explications peuvent être proposées.

Une première réponse (naïve) qui vient tout d'abord à l'esprit, et en particulier à l'esprit des théoriciens, est que les praticiens ont tort et qu'ils ignorent ou sous-estiment l'efficacité du maniement des prix. Il y a une part de vérité dans cette réponse. Dans tous les pays, les "praticiens" ont une formation d'ingénieur ou de juriste. Le fonctionnement du marché des prix est finalement assez complexe, ou pour mieux dire, assez abstrait, et on peut penser que des administrateurs à qui on ne l'a jamais expliqué ont quelque difficulté à le comprendre véritablement. Le détour que représente le passage par les signaux des prix leur paraît à la fois long et incertain et ils préfèrent l'action directe en application de l'adage: "un tiens vaut mieux que deux tu l'auras."

On peut aller plus loin et noter avec Alexandre et Barde (1973, p. 121) que les administrateurs ont intérêt à préférer la contrainte à l'incitation. La contrainte satisfait mieux leur volonté de puissance. Elle leur permet de discuter d'égal à égal, ou même de supérieur à inférieur, avec les patrons des entreprises polluantes. Il est sans doute plus exaltant de recevoir dans un bureau tel P.D.G. influent venu quémander que de modifier l'assiette d'une taxe. Les bureaucrates peuvent ainsi, non seulement exercer leur volonté de puissance, mais le faire au nom de l'intérêt général, et donc avec une entière bonne conscience. Ils tirent donc de l'action discrétionnaire qui caractérise souvent la mise en oeuvre des instruments directs, des avantages psychologiques considérables qui ne peuvent pas manquer de jouer un rôle dans l'idée qu'ils se font et dans le choix qu'ils font des instruments d'intervention.

L'idéologie dominante peut-elle être un facteur explicatif de la préférence pour les normes? Les économistes marxistes et les anti-économistes ont insisté sur le caractère apologétique de la théorie néo-classique. Cette théorie, soutiennent-ils, a pour principale fonction de justifier le système capitaliste qui, réciproquement, impose la théorie néo-classique. L'idéologie dominante qui imprègne (par définition) l'esprit des décideurs devrait donc les entraîner à préférer des systèmes d'incitation. On a vu que les décideurs préfèrent en réalité les systèmes d'interdiction. L'explication par l'idéologie dominante est peut-être pourtant éclairante, à condition d'être retournée complètement. Il est bien possible en effet, que l'idéologie dominante soit en réalité planificatrice. La vérification de cette hypothèse demanderait des développements qui n'ont pas leur place ici. Mais cette hypothèse permettrait de comprendre la préférence pour la contrainte qu'il faut bien enregistrer.

L'intérêt des pollueurs est un dernier facteur explicatif. Les entrepreneurs privés devraient, en tant que défenseurs de l'économie de marché, préférer les systèmes d'incitation, qui ressortissent à ce type d'économie et qui laissent intacte leur liberté de décision. En fait, ces entrepreneurs privés ne sont pas les moins ardents défenseurs des systèmes de contraintes. Comment expliquer ce paradoxe, sinon par le fait que les systèmes de normes sont finalement ceux qui leur coûtent le moins cher. On sait que les redevances mettent à la charge des pollueurs non seulement les coûts de dépollution, ainsi que le font les normes non assorties de subventions, mais aussi tout ou partie du coût résiduel de pollution. Dans une analyse intéressante mais limitée (par une hypothèse irréaliste: la constance des processus de production), Buchanan et Tullock (1975) ont montré que la réduction directe de production, au moyen de quotas, était plus intéressante pour les firmes en place, que la réduction indirecte au moyen de taxes. La réduction directe donne en effet aux entreprises en place une sorte de rente. On peut sans doute généraliser cette observation et avancer, au moins à titre d'hypothèse, que l'action directe par le plan est plus conservatrice que l'action indirecte par les prix. La première contrôle ou modifie l'existant, et ce faisant, le consolide. La seconde contrôle ou modifie les conditions d'existence, entraînant des disparitions et des créations, et ce faisant, bouleverse l'existant. Ceci pourrait expliquer que les forces en place, et au premier rang d'entre elles, les pollueurs, préfèrent les instruments directs aux instruments indirects.

IV. Conclusion

La fiscalité, sous la forme de taxes internalisantes, semble un instrument particulièrement bien adapté à la lutte contre les pollutions et les encombrements, qui est elle-même un élément essentiel des politiques urbaines et régionales. Il n'y a rien là de très original: les économistes savent cela depuis Pigou. Mais les administrateurs ne le savent pas encore. Rien, pourtant, n'infirme l'idée que, dans ce domaine, la manière douce, c'est-à-dire l'instrument fiscal, est préférable à la manière forte, c'est-à-dire à l'instrument contraignant.

References

Alexandre, A. et Barde, J. P. (1973), *Le Temps du Bruit,* Paris, Flamarion, 232 p.

Alexandre, A. et Barde, J. P. (1974), "Aircraft Noise Charges," *Noise Control Engineering,* vol. 3, n°2.

Baumol, W. J. and Oates, W. E. (1971), "The Use of standards and prices for the protection of the environment," *The Swedish Journal of Economics,* vol. 73, n°1 pp. 42–54.

Buchanan, J. and Tullock, G. (1975), Polluters, profits and political response: direct control versus taxes, *American Economic Review,* n°65, pp. 139–147.

Hoch, I. (1974), "Interurban differences in the quality of life," *in:* Rothenberg, J. G. and Heggie, I. G., ed. *Transport and the Urban Environment,* London, Macmillan, pp. 54–98.

Kneese, A. and Bower, B. (1968), *Managing Water Quality, Economics, Technology, Institutions,* Baltimore, Johns Hopkins University Press, 328 p.

Mercadal, G. (1972), "Peut-on tirer un enseignement des essais français de modélisation du développement spatial urbain?" *Revue Economique,* vol. 23, pp. 952–991.

Prud'homme, R. (1980), *Le Ménagement de la Nature,* Paris, Dunod, 212 p.

Rose-Ackerman, S. (1973), "Effluent charges: a critique," *Canadian Journal of Economics,* vol. VI, n°4, pp. 512–528.

Rothenberg, J. (1970), "The Economics of congestion and pollution: an integrated view," *American Economic Review,* vol. 60, n°2, pp. 114–121.

Smeed, R. J. *et al* (1964), *Road Pricing: The Economic and Technical Possibilities,* London, Ministry of Transportation, H.M.S.O.

Summary

Besides conventional taxes which are justified because they permit to cover public expenditures, one can envisage others whose justification stems from the changes they cause in behavior. Urban economics and environmental economics are fields for this type of taxes.

This paper indicates at first the same underlying source of the congestion and pollution phenomena, which generally appear simultaneously. After we have shown how taxes, designed to internalize externalities, reduce the latter, the paper then compares the advantages of internalizing taxes versus other policy tools in the fight against congestion and pollution. If conventional instruments used serve as a norm, it is found that in most cases taxes are superior instruments.

Finally, the paper examines cases in which internalizing taxes have been used. These taxes have since long left the realm of economic theory and are now effectively utilized. It must nevertheless be recognized that cases of utilization are still relatively rare and that economic policy relies much more on conventional policy instruments of the norm type.

The question then arises why instruments which are the best ones are the least utilized ones. The present paper suggests several reasons, most of them of a sociological rather than economic nature.

Fiscal Measures against Pollution: Are Effluent Taxes and Abatement Subsidies Equivalent?

*Hirofumi Shibata**

I. Introduction

Until recently, regulation and moral suasion have been the only major means for controlling environmental pollution. Outside of continental Europe, little has been heard of fiscal measures against pollution, except for such stereotyped means as construction subsidies and accelerated depreciation allowances on pollution abatement facilities,[1] even though a successful application of an effluent discharge tax has been in existence in Germany for some time.[2]

Lately, however, one hears suggestions that effluent taxes and pollutant abatement subsidies should be used as substitutes for regulation, and one hears of schemes based on these suggestions being implemented.[3] The supporters of these suggestions are mainly economists. They perceive environmental pollution as a phenomenon of market failure due to the absence of prices on pollutants and pollution-generating activities. In the absence of prices on pollutants emitted into common properties such as air, water, and publicly owned land, users tend to neglect the fact that the use of these properties imposes costs on others. Accordingly, economists have reasoned that the introduction of substitutes for prices of pollutants would solve the problem. The substitutes thus recommended are taxes and subsidies.

Effluent taxes and abatement subsidies provide polluters with incentives to curtail their emission of pollutants. These means appeal less to the polluters' conscience than to their natural desire to increase their profits and personal well-being. Since profit motives usually compel

*I would like to thank Professors Dieter Biehl, Sei Fujita, Alan Tait, Kazuyuki Tanaka, Henry Tulkens, Remy Prud'homme and Masatoshi Yamade for helpful comments, and Kikawada Memorial Foundation, Tokyo, for financial support.

Public Finance and Economic Growth. Proceedings of the 37th Congress of the International Institute of Public Finance. Tokyo, 1981, pp. 399–418

people more often than their law-abiding spirits, the tax subsidy approach is thought to be much more effective than regulation in controlling environmental pollution.

One of the most remarkable tenets held by the supporters of this tax-subsidy approach is the equivalence of the allocative effects of taxes and subsidies. An effluent tax charged at a given rate on each unit of pollutant emitted and a subsidy given at the rate equal to the tax for each unit of pollutant withheld from emission are expected to produce equal resource allocation in the absence of income effects. Let us refer to this argument as the equivalence theorem hereafter. Since the time when Coase (1960) introduced a theorem which germinated this idea and subsequently Kneese (1964) formalized it in the context of taxes and subsidies, the equivalence theorem gained wide acceptance among economists. Indeed, it so firmly established itself in the profession that it has begun to be included as a standard economic principle in many textbooks.[4] However, a series of articles have persistently questioned the validity of this theorem. It has evolved in two strands of arguments.

Kamien, Schwartz, and Dolbear (1966) argued that when a polluter anticipates the effect of his polluting actions on a regulatory authority's estimate of his contribution toward pollution reduction, a subsidy scheme may prompt him to emit more pollution than he otherwise would have in order to qualify for larger subsidy payments. But, they argue by implication, a tax scheme would not induce such a strategic behavior.[5]

Bramhall and Mills (1966) have pointed out the possibility that a firm which would be unable to survive under a tax scheme might become profitable under a subsidy scheme. Expanding this line of argument, Baumol and Oates (1975) have demonstrated that in a competitive industry where pollutant emission is a fixed and rising function of the industry's output, "equal tax and subsidy rates will normally *not* lead to the same output levels or to the same reduction in total industry emissions. Other things being equal, the subsidy will yield an output and emission level not only greater than those that would occur under the tax, but greater even than they would be in the absence of either tax or subsidy" (1975, p. 183).[6]

In this paper I shall attempt to examine the following issues. First discussed will be the type of strategic behavior with which Kamien, Schwartz, and Dolbear were concerned: this behavior depends on whether the authority's decision on the benchmark in determining the tax or subsidy base of a polluter is independent of the polluter's pretax or presubsidy emission level. If it is not independent, both a tax and a subsidy induce the polluter to behave strategically in spite of these authors' implicit claim that a subsidy alone induces such behavior. If the decision is independent, as it could be, then neither induces strategic behavior. Next the so-called long-run effect will be discussed. The argument of Baumol and Oates is correct under the conditions which they specified, but I argue that the equivalence theorem should be reestablished as valid under more general conditions, those in which distributional effects of the tax revenue and the subsidy monies are taken into account. Third, I shall introduce a new argument that considerably weakens the validity of the equivalence theorem in practice. I shall compare a tax on pollutants emitted and a subsidy on pollutants retrieved, both at the same rate. My conclusion is that in general the former will be more efficient than the latter.

II. Effluent Tax Experiments

Before I start theoretical discussions, let me introduce actual examples that demonstrate rather dramatically the effectiveness of tax incentives for pollution abatement.

In 1971, the State of Oregon enacted the so-called Bottle Bill. The bill required, among other things, that (1) all carbonated-beverage containers sold in the state must carry a minimum refundable deposit of five cents and (2) the deposit on any such container must be refunded by any retailer or wholesaler selling that kind, brand, and size of beverage. The intent of the bill is obvious: (1) promotion of the reuse of beer and soft drink containers and (2) reduction of container littering.[7] The bill has worked marvelously to produce the intended results. The use of refillable containers increased from 45 percent in 1972 to over 91 percent in 1973 and 1974.[8] But our major interest in this paper is the bill's stunning success in cleaning up the state's container pollution on highways, beaches, and mountains.

The Oregon State Highway Department has carefully monitored roadside litter along Oregon Highways since October 1971. The department discovered a 72 percent reduction in roadside litter when the Bottle Bill became effective in October 1972. An 88 percent reduction in the number of beverage containers found in the state's solid waste went with it when the bill became effective,[9] implying a substantial reduction in litter pollution in general.[10]

Impressed by the Oregon experience, Yosemite National Park in California experimented with the same method during the summer of 1976. The park's concessioners imposed a five-cent deposit on each bottle and can sold. In the absence of a bottle bill in California, the main objective of the Yosemite experiment was eradication of container pollution in the park. The return rate of the used bottles and cans was reported to be close to 80 percent. Park officials were quoted as saying that they found "people from five to ninety-five out picking up the cans."[11] In both experiments the effluent tax on bottles and cans has proven itself to be strikingly effective as an antipollution measure.

III. The Socially Optimal Level of Pollution

Let us use the Yosemite experiment as our example and compare it with the situation where a subsidy of the same rate replaces the effluent tax. Note that any other pollutant can replace cans and bottles in our discussion, provided certain conditions are met,[12] and therefore the conclusions in this paper are not restricted to this specific example.

Before the effluent tax was introduced, there were, of course, regulations prohibiting littering in the park. But a regulation usually permits tacitly, if not expressly, some level of pollution, for complete elimination of pollution would be very costly to obtain relative to the benefits achievable. Let the socially optimal level of pollution be 9 bottles (or cans) per park visitor, and assume, albeit unrealistically, that the regulation is effective in holding that level at a negligible enforcement cost. This pollution level is optimal in the following sense. Before he comes to Yosemite Park, the potential visitor evaluates his utility of visiting Yosemite and compares it with the utility to be gained from other alternatives. In this evaluation, he must include, among other factors associated with the park, the possible disutility of encountering scenes littered with discarded cans and bottles. At the same time he will value positively the factor that he is not restricted excessively from disposing of his own empty bottles in the park. If the number of visitors who decide to visit Yosemite after such an evaluation exceeds the "capacity" of the park, an admission fee may be charged in order to relieve congestion.[13] Thus both the number of bottles per person which are permitted to be left as litter (which in turn determines the level of bottle pollution in the park) and the admission fee charged at the gate affect the number of visitors to the park. Following the mandate given to national parks, the park authority determines, along with the other variables, these two variables (the number of bottles per visitor permitted as litter and the admission fee) so as to maximize the aggregate utilities of the visitors. Let *N* stand for the optimal number of visitors thus determined.

Figure 1 illustrates this situation. The horizontal and vertical axes measure the number of bottles and dollar values, respectively. For the sake of simplicity, let us assume that all potential visitors are identical and that each would toss away 20 bottles per visit if there were no hindrance whatsoever to this behavior. Each will do so because retrieving empty bottles involves costs in terms of the visitor's effort, time, and money. Let the visitor's marginal retrieval cost schedule be AB, which increases as he attempts to reduce the number of bottles that he leaves behind. Looking at this schedule from the point of view of a visitor's motives for discarding bottles, that is, in terms of the benefits that he derives from littering, schedule AB is his marginal utility schedule of littering. Schedule OC, on the other hand, measures his marginal disutility of encountering unsightly areas in the park littered with discarded bottles. It increases as the quantity of the garbage increases. We assume that these bottle-related costs are such a small portion of the visitor's total income that schedules AB and OC are invariant with respect to a change in his income. (The disutility is measured in terms of money, that is, the money that he would require if he were exactly compensated for the unpleasantness of seeing these scenes.)

When we have *N* identical visitors, the number of bottles discarded will be 20*N* in the absence of any pollution control, and the individual visitor's total disutility from the bottle pollution is represented by areas OCE. This disutility is pitted against the total utility that the individual receives from littering, area OBA. His net bottle-related utility is therefore area OBA minus area OCE, an amount which is most likely negative. If net utility is negative, bottle pollution becomes a factor that deters a potential visitor from visiting Yosemite, and if it is positive, being able to litter becomes a factor that encourages his visit.

Since bottle pollution is a "public bad," that is, because all visitors will suffer from having to cope with the same number of discarded bottles, the vertical sum of all such OC schedules for all visitors constitutes the aggregate marginal disutilities of all the visitors and is given by schedule OC′ in figure 2. On the other hand, since the benefits of littering represent a "private good," the horizontal sum of the AB schedules for all visitors composes the aggregate utility of littering and is given by schedule EF in figure 2. The intersection of these two schedules gives the socially optimal pollution level, OK (the society being all park visitors).[14] This level is 9*N* discarded bottles in our example. Here a perfectly inelastic demand for the contents of the bottles, say beer, is assumed. The assumption will be relaxed in section VII.

IV. An Equivalence Theorem

Now let an effluent tax of the rate equal to $OT per bottle replace the bottle regulation. The park authority imposes a refundable tax of $OT on each beverage bottle that visitors bring into or purchase in the park and refunds the same amount when they present used bottles at specified receiving sites in the park.[15] Since the deposits on them are refundable, each consumer finds it worthwhile to retrieve bottles as long as the effort involved in retrieving an additional bottle is less than the tax. As his marginal retrieval cost increases, he finds bottle fetching less and less attractive. He accumulates and searches for empty bottles up to the point at which the marginal cost of retrieving equals the tax rate. Figure 1 indicates that an individual's marginal retrieving cost equals the tax rate, $OT, at 11 bottles. Hence, the visitor will abandon 9 bottles rather than retrieve them. With *N* visitors, the total number of bottles left in the park will be 9*N*, the socially optimal level of pollution.

It is apparent that the result will be the same and administratively much simpler if the park authority substitutes for the effluent tax a subsidy on cleaning the park. The park now grants a $OT subsidy on each empty bottle returned at specified receiving sites. The subsidy given in this way differs from the tax only by the fact that the visitors are no longer required to leave deposits on bottles and cans. Forfeiting a deposit is in fact equivalent to paying the tax under the tax scheme, but not receiving a subsidy does not constitute payment of a tax under the subsidy scheme. One can easily recognize that the same desire to maximize the net difference between the money received and the retrieving effort compels a visitor to fetch up to 11 discarded bottles as before. The decision process that determines this equilibrium quantity works exactly the same as under the tax scheme. Hence the number of bottles left behind in the park will be again the same (9*N*). This is the logic behind a simple version of the equivalence theorem.

V. Evaluation of a Nonequivalence Theorem: Strategic Behavior

Kamien, Schwartz, and Dolbear (1966) argue that the subsidy scheme encourages polluters initially to pollute more than they would under the tax scheme in order to qualify for larger payments in a system in which the base of the subsidy is the difference between the polluter's presubsidy and postsubsidy emission levels.

However, in determining the benchmark from which it may count the number of bottles qualifying for subsidies, the authority need not choose the polluters' presubsidy emission level. It can choose the benchmark number of bottles arbitrarily and make it invariant with respect to the polluters' strategically determined presubsidy emission levels. As long as the benchmark chosen is greater than the optimal pollution level, the subsidy scheme works because only the payment on the marginal bottle is crucial in the polluters' maximization decisions. For example, if the park authority declares that it will subsidize only the returned empty bottles exceeding two bottles per person per day (or at a time), the same number of bottles will be retrieved as in the full subsidy case because to obtain a subsidy on one bottle, a consumer must return at least three bottles. If the individual's marginal retrieving cost for the third bottle is still smaller than the subsidy per bottle, he will continue to retrieve until his marginal retrieving cost equals the subsidy—that is, until he has collected 11 bottles in our example. Thus the authority can achieve the same socially optimal pollution level without subsidizing the entire reduction in pollution as long as the subsidy policy does not reduce the consumer's gross receipts of subsidies to less than his gross disutility of his retrieving efforts.

Similarly, although it has not been recognized in the literature, the benchmark from which the authority counts the number of pollutants for tax purposes can also be determined arbitrarily without affecting the optimality. For example, the park authority may declare that it will refund the deposited effluent taxes on any number of retrieved bottles exceeding, say, two bottles per person per day. The same logic of the consumer's decision processes leads to the conclusion that the optimal number of bottles to be retrieved by all consumers will remain the same as under the full refund regime, provided that the marginal retrieving cost schedule remains unchanged and the gross conditions mentioned above are met. If, however, the regulatory authority chooses the number of bottles to be excluded from those qualifying for refunds to be a positive (negative) function of the number of bottles abandoned in the absence of any control, the polluter may start off by emitting a smaller (larger) quantity of pollutants than he would otherwise and increase (reduce) his emission level after the exclusion number has been chosen. Thus under systems in which the polluter's pretax emission level influences the authority's decision on the benchmark, the basic symmetry between the tax and subsidy schemes remains intact.

VI. Evaluation of a Nonequivalence Theorem: Income Effects

Recall that the validity of the equivalence theorem was proven for the short-run point of view. That is, the proof proceeded on the assumption that the number of park visitors was fixed. However, the choice of a control scheme most likely affects the number of visitors, for it influences the potential visitor's decision calculus.

If a subsidy scheme is used, a potential visitor will expect the extra benefits that he obtains from the subsidy to equal the area AUG in figure 1; these benefits are in addition to those that he would obtain under the regulation system, the area OBGH minus area OKI. If, on the other hand, a tax scheme is used, a potential visitor will expect that the utility he derives from visiting the park would be less than that derived under the regulation regime by an amount equal to area OTGH. Consequently, a subsidy scheme will increase (a tax scheme will reduce) the number of visitors above (below) the socially optimal number.[16] In other words, some visitors who would come to Yosemite Park under a subsidy scheme would reject visiting the park under a tax scheme. The two systems are then apparently not equivalent.

Bramhall and Mills (1966) and others have pointed out this type of asymmetry between the tax and subsidy schemes. Baumol and Oates (1975) pursued this line of argument and concluded that under the subsidy scheme the aggregate amount of pollution occurring would exceed the level that would result in the absence of either tax or subsidy (p. 183). Since the number of visitors under the subsidy scheme, say N', is greater than N, it is possible that the pollution level of $9N'$ is greater than $20N$.

It may be obvious that this type of nonequivalence is the direct consequence of the implicit assumptions of the Bramhall-Mills and Baumol-Oates arguments that a tax scheme removes from the park the revenues derived from the taxes while a subsidy scheme injects funds from outside to finance the subsidies. If intragroup transfers replace the intergroup transfers of the tax revenues and the subsidy funds, the situation is clearly different. Let's assume now that the revenue collected under the effluent tax plan is returned to the visitors of the park as a lump sum and that the monies needed to finance subsidies are raised from the actual visitors as a lump sum. All visitors' expected net utility gains from reduced bottle pollution would then be the same under both schemes. Thus, the equivalence theorem reestablishes itself in this broader framework. In our case, this equivalence could be achieved simply by lowering the admission fee to the park if the tax is employed and by raising it if the subsidy is used in an amount equal to the lump-sum transfers, assuming all visitors' utility functions are identical.

In this connection, Baumol and Oates argue somewhat differently. They state that in order to make lump-sum payments not contingent upon the potential polluters' entry and exit decisions, a lump-sum subsidy must be given to *all* polluters, whether potential or actual. Since "the administrative infeasibility of such a system of payments is evident" subsidy payments in any period must be limited to firms that are actively in business and thus generate pollution during this period (1975, p. 178). Hence, they argue that the subsidy scheme encourages new firms to enter the pollution-generating industry and increase the overall pollution level.

Although their argument concerning the need for subsidizing *all* polluters (whether potential or actual) in order to produce a true lump-sum subsidy scheme is correct, it seems to me to be unnecessarily restrictive and to preclude all possible practical applications of lump-sum subsidies. A firm's decision to enter or exit the polluting industry or any other industry depends upon net expected gains from entering or remaining in the industry relative to opportunities available to the firm elsewhere. Therefore, imposition (granting) of a lump-sum tax (subsidy) to the actual entrants as an entry condition into that industry neutralizes the artificial encouragement (discouragement) given by the subsidy (tax), just as a change in the admission fee neutralizes the artificial stimulus to visit the park. The lump-sum tax may take the form of a license fee, and the lump-sum subsidy may be given as an investment subsidy to the firms which actually construct facilities specific to the polluting industry. There seems no need for granting a lump-sum subsidy to all the potential and actual polluters.

VII. A Case of Nonequivalence

I now turn to a discussion of what seems to me a practical, significant, albeit as yet undiscussed factor causing nonequivalent results between an effluent tax and an abatement subsidy. Recall that the proof of the equivalence of their effects was derived on the implicit assumption that the quantity of beer consumed is the same under either the tax or the subsidy scheme. It amounted, as it will become clear, to assuming a perfectly inelastic demand for beer. Let us consider the situation where the demand for beer is not perfectly inelastic.

In figure 3, the horizontal and vertical axes measure the number of beer bottles and dollar values, respectively. The vertical distance OP measures the market price of beer per bottle, which is unaffected by the number of beers visitors of the park imbibe. Curve PB is the representative consumer's marginal cost of retrieving empty bottles

Figure 1.

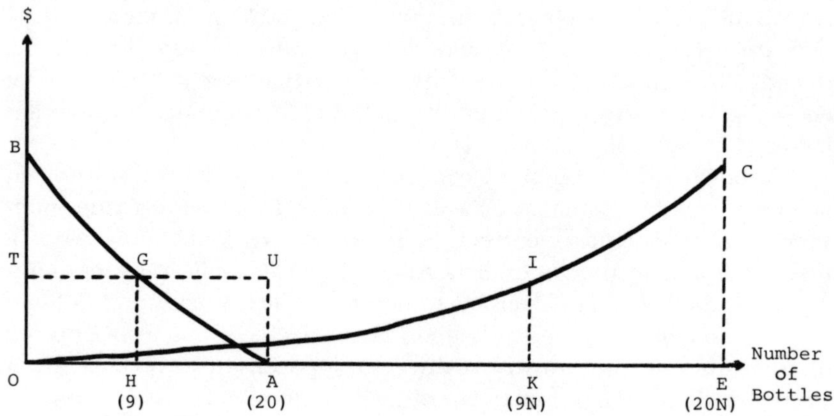

Private benefits and costs of littering

Figure 2.

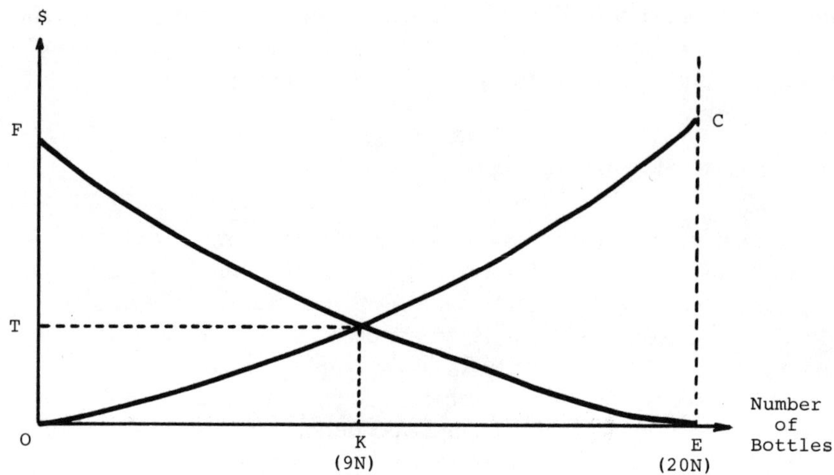

Social benefits and costs of littering

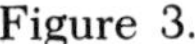
Figure 3.

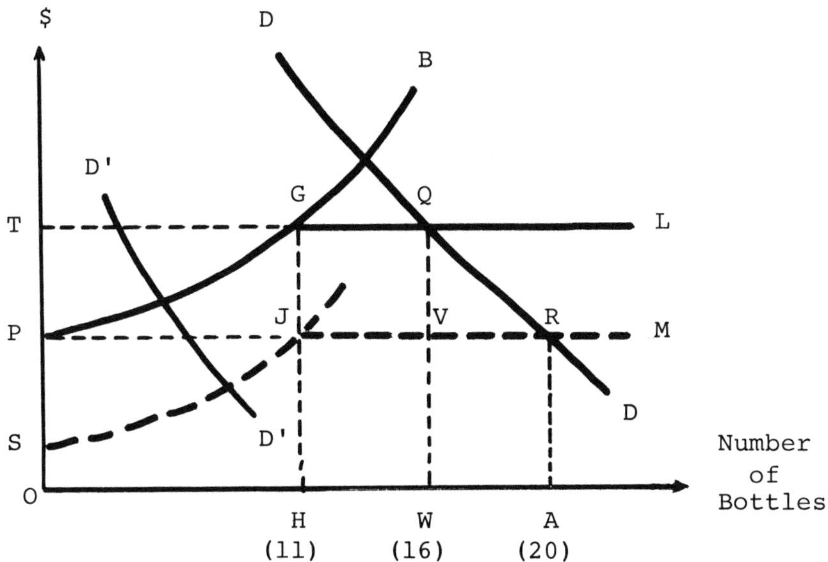

Pollution levels under an effluent tax and under an abatement subsidy of an equal rate

Figure 4.

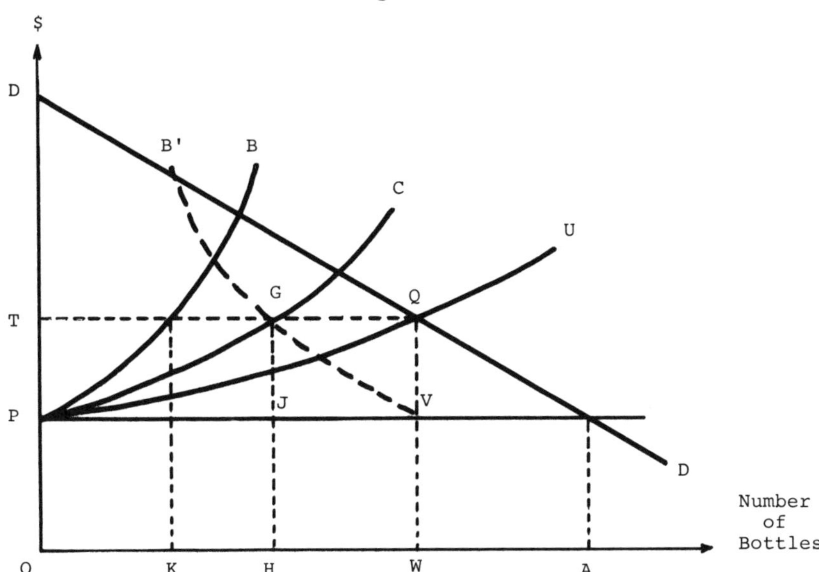

The Socially optimal levels of consumption, pollution and the effluent tax

and, as before, is assumed to be an increasing function of the number of bottles of beer retrieved. The distance PT measures the refundable effluent tax per bottle. From the point of view of the beer consumer, the marginal cost schedule of drinking beer will appear as the thick, kinked curve PGL under the tax scheme: when his marginal retrieval cost is less than the amount of the tax, the marginal cost of beer consumption is the market price plus this marginal retrieval cost. As the drinker's marginal retrieval cost increases, his marginal cost of drinking also increases. However, when his quantity consumed reaches or exceeds OH, it becomes cheaper for him to pay the tax rather than to retrieve used bottles. Thus, the marginal cost of beer consumption for him becomes OT (the market price plus the tax) thereafter.

Suppose now that the consumer's demand schedule for beer is given as curve DD, and let DD be invariant with respect to his income (as we assume that the cost of beer consumption is only a small portion of the consumer's income). His beer consumption declines under the tax from OA, the quantity under the absence of any control, to OW. This decline reflects the substitution effect generated by the tax. He also retrieves quantity OH of bottles, leaving behind him quantity HW of empties. The total reduction in the quantity of pollutants he leaves behind from 20 to 5 is thus the result of two effects: (1) a decline in the emission of the pollutants (4 bottles) and (2) cleaning up of already emitted pollution (11 bottles). If there are *N* visitors to the park, the total pollution level will be 5*N*. If the demand schedule cuts the consumer's cost curve between P and G, as in the case of D′D′, the consumption of beer will decline under the tax and all of the empty bottles will be retrieved, leaving no empties in the park.

On the other hand, thick broken lines in figure 3 depict the situation under a subsidy on the returned bottles. If we deduct the vertical differences between the marginal retrieval cost and the subsidy per unit, represented by the vertical distance PS (=PT), from the market price of a bottle of beer (OP), we obtain the schedule shown by the thick, broken curve, SJM. This schedule represents the marginal cost of drinking beer from the consumer's point of view under the subsidy plan. In other words, his marginal cost of beer equals the market price plus the cost of retrieval per unit minus the subsidy when the retrieval cost is less than the subsidy, and equals the market price when the retrieval cost exceeds the subsidy. This schedule indicates that, given demand schedule DD, the consumer would consume 20 bottles of beer under the subsidy scheme as he would under the regulation scheme. Out of 20 discarded bottles, he would retrieve 11 bottles. Accordingly, the number of empties left behind would be 9: bottle pollution is greater under the subsidy than under the tax scheme when they are imposed at the same rate, provided that the total number of visitors remains unchanged. If the consumer's demand for beer is much smaller relative to his retrieval cost schedule and is represented by a schedule like D′D′, the subsidy scheme increases the consumption of beer, but all the empty bottles will be retrieved, leaving no bottle pollution in the park. But this amounts to subsidization of beer consumption as well as retrieval of empty bottles.

An economic analysis would not be complete without assessing the relative efficiencies of the policies suggested. In this respect, the preceding comparison of pollution levels is rather unsatisfactory because it does not clearly tell aggregate welfare levels under the tax and the subsidy. However, a more straightforward method of comparison is available. General economic principles tell us that if there are a number of methods of attaining a given reduction in pollution, all methods should be used simultaneously; the optimal combination of these methods is attained when the marginal costs of reducing pollution are equal for all methods used, provided that the cost functions of all methods are independent of each other.[17]

Let us retain the assumption that the possible intergroup distributive effects of collecting tax revenues through an effluent tax and of subsidization of retrieval are neutralized by a reduction and an increase in the admission fee, respectively. The optimality is shown in figure 4. The measurements of the horizontal and vertical axes are the same as in figure 2, except for the market price of beer, OP, added to the vertical axis. Curve PC is, as curve OC, in figure 2, the social cost of pollution, and curve PB depicts the social cost of retrieval (that is, the horizontal sum of individual polluters' retrieval cost schedules). The curve PU is the horizontal sum of curves PC and PB and curve DD is the visitors' aggregate demand for beer. The intersection of the curves PU and DD, denoted by Q, indicates the socially optimal consumption of beer, OW, and the social cost of beer, WQ. Hence the optimal effluent tax rate is PT (WQ minus the market price of beer). The points at which the pollution cost and retrieval cost schedules equal the social price of beer indicate the socially optimal level of pollution (OH) and the optimal quantity of empty bottles retrieved (OK), respectively. Note that OK equals WH.[18] The aggregate consumers' surplus is the area DQP.

In our example, curtailment of the consumption of beer is clearly one method of reducing pollution, as is the retrieval of empty bottles. An effluent tax of $PT induces consumers to curtail their consumption of beer from OA to OW bottles in figure 4. The marginal net disutility suffered by a consumer from curtailment is $VQ (portion $WV is offset by the amount of money that he saves by not purchasing the beer) at equilibrium. The marginal disutility resulting from the individual's retrieving empty bottles is $JG. Since $VQ = $PT = $JG, the effluent tax induces an optimal mobilization of all the pollution abatement methods available in this example. On the other hand, a subsidy on returned bottles mobilizes the retrieval method only. Consumers' equilibrium marginal costs of retrieval are $JG as they were under the tax scheme, but their equilibrium marginal disutility of pollution reduction through curtailing beer consumption is zero. Evidently, the subsidy device by itself will not activate the second useful pollution abatement device. Because the effluent tax achieves what general economic rationality requires, while the subsidy on returned bottles does not, we can conclude that the tax on pollutants emitted is more efficient than the subsidy on pollutants retrieved in reducing pollution.

However the following words should be added lest the above conclusion be taken as a general indictment of subsidy schemes. A more elaborate set of subsidies would, at least theoretically, produce the same economic effects as the effluent tax. A subsidy on curtailment of consumption of bottled beer, for example, may be combined with the subsidy on retrieved bottles. Let the number of bottles retrieved, plus the number of bottles that corresponds to the difference between the number of bottles that would have been consumed in the absence of the subsidy and that consumed in the presence of the subsidy, be made the basis of a subsidy. Or, alternatively, let the difference between an arbitrarily determined benchmark number of bottles (assuming that the benchmark number is greater than the socially optimal pollution number) and the number of bottles actually discarded in the park under the subsidy scheme be made the basis of a subsidy. Under such a scheme, a subsidy produces an economic effect equivalent to that of an effluent tax of an equal rate. However, these schemes require identification of the number of bottles actually consumed in the first example and the number actually discarded in the second example. Any visitors desirous of increasing the sum of subsidies receivable are tempted to misrepresent these numbers. The effective administration of these systems requires, therefore, policing of these numbers. One method may be that the park authority issues every visitor a fixed number of coupons (equal to the benchmark number) and requires him to present one coupon upon purchase of each bottle of beer.[19] The authority then grants a subsidy equal to the socially optimal tax rate on unused coupons plus the number of retrieved empties. Because this method must handle coupons in addition to beer bottles, it is more cumbersome to administer than the bottle law. Accordingly, practical implementation of a subsidy that can produce an economic effect equivalent to that of an effluent tax may have to await an innovation the ingenuity of which can match the bottle law.

A few words on the control of pollution through regulation may be in order at this point. I have postulated regulation as a method which achieves the optimal outcome throughout the paper. But I do not claim that regulation will in fact produce such an outcome. Regulation has been cited simply to establish the optimal outcome with which the tax and the subsidy schemes can be compared. In reality, regulation will most likely be less efficient than the other two methods. For example, assume that the park authority issues a decree that each visitor must retrieve at least 11 empty bottles for presentation at the gate before he leaves the park. This decree may be accompanied by a severe penalty for violation.

Despite the fact that actual activities needed to comply with this decree are almost identical to those needed under the tax or the subsidy scheme, the decree may be observed with much unhappiness. People who would diligently and happily comply with the same procedure if it resulted in the refund of deposit money or in the receipt of a subsidy which they considered themselves to have earned would tend to complain if they received "nothing" in return for their actions. If penalties were actually imposed on violators, they would certainly protest, for many of them would be likely to feel that such a decree was unjust, and some might even embark upon long court battles. Such a prospect may delight lawyers (incidentally, lawyers in general favor regulation), but it certainly spells wastefulness with respect to resource use for the rest of us. It is reported that while there is much tax litigation, the bulk of excise taxes—which most resemble effluent taxes—are paid without legal struggle.[20] The regulation approach seems a poor substitute for the effluent tax and abatement subsidy approaches.

VIII. Summary and Conclusions

If we take for granted the superiority of the tax and subsidy approaches over the regulation approach in controlling pollution, we must still decide which of the two types should be employed. The remarkable proposition that a tax and a subsidy of equal rates are equivalent as means of achieving a desired reduction in pollution is longstanding and widely accepted. However, two major arguments have been presented which challenge the proposition. The first is that a subsidy scheme may induce polluters initially to emit more pollutants than they would otherwise in order to qualify for larger subsidy payments. The second contends that the subsidy scheme encourages the entry of new firms into the pollution-generating industry and thereby increases pollution to a level higher than the level that would have been reached not only under the tax but in the absence of any control.

Upon reviewing both arguments, the present paper finds that if the polluters anticipate that their pollution levels affect the authority's decision on the benchmark to be used to calculate subsidies, they will behave strategically, and, if that is indeed the case, similar strategic behavior appears under the effluent tax as well. Therefore, the basic symmetry of the two schemes remains intact. Moreover, strategic behavior may be avoided by fixing arbitrarily the benchmark by which the authority counts the subsidy base or the tax base.

With respect to the second argument, this paper finds its validity conditional. The logic of the argument depends on the implicit assumptions that the revenues raised by the effluent tax on pollutants are transferred from the taxpaying group to other groups, and that the funds needed to finance the subsidy scheme are transferred to the subsidy-receiving group from other groups. If lump-sum intragroup transfers accompany the tax and subsidy schemes and eliminate the necessity of intergroup transfers of tax revenues and subsidy funds, the equivalence of tax and subsidy is reestablished. Such lump-sum intragroup transfers are, in fact, feasible in many cases and, therefore, the equivalence theorem should not be abandoned so readily on grounds that such intragroup transfers are infeasible.

After assessing the validity of earlier discussions, the paper presents its own reasons for the nonequivalence of the effluent tax and the abatement subsidy when the demand for the activity generating the pollutant in question is not perfectly inelastic. It points out that under an optimal effluent tax rate, polluters not only utilize their own pollution abatement methods but also curtail the activities that generate pollution, for the tax raises the price of such activities. In short, the effluent tax induces the optimal utilization of all abatement methods under the polluters' control.

In contrast, the pollutant retrieval subsidy will not change the price of the pollution-generating activity and, therefore, it will not alter the extent to which people indulge in such an activity. Consequently, the tax and the subsidy, although at equal rates, do not necessarily produce equal reductions in the overall pollution level. Moreover, since the subsidy method thus fails to mobilize at least one important pollution abatement mode, it is less efficient than the tax method unless demand for the activity generating pollution is perfectly inelastic.

Finally, this paper points out that a set of subsidy schemes does exist that would produce economic effects equal to those of an effluent tax of an equal rate. Implementation of such subsidies would, however, encounter many practical difficulties and must await an innovation that matches the bottle bill for ingenuity.

Notes

[1]These subsidies and depreciation allowances can never by themselves make pollution abatement investment profitable. Hence, unless pressures to make such investments exist, these measures alone will never effectively reduce pollution. For further criticisms on such measures, see Kneese and Bower (1968, pp. 175–178).

[2]For the German Effluent discharge tax, see: Der Rat von Sachverständigen für Umweltfragen, Die Abwässerabgabe—Wassergüterwirtschaftliche und gesamtökonomische Wirkungen, 2. Sondergutachten, Stuttgart und Mainz, 1974.

[3]Information as to existing pollution taxes is contained in OECD (1980).

[4]See, for example, Seneca and Taussing (1979).

[5]Beside Kamien, Schwartz and Dolbear, authors who have pursued this strand of argument are Freeman (1967), Mumey (1971), Dick (1976), Burrows (1979), Sims (1981), and others.

[6]Some other articles discussing this type of difference in the long-run effects between taxes and subsidies are Calabresi (1965), Page (1973), Kneese and Mäler (1973), Porter (1974), Dick (1976), Holterman (1976), Dewes and Sims (1976), Polinsky (1979), Mestelman (1981), and others.

[7]Another objective of the bill is to encourage standardization of containers used by different beverage manufacturers to reduce the cost of sorting and returning the empty containers. The bill therefore includes a provision that refillable containers used by more than one beverage manufacturer may have a minimum deposit of two cents instead of five cents upon certification by the Oregon Liquor Control Commission.

[8]See Don Waggoner (1975, pp. 21–22), and William J. Baumol and Wallace E. Oates (1979, pp. 268–270).

[9]See Charles M. Gudger and Jack C. Bailes (1974), and William J. Baumol and Wallace E. Oates (1979, pp. 268–270).

[10]It is reported that the containers account for over 60 percent of the volume of litter. See William J. Baumol and Wallace E. Oates (1979, p. 269).

[11]See Jerry Uhrhammer (1976, pp. 42–46).

[12]The conditions required are identifiability of pollutants and their countability as the basis of taxation or subsidization. I accept Professor Alan Tait's criticism that these conditions will not be met by many cases of pollution, but they are conditions implicit in Professor Pigou's seminal analysis and are traditionally employed by the analyses followed. In any case, I claim that my analysis is applicable not to all types of pollution but to those cases where these conditions can be met.

[13]We set aside legal issues that may prohibit, in principle, charging an admission fee on entry into a "publicly owned" land.

[14]Here we assume that personal retrieving is the most efficient method of collecting discarded bottles and cans. If other methods are available, the personal-retrieving method should be used along with them or be abandoned, depending upon the efficiency of that method relative to the efficiencies of other methods.

[15]Refunds need not be on the empty bottles. However, it would be unusual for a consumer to turn in a filled bottle for a refund which is only a small portion of the price of the filled bottle. Of course, deposits on the filled bottles removed from the park area should be refunded.

[16]In the context of entry and exit decisions of firms, Ackerman (1973) has argued that an effluent tax may make firms unprofitable and may induce their exit from the polluting industry.

[17]See Shibata (1977) for a proof. See also Mishan (1971). I analyzed the case where individuals' marginal retrieving cost schedules are independent of each other not because I believe that they always are, but, Professor Tait's criticism notwithstanding, they often are particularly when the retrievers are those very people who consume the content of the bottles which they retrieve. Interdependence of marginal retrieving cost schedules does occur, but a thorough analysis of such cases would require more space than that alloted to this paper. Those interested in such cases are invited to see Shibata (1977) and Shibata and Winrich (1981), where the problems arising from interdependence are analyzed.

[18]One can draw the social retrieval cost schedule from point V as depicted by the broken-line curve VGB′, which is the mirror image of schedule PB: Consumers drink under the tax quantity OW of bottles of beer and retrieve quantity WH of empties leaving quantity OH of empties in the park.

[19]On this point I benefited from the suggestion of Professor K. Tanaka.

[20]See Kneese and Schultze (1975, pp. 91).

References

Ackerman, R. S. "Effluent Charges: A Critique." *Canadian Journal of Economics*, 6 (November, 1973), 512–528.

Baumol, W. J. and Oates, Wallace E. *The Theory of Environmental Policy: Externalities, Public Outlays, and the Quality of Life.* New Jersey: Prentice Hall, 1975.

———, *Economics, Environmental Policy, and the Quality of Life.* New Jersey: Prentice Hall, 1979.

Bramhall, D. E. and Mills, E. S. "A Note on the Asymmetry between Fees and Payments." *Water Resources Research* II, No. 3 (1966): 615–616.

Burrows, R. Pigovian Taxes, Polluter Subsidies and the Size of the Polluting Industry, *Canadian Journal of Economics,* 1979, 494–501.

Calabresi, G. The Decision for Accidents; An Approach to Nonfault Allocation Costs, *Harvard Law Review,* 78, 1965, 713–730.

Coase, R. H. "The Problem of Social Cost." *Journal of Law and Economics* III (October, 1960), 1–44.

Dewes, D. N. and Sims, W. A., *The Symmetry of Effluent Charges and Subsidies* for Pollution Control, *Canadian Journal of Economics,* 1976, 323–331.

Dick, D. T. The Voluntary Approach to Externality Problems: A Survey of the Critics, *Journal of Environmental Economics and Management,* 1976, 2, 185–195.

Endres, A. Nonseparability and the Voluntary Approach to Externality Problems, *Journal of Environmental Economics and Management,* 1977, 4, 209–213.

Freeman, A., III. "Bribes and Charges: Some Comment." *Water Resources Research* III, No. 1 (1967), 287–288.

Gudger, C. M. and Bailes, J. C. *The Economic Impact of Oregon's "Bottle Bill."* Corvallis, Ore.: Oregon State University Press, 1974.

Holterman, S. Alternative Tax Systems to Correct for Externalities and the Efficiency of Paying Compensation, *Economica,* 1976, 1–16.

Kamien, M. I., Schwartz, N. L. and Dolbear, F. T. "Asymmetry between Bribes and Charges." *Water Resources Research* II, No. 1 (1966), 147–157.

Kneese, A. V. *The Economics of Regional Water Quality Management.* Baltimore: The Johns Hopkins University Press, 1964.

Kneese, A. V. and Bower, B. T. *Managing Water Quality: Economics, Technology and Institutions.* Baltimore: The Johns Hopkins University Press, 1968.

Kneese, V. and Schultze, Charles L. *Pollution, Prices and Public Policy*. Washington, D.C.: The Brookings Institution, 1975.
Mestelman, S. Corrective Production Subsidies in an Increasing Cost Industry, *Canadian Journal of Economics*, 1981, 124–130.
Mishan, E. J. "What is the Optimal Level of Pollution?" *Journal of Political Economy*, 82 (November/December, 1974): 1278–1299.
Mumey, G. A. The "Coase Theorem," a Re-examination, *Quarterly Journal of Economics* 85, 1971, 718–723.
OECD (Ed.), *Pollution Charges in Practice*, Paris, 1980.
Page, T. "Failure of Bribes and Standards for Pollution Abatement," *Natural Resources Journal*, 13, 1973, 677–704.
Polinsky, A. M. Notes on the Symmetry of Taxes and Subsidies in Pollution Control, *Canadian Journal of Economics*, 1979, 75–83.
Porter, R. C. "The Long Run Asymmetry of Subsidies and Taxes as Anti-Pollution Policies," *Water Resources Research* 10, 1974, 415–417.
Shibata, H. "What is the Optimal Control of Polution?" *Osaka Economic Papers*, 27 (December, 1977), 104–107.
Shibata, H. and Winrich, S. J. "Control of Pollution when the Offended Defend Themselves." *Economica*, forthcoming; also presented at the 51st Annual Conference of the Southern Economic Association, November 1981.
Sims, W. A. "The Short Run Asymmetry of Pollution Subsidies and Charges," *Journal of Environmental Economics and Management*, 1981, 395–399.
Seneca, J. J. and Taussing, M. K. *Environmental Economics*, 2nd Ed. New Jersey: Prentice Hall, 1979.
Uhrhammer, J. "The Point of No Return." *Sports Illustrated*, August 2, 1976, 42–46.
Waggoner, D. *Oregon's Bottle Bill Two Years Later*. Oregon Environmental Council. Portland, Ore.: Columbia Group Press, 1975.

Résumé

Le théorème selon lequel les résultats économiques d'allocation sont égaux pour un impôt levé sur chaque unité de polluant rejeté et pour une subvention de même taux attribuée à chaque unité de polluant non rejeté est largement admis mais il continue à rencontrer deux domaines de critiques. Cet article étudie d'abord ces deux groupes de critiques—l'un concernant le comportement stratégique des pollueurs qui est appelé à apparaître dans les cas d'un programme de subvention à la différence d'un programme d'imposition, et l'autre concernant les effets à long terme associés aux transferts de recettes fiscales et aux fonds nécessaires pour financer la subvention—la conclusion est que ces critiques entachent peu la valeur de ce théorème. L'article montre ensuite qu'une imposition sur les déchets chimiques et une subvention donnée pour chaque unité de polluant émise et retirée de l'environnement sont respectivement équivalentes quand la demande pour les activités génératrices de pollution est parfaitement inélastique, mais non équivalentes lorsqu'elle est élastique. Ces résultats soutiennent le point de vue de cet article selon lequel un programme de subvention est plus simple à mettre en place qu'un programme d'imposition quand la demande pour les activités génératrices de pollution est parfaitement inélastique, mais est bien plus difficile à appliquer et moins efficace quand la demande est élastique, si les deux programmes sont conçus pour produire le même effect économique.

La discussion commence par la présentation de la loi connue sous le nom de "Oregon's Bottle Bill" et elle se poursuit par l'analyse de cette méthode.

Public Finance and the Cultural Factor in Economic Growth

Jack Wiseman

INTERVIEWER: Vous pensez aussi que le roman classique est mort?
ALBERTO MORAVIA: Pas absolument . . . Mais le monde moderne n'a plus le temps de lire.
(Moravia, 1967).

I. Introduction

The above quotation is taken from one of the few modern sources that I have discovered which deals seriously with the relation between culture and economic growth. (Linder, 1970, p. 94). A further quotation, this time from Linder himself, underlines the profound difficulty that faces anyone asked to write to a title such as the one I have been given:

> The Cultivation of the mind and spirit is generally accepted as being the supreme goal of human effort. These pursuits supposedly raise our civilization above anything our inferiors in the Darwinian chain can achieve. This is the attitude reflected in the Latin sentence: *Horas non numero nisi serenas*—only peaceful hours count.
> (Linder, 1970, p. 94).

Which is to say that the "cultural factor"—presumably, the cultural pursuits of the members of any society—is not something distinct from economic growth, properly defined, but is a part of that growth. Insofar as people find pleasure in cultural pursuits, the "utilities" concerned are as real and relevant as, for example, the utilities associated with a rise in car ownership. Indeed, the two are formally

Public Finance and Economic Growth. Proceedings of the 37th Congress of the International Institute of Public Finance. Tokyo, 1981, pp. 419–427

identical if we define value *subjectively*—as the enjoyment of experiences that may or may not involve objects—rather than *objectively*—as the accumulation of goods and personal services, measured by their market prices as a convenient proxy.

Thus, at what might pompously be called a quintessential level, "cultural" values and "economic" values are not distinguishable: and I should write no more. I do so partly because I have an obligation to fulfil, and partly because it is not a trivial matter to invite economists to consider the practical deficiencies of their conception of the economic problem, and not least of the economic growth problem.

In terms of the history of thought, "economic progress" has tended to be regarded as automatically encouraging "cultural progress": the reduction in the time needed to satisfy physical wants would automatically increase the time available for cultural activities. This proposition implies the need for definitions, and the ones I shall use from now on, albeit reluctantly, are the standard ones used by the present generation of economists. Essentially (and I know that I am simplifying) the growth rate that interests economists is the rate of increase of output per head, where output is defined as the market value of goods and services produced during the relevant period. Goods (satisfactions, utilities) that are not marketed, or not conceptually capable of being related to market-oriented criteria are ignored: normally, by being treated as "inputs" to the (customarily-defined) rate of economic growth.

In what follows, I shall accept the customary definition of economic growth (the *per capita* increase in the measure of marketed output, subject to the usual qualifications). But I do so only to develop a theme, not because I believe that the definition is in any way adequate for the evaluation of human well-being. Nor, of course, do I suggest that I am the first economist to observe that cultural concepts fit uneasily into the economists' orthodox models: I suggest only that there is a continuing gap between recognition of the problem and its satisfactory intellectual resolution. (For example, Marshall writes of chivalry as well as of the condition of the labouring classes, Keynes' essays reveal a clear sensitivity to the problem, and, above all, the work of Schumpeter postulates the "overspill" of the newly-emerging capitalist economy into cultural change (Schumpeter 1943, particularly Chapter XI).)

Subject to this reservation we can discuss the relation between "culture," and (narrowly-defined) growth, and the relevance of public finance to both.

Within the confines of a short paper, and of my own intellectual limitations, I cannot hope to reach definitive general conclusions about a problem to which economists have made insightful but individual contributions which nevertheless, it is fair to say, fall short of a persuasive rationale. I shall seek only to provide further insights, and to suggest ways in which the relation between culture, growth, and public finance might fruitfully be further researched. I start from the proposition that the relation between "cultural" activities and "growth" activities within the simplified definition of growth, is more complex than is normally assumed.

The extreme view among economists is that economic growth, defined in the narrow (materialistic) fashion, is an interesting end in itself, and one which it is legitimate for them to study positively without concern for whether its achievement is interesting to other members of the community or not. A more sophisticated view acknowledges the inadequacy of economic growth as customarily defined as a proxy for human aspirations, but treats the two as positively correlated. Within our present context, economic growth, it is argued, promotes cultural activity, because the easier fulfilment of material wants increases the time available for cultural pursuits. The result of growth, according to the prophets, would be to provide time for the "leisurely and philosophical contemplation of the world and its wonders" (Scitovsky, 1964, p. 209). But as the quoted authors point out, the world does not work like that. Material growth, as now defined, frees time for cultural pursuits. But it also raises their opportunity-cost. The greater the materialistic (growth-related) yield to an hour's input of effort, the more an individual can "afford" to devote time to cultural activities rather than to "material" income-acquisition. But at the same time, the greater the product of an hour's input in improving material well-being, the greater the cost of sacrificing material benefits in order to devote time to cultural activities. Using the narrow definition of economic growth, then, we find ourselves faced with a special, and sophisticated, example of conflicting income and substitution effects. Growth (materialistically defined) implies a fall in the relative "price" of non-cultural activities, which would predict an increase in the share of "non-cultural" consumption in total consumption. But the income effect may be contrary to this, depending on the income elasticity of demand for "cultural consumption."

These formalizations are perhaps useful pedagogically. But it is difficult to translate them into quantifiable form: cultural activities are things people "do": attitudes of mind: not (or frequently not) activities that involve market transactions. "Culture" is a man enjoying a sunset. No doubt, "economic" inputs will have contributed to him being where he is. But how to model his valuation of sunsets in relation to "material" growth, and how to relate the two to public finance, is a vexing question. It is not a question that I shall pretend that I can solve in this paper. I shall offer some speculations, based on a very narrow conception of culture, and use these to suggest a research scenario: not one that I ever expect to have time to pursue myself, but one that might encourage someone to give time to this difficult but potentially rewarding problem.

II. Culture as a Set of Attitudes

The interest of men in "the cultivation of the mind and spirit," and in the particular forms of that cultivation is of course the result of conditioning: we are not born with our cultural tastes and preferences ready-formed, any more than we are born without tastes and preferences for goods already established. We are born into a family and a society, and the institutions of society influence both our cultural and our narrower "economic" attitudes and behaviour. Nor are these constant. All of life is a learning process (of which formal education is but a part) and experience changes preferences and behaviour. The process is not a simple one: I have little sympathy with the attempts to describe it in terms of grand generalisations said to define the "good society." The richness and diversity of human cultures is not to be so constrained, nor is it accidental that attempts to do so frequently result in attempts to impose cultural conformity from "above," in the interests of human freedom. This is not to deny that elites and power are significant for cultural as for economic development. But as Bottomore (1964) points out, there can be many kinds of elites (political, intellectual, managerial, bureaucratic), they can relate to each other in a variety of ways (which can and do differ from one society to another), and there is no reason to expect them to form a unified power structure or a system of cultural norms to which citizens will wish or feel obliged to conform.

Once again, we have reached a position of despair. What that is useful can economists say? The answer is: nothing definitive: but we can perhaps simplify or clarify the issues. I shall try to do so by concentrating on one aspect of culture: religion. In so doing, I do not imply that culture and religion are synonymous, or that the relations between the two are simple. But we need to get a handle on the problem, and religion is a way to begin.

The generalisations which follow are just that: generalisations. Indeed, they are fairly wild generalisations, for which I would not like to be asked for supporting evidence. But I think they are practically interesting.

The Muslim religions place heavy emphasis on the security of the family, and so encourage risk-avoidance. This does not encourage entrepreneurship and innovation (I once read, as external examiner, 400+ answers to a question: What are the cultural obstacles to economic growth in country X? I thought the first answer excellent. The four-hundredth was identical with all the others. The examiners were practising the risk-aversion they were condemning.)

The Christian ethic, in at least some of its manifestations, identifies moral rectitude with economic initiative: groups such as the Quakers have seen the obligation to care for others, and the obligation to pursue economic well-being, as joint rather than as competitive obligations. This relationship has of course been thoroughly investigated, for example by Max Weber and R. H. Tawney, in respect of the relation between the Protestant ethic and the spirit of capitalism.

Equally, the Jewish religion, with its emphasis on family and self-sufficiency, encourages an identity of attitude to "material" growth and cultural development.

In the socialist countries, religion is largely replaced by a different dogma, which emphasizes the individual citizen's obligation to the state. The implications of this for "material" growth depend upon the interpretation placed upon the obligation. Just as Muslim communities may be averse to entrepreneurial risk, so socialist communities may be discouraging to the innovation that stimulates growth. They will solve defined technical problems, but may be inhibited in producing innovations valued by consumers insofar as private consumption is itself not a major objective of economic policy.

These are parodies, and should be so evaluated. They are also deficient because society and religious belief are not coterminous. There are many countries in which Jews are a minority, but preserve their "culture," and through it influence the country's culture and economy. The Indian Asians fulfill a similar role in the Far East: my Indian friends tell me that they are a sub-set of the Indian community, and in no way typical of the country as a whole. (Perhaps that is a pity, so far as economic growth is concerned.) But the parodies do perhaps give us a way of beginning to think about public finance and "culture."

III. The Role of Public Finance

In any society, the pursuit of economic growth, narrowly defined, is in actual or potential conflict with other objectives, including cultural ones. Growth implies change: new ways of doing things, or better ways of doing existing things. The process of change (technological improvement and changes in the preferences of demanders), is an integral part of economic growth. Change implies displacement. The more rapid the rate of economic growth, the greater the economic risks to which citizens are likely to be exposed. Thus, implied in the espousal of material growth as an appropriate objective of a community, there is some form of "social contract" between its members which commits them to care for those displaced by change. "Caring" is a necessary concomitant of material growth: without it, the penalties of growth for the unfortunate will lead to rejection of the society's *mores* or its goals. There is nothing incompatible, for example, between what is called the capitalist system and "caring." The belief that there is rests upon the identification of competition with selfishness. But both parties gain from trade freely undertaken, and I have already pointed out the importance of the Protestant ethic in the evolution of capitalism. Put very briefly, self-help is a virtue, but men also have a moral duty to care for the unfortunate.

The interesting questions concern less the existence of caring than the form it takes, and the relationship of these to interest in material wealth and to public finance. I shall continue to use religion to illustrate, though without suggesting that religion and culture in the broader sense can in any way be treated as identities. Nor am I describing anything more than *tendencies*: individual countries differ one from another in ways much more subtle than I can describe here, and nothing I have to say is intended to be descriptive of any actual country.

If the head of the family has a duty to protect the family from risk, children absorb a set of values generally inimical to innovation and entrepreneurship. The fiscal and property rights systems are related to traditional socio-religious values rather than material growth. The elite groups in such countries tend to be identified by superior (often privately-provided) education, strong family linkages, and, in the case of the entrepreneurial/managerial elite, a commitment to "foreign" values/cultural attitudes which may conflict with traditional ones. There may be wide dispersions of income and wealth in such countries, but redistribution of income by means of the tax system is frequently hypothetical rather than real because of endemic avoidance and evasion. "Caring" is a family matter, and the need for growth-related "caring" through the fiscal system is avoided by a weak commitment to growth.

In contrast are the Protestant and similar ethics, where either the commitment is to a community broader than the family, or the family commitment is one of self-help rather than protectiveness. Communities in which these attitudes are important seek means to achieve the "caring" necessary for social stability without inhibiting material growth and innovation. The form and extent to which public finance is used for this purpose differs considerably between countries, but all (e.g.) Western-type capitalist economies rely upon it to an important extent. Debate focusses upon *method*, and in association with this upon the relative weight to be given to particular broad objectives. Thus, the most comprehensive way to care for those adversely affected by socio-economic change may be by government social security arrangements, and some rich high-growth countries have highly-developed schemes of this kind (they are commonly financed by "contributions," but often lose all semblance of compulsory insurance and become rather a form of taxation, because there is no or little financial nexus between contribution and entitlement). But those who attach great importance to the notion of self-help resist the undue integration of such arrangements with the redistributive objectives of general tax policies. They support contributory against non-contributory arrangements, for example, and the restriction of subsidised benefits to subsistence levels. They regard compulsory insurance against the risks of change as the (self-help) "trade-off" for the community's commitment to care for those who nevertheless fall in need. In such communities, fiscal means are frequently sought to encourage innovation (e.g. by the subsidisation or tax relief of research and development). "Culture" in the broader sense is regarded as a form of consumption, though one that may merit subsidisation. (But in some such countries at least the subsidised consumption tends to be that of the elite rather than that of the majority.) The fiscal encouragement of private "caring" activities (e.g. organised charity) is also common.

There is also diversity among the socialist countries, and my description can again only be illustrative. The essential point is that, insofar as the growth objectives of such a community are centrally-determined, policies towards "caring" will be decided at the same time and in the same fashion. I do not have enough information to comment very usefully on this. Superficial observation suggests that these arrangements will be better at dealing with specified technological problems than in using fiscal means to encourage broader (consumption-related) innovation. But I hope colleagues from socialist countries will improve my knowledge.

To complete this Section, I would like to comment on arrangements in our host country. I am not an expert on Japan. But my little knowledge suggests that it differs strikingly from any of the prototypes I have been describing. Given Japan's phenomenal record of economic growth, I would like to know more. I will give my impression briefly, in the hope that my Japanese colleagues will amplify and correct it. The fundamental difference seems to be that, where in other countries, culture and growth are related through (e.g.) religion and family or community "caring," the primary growth-related "caring" institution in Japan is the firm itself. Employers have a moral obligation to keep their work-force in employment, and failure to do so is not just "economic failure" of the enterprise but "social" failure of the employers. Thus the firm is a much more significant *cultural* institution in Japan than elsewhere, and I suspect that this contributes in an important degree to the relatively low ratio of taxation to GNP: enterprises can be relied upon to perform "caring" functions which in other countries are transmitted through the system of public finance. (as an aside, it may also explain Japanese success in development—the translation of basic innovation into final products). It is perhaps noteworthy that the process whose existence I suspect would imply that, while the success of Japanese economic enterprises may have been culturally conditioned, a reverse process may now be at work, in that the relationships and attitudes of the workplace are invading other cultural spheres. Insofar as this is true, Japan may differ from the prototypes I have offered, but my argument nevertheless parallels that of Schumpeter, who saw the concepts of logic and rationality thrown up by emergent capitalism invading other cultural spheres (Schumpeter, 1943).

IV. Apologies and Suggestions

I am very conscious of the inadequacies of this paper. The topic is a difficult one, and I had to write it at short notice. It is little more than a set of reflections and (perhaps) provocations.

In the course of writing it, I have come to think that a more formalized and interesting way of approaching the problem might be to try to evolve a set of "cultural indicators" which could be compared with growth indexes and with indexes of change in fiscal arrangements. Such an approach, using divergences in "social indexes" (GNP per head, number of graduates per head, etc.) has been used to identify countries "at risk" of social disruption, with interesting results. The most difficult task, of course, would be to find a satisfactory set of "cultural indexes." For, returning to my beginning theme, I find myself in the unusual position of being in complete sympathy with Joan Robinson (1962), when she writes that economists have an obligation "to combat, not foster, the ideology which pretends that values which can be measured in terms of money are the only ones that ought to count." (p. 147). Nothing follows for public finance policy from the discovery that cultural values are inhibiting economic growth, except the observation that the country concerned should be aware of the evidence. Material and cultural well-being may be correlated: they are surely not identical.

References

Bottomore, T. B. (1964), *Elites and Society*, London, C. A. Watts and Co. Ltd., (The New Thinker's Library)

Linder, S. B. (1970), *The Harried Leisure Class*, New York and London, Columbia University Press.

Moravia, G. (1967), Interview reported in *La Tribune de Geneve*, September 9–10.

Robinson, Joan (1962), *Economic Philosophy*, London, C. A. Watts and Co. Ltd. (The New Thinker's Library)

Schumpeter, Joseph, A. (1943), *Capitalism, Socialism and Democracy*, London, Allen & Unwin.

Scitovsky, T. (1964), *Papers on Welfare and Growth*, London, Allen and Unwin Ltd.

Tawney, R. H. *Religion and The Rise of Capitalism*.

Weber, M. (1947), *Der Bourgeois*, and *From Max Weber*, (ed. H. H. Gerith and C. Wright Mills), London, Kegan Paul.

Résumé

Cet article explique la difficulté que rencontrent les économistes lorsqu'ils essayent d'intégrer un changement culturel dans leurs modèles orthodoxes de croissance. La culture est un ensemble d'attitudes plutôt qu'un ensemble de "valeurs" au sens que donnent les économistes à ce terme. Mais ces deux ensembles sont étroitement liés quoique d'une façon subtile difficile à appréhender.

Cet article considère la religion comme une "représentation" de la culture à titre général et propose de voir des liens très simplifiés entre la culture entendue comme religion et des phénomènes économiques comme la croissance. Son objectif est de stimuler l'esprit plutôt que d'affirmer une position intellectuelle bien que naturellement des auteurs plus anciens aient soutenu (par exemple) que l'émergence du capitalisme était liée à l'acceptation de croyances religieuses particulières.

Les finances publiques s'inscrivent dans un tel système culturel grâce au support que celui-ci apporte à des types particuliers de "relations sociales": par exemple, le rôle "d'assistance" que joue la famille peut trouver son reflet dans l'utilisation ou le rejet de modes "paternalistes" d'intervention de l'Etat dans l'économie ou le budget.

En conclusion, cet article souligne notre profonde ignorance en la matière et pose des questions qui nécessiteraient d'en savoir davantage sur le Japon qui semble se détacher des archétypes décrits dans cet article, bien qu'il soit tout à fait possible que l'on puisse l'expliquer en gros de la même façon que SCHUMPETER explique l'effet culturel du capitalisme à ses débuts sur la société occidentale.

Anciens Dirigeants/Former Officers

Anciens Présidents/Former Presidents

Edgar Allix, France	1937
William Rappard, Suisse/Switzerland	1938–1940
Max Léo Gérard, Belgique/Belgium	1948–1950
Carl S. Shoup, Etats-Unis/USA	1950–1953
Ugo Papi, Italie/Italy	1953–1956
Fritz Neumark, République Fédérale d'Allemagne/Federal Republic of Germany	1956–1959
Maurice Masoin, Belgique/Belgium	1959–1962
Bernard Schendstok, Pays-Bas/Netherlands	1962–1965
Alan T. Peacock, Royaume-Uni/United Kingdom	1965–1968
François Trevoux, France	1968–1971
Otto Gadó, Hongrie/Hungary	1971–1975
Jack Wiseman, Royaume-Uni/United Kingdom	1975–1978
Horst-Claus Recktenwald, République Féderale d'Allemagne/Federal Republic of Germany	1978–1981

Anciens Vice-Présidents/Former Vice-Presidents

Lord Beveridge, Royaume-Uni/United Kingdom
D. Diachenko, URSS/USSR
J.-C. Dischamps, France
Francesco Forte, Italie/Italy
C. Lowell Harriss, Etats-Unis/USA
Lady Ursula K. Hicks, Royaume-Uni/United Kingdom
P. Jacomet, France
Fritz Neumark, République Fédérale d'Allemagne/Federal Republic of Germany
Ugo Papi, Italie/Italy
H. de Peyster, France
Günter Schmölders, République Fédérale d'Allemagne/Federal Republic of Germany
E. Seligman, Etats-Unis/USA
Carl S. Shoup, Etats-Unis/USA
E. da Silva, Portugal
Stepan Sitaryan, URSS/USSR
Lord Stamp, Royaume-Uni/United Kingdom
Conte Volpi, Italie/Italy
Jack Wiseman, Royaume-Uni/United Kingdom

Anciens Secrétaïres Généraux/Former Secretaries-General

André Piatier, France	1937–1948
Maurice Masoin, Belgique/Belgium	1948–1959
Paul Senf, République Fédérale d'Allemagne/Federal Republic of Germany	1959–1974

Présidents Honoraires et membres Honoraires
Honorary Presidents and Honorary Members

Présidents Honoraires/Honorary Presidents

Otto Gadó, Hongrie/Hungary
Lady Ursula K. Hicks, Royaume-Uni/United Kingdom
Richard A. Musgrave, Etats-Unis/USA
Fritz Neumark, République Fédérale d'Allemagne/Federal Republic of Germany
Ugo Papi, Italie/Italy
Alan Peacock, Royaume-Uni/United Kingdom
Horst-Claus Recktenwald, République Fédérale d'Allemagne/Federal Republic of Germany
Paul Senf, République Fédérale d'Allemagne/Federal Republic of Germany
Carl S. Shoup, Etats-Unis/USA
François Trevoux, France
Jack Wiseman, Royaume-Uni/United Kingdom

Membres Honoraires/Honorary Members

C. Lowell Harriss, Etats-Unis/USA
Motokazu Kimura, Japon/Japan
Paul Schütz, République Fédérale d'Allemagne/Federal Republic of Germany
Stepan Sitaryan, URSS/USSR

DATE DU